PRAISE FOR *FOUNDING A MOVEMENT*

FOUNDING A MOVEMENT

Women's World Banking, 1975–1990

FOUNDING A MOVEMENT

WOMEN'S WORLD BANKING
1975–1990

Michaela Walsh

**with Shamina de Gonzaga
and Financial Strategy by Lilia C. Clemente**

Cosimo Books
NEW YORK

Cosimo aims to publish books that inspire, inform, and engage readers world-wide. We use innovative print-on-demand technology that enables books to be printed based on specific customer needs. This approach eliminates an artificial scarcity of publications and allows us to distribute books in the most efficient and environmentally sustainable manner. Cosimo also works with printers and paper manufacturers who practice and encourage sustainable forest management, using paper that has been certified by the FSC, SFI, and PEFC whenever possible.

Ordering Information:
Cosimo publications are available at online bookstores. They may also be purchased for educational, business, or promotional use:
Bulk orders: Special discounts are available on bulk orders for reading groups, organizations, businesses, and others.
Custom-label orders: We offer selected books with your customized cover or logo of choice.

For more information, contact us at:

Cosimo, Inc.
P.O. Box 416, Old Chelsea Station
New York, NY 10011

info@cosimobooks.com

or visit us at:
www.cosimobooks.com

To every person who supported and continues to work toward fulfilling the dream of women owning their own production—and reproduction— and who worked so hard to create the Women's World Banking movement.

CONTENTS

With Deep Gratitude   *x*

About This Book   *xi*

Abbreviations and Acronyms   *xii*

Prologue   *xiv*

Timeline   *xvi*

1 From Kansas City to Mexico City   1

2 From Inspiration to Reality   14

3 Amsterdam 1980: Women's World Banking Takes Shape   32

4 Women's World Banking Gets Down to Work   53

5 Letting the Flowers Bloom: A Multitrack Structure Evolves   67

6 Bilderberg: Building a Global Network   84

7 Regional Leadership Grows Stronger   94

8 Coming to Maturity   116

9 End of an Era   129

10 Getting There from Nowhere (*by Lilia Clemente*)   145

11 Reflections   163

Notes   *179*

Aids and Documents   *180*

SWWB Organizing Committees and Working Groups , 1975–1980   *181*

SWWB Global and Trustees Meetings, 1980–1990   *182*

SWWB Trustees, 1980–1990   *184*

SWWB Consultants, Volunteers, Staff and Interns, 1980–1990   *187*

SWWB Affiliates and Affiliates-in-Formation, 1975–1990   *188*

Key to Acronyms, by Chapter   *190*

Index   *335*

About the Author   *345*

WITH DEEP GRATITUDE

This history could not have been written without the wisdom, professional experience, and dedication of many people who believed in and contributed to my personal efforts in creating Women's World Banking and in documenting its early years through this publication.

Special thanks to my collaborators—my coauthor, Shamina de Gonzaga; my chief editor, John C. Long; my contributing editor and longtime friend, Nancy Carson; and Lilia C. Clemente, my colleague and friend, who stepped up to provide a complete history of our collaboration and WWB's financial history during its first decade.

I would also like to express my appreciation to my generous sponsors, and to those who provided special guidance and advice, whose invaluable support enabled my endeavors to come to fruition.

Thanks also to numerous students and interns who worked tirelessly to transcribe the many, many hours of interviews and helped me compile endless lists and documents; to WWB staff members; and to those who took time to give me excellent feedback and encouraged me to persevere. Among them are Meg Chappell, Alex Paulenoff, Sadis Sequeria, Vanessa Singh, Elizabeth Walsh, and Katherine Wessling.

On a more personal note, certain individuals played central roles in my life by giving me a sense of freedom to dedicate myself to something I loved. Jerry, my brother, and Dorothy Lyddon, a mentor and friend, provided crucial help in the early days of WWB. Bill Bohnett has been a rock throughout the writing of this history. Three generations of my family and lifelong friends have enriched my life and have given me the inspiration to follow my dreams.

To each of you who are not mentioned by name—you know who you are—I love you and I thank you for all your support.

—*Michaela Walsh*

ABOUT THIS BOOK

JUST AS WOMEN'S World Banking emerged from collective efforts, this book also evolved through the continued input of interviewees, writers, editors, collaborators, and friends across generations who value the searches and insights that characterize the early days of Women's World Banking (WWB).

This effort began as my project to interview the founders of WWB and those who contributed so much in the years 1975 to 1990. Those interviews yielded vivid personal memories and a treasure trove of information on how something entirely new was developed. Telling the full story then seemed a necessity. In early 2010, a group of us who believed in the project met for three days to outline parameters for the book.

The pages that follow are not intended to support or critique what is currently known as "microfinance," or "inclusive finance," but rather to offer an understanding of the rich context in which these practices were developed and took form, through the prism of the organization WWB and the individuals who had a pioneering role in that field at a global scale. As WWB is a network united by a communications hub and composed of independent affiliates around the world, affiliate management is not discussed in this document, except for comments from interviewees and historical records.

Information is taken from the personal files of Michaela Walsh and other WWB founders and members; WWB archives at Princeton University's Seeley G. Mudd Manuscript Library; files located at WWB offices in New York City; videotapes of the 1980, 1981, and 1990 WWB Global Meetings filmed by Martha Stuart, president of Martha Stuart Communications, and her company; and from Lilia Clemente's financial strategy and timelines. Every effort has been made to identify all individuals who were involved in the founding years and to verify the accuracy of our memories.

Unless otherwise noted, quoted material has been adapted from interviews conducted for this project between 2008 and 2012. Descriptions of projects and events vary from brief to extensive, largely reflecting the information available from the interviews. Interviewees are identified in the documentation section, and original interviews are accessible at the Mudd Library as audio recordings and transcriptions. Videos are also at the library.

WWB is officially the Stichting to Promote Women's World Banking, or SWWB, because that is the corporate name under which the group is registered—in the Netherlands. (*Stichting* is Dutch for "foundation.") But we are known around the globe as Women's World Banking (WWB). That is our brand, and that is the name we will generally go by throughout the book.

ABBREVIATIONS AND ACRONYMS

AAAS—American Association for the Advancement of Science
ACWF—All-China Women's Federation
ADB—African Development Bank
ADIEF—Association pour le Développement des. Initiatives Economiques pour les Femmes
ADOPEM—Asociación Dominicana para el Desarrollo de la Mujer
BSc—Bachelor of Science
CARD—Centre for Agriculture and Rural Development
CGAP—Consultative Group to Assist the Poor
CIDA—Canadian International Development Agency
CPA—Certified Public Accountant
DAWN—Development Alternatives with Women for a New Era
DESAP—Desarrollo del Pueblo
DFC—Development Finance Consultants, Ltd.
ECOSOC—Economic and Social Council
EEC—European Economic Community
EIU—Economic Intelligence Unit
FCEM—Femmes Chefs d'Entreprises Mondiales
FHAF—Fonds Haitien d'Aide à la Femme
FIG—Foreign International Group
FINCA—Foundation for International Community Assistance
FWWB/USA—Friends of Women's World Banking USA
GAWF—Gambia Women's Finance Trust
GAWFA—Gambia Women's Finance Association
GNP—Gross National Product
GSL—Global Student Leadership
IDB—Inter-American Development Bank
IFC—the World Bank Group's International Finance Corporation
INSTRAW—The International Training and Research Center for the Advancement of Women
IPPF—International Planned Parenthood Foundation
IPS—Institute for Policy Studies
JPM—JP Morgan
K-REP—Kenya Rural Enterprise Program
KWFT—Kenya Women's Finance Trust
MBA—Master of Business Administration
MFIs—Microfinance Institutions

MIT—Massachusetts Institute of Technology
NABOW—National Association of Business Owner Women
NGO—Non-Governmental Organization
NMB Bank—Nederlandsche Middenstands Bank
NORAD—Norwegian Agency for Development Cooperation
NYSE—New York Stock Exchange
OECD—Organization for Economic Cooperation and Development
OEF— League of Women Voters Overseas Education Fund
OPEC—Organization of Petroleum Export Countries
OPIC—Overseas Private Investment Corporation
OTA—Congressional Office of Technology Assessment
PPM—Private-Placement Memorandum
PRI—Program Related Investment
PTAs—Parent-Teacher Associations
RBF—Rockefeller Brothers Fund
RR—Regional Representative
SEWA—Self-Employed Women's Association
SIACO—Trade Union of Swedish Academics
SIDA—Swedish International Development Agency
SWWB (1979)—Stichting Women's World Banking
SWWB (1985)—Stichting to Promote Women's World Banking
TB—Triodos Bank
UNCTAD—United Nations Conference on Trade and Development
UNDP—United Nations Development Program
UNICEF —United Nations Children's Fund
UNIFEM—United Nations Fund for Women
UNGA—United Nations General Assembly
UNITAR—United Nations Institute for Training and Research
UN—United Nations
USAID—United States Agency for International Development
UWFT—Uganda Women's Finance Trust
WID—Women in Development
WIFE—Women in Finance and Entrepreneurship
WINTRAC—Women in Trade and Commerce
WWB—Women's World Banking
WWE—Women's World Enterprise

PROLOGUE

THIS BOOK TELLS the story of the founding of Women's World Banking. It tells the story as I experienced it, but my story is enriched by the participation and opinions of many others who conceived, created, launched, and built WWB into a movement that helped change women's lives around the globe.

My goal was to shine a light on the value that women contribute through work, and through their support of one another to become full participants in the economy, through access to financial institutions and services and everything that goes with that access. When some of us first met one another at the first United Nations World Conference on Women in Mexico City in the summer of 1975, the work of roughly half of the citizens of the world was invisible. Women were routinely denied commercial banking privileges, and even in the United States, many women could secure working capital only with the endorsement of a man. This had to change.

The change we envisioned came from our backgrounds as lawyers, as bankers, as trade-union organizers, as entrepreneurs, as nonprofit executives, as economists, and as international-development professionals. It came from realizing that our different cultures and backgrounds gave us strength. As we met and talked and dreamed, we saw that women could work together in a whole new way.

For me, the Mexico City experience was a whirlwind of energy and color. Colors of skins, colors of garments, colors of speech. We did not gather in dark suits to rubber-stamp preset agendas. Our meetings had the color of emotion, of passion, of disagreement. We listened, we worked, we ate, and we danced and sang; we were driven by hopes for our children and our world. It was not easy or simple.

Many times we were told that what we had in mind was impossible, that there would be no funding for the effort, that we could not conceivably proceed unless we adopted a traditional development-project model, and that women could not be full participants in the economy. I never, never accepted these comments. The women who founded Women's World Banking were for the most part visionaries, dreamers, people unafraid to create something new. We knew we had to work within each culture, not distort beliefs based on a Western idea of what was best. Our working model was a wheel—a hub for communication and coordination with many spokes reaching out, each spoke essential for the integrity of the wheel. We knew we could not use a top-down model. We had to work together to connect women around the world and support each other.

This book covers the Women's World Banking experience from 1975 to 1990, when I had major responsibility for leading and managing the core organization. My voice as narrator in this book recounts my experience and impressions. I didn't want this to be my biography, but in telling the story of an organization I was so intricately involved with, the personal and the professional are interwoven in my memory. Perhaps that is why I have emphasized so many other voices as well. I hope that the diverse experiences recounted offer some insights about the weaving of not just one life or institution, but of the expansive tapestry we create when we listen, learn, connect, and follow our hearts and inspiration.

This history affirms that each one of us would tell the story differently. I am grateful to every woman and man who worked hard to make Women's World Banking a reality. I am also grateful for the young people around the world today who are finding their own new ways to make things better.

Looking back over all these interviews, meeting minutes, reports, and memories, I see clearly that my vision and my struggle was for WWB to support a movement, not to build an institution; to keep it open, not exclusive; to serve women rather than serve an organization. I fought for banking for women, never for an international bank. Others had different beliefs about what could work. It is my profound trust that the movement of women helping each other gain full control over their economic destinies is the basis of how the world will change for the better, and that it will continue long after my voice is silent.

—Michaela Walsh
New York City, July 2012

TIMELINE

A SENSE OF HISTORY

1974

- Ghanaian market women meet at State House, Accra and affirm that "women's access to credit" is the key factor impending their productivity.

Origins

While Mexico City 1975 is most often cited as the spot where WWB got its start, there is a sound basis for suggesting that WWB actually has its roots elsewhere.

In 1974 Ghana's First Lady called the country's market women to State House, Accra for a special women's meeting, organized with the National Council of Women. The main aim of the meeting was to "brainstorm" with local women entrepreneurs in order to bring their most immediate concerns to the UN Women's Conference in Mexico City.

What was the main issue they'd like conveyed at the Conference? The market women's response was singular and unequivocal: Above all else, small business women like themselves never succeeded unless they had *access to credit!*

Access to credit was first and foremost in their minds—not better education, housing, health care or family planning, nor development, equality or peace. They said their needs were simple: Once they had credit, they could use that to generate the funds they required to satisfy all their other needs.

Fortunately, their views were conveyed to the Mexico City meeting by Ghanaian women leaders Justice Annie Jiagge and Dr. Esther Ocloo, both of whom became "founding mothers" of WWB (along with 13 others). Esther was elected the first chairperson of WWB's Board of Directors.

1975

- Mexico City: At the United Nations International Women's Conference, women declared the need for a "mechanism" or means to ensure women's access to credit.

1976

- United Nations Women's Decade (1976–'85) launched
- US/Pennsylvania organizes Women's Association for Women's Alternatives. WAWA sets up training and counselling programs.

1977

- 15 founding members become the "Committee to organize Women's World Banking" The 15 were:
  Martha Bulengo ✓
  Patricia Cloherty ✓
  Gasbia El Hamamsy ✓
  Annie Jiagge ✓

Lucille Mair
Bertha Beatriz Martinez-Garza
Esther Ocloo
Caroline Pezzullo
Virginia Saurwein
Leslie Sederlund
Leticia Ramos Shahani
Margaret Synder
Martha Stuart
Zohren Tabatabai
Michaela Walsh

1979

- Stichting to Promote Women's World Banking incorporated on May 11 in the Netherlands.
  Friends of WWB/USA, Inc. was initially formed to act as a liaison between the Netherlands and the New York Service Center. In 1986, the affiliate was reorganized with a view to encouraging affiliate development in the United States.

1980

- First International Workshop of Women Leaders in Banking and Finance held in Amsterdam, March 12–15. The women leaders in Banking and Finance represented 27 countries and agreed to launch an organization that would:
  - ► increase women's involvement in the financial workings of their countries, both as entrepreneurs and as decision-makers;
  - ► develop a global network of women in banking and business;
  - ► establish initially a loan guarantee fund as an incentive for lending institutions to extend credit to women;
  - ► create a network of cooperating institutions, or "intermediaries," in each participating country;
  - ► develop a system flexible enough to adapt to varying national needs and conditions;
  - ► offer education and training when needed, prior and/or simultaneous to the delivery of credit;
  - ► seek out enterprising women;
  - ► provide small-scale credit;
  - ► provide start-up credit as well as expand existing credit;
  - ► assist enterprises that will have both an economic and a social impact;
  - ► focus on income-generating activities of low-income women, urban and rural;
  - ► work with cooperative endeavors and group enterprises when feasible;
  - ► cooperate with national and international agencies to broaden the impact.

In essence, the basic objectives have not changed since then, although they have been refined as women have worked to put their ideas into practice.

- Stichting to Promote Women's World Banking is launched, and the first Board of Directors elected:
  ELA BHATT
  SEWA, INDIA
  LILIA CLEMENTE
  Clemente Capital Consultants, Inc.,
  NEW YORK
  OMAYMAH DAHHAN
  University of Jordan, JORDAN

BEATRIZ HARRETCHE
Inter-American Development Bank,
WASHINGTON, DC
ANITA KALFF
Worst & Van Haersolte,
THE NETHERLANDS
GLORIA KNIGHT
Urban Development Corporation,
JAMAICA
ESTHER OCLOO
Nkulenu Industries Ltd., GHANA
ANN ROBERTS
Rockefeller Family Fund,
NEW YORK
VIRGINIA SAURWEIN
Chief, NGO Section/UN,
NEW YORK
MICHAELA WALSH
Rockefeller Brothers Fund,
NEW YORK

Others who have served on the Board:
BERIT AS
University of Oslo, NORWAY
FLORIS BANNIER
Nauta Van Haersolte
THE NETHERLANDS
NANCY BARRY
The World Bank, WASHINGTON, DC
CHRISTINE B-BINDERT
Shearson Lehman Bros.,
NEW YORK
ARTHUR BROWN
United Nations Develop. Prog.,
NEW YORK
DO SONG CHANG
Cho Hung Bank, KOREA
CHINDA CHARUNG-
CHAROENVEJJ
Bangkok Bank, THAILAND
LOURDES LONTOK CRUZ
Paluwagan Ng Bayan S/L Assoc.,
THE PHILIPPINES
BARBRO DAHLBOM-HALL
Management Consultant, SWEDEN
MANILA CHANETON DE VIVO
Artisans Consultant, BRAZIL
FRANS A. ENGERING
Ministry of Finance,
THE NETHERLANDS
SYLVIA FLETCHER
Credimujer, COSTA RICA
BARBARA FLYNN-WILLIAMS
Bajata Agencies, GHANA
MARGARITA GUZMAN
Business Consultant, COLOMBIA
SASKIA HOLLEMAN
Nauta Van Haersolte,
THE NETHERLANDS
J. BURKE KNAPP
The World Bank, WASHINGTON, DC
GEERTJE LYCKLAMA
Institute of Social Studies,
THE NETHERLANDS
RUDOLF S.H. MEES
Nederlandsche Middenstandsbank,
THE NETHERLANDS
ROSMARIE MICHEL
Confiserie Schurter, SWITZERLAND
BABACAR N'DIAYE
African Development Bank,
IVORY COAST
HELEN B. O'BANNON
University of Pennsylvania,
PHILADELPHIA
MARY OKELO
African Development Bank, KENYA
MODUPE IBIAYO OKOJIE
Finance Consultants, Ltd., NIGERIA

ANN PARTLOW
Rockefeller Co., Inc., NEW YORK
DEANNA S. ROSENSWIG
Bank of Montreal, CANADA
DAVID SAMBAR
Sambar Int'l., ENGLAND
MARTHA STUART
Martha Stuart Communications, Inc.,
NEW YORK
NELLIE TAN-WONG
WINTRAC (WWB/Malaysia),
MALAYSIA

- WWB's Business Plan prepared by women from Yale School of Organization and Management.
- WWB/Cali, Colombia and WWB/Western India organized.
- Copenhagen: World Conference of the United Nations Decade for Women.

1981

- Second International Workshop of Women Leaders in Banking and Finance held: 23 countries represented.

At this 1981 meeting:

"It was the best of times, it was the worst of times . . .we had everything before us, we had nothing before us. . ."
*Lila Clemente
(alias Charles Dickens)*

- 1st Regional Workshop for Latin America and the Caribbean, held in May in Cali, Colombia: 11 countries represented.
  Set against an atmosphere of "economic insecurity," the second women leaders workshop is as exciting as the first. Women from 23 countries reaffirm their commitment to WWB's objectives. Progress reports indicate the following:
  - ► WWB's first Loan Guarantee program begins in Cali, Colombia in May 1981;
  - ► WWWB is about to make a direct loan to the Self-Employed Women's Association (SEWA) Cooperative Bank in Ahmedabad, India. This, plus funds raised by Friends of WWB/Western India, will be used by SEWA to strengthen its lending services to women;
  - ► WWB programs are proposed in Brazil, Ghana, the Philippines, Thailand, the United States as well as in Egypt, Kenya, Nigeria and Uruguay;
  - ► WWB office is established in New York City;
  - ► The Workshop spurs on WWB program development in other cities of Colombia and in the Dominican Republic, Haiti, and Uruguay. Trinidad, Venezuela and Jamaica are also interested in WWB.
- Second WWB Program begins at SEWA in India as WWB completes successful negotiations with Reserve Bank of India, and WWB/Western India is incorporated
- First Asia Regional Workshop in December in Ahmedabad, India advances WWB programs in Bangladesh, Indonesia, the Philippines, Sri Lanka and Thailand.

TIMELINE
A SENSE OF HISTORY

1982

- Africa Regional Workshop held in Nairobi attended by representatives of 3 countries: Kenya, Ghana and Cote D'Ivoire.
- Friends of WWB/Nigeria formed.
- WWB Affiliation:
  - Fundacion Banco Mundial de Mujeres (WWB/Cali)
  - Asociacion Dominicana para el Desarollo de la Mujer (ADOPEM), (WWB/Dominican Republic)
  - Friends of Women's World Banking/Ghana Ltd.
  - Fonds Haitien d'Aide a la Femme (FHAF), (WWB/Haiti)
  - Kenya Women Finance Trust Ltd. (KWFT)
- ADOPEM starts programs in training, loan guarantee, direct lending, marketing, health insurance and planning.
- SEWA programs are strengthened with WWB assistance: training, direct lending, savings, marketing.

1983

- Affiliate self-assessment process introduced.
- WWB Affiliation:
  - Fundacion Uruguaya Women's World Banking (WWB/Uruguay)
  - Friends of WWB/Jamaica Ltd.
  - WINTRAC (WWB/Malaysia), Women in Trade & Commerce
  - WWB/Liberia Ltd.
  - Women in Finance and Entrepreneurship Inc. The Philippines (WIFE)
- WWB Loan Guarantee Programs launched at ADOPEM (Dominican Republic) and FHAF (Haiti)

1984

- Third International Workshop for Women Leaders in Banking and Finance in Oosterbeek, the Netherlands held.

  Representatives from 40 countries who attended the Workshop observed that WWB had 21 affiliates geographically dispersed and 19 in formation. The progress WWB has made over the last 2 years is impressive; it is also overwhelming proof that WWB is on the right track, devising practical means whereby women may have equal access to the benefit of the formal economy.

  With the end of the Women's Decade so close at hand, Dr. Esther Ocloo's opening remarks to the 3rd Women's Workshop are salient:

  "The goals of the United Nations Women's Decade are peace, development and equality. In my mind, none of these will be possible without money. Women must have a solid economic foundation. . . . We are here to think of ways of getting economic power into the hands of women throughout the world."

- WWB receives the PAUL HOFFMAN AWARD:
  "For outstandingly significant work in national and international development which serves the human aspiration for a world based on

universal opportunity and justice and demonstrates that mankind, through cooperative endeavour, can achieve this vision of the future society, and for encouraging direct participation of women in the money economies of their countries through loan guarantees which help finance women's income-producing activities."

- WWB Affiliation:
  - FWWB/Thailand
  - Associacao Brasileira para o Desenvolvimento da Mulher-Banco da Mulher (WWB/Brazil)
  - Credimujer (WWB/Costa Rica)
  - Fundacion Honduena para el Desarollo de la Mujer (FUNHDEMU) (WWB/Honduras)
  - UWFCT (Uganda)
  - WWB/West Virginia Affiliate, Inc.
  - Femin' Autres (WWB/France)
- WWB Loan Guarantee Programs launched:
  - WWB/West Virginia Affiliate, Inc.
  - FWWB/Thailand
- Programs initiated:
  - FWWB/USA: information
  - FWWB/Thailand: training, loan guarantee, direct loan, marketing
  - UWFCT: technical assistance

1985

- Africa Regional Operation established in March

  The opening of the Africa Regional Operation by Mary Okelo was a turning point for women in Africa as well as for WWB at large. For WWB as a whole, the opening of WWB/Africa was clear proof that we were serious about decentralizing decision-making and developing a truly democratic global institution.

- United Nations End of Women's Decade Conference and WWB Workshop held in Nairobi
- WWB Workshop for Women in Banking held in New York. Sponsored by Friedrich-Naumann Foundation
- WWB/African Development Bank Seminar in Abidjan
- WWB Affiliation:
  - Corporacion Banco Mundial de la Mujer/Medellin (Colombia)
  - ADIEF (WWB/France)
  - Associazione per la Women's World Banking in Italia
  - Zimbabwe Women's Business Promotion Pvt., Ltd.
- WWB Loan Guarantee Program launched: Kenya Women Finance Trust

1986

- WWB Workshop, Rio de Janeiro (May)
  Rio will be remembered for one main reason. It was where WWB laid down a

clear-cut policy defining the terms and criteria for affiliation with WWB. Before the Rio meeting, affiliation procedures had been flexible to a fault. Now we needed firm and legally binding commitments from women to ensure the long life and credibility of the world's first women-oriented international financial institution.

- Africa Regional Seminar in Nairobi: 15 countries represented
- WWB/ADB Seminar on "Women's Access to Credit"
- WWB Affiliation:
  - National Association for Resource Improvement: NARI (Bangladesh)
  - Banco Mundial de la Mujer/Bucaramanga (Colombia)
  - Association pour l'Integration de la Femme dans l'Economie Malienne: AIFEM (Mali)
  - Societe Senegalaise de Garantie d'Assistance et de Credit: SOSEGAF (Senegal)
  - Women in Finance and Entrepreneurship: WIFE (Nigeria)

1987

- North American Regional Workshop in Charleston, W.Va.
- WWB Affiliation:
  - Women's Finance Trust of Zambia
- Loan Guarantee Scheme launched:
  - WWB/Ghana

1988

- Appointment of WWB Regional Coordinators
  Regional coordination has always been one of WWB's goals. This dimension of WWB's work is now beginning to be realized as cost effective and helpful by partners of WWB.
- WWB Asia Regional Meeting (Malaysia)
- WWB Management Institute preparatory work begins
  The first WWB Management Institute preparatory meeting is held in the Netherlands to broadly outline MI's objectives and define the work of Educational Training Consultants (ETC), which will help to design the training curriculum and syllabus.
- WWB Exchange Trip to Grameen Bank in Bangladesh and SEWA bank in India by several affiliates.
- WWB trip to People's Republic of China
- WWB Affiliation:
  - Fundacion Boliviana para el Desarollo de la Mujer (Bolivia)
  - Association of Women Entrepreneurs of Karnata (AWAKE) India
  - WWB/Philadelphia (USA): Women's Association for Women's Alternatives (WAWA)
  - Women Entrepreneurs Resource Development Agency (WERDAN) (New Delhi, India)
  - Femmes et Initiatives pour le Developpement Economiques de la Guadeloupe (FIDEG)
  - Gambia Women's Finance Company
  - Basali Boitjarong (WWB/Lesotho)
  - Duterimbere (Rwanda)

- WWB Loan Guarantee Program:
  - Fundacion Uruguaya De Ayuda Assistencia a la Mujer (FUAAM): Uruguay

1989

- WWB Africa Regional Seminar in Nairobi: 11 countries represented
- WWB Ten Years Assessment and Partners Review (May–July)
  The Ten Years Assessment and Partners Review begins in May, as a team of independent consultants from Development Finance Corporation (DFC) carry out an unprecedented exercise. At WWR's request, DFC will assess the progress and performance of WWB by focusing on 12 affiliates and analyzing them in depth. DFC treks around Africa, Asia, Latin America and the Caribbean collecting data. After digesting it, DFC delivers its report in November in the Netherlands.
- First WWB Management Institute course conducted (July)
  WWB conducts its first course— Affiliate Management Support Course attended by senior managers from 10 affiliates. The aim of the project is to ensure that the curriculum is based on actual WWB affiliate experience.
- WWB/Europe helps coordinate 5th Management Symposium for Women in Zurich, Switzerland (September)
- WWB Affiliation:
  - Association pour le Promotion Economique de la Femme (APEF) Burundi)
  - Corporacion WWB Filial Chilena de Women's World Banking (Chile)
  - Women's World Finance/Cape Breton Association (Canada)
  - Corporacion Mundial de la Mujer (Bogata, Colombia)
  - Fundacion Mundo Mujer–Popayan (Colombia)
  - Corporacion Femenina Ecuatonana (CORFEC) (Ecuador)
  - Fundacion Laboral WWB en Espana (Spain)
  - Women's Entrepreneurial Growh Organization (Ohio, USA)
  - Women's Economic Assistance Ventures (Ohio, USA)
- WWB/Africa holds its first Technical Support course in December on 'Food Processing'

1990

- WWB's Management Institute Affiliate Management Training syllabus finalized in Oosterbeek, The Netherlands.
  In February, the managers of nine affiliates who attended the WWB Management Institute's first course meet to review the courses and to help prepare the second and third course syllabus to be held for 20 more affiliates. The course is regarded as an overwhelming success.
- WWB Affiliation:
  - Women's World Banking Trinidad & Tobago Ltd.
- WWB Fifth Biennial Affiliates and Trustees Meeting and Tenth Anniversary Celebration in Atlanta, Georgia, USA: "GIVE WOMEN CREDIT," April 21–28

■ BANGLADESH
National Association for Resource Improvements
Friends of WWB in Bangladesh (NARI)
1982–1987
- coordinated training through government
- increased women's employment

1988–1989
- hosted WWB affiliate exchange—Grameen Bank and SEWA—1988
- negotiated WWB loan guarantee agreement with Janata Bank
- organized annual Handicraft Bazaar for products of women entrepreneurs
- provided loans/grants to 8 women's cooperatives
- purchased store-front to retail women's products

■ BOLIVIA
Fundacion Boliviana para el Desarrollo de la Mujer
1982–1987
- attended WWB meeting in Rio, 1986

1988–1989
- affiliated with WWB 1988
- began negotiating WWB Loan Guarantee Agreement
- cooperated in design of management training and funding program for entrepreneurs in slum areas
- held "custom fair" for products made by women

■ BRAZIL
Banco da Mulher –
Associacao Brasileira para o Desenvolvimento da Mulher
1982–1987
- opened 6 branch offices
- signed agreements to launch loan programs with local banks
- cohosted second LA/C regional meeting and Trustees and affiliate meeting in Rio, 1986
- cooperated in technical assistance/trade program—reached 17,500 people

1988–1989
- extended 379 loans valued at US$142,000 at year-end in 1989
- opened 7th branch office
- applied for WWB start-up loan to support branch offices
- obtained US$498,000 grant from IDB to support credit training, and counselling to low-income women entrepreneurs
- 3,092 people reached through information services; total number pople trained in management and marketing skills—2,339

■ BURUNDI
Association pour la Promotion Economique de la Femme (APEF)
1988–1989
- affiliated with WWB 1989
- finalized WWB Loan Guarantee Agreement
- raised US$47,168 local guarantee fund

■ CANADA—CAPE BRETON
Women's World Finance/
Cape Breton Association
1988–1989
- affiliated with WWB 1989
- held mini-conference to launch affiliate, promote WWB and meet with bankers from Cape Breton—May, 1989
- participated in WWB Management Institute
- negotiated WWB Loan Guarantee Agreement

■ CHILE
Corporacion WWB
Filial Chilena de
Women's World Banking
1988–1989
- affiliated with WWB 1989
- negotiated WWB Loan Guarantee Agreement
- established direct lending program; disbursed 6 loans valued at US$9,000
- completed study of women and enterprise in Santiago

■ COLOMBIA—BOGOTA
Corporacion Mundial de la Mujer—Colombia
1988–1989
- initiated credit program for solidarity groups in July, 1989; disbursed 279 loans valued at US$37,400
- opened office with two full-time staff
- trained 1046 people in business administration and accounting
- held trade show for clients to promote their products

■ COLOMBIA—BUCARAMANGA
Fundacion Mundial de la Mujer—Bucaramanga
1982–1987
- participated in staff and clients exchange with Medellin and Cali

1988–1989
- continued direct lending program
- provided borrowers with training in business management
- organized solidarity groups for borrowers
- completed study of local markets and micro credit
- began negotiations for WWB Loan Guarantee Agreement

■ COLOMBIA—CALI
Fundacion WWB–Colombia–Cali
1982–1987
- extended first WWB guaranteed loan
- made contacts to develop affiliates in other cities in Colombia
- extended loans through direct loan program and WWB loan guarantee program
- visited other WWB affiliates in LA/C, Africa, Europe and Asia
- opened 2 branch offices
- participated in staff and clients exchange with Bucaramanga and Cali

1988–1989
- expanded lending activities—nearly 26,000 loans extended; cumulative value US$3,090,227
- developed solidarity group mechanism for borrowers
- developed training and savings programs
- negotiated guarantee agreement with Banco de Occidente
- helped group in Popayan to gain independent status as WWB affiliate after three years as branch office

■ COLOMBIA—MEDELLIN
Corporacion Mundial da la Mujer—Medellin
1982–1987
- established direct loan program
- participated in staff and clients exchange with Bucaramanga and Cali

1988–1989
- increased training and promotional activities for women entrepreneurs
- expanded lending activities— disbursed 3,867 loans valued at US$178,000 by year-end 1989
- offered medical insurance to cients
- obtained grant to purchase house for offices
- developed 260 solidarity groups for over 800 micro-entrepreneurs
- began negotiations for WWB Loan Guarantee Program

■ COLOMBIA—POPAYAN
Fundacion Mundo Mujer—Popayan
1982–1987
- established branch office of WWB affiliate in Cali

1988–1989
- affiliated with WWB Nov. 1989
- increased lending and management training programs for small-scale women entrepreneurs; total loan portfolio valued US$77,000 at year-end 1989
- expanded promotional activities

■ COSTA RICA
Credimujer
1982–1987
- established 2 direct loan programs
- created jobs through lending activities

1988–1989
- established training program to complement loan program
- hit break-even point 1989
- disbursed over 300 loans valued at US$200,000

■ DOMINICAN REPUBLIC
Asociacion Dominicana para el Desarrollo de la Mujer (ADOPEM)
1982–1987
- established WWB Loan Guarantee Program
- developed shopping center/bazaar for borrowers' products
- expanded lending activities to five other areas in D.R.
- held banking seminar with WWB/NY

1988–1989
- increased loan portfolio 45% over 1988; total of 1992 loans valued at US$397,600 extended through direct loan program, while 1,685 loans valued at US$1,039,149 extended through WWB Loan Guarantee Program
- held training sessions in business management reaching over 3,055 women
- organized three trade fairs with ADOPEM clients from entire country
- cohosted third LA/C regional meeting—April, 1988
- participated in pilot technical and financial assistance program for women entrepreneurs with USAID and IESC (International Executive Service Corps)

■ ECUADOR
Corporacion Feminina Ecuatoriana (CORFEC)
1982–1987
- provided training and recreational activities to women entrepreneurs nd their families

1988–1989
- affiliated with WWB 1989
- applied for start-up loan to expand training activities and loan operations
- provided training to 210 women micro-entrepreneurs
- established direct lending program; disbursed 13 loans valued at US$2,500
- organized trade exhibition for women micro-entrepreneurs

■ FRANCE
Association pour le Developpement des Initiatives par les Femmes (ADIEF)
1982–1987
- worked to heighten awareness of government and private sectors concerning women in business
- promoted formation of WWB affiliate in Guadeloupe

1988–1989
- program priorities —creation of financing tool for disadvantaged women and information exchange among businesswomen
- participated in government business advisory program for women

■ FRANCE
Femin'Autres
1982–1987
- provided consultancy services to organizations in West Africa

1988–1989
- developed new training program for women in France and West Africa
- began negotiations for WWB Loan Guarantee Program with Credit Lyonnais
- developed program for small group lending
- participated in group studying effects of savings on local development

■ GAMBIA
Gambia Women's Finance Company (GWFC)
1988–1989
- affiliated with WWB 1988
- collaborating with World Bank—Private Sector Development Project to establish credit and technical assistance program for women entrepreneurs
- received technical support from WWB through Elizabeth Littlefield, consultant from J.P. Morgan, Paris
- negotiated WWB Loan Guarantee Agreement
- held workshop on business management for women in 3 local languages

■ GHANA
Friends of Women's World Banking Ghana, Ltd (WWBG)
1982–1987
- established direct loan portfolio
- provided technical assistance and promoted markets for women entrepreneurs

1988–1989
- completed US$100,000 grant from Foundation for administration, trai and capital fund
- established savings program for market women (SUSU) to circumve exploitation by informal money bro
- disbursed 18 loans valued at US$44,308 through WWB Loan Guarantee Program
- expanded services to rural areas
- participated in WWB Management Institute

■ GUADELOUPE
Femmes et Initiatives pour le Developpement Economique de la Guadeloupe (FIDEG)
1982–1987
- raised capital fund through sale of members' personal items

1988–1989
- affiliated with WWB 1988
- established training program with volunteer staff
- organized trade fair for women's handicrafts (due to Hurricane Hugo postponed until December, 1990)
- offered training in employable/job creating skills

■ HAITI
Fonds Haitien d'Aide a la Femme (FH
1982–1987
- signed two WWB Loan Guarantee Agreements and extended loans fo US $323,000
- sponsored seminars on manageme training
- established direct loan program
- procured medical insurance plan fo borrowers and families

1988–1989
- expanded direct loan program
- expanded management services to clients
- 4 women received loans from Banc Nationale de Credit on strength of FHAF's recommendation
- held trade exhibition for clients' products

■ HONDURAS
Fundacion Hondurena para el Desarr de la Mujer (FUNHDEMU)
1982–1987
- procured funds for direct lending
- started portfolio for home/business site improvement

1988–1989
- initiated major data collection progr aimed at measuring impact and setting future direction for FUNHDE
- increased lending program; 1,294 loans for US$361,165 extended
- offered training in bookkeeping and business management to clients

■ INDIA—AHMEDABAD
Friends of WWB–India
1982–1987
- received WWB loan for US$25,000
- raised US$50,000 to leverage funds with participating local banks in WW direct lending program
- provided technical and management assistance
- promoted savings
- organized exhibition and sale event promote borrowers' products
- conducted village seminars to educa people on available banking facilitie

omplishments of WWB Affiliates

8–1989

- rengthened training and lending
  ctivities; more than 2,000 loans
  tended through direct lending
  ogram
- hosted WWB Exchange Visit
  rameen Bank and SEWA Bank—
  angladesh and India
- ained 70 leaders of 40 SEWA Bank
  vings groups in accounting
  ocedures
- ised US$160,000 for revolving loan
  nd
- negotiated WWB India Fund
  greement to provide loans to 50
  oluntary women's groups throughout
  dia as part of networking activities

NDIA—BANGALORE
ociation of Women Entrepreneurs in
ataka (AWAKE)
2–1987

- eld comprehensive 6-week
  ntrepreneurial development program
- chnical assistance to women in
  art-up businesses

3–1989

- filiated with WWB 1988
- egotiating WWB Loan Guarantee
  greement
- ceived K.L.N. Award for outstanding
  ontribution toward entrepreneurship
  evelopment among women
- usiness training and counselling
  rvices to 350 women

NDIA—NEW DELHI
men Entrepreneurs Resource
elopment Agency (WERDAN)
8–1989

- filiated with WWB 1989
- ised capital fund of US$20,000 in
  st year
- ained 180 women in entrepreneurial
  d managerial strategies

TALY
ociazione per la Women's World
king in Italia
2–1987

- ed capital of US$35,000
- ganized unemployed young women
  provide training and promote
  ntrepreneurship

8–1989

- ovided financial and credit
  ounselling
- eld training program for women
  ntrepreneurs in Milan
- ounselled women high school
  aduates on employment
  pportunities
- articipated in WWB Management
  stitute

MAICA
nds of Women's World Banking
aica, Ltd.
2–1987

- gned Loan Guarantee Agreement
  ith WWB

8–1969

- unched direct lending program,
  xtending 14 loans for US$18,565 by
  ear-end 1989
- ursued fundraising activities to
  crease funds for lending program
  nd to assist borrowers who suffered
  sses during Hurricane Hugo

KENYA
ya Women's Finance Trust (KWFT)
2–1987

- stablished direct lending program
- ained clients in basic business
  anagement
- gned WWB Loan Guarantee
  greement with Barclay's Bank
- pened two rural branch offices

8–1989

- 29 loans for US$144,438; 35 loans
  alued at US$74,875 extended through
  WD Loan Guarantee Program
- articipated in WWB Management

Institute

- negotiated WWB Loan Guarantee
  Agreement with Barclay's Bank
  (Barclay's increased its % of
  guarantee)

■ LESOTHO
Basali Boitjarong (Women for Self
Reliance)
1982–1987

- more than 450 members countrywide
- raised capital fund of US$10,000 from
  membership fees

1988–1989

- affiliated with WWB 1988
- started negotiating WWB Loan
  Guarantee Agreement
- compiled financial resources guide for
  local businesswomen
- developed proposal for technical
  assistance

■ MALAYSIA
WINTRAC (WWB/Malaysia)
Sdn. Bhd. Women in
Trade and Commerce
1982–1987

- raised capital fund of US$100,000
- started dealership for Toshiba and
  opened showroom in Seremban
- started project to invest and operate
  hotel
- provided management counselling and
  seminar organization to local
  companies

1988–1989

- direct lending program
- cohosted SWWB Annual Board of
  Trustees meeting and 1st Asia
  Regional Meeting in 1988
- acted as interim WWB regional
  coordination office
- collected information from WWB Asian
  affiliates on status of women in work
  force in Asia
- organized regional WWB/Asia Seminar
  to be held in late 1990

■ MALI
Association pour l'Integration de la
Femme dans l'Economie Malienne
(AIFEM)
1988–1989

- structured lending program with
  assistance of Ms. E. Littlefield,
  WWB/consultant
- negotiating WWB Loan Guarantee
  Agreement with Banque Malienne de
  Credit et de Depots

■ NETHERLANDS
Stichting WWB/Nederland
1982–1987

- cohosted WWB meeting in Oosterbeck
  1984
- organized first WWB European
  Regional meeting 1987
- produced WWB video shown at World
  Bank for marketing and promotional
  purposes
- helped raise capital for SWWB and
  affiliates

1988–1989

- helped WWB affiliates apply for grants
  to Dutch government
- hosted cultural event for participants
  in WWB Management Institute
- hosted WWB and Donor Review
  meeting

■ PHILIPPINES
Women in Finance and Entrepreneurship
(WIFE)
1982–1987

- established Big Sister–Small Sister
  program in rural areas
- provided financial and technical advice
  to clients
- established links with similar
  organizations for joint training and
  development programs

1988–1989

- developed proposal for direct lending
  program

- started negotiating WWB Loan
  Guarantee Agreement
- obtained grant with help from
  WWB/NY from Church of the Brethren
  for operations
- participated in WWB Management
  Institute
- opened office; increased membership
- cosponsored three-day Trade Fair for
  300 community projects and
  micro-entrepreneurs

■ RWANDA DUTERMIBERE
1982–1987

- obtained start-up assistance from
  UNICEF
- promoted WWB through "Awareness
  Seminars"

1988–1989

- affiliated with WWB 1988
- devised and implemented credit
  training and technical assistance
  program
- began construction of 4-story building
  to house affiliate and provide rental
  income
- finalized guarantee agreement with
  local bank—bank to cover 65% on
  loans administered by DUTERMIBERE
- granted 8 loans for US$12,500

■ SENEGAL
Societe Senegalaise de Garantie
d'Assistance et de Credit (SOSEGAF)
1988–1989

- worked toward setting up Women's
  Bank in Senegal
- held WWB Awareness Seminar
  attended by hundreds of women and
  developed promotional brochure
- networked with other women's
  organizations in Senegal

■ SPAIN
Fundacion Laboral WWB en Espana
1988–1989

- affiliated with WWB 1989
- opened office October, 1989
- raised funds to develop training course
  on self-empowerment for women
- approved 6 guarantee applications
  valued at US$135,000 through
  agreement with Caja de Ahorros
- held 1st Annual Trade Fair of Products
  and Services of Women-Owned
  Businesses—November, 1989, Madrid

■ THAILAND
Friends of WWB Association in Thailand
(FWWBT)
1982–1987

- established WWB loan guarantee
  program
- opened 2 branch offices in northern
  and southern rural regions
- established Women's World Enterprise
  as marketing arm for clients

1988–1989

- obtained USAID grant to expand
  training and administrative support for
  clients
- organized trade show for over 100
  village women handicrafters
- extended 2,308 loans valued at
  US$886,813 (cumulative) through WWB
  Loan Guarantee Program and direct
  lending program
- participated in WWB Management
  Institute

■ UGANDA
Uganda Women's Finance and Credit
Trust (UWFCT)
1982–1987

- raised local and international support
- secured line of credit of US$15,000 for
  borrowers

1988–1989

- operated direct lending and training
  program for women entrepreneurs
- extended 85 direct loans totalling
  US$69,731
- began negotiations for WWB loan
  guarantee scheme with Uganda
  Commercial Bank

- ran management training sessions
- established savings scheme for clients
- participated in WWB Management
  Institute

■ URUGUAY
Fundacion Uruguaya de Ayuda y
Asistencia a la Mujer (FUAAM)
1982–1987

- raised seed capital US$52,000
- established direct lending program

1988–1989

- office space in local bank
- signed WWB Loan Guarantee
  Agreement for US$100,000 with Banco
  de la Republica
- extended 30 loans valued at US$79,588
  through direct lending program
  (cumulative)
- counselled clients on business
  management
- completed market survey to define
  targeted programs

■ USA—OHIO (AKRON)
Women's Entrepreneurial Growth
Organization (WEGO)
1982–1987

- attended WWB/West Virginia affiliate
  seminar—How to Start a WWB
  Affiliate—1987

1988–1989

- affiliated with WWB 1989
- developed comprehensive business
  management course for clients
- designed credit program structure
- expanded staff to 3 full-time paid staff
  and 3 volunteers

■ USA—OHIO (YELLOW SPRINGS)
Women's Economic Assistance Ventures
(WEAV)
1988–1989

- affiliated with WWB 1989
- obtained tax exempt status and
  launched local capital fund
- one-day seminar "So You Want to
  Start a Business"

■ USA—PENNSYLVANIA
Women's Associacion for Women's
Alternatives
1982–1987

- offered programs in housing, child
  care, career counselling and job
  placement to women

1988–1989

- affiliated with WWB 1988
- started negotiating WWB Loan Guarantee Agreement with six local banks
- chosen by State of Pennsylvania as
  one of 3 demonstration sites to
  provide training and assistance to self-
  employed low-income women
- held two 16-week training courses for
  women entrepreneurs

■ USA—WEST VIRGINIA
Women's World Banking,
West Virginia Affiliate, Inc.
1982–1987

- provided management counselling to
  women entrepreneurs
- signed WWB Loan Guarantee Agreement; extended 4 loans for US$23,148
- hosted meeting on how to start WWB
  affiliate for interested groups in North
  America—1987

1988–1989

- worked to strengthen mgmt. structure
- obtained grant of US$44,000 for credit
  program
- developed 4 programs around state to
  work with applicants for loan program
- contracted with local bank to
  guarantee small loans on 50/50 basis

■ ZAMBIA
Women's Finance Trust of Zambia, Ltd.
(WFTZ)
1982–1987

- raised seed capital

1988–1989

- negotiated WWB Loan Guarantee
  Agreement with Zambia National
  Commercial Bank
- hosted two-day National Seminar on
  Women and Credit
- provided input on Women and
  Development to Zambia Government
  National Development Plan

■ ZIMBABWE
Zimbabwe Women Finance Trust Ltd.
(ZWFT)
1988–1989

- raised seed money for capital fund
- started negotiating WWB Loan
  Guarantee Agreement with Barclay's
  Bank, Zimbabwe
- designed training program linked with
  credit program
- 1989 registered as non-profit
- purchased property for office and
  training center

1

FROM KANSAS CITY TO MEXICO CITY

"Too high-risk for women"

HOW DID A young woman from Kansas City end up participating in a global movement to ensure women had ownership over their production and reproduction, and eventually help assemble and lead an institution to accomplish this? Looking back over my life, I can see how experience and attitude shaped me for this role.

One of the fundamental threads that weave through my life tapestry is that of interconnection. Just as I could never have started Women's World Banking alone, I would not have ended up where I did if not for the influence of my family, particularly my family's history of working toward social justice. I knew from the age of seven that I didn't want to be a stay-at-home mom, and that I wanted to travel. In high school, I did a lot of volunteer work. I was especially motivated by the work of my grandfather, Frank P. Walsh,[1] who became one of the social leaders in this country during the late nineteenth and early twentieth centuries. He co-wrote the congressional proposal for the child-labor law and for the eight-hour workday, and worked all his life for businesses to give living wages to their workers. He was a strong voice for social and legal justice at a time when factory workers often didn't earn enough to pay rent and buy food for the family.

Another life thread is my connection to the environment. As a child, I had my own garden, and I loved to walk through the woods at my grandparents' farm, pick wild strawberries and raspberries, and follow streams. I still have my freshman Biology course report on the variety of trees in Kansas City, Missouri—dedicated to President Harry S. Truman—which my father took to the White House and had autographed by the president. One of my motivations to work with Women's World Banking was my belief that until experts connected and communicated with people at the grass-roots level, there was no real hope of saving the planet. Early in my career, I was charged with helping give grants to environmental organizations, and the motto of one group, the New Alchemy Institute, was "to learn to live more gently on the earth." This thinking resonated with my vision. This experience of bottom-up influence translated into one of the cornerstones of Women's World Banking.

Another truth about me is that I always felt like the black sheep in my family; the one who did things differently and saw things in different ways. With hindsight, I think I must have had a learning disability, maybe dyslexia, which helped make me a good listener. Above all, I learned to trust my instincts.

After college, I went into finance, because that's where the power was, and I was fascinated by how one could use power to make people's lives better. My first job was as a sales assistant for Merrill Lynch in Kansas City. When I decided to move to New York City, Bates Huffaker, manager of the firm's Kansas City office, suggested that I transfer to the Merrill Lynch headquarters on Wall Street while I decided my next steps. In 1957 I got a job as the assistant to the manager of Merrill's New York City Foreign Department. Merrill Lynch International had just been launched with offices in Geneva and Paris.

I attended night school at the New York Institute of Finance to become a registered representative of the New York Stock Exchange. Then, in 1960, when Merrill Lynch was planning to open in Beirut, Lebanon, staff going to the Beirut office encouraged me to join them. But the personnel office of Merrill Lynch said "no." When I asked why, I was told it was too high-risk for women.

Confronted with that refusal, I resigned from Merrill Lynch USA and paid my own way to Beirut. That's how different it was to be a woman in finance in 1960! My route took me through Spain, where I was held for six weeks because I did not have a visa for Lebanon. I was offered a job in the Madrid Merrill Lynch office, but although I wanted to learn Spanish, I knew that if I did not go to Beirut I would always wonder what I missed. Finally they understood that I was determined. My visa was granted, and I went to Beirut and was hired by Merrill Lynch International.

My time in Beirut (1960–64), followed by a stint in London (1964–65), changed my life. It exposed me to the world, to different cultures and ideas, to new technologies and the beginnings of global finance. As soon as I stepped off the plane in Beirut, I felt as if I were walking into a cloud of passion. The heat and the dynamics of people, even the way people walked and related to each other on the street, were markedly different from my own culture. I was 26. For the first six months of my stay, I worked seven days a week, sometimes ten hours a day. I was working in a language I did not speak, and teaching myself procedures I did not know. After a while I got to know people, and then

ROCKEFELLER CENTER EMPLOYEE ID CARD

after long days at work, I would change my clothes, go out dancing, come home, take a shower, and go back to work. For nearly five years, I barely slept. Although I had never before lived in an environment with security checks near my home and on all major roads, I never felt fear or violence. Life was full of long hours of work and play.

Many people from my time in Beirut remain friends: Myrtle Haidar, with whom I shared an apartment with balconies overlooking the sea and the mountains; David Sambar, a distinguished international banker and financial expert who eventually became a WWB trustee; and Genevieve Maxwell, an American journalist with Beirut's English-language newspaper, *The Daily Star*. Genevieve remained a mentor until her death in 2004. My years in Beirut gave me my adult sense of identity and a lifelong love of the Middle East.

Working in a totally new culture, I realized that I could learn how to manage and gain the confidence to do a job that I had never done before. It was learning by doing rather than from a textbook. This observation played a role later when I began to work with women around the world.

I also learned to question my own assumptions. A turning point came when an office boy said to me, "*Why do I have to do it your way? We've always done it this way.*" I was struck by my own sense that the American way was the only way, and at that moment it became clear to me that there are many ways to arrive at a successful outcome—another principle that would be fundamental in the architecture of WWB more than a decade later.

As acting operations manager of Merrill Lynch Beirut, I learned to handle back-office operations and communications with the New York home office and with the sales force, who were coping with a uniquely active commodities market. We introduced a direct wire from New York to Beirut. Real-time investing and trading was a first-time phenomenon in that part of the world; it was the beginning of global finance. Men, and only men, came and traded from all over the Middle East. As a woman running the office, I was something of an oddity. Later on, I found out that I was regarded with intrigue and that there was a lot of talk about what I was "really about," since I was a member of the NYSE (New York Stock Exchange), and wasn't a dancer at the Kit Kat Club down the street or attached to a sheikh or ambassador.

As I was getting ready to leave Beirut in 1964, Merrill Lynch offered me an opportunity to work in its newly opened City of London office. The Bank of England had recently changed the laws to allow foreign brokers to do business in London. The international financial-brokerage community was just beginning to form, in contrast to forty-some years later, when fifty percent of British revenue would come from the financial sector. Other than secretaries, there were no women in the City. Merrill Lynch was one of the first international brokerage offices to be opened in London, at 10 Fenchurch Street, and it had hired an advertising company to market brochures on *How to Buy Stocks* and *How to Read a Financial Report*. Unbeknownst to Merrill Lynch, the British were crazy about advertisements and clipping coupons, and the office was soon inundated with thousands of requests. So my work was to train personnel to handle these "prospective clients." After many memorable experiences in that foggy and lovely city, I returned to New York. There were no opportunities for advancement at Merrill Lynch, so I joined a firm that was representing one of the first hedge funds, City Associates, and ultimately became a partner of Boettcher & Company, the firm that traded the first mutual fund on the New York Stock Exchange. At the same time, I enrolled in Hunter College and completed my undergraduate degree.

All of these experiences helped me understand how little access women had to the economy. It would be years before I would pursue that idea, but I did learn to work with groups outside the formal work environment. During my time in Beirut, I helped start the Financial International Group (FIG); we were the first group to create monthly social gatherings for expats who were neither presidents of organizations nor ambassadors. We made exciting field trips to Syria, Jordan, Greece, Egypt, and Cyprus. When I returned to New York, I was one of the early vice presidents of the Financial Women's Association on Wall Street. Other than the Women's Bond Club, there were no financial women's associations, and we were trying to encourage the development of a network for women. I remember writing out questions for women to stand up and ask when we had guest speakers at lunch, since women were reticent to ask questions in public. It was a different world!

In the 1970s, while volunteering to teach high-school equivalency on Manhattan's Lower East Side to teenagers who had dropped out of school because of drugs, I helped start a program on drug education at the New York Junior League. We produced a book on all the drug and alcohol information and rehabilitation facilities in the New York City area and then put together educational programs for Parent-Teacher Associations (PTAs) with medical professionals. In those days, there was so much denial, and such a lack of information about drugs and alcohol.

It was becoming clear to me that there was a gap between my personal values and my work on Wall Street. Although I had had conversations about investments with a woman at the Ford Foundation, I knew nothing about the nonprofit world. (That woman was Lilia Clemente, then an investment officer at the foundation. Years later Lilia managed WWB investments.) Through my volunteer work in drug education on the Lower East Side, I began to learn about the work of foundations in New York City. Jane Lee Eddy, executive director of the Taconic Foundation and a colleague in the drug-education effort, introduced me to people from the Rockefeller Family Fund offices.

Without looking for the next phase in my life, it just happened. In 1972 I became a program associate at the Rockefeller Brothers Fund (RBF). Walking into the Rockefeller offices was like entering grad school; it opened up a world of information, ideas, and people that I had never encountered. William (Bill) Dietel, former president of Rockefeller Brothers Fund, stands out as a mentor and someone who had a lasting impact in changing my life's direction. He could identify people's strengths and help them develop their potential. His influence on me was one of the major influences on my life that paved the way for my role in Women's World Banking.

As part of the civic and cultural values program at the RBF, I was again working in a totally new environment full of new ideas, intellectual challenges, and with a team of diverse professionals focused on policy and social change. My assignment was to bring new ideas to program officers. The appropriate-technology movement was evolving. New ideas were everywhere. I was

IN MEXICO CITY IN 1975; FROM LEFT, MICHAELA WALSH, ELA BHATT, HAMIDA HOSSEIN, ROUNAQ JAHAN, ADRIENNE GERMAIN, DEVAKI JAIN, AND JOAN DUNLOP, WHO DIED JUNE 29, 2012

assigned to visit the Lindisfarne Association community established on Long Island by William Irwin Thompson, a former Massachusetts Institute of Technology professor and author of *At the Edge of History*. Lindisfarne incorporated meditation and teachings from diverse spiritual traditions and applied learning through community labor. This was perhaps my first encounter with the connection between globalization, innovative learning, and holistic thinking. I remain connected as a Lindisfarne Fellow and deeply value what I continue to learn from our annual Fellows meetings.

In addition to learning more about appropriate technology, I was exploring other issues. John D. Rockefeller 3rd and his associate Joan Dunlop, who has been a valued friend over many years, briefed the staff about his groundbreaking speech at the Bucharest World Population Conference in August 1974. One of my colleagues and I were seeking new ideas on how to help improve the economic status of women and how the Foundation might support that goal. I met Arvonne Fraser in the office of her husband, Congressman Don Fraser; she was interested in economic policies that would serve as a social safety net for all women, regardless of their economic or social status. These introductions, and many others as well, put me in touch with people involved in plans for the first United Nations World Conference on Women.

Talking with Bill Dietel many years later, I discovered that in addition to his own predisposition to encourage people to pursue their dreams, there was institutional support for innovation available at that time from the Rockefeller Brothers Fund.

Bill Dietel

In 1970, and the immediate years thereafter, the Rockefeller brothers were at their peak, in terms of energy, time, and funds to invest in their nonprofit activities. Prompted by the failing health of Dana Creel, the long time president, the brothers decided that they needed to take a fresh look at what they were doing with the Brothers Fund. I had a special assignment to understand what the big emerging issues were and, after about three years, my findings were issued in a report to the board by President Creel. So by the time of the 1975 Mexico City Conference, we had the board's approval for a shift in our thinking. That took place against a background: Richard Nixon was into the business of thinking about the future. It sounds improbable now, but it was possible, even in certain conservative circles, to tackle problems from a fresh perspective. The Club of Rome was active, Jay Forrester was doing his system-dynamics work at MIT, and we, along with the younger generation of Rockefellers, were plugged into these developments that characterized the social changes of that time. There was a readiness to take action, even though some of the elders thought their children were crazy. It was very clear to me that as a foundation staff we were too wedded to our desks and needed to get out and see what was going on. We encouraged a lot of our staff people to break out of that little mold.

Sending me to the first World Conference on Women in Mexico City was part of that strategy. I had not expected to go to the conference, and didn't initially understand how I would contribute to such a meeting, but I was excited to attend—I knew little about the world of international development and had never been to Mexico.

When the UN began planning the Mexico City conference, Joan Dunlop and I met with Zohreh (Zuzu) Tabatabai, who was then a young diplomat working at the Iranian Mission to the UN and supporting the work of the conference chair, Princess Ashraf ul-Mulki Pahlavi, the sister of the Shah of Iran. The conference agenda hadn't been set, and Zuzu proved to be someone who influenced meetings and helped me understand how things really worked.

The declaration by the UN General Assembly of 1975 as International Women's Year was a response to rising feminist efforts around the world. The February-March 1974 International Forum on the Role of Women in Population and Development at the UN's New York Headquarters was preceded by regional conferences that helped define the role of women in population and development for the International Decade for Women. The World Food Conference talked about population and food, and Africa's input mentioned husbands' roles. A study conducted in advance of the 1975 UN Women's Conference in Mexico City demonstrated that men tend to spend money on themselves first, while women prioritize spending on their children and family.

Mexico City in the summer of 1975 helped reflect new understanding of the economic condition of women. Ester Boserup, a Danish economist and writer who worked for the United Nations, had published an analysis in 1965 questioning the assumption of gender neutrality in the costs and benefits of development. Boserup pointed out that, "Women perform over sixty-five percent of the world's work, earn only ten percent of the income, and own less than one percent of the world's property."[2] This study affected the understanding of women's role in the workforce and human development. Women's work had never before been included in the GDP (gross domestic product).

I am grateful to Anne Walker (International Women's Year Tribune Center), Judith Bruce (Population Council), and Jacqui Starkey (Consultants in Development and Planning Assistance Inc.), as well as to Rosaline Harris (co-director of the NGO Tribune with Mildred Persinger), for the insightful historical stories of the leading roles they played in helping to make the NGO conference an event that, despite having had no formal agenda, would positively affect the future of women in development worldwide.

Jacqui Starkey

After the Mexico City conference and at its urging, the years 1975–85 were declared the UN Decade for Women. The World Conference on Women was held from July 19 to 21. The International Women's Year Tribune (IWY), a meeting for nongovernmental organizations, ran concurrently with the UN conference. This is well-explained in the report of a seminar held June 20, 1975, at the IWY Tribune, Mexico City, "Third World Craftsmen and Development":

> International Women's Year, proclaimed for 1975 by the United Nations, had as its climax two conferences that were held at the same time in Mexico City, from June 19 through July 2. Although not competing conferences, the two were quite different in organization and constituency. The 1975 World Conference was a closed conference to which only officially designated governmental representatives were accredited. The Tribune (NGO Forum for International Women's Year) was an open conference in which all interested people and organizations were welcome to participate.

The American Association for the Advancement of Science (AAAS), along with the United Nations Institute for Training and Research (UNITAR) and the United Nations Development Program (UNDP), convened an international seminar in Mexico City on Women in Development (WID) immediately preceding the UN Conference. The seminar, organized by Irene Tinker, was intended to consider a bibliography of studies and data she had collected, which indicated that development programs may have had a negative impact on women. It was during discussions of the seminar's Food Processing and Small Technology Committee that the idea of an "International Women's Development Bank" originated. A small steering committee was then formed to further explore the idea, including drafting language to be incorporated in a UN General Assembly resolution.

During my two weeks in Mexico City, I met many remarkable women. One night I had dinner with Joan Dunlop, Adrienne Germain (Ford Foundation), Devaki Jain (India), Rounaq Jahan (Bangladesh), and others—all leaders in articulating the women's movement, especially as it related to women's reproductive rights. Some in the group would lead the groundbreaking International

Women's Health Coalition. There I met Ela Bhatt, who had launched SEWA (Self Employed Women's Association) in India. Ela became a founding member of WWB in 1980, served as chair of the Board of Trustees in the 1990s, and remains a member of WWB today.

Esther Ocloo, a businesswoman from Ghana who participated in the AAAS seminar, described how its discussions evolved in her *History of Women's World Banking*.

Esther Ocloo

One of the subcommittees at the AAAS conference was on problems of women as farmers, chaired by ChoKyun Rha of Korea. It came out during the discussions . . . that access to credit due to lack of collateral was one of the basic problems women face. It was at this point that I made a passionate appeal for setting up a women's bank. The idea was received with such excitement and applause that the six women participants of the subcommittee were encouraged to take up the challenge. They were Gasbia el Hamamsy (Egypt), Chokyun Rha (Korea), Bertha Martinez Garza (Mexico), Esther Ocloo (Ghana), Margaret (Peg) Snyder (UN Economic Commission for Africa), and Virginia Saurwein (ECOSOC) [United Nations Economic and Social Council]. . . . One had to be in Mexico to believe the level to which the declaration of the International Women's Year raised the consciousness and solidarity of women. . . . It seemed as if there was a strong call to all men and women: "All hands on deck"—to save the world through women. The WWB idea was considered as one of the major solutions to the problems facing women.

ZuZu Tabatabai describes the inside story of the UN World Conference on Women.

Zohreh (ZuZu) Tabatabai

I was a delegate (third secretary, then second secretary) at the Iranian Mission to the United Nations. As I was a woman, the mission figured I could follow the issues related to the women's conference. None of the member states wanted to host the women's conference; then Mexico came forward. The princess of Iran was furious that Iran didn't host it, so the prep com (preparatory committee) was created so that Iran could play a role. It was put together at the last minute—no one was prepared for what we were supposed to do. The prep com was a brief two-three day meeting that gave delegates an opportunity to meet and become familiarized with the issues that would be on the agenda in Mexico City, but the big divide came when it turned out that the participants in the prep com would not necessarily be attending the Women's Conference in Mexico.

The Secretariat for the women's conference had prepared a ton of documents. All the delegates needed to be prepared, so I formed a working group of young delegates, as well as NGO representatives and the Secretariat. We sat down together and came up with twelve sets of issues that we thought were main questions and problems, and that became a draft paper that we presented at the prep com. Elizabeth Reid (the first gender adviser to a head of government—the Australian Labour Prime Minister Gough Whitlam, chief of the Australian delegation to the women's conference), who chaired the sessions, picked our simple one-page document out of a basket full of different materials, and thought it would be a good basis to begin the discussions, as we had articulated a brief statement of the problems to be addressed along with bullet points covering the main issues like women's health, participation in politics, etc. The Indian delegation agreed with her.

Because of my work on the draft paper and Iran's chairmanship, many NGOs that wanted to help started appearing at the Permanent Mission of Iran. Michaela Walsh and Joan Dunlop came to find out how they could help. So, we walked through what we thought would happen; it was one of the first major conferences of the UN, so there weren't many precedents to draw on, everyone had their own views as to what should take place. I explained that Iran would chair the second committee, which focused on development issues, but it was only once we were in Mexico that I discovered that NGOs were being kept as far away as possible from the formal proceedings. In those days, member states were worried about NGOs being radical revolutionaries; the idea that they might be cooperative was not seen as an option, they were viewed more like rabble-rousers. I thought there had to be a dialogue among all parties and hoped everyone could participate, but all the delegates were in the main conference center, while the NGOs and foundations were at another center all the way across town. At one point, the delegates started whispering, "The NGOs are coming." The Mexicans were wondering what was going on. Bella Abzug and a group of women had decided they would come to the main conference and make their views known.

The real wheeler-dealers were the male delegates who knew their way around the General Assembly and had come to the conference from UN Headquarters. In contrast, many of the other members of delegations were coming from capitals and had no UN experience, so it was all very novel for them. The minute the discussions became political, the men climbed over the women's heads to take the floor. That's how the discussion wound up turning around to "Zionism is racism," etc. The women weren't focused on that, but we still hadn't learned how to take over the mike, so at night the women got into huddles to figure out how to make something come out of the meeting. In the second committee, we discussed all the issues that women wanted discussed, including access to credit, the fact that women couldn't have their own businesses. . . and we were working on a draft declaration that would come out of Mexico. We were totally disillusioned and exhausted.

Eventually a group of NGO women got together with some of the delegates, including myself and the Jamaican, Indian, and Scandinavian delegates, to discuss how we could get something useful out of the conference. One of those discussions revolved around how women could have access to power, and I recall Michaela chimed in and said, "Unless women have access to money and credit, they're not going to have the power." Michaela was one of the few women at the meetings who had actually worked in finance and banking. The women explained how the banks didn't loan them money.

Michaela had this bee in her bonnet: only through the real economy would women have power. A handful of us who were there bought into her idea, and she kept in contact. The idea excited us, but it was so overwhelming. I don't think any of us thought it would really happen, but Michaela was so persevering . . .; she was like a beacon working from beginning to end. All of us worked peripherally, *but she continued to push the envelope. I think we were all amazed that it happened, because there were so many stumbling blocks.*

Experiencing the extraordinary diversity and the powerful level of energy that existed in Mexico City among women around the world opened my eyes to a new reality. When I saw conference delegates clad in magnificently colored African dresses and Asian saris instead of black suits, it was clear to me that the world was changing. One thing was certain: my vision of the world had altered dramatically. I had worked in banking until then. I hadn't reflected on how you could have a developing economy when fifty percent of the workforce had no access to the tools of production. Mexico City was a game-changer for my life, a complete paradigm shift.

ChoKyun Rha, professor of biomaterials science and engineering at MIT, remembers how she, too, was taken aback by the points that emerged in Mexico City.

ChoKyun Rha

I was asked to attend the conference as a representative of Far Eastern countries. Everyone was discussing what the critical issues were for women's development and giving personal examples to illustrate their points. Esther Ocloo shared how she had been penniless and orphaned as an adolescent and had received one quarter in cash from an aunt. That was the first money she had ever possessed, and she was determined to make something out of it to change her future. So she bought a glass jar and went around collecting berries or fruit and made jam and sold it. . . . That was how she became an entrepreneur, and understood the importance of having financial means to get started. The idea of a women's bank developed from there.

Margaret (Peg) Snyder, who was working at the UN Economic Commission for Africa, providing nominations of regional delegates to the conference, offered additional background on how the impetus for the resolution on women's access to credit emerged.

Margaret (Peg) Snyder

We had just established the African Training Research Center for Women in Addis Ababa within the UN Social Development Division. Women were our main concern, and the issues they cared about were along the lines of social justice and apartheid, recognizing that women couldn't advance if the whole society was kept down. Whereas women from the North were talking about women's equality in the workplace and in the home, women in the South had a different perspective; they were talking about social justice for everyone, and especially for women. In our advocacy, we resisted using any of the "women's lib" terms, like the word "empowerment," for example, because they frightened people, when what the women were actually concerned with was improving the supply of food and the education system for their children and for their country. The issue of access to credit was also on their minds, because, in the rare situations when women had access to credit, it was from moneylenders who charged 100 percent interest. When I first went to the Economic Commission in '71, there was already a fellow working for the International Labor Organization (Al Major) who was pioneering credit in Swaziland as a buffer against women having to turn to the "terrible moneylenders."

The resolution on access to credit by women that was formulated at Mexico City and later adopted by the General Assembly[3] was passed thanks to people like Virginia Saurwein, the chief of the NGO Section at the UN; Lucille Mair of Jamaica; Leticia Shahani from the Philippines; and Mrs. Justice Annie Jiagge, who was the first woman Superior Court justice in Ghana, among other strong women who held important positions in their government and were able to get support from the men on their delegations as well. There was, of course, an educational process, and a constant mindfulness to frame the resolution in such a way that it was directed more towards rural women, thus eliciting some sympathy in the context of food production, which men could relate to in terms of its importance to society overall. The voices of women like Esther Ocloo from Ghana, who emphasized the detrimental impact of lack of credit on the activities of women farmers, were vital in that regard. In fact, I think the idea first came up at the American Association for the Advancement of Science, when Esther Ocloo said, pounding her fists, "I'm so tired of these moneylenders; what we need is a women's world bank!" And wow! Everybody lit on that, and we ran to a hotel room after the meeting and we started drafting this resolution. (See the text of the resolution, p. 192.)

It was the first global UN conference that had a majority of women delegates representing the governments. I remember how the United States was going to send a man, until Republican women like Patricia Hutar, Virginia Allan, and others protested so loudly that the situation changed, and the delegation was led by women. All of the women realized that while the movement they were creating in Mexico City constituted an amazing step, institutions were needed to carry it forward. That's why UNIFEM (the United Nations Fund for Women), INSTRAW (the International Research and Training Institute for the Advancement of Women), WWB, and the International Women's Tribune Center were created. In our efforts to get these institutions established, it was a kind of "let's get resources where we can find them" situation. For example, we had money from the Economic Commission in Africa, the Ford Foundation, the UN, and governments, but none of them dictated exactly how the money should be spent, so we proposed what would be done, and they agreed. It was an era of new ideas before the turf wars among and within institutions set in. Everybody wanted to join this lively thing that was happening, and there was a very good network of UN civil servants to support that momentum. I once was quoted as saying that the UN was the unlikely godmother of the global women's movement, and in some ways, I think it's true.

Leticia Ramos Shahani, who had worked for the UN Section on the Status of Women prior to joining the foreign service of the Philippines and represented her country at the Commission on the Status of Women and at the Mexico City conference, recounts her experience in her essay for *Developing Power.*[4]

Leticia Ramos Shahani

The demand from the developing countries for emphasis on development issues at the UN slowly brought more focus on women. The Western emphasis on human rights—that is, civil and political rights—was not adequate to convince the poor countries that this was the main issue for women. In order for human rights to be realized and exercised, observed those in developing countries, the proper economic and social conditions—such as the rights to education, employment, and freedom of expression—had to be created and put in place. Development would create these conditions. . . . The organization of the series of global conferences on women forced governments to take the women's issue seriously and gave the NGOs all over the world unprecedented support at all levels for their efforts. Although the word "networking" was not officially adopted until the Nairobi conference in 1985, the ease and speed with which women communicated with each other along informal and flexible lines had already been discovered and put in motion in the 1970s. The phenomenon of networking by and among women was born then.

Comfort Engmann, who was a member of the National Council of Women and Development in Ghana, and went on to become one of the founders of WWB-Ghana, recalled her experience.

Comfort Engmann

In advance of the Mexico City conference, we brought women together from all over the country who were operating "micro-businesses." We thought what they needed was education. They pointed out that their daughters who had gone through school were powerless because they didn't have capital, so they couldn't work. They thought that money in the poor person's pocket was the answer. The women made me humble. When I went among them in the markets, they gave me wisdom. I saw that they were right.

Just as the conference was an unprecedented platform for women from the South, it was an equally transformative experience for women from the North. Barbro Dahlbom-Hall, a Swedish pioneer in management training whom I would first meet and collaborate with several years later when WWB was getting off the ground, also attended the women's conference.

Barbro Dahlbom-Hall

In 1975, following my encouraging the Trade Union of Swedish Academics (SIACO) to engage themselves in management training, they decided to send five of their most well-known women to Mexico. A much bigger trade union sent ninety-three journalists, representing all the big papers. Only one of the journalists was a woman. We were there for three weeks. It was unbelievable for me to see women from around the world fighting to come on the stage and discuss their issues. However, what's even more unusual is that, for the five women from SIACO, it was the first time we had ever come together to talk about women's issues and leadership!

In addition to the amazing women in Mexico City, there were extraordinary men. Jan Pronk, an economist who was appointed head of the Ministry of Development in the Netherlands in 1973, counts the Mexico City meeting as a "major education," as he indicated in our recent conversation. He remained involved and in later years played a role in helping fund the women's movement.

Jan Pronk

I was interested in non-Western socialization as related to development. In the 1970s, I realized I knew little about two important issues: environment and development, and gender and development. Prior to the Mexico City meeting I asked a gender specialist, Prof. Els Postel, to organize a group including younger women and teachers to prepare a report on these issues for his development policy. Then there was a major debate about who should lead the delegation; there was even a contest within the cabinet. I won the battle because of the development issues and I claimed the lead. I learned a lot about development terms and issues. In Holland, gender issues mostly focused on women's emancipation. At Mexico City, the focus among developing countries was very different.

After Mexico City I sent a policy paper on all of this to Parliament. After leaving the government following a Cabinet change in 1977, I was at the Institute of Social Studies in The Hague and then became deputy director of UNCTAD (United Nations Conference on Trade and Development). From 1980 to 1986 we dealt with macroeconomics and women's issues on trade and development. These issues had never reached the UN before.

I first became directly involved in these efforts during the Mexico City conference when Martha Stuart, the independent video producer (*Are You Listening? Key Women at International Womens' Year* and *Are You Listening/Journalists at International Women's Year*), and her son, Barkley, suggested that I meet with a group of women who had formed a steering committee to draft a UN resolution to provide women with access to credit. I had dinner with two members of the steering committee, Margaret (Peg) Snyder and Virginia Saurwein. I was inspired by their commitment to development, and by the momentum of this new idea. But as someone who had lived in the for-profit world and knew something about capital markets, it was clear to me that at the UN there was no history or understanding of women in banking at that time. The international development community, Washington, D.C., and the United Nations were all different worlds I was struggling to understand.

2

FROM INSPIRATION TO REALITY

"Dissent keeps things alive"

BACK AT THE Rockefeller Brothers Fund with new insights and a new enthusiasm for exploring ways to link women with the financial system, I continued to meet wonderful people who taught me more than I could have imagined. So many people shared their experience, volunteered to help, and accelerated our burgeoning network.

Because I already felt the power of this idea, I agreed to work with a group of women at the UN, led by Virginia Saurwein, director of the NGO section of ECOSOC. One of the reasons for my commitment was Virginia's deep belief in the United Nations process and her unique ability to listen to and learn from diverse and differing voices. The group included Margaret (Peg) Snyder, Lucille Mair, and Leticia Shahani from the UN, as well as Caroline Pezzullo, Leslie Sederlund, Martha Stuart, and others from New York City. The group was working toward defining a legal structure that would bring women into the formal financial system. I felt that I had some knowledge that could help accomplish what was needed. But I recognized that it would be a challenge to identify money to capitalize such an institution, and I knew of no women bankers who could run a global bank. We decided to pursue the idea of creating some kind of international development institution that would help give local women access to the tools of production. Bill Dietel approved my work on the project.

Over the next couple of years, our working group—later to become the Committee to Organize Women's World Banking—met regularly, sometimes at Virginia's house in the country, often in my offices in Rockefeller Center, or at Peg's apartment. Each of us identified people who could offer suggestions and ideas. I had access to files about the creation of the World Bank, and was able to see that the Bretton Woods institutions had grown out of relationships among a small number of people. This impressed me because it was at the same time that I read a quote from Margaret Mead: *A small group of thoughtful people can change the world. Indeed, it's the only thing that ever has.* That understanding energized me in my conviction to help get our efforts off the ground.

Each of us had a somewhat different way of working, as in any group. I was on a fast learning track regarding international development and NGO experiences. Others were thinking in terms of the World Bank and various regional development banks. It was clear to me that there were no women in international banking we could tap and certainly no source of capital to finance an international institution such as we were envisioning. We had long discussions about where the institution should be located. Debates were ongoing about whether New York City would be logical because of our group's potential relationship to the United Nations, or if it would make more sense to be based in Africa. And at every meeting we came up with a new possible name: Women's Finance International; International Women's Fund; International Women's Development Bank; and others.

As I worked with these capable and committed women, I was also influenced by a book that I still reread each year. *Toward a New Psychology of Women*, by Jean Baker Miller, published in 1976 by Beacon Press, presented an entirely new way of thinking about understanding women, a way of thinking not defined by women as pale imitations of men.

My strong belief in this idea, plus my experience in learning I could do new things, gave me a power that I had not realized. Russell Phillips, former vice president of the Rockefeller Brothers Fund, recalled how unusual all of this was.

Russell Phillips

Michaela and I. . . came to know one another and I had the chance to observe her. This whole thing has a much broader context because we had had only one woman on the professional staff prior to that. . . . The women in the office were all what we then called "secretaries."

Michaela came back from Mexico City with this idea of creating some kind of finance mechanism that would focus on women, be organized by women, and run by women. I remember thinking it was a really crazy idea. If this kind of thing needed to be done, the men would organize it. (I am really sounding like a dinosaur.) The men would recognize that, and it would be organized in the traditional way, and that would give it respectability and make it function. Michaela and her colleagues kept insisting this is going to be a different way of doing things. . . . I remember particularly thinking Michaela was crazy to go out and get all these international women on the board. "How are you going to control them?" That was not the idea. The idea was to have them bring their perspective on what it was the organization was trying to do rather than have a group of New Yorkers sit in judgment on all kinds of projects. . . . That was a really, really gutsy move. When you are starting a new organization, to let it run the risk of getting so far out of your control early on means you might miss achieving your objective.

I was certain that any new plans would require a top international law firm and a top accounting firm, so I made an appointment with Donal O'Brien, the chief legal counsel for Rockefeller Family and Associates, to talk about the concept of a global financial institution for women. He made an appointment for me at Milbank, Tweed, Hadley & McCloy, an international law firm in New York City. There I met with a Dutch lawyer, G.J.S. Postma, who suggested that it might be appropriate for WWB to be registered in the Netherlands, given the country's long history of global trade and finance, its relevant tax structures, and the newly approved Triodos Bank, a different type of bank that shared similar objectives.

In Mr. Postma's March 7, 1977, letter, he suggested the type of legal structure under Dutch law that the Women's International Loan Guarantee Association (yet another name we had identified for our institution) could consider. He sent a copy of his letter to Floris Bannier, the managing partner of Nauta Van Haersolte, whose involvement, upon becoming general counsel, would be vital in the establishment of the organization and throughout the two decades that followed.

Asked why the Netherlands was a propitious environment for organizations interested in developing an innovative approach to banking services (such as Triodos Bank and WWB) to emerge, Peter Blom, Triodos Bank's current managing director, explained.

Peter Blom

The Netherlands is a small nation that has been highly dependent on trade for many centuries. Situated in the delta of the Rhine—the main river in Europe—the Netherlands connected Europe with the rest of the world for almost a century. That was almost 400 years ago, and the Netherlands was one of the most powerful nations at that time. Although this role has changed, that deep awareness of international interdependence is very much engrained in our culture. Dutch culture was clearly amenable to the kind of enterprise WWB was envisioning because we are very interested in what's happening outside the Netherlands.

My friend Charlie Johnston, a vice president at Chase Manhattan Bank, had introduced me to Tom Hunter, an accountant who worked with international clients and remained the CPA and personal adviser to WWB throughout my tenure. Charlie took me to lunch to introduce me to a young marketing executive from Norway, **Carlos Joly**, who was working on a fresh message for Chase. Charlie thought he might have ideas about people who could help us. At the lunch, Carlos suggested the name Women's World Banking. When I spoke with Carlos in 2010 to ask if he remembered that conversation, he said he did not remember it clearly, but the name would make sense in terms of the way he worked: "*Ideas come from any number of places, but names should be descriptive of what the business was or should be doing. Women's World Banking: Women (who is doing it and for whom); World (global); Banking (registered as a bank and not some pseudo, nonfinancial company).*"

One of the wonderful experiences in those years that would be a continuing influence in Women's World Banking was a trip to Chicago to meet with Ron Grzywinski, at the suggestion of my sister, who had worked with him at the Adlai Stevenson Institute. Ron, two African-Americans, and his colleague Mary Houghton had taken over South Shore Bank in 1973, to provide banking services to a local community that was underserved. During my meeting with Ron, explaining what we were trying to do on an international level, he suggested that a global capital fund could be used as a guarantee to local financial institutions to encourage them to provide women with access to banking services. That idea would become central to the development of Women's World Banking. I remain indebted to Ron for his vision and for his penetrating questions, and to Mary for her continued belief in WWB.

In an excerpt from his essay "The New Old-Fashioned Banking" in the *Harvard Business Review* of May–June 1991, Ron explained the background to the establishment of South Shore.

Ron Grzywinski

In the late 1960s, Mary Houghton, Milton Davis, Jim Fletcher, and I, who now make up the management team at the bank and its holding company, Shorebank Corporation, were all about thirty years old. During the day, we worked together doing successful minority lending at a bank in the Hyde Park section of Chicago. Most nights, we did volunteer work in community organizations, addressing things like better housing, crime prevention, child care—the whole litany of neighborhood needs. On Friday nights, however, we'd go to the Eagle Bar and talk about inner cities and what to do about them. . . .

We saw that community organizations had identified the right issues but lacked the capital and the technical competency to make a real difference. . . . The answer to rebuilding neighborhoods had to be some kind of business. It had to be self-sustaining; it had to have the independence of a capital base and the discipline of a for-profit motive. What we were imagining was a development bank—a bank that could be tough-minded about loans, qualify borrowers according to strict standards, satisfy the most demanding federal bank examiners, make a profit, and still transform an inner-city neighborhood without driving out those who lived there.

In an interview with Ron, he added that to make a difference, "*You didn't ever need a majority of people on a board of directors, but you needed at least one member to make a change.*" He also reminded me about some of the most fundamental questions around money and power, and about the democratizing of capital.

But the question is, is it worth even imagining a future in which financial capital is networked in a way that we don't lose control? When you give your money to a bank you lose control of it. When we were starting Shore Bank a union organizer said to me, "What you're really trying to do is what we tried to do through the '20s, and '30s—we tried to organize people and their money together, and we failed. We did not succeed at that." And while that wasn't the original notion of Shore Bank, it was the way he saw it.

Well, I'm just trying to raise questions. Regarding the issue of working a loan and using it to raise talent, we've had people break off from Shore Bank. We've had other people from inside Shore Bank create new institutions —they've been provided the freedom and they have the will and the desire to do that. So it's easier to use capital to develop talent. It's when you come to the capital issue, are there ways to think about networking capital and not losing control? Then there's also just trying to think about human-scale capital. You can use capital for consumption purposes or for development purposes, whatever you want to call it, or for investment purposes.

Until a couple of years ago we thought that the existing systems really had consumption capital down cold—credit cards, mortgage loans, that sort of thing. They can build big systems that can do that, and you need large amounts of capital if you're going to finance nations. But are there things like enterprise formation or other things that are really consumption capital, mortgage loans even, that need to be on a human scale and not on an institutional scale?

Mary Houghton has vivid memories as well.

Mary Houghton

In 1967 or '68, Adlai Stevenson III, treasurer of the state of Illinois, said he would move money to state banks that did something to invest in low-income communities. In 1968 we put a press release out saying that we were making loans to African-American businesses, and the phone never stopped ringing. A couple of years later, we realized there was a big market for this, but that Hyde Park Bank wasn't the best place to do it, because they were too business-oriented, and perhaps there was something bigger and better out there. Milton and Jim were African-American, and Ron and I were white, so we were a wonderful but odd group. We decided that we would raise enough money to write a business plan for an idea that was to make a bank into an anchor for community development in a neighborhood. Thanks to changes in bank-company holding laws around that time that made community development a permissible activity in banking, we were encouraged and put together an investment program, determined to raise three million dollars in capital. Then we set out to find the right neighborhood to establish ourselves. South Shore had been one hundred percent white in 1960, seventy percent black in 1970, and ninety-seven percent black in '72–'73—so it had changed racially, but had not had a long period of disinvestment. South Shore Bank had wanted to move downtown, but the neighborhood resisted that, and finally the controller of the currency told the bank it couldn't move, so it came up for sale. We took over in 1973.

Leslie Sederlund, who had worked with me at RBF and the Office of Technology Assessment of the US Congress (OTA) and served on the Committee to Organize WWB, remembers the brainstorming process involved in determining what form WWB would assume.

Leslie Sederlund

There was a lot of dialogue back and forth about what would be the most effective way to bring women into the economy, and early ideas had included a bank, until finally we all coalesced around the idea that there was no need to replicate existing resources. We could build this "Women's World

Banking" by leveraging existing resources and working with local and national banks, serving as a loan guarantor. Looking back, it seems like a no-brainer, but it really did take a lot of clearing of the forest to get to that. Another difficulty was the use of the word "banking" in our title. It's a gerund, not a noun. We wanted it to bespeak a system, an active exchange process, not brick and mortar. Women's World Banking was really conceived as a living organism that, if stopped in one part of the world, could still continue to actively engage in other parts of the world, because it was not under the thumb of any one institution, government, or international agency, and so could not be easily attacked.

As I continued to work on the project, my professional life shifted again. In 1978, I was appointed by Russell Peterson, the director, and Hazel Henderson, an OTA adviser, to a position at the Congressional Office of Technology Assessment to conduct a study on appropriate technology (*Assessment of Technology for Local Development*). OTA provided scholarly, nonpartisan studies for the major standing committees of the US Congress. Appropriate technology was an area of emerging thinking and design that I had been exploring at RBF. Moving to Washington gave me the opportunity to try to relate some of these ideas to Congress and the international development community, as well as to continue working on the development of WWB. In October 1979, I was invited to the Club of Rome meeting in Berlin and went with Hazel Henderson, who remains a mentor, colleague, and friend. En route, I made a detour to the Netherlands to meet with Floris Bannier. His positive reception led me to encourage Virginia Saurwein to meet with him later that year on her next trip to Europe. He recollects his introduction to WWB.

Floris Bannier

A legal assistant, Anita Kalff, came to my room and said that one of my colleagues who had been at Milbank, Tweed in the US had been contacted by a member of the Committee to Organize Women's World Banking about starting a global financial institution for women, and had passed the matter on to her, because he thought a woman should attend to it, but he hadn't understood what was being created—he thought it was going to be a bank. He and his colleagues, the American lawyers, believed that it was advantageous for groups that operate in different countries, and banks in particular, to establish a headquarters or holding company in the Netherlands, for tax reasons. So the first message to us was, "there is another bank, this time a women's bank," but to the banking world that doesn't make any difference. Anita asked me what she should do; she had no idea how to approach it, as she'd only been a lawyer for about a year. Based on the information we had received, I thought of it as a routine thing that I had done a number of times, and started working, but on a totally incorrect footing.

It took me about one year, and numerous discussions, first with Virginia Saurwein, who was the chief of the NGO Unit at the UN Secretariat, and then mostly with Michaela Walsh, to understand what the plan really was. Once I understood that it was not going to be a bank, but something totally new—an institution to help women, especially small-scale female entrepreneurs, enter the financial world, be able to have bank accounts and get credit that they wouldn't have been able to access otherwise—I saw it as a beautiful idea. It was thought that any money invested in women entrepreneurs would come back into the economy and not be spent by men for personal purposes like going to a football match or a pub. It was new, and the dedication of these women was quite forceful. As I have three daughters, I had some feeling of personal involvement and became very enthusiastic. We decided to give it the form of a nonprofit institution/foundation, "stichting" in Dutch, and I'm happy to say, the tax reasons didn't play any role at all in the end.

The 1979 registration of our organization or *"stichting"* in the Netherlands (it is legally registered as "Stichting Women's World Banking" or SWWB) provided a solid legal foundation on which we could build. There was, however, some skepticism vis-à-vis WWB. Geertje Lycklama, the first coordinator of International Women's Affairs at the Ministry for Development Cooperation in the Netherlands described the Dutch government's initial position regarding women in development. (See the charter and bylaws, pp.198–210.)

Geertje Lycklama

In 1977 I was appointed the first coordinator of International Women's Affairs at the Dutch Ministry of Foreign Affairs, in which the Ministry for Development Cooperation is located. Prior to that, I had worked in Pakistan. I didn't start out as a feminist, but in Pakistan my eyes were opened, because it was such a segregated society, and it was not clear what could be done to help.

In the Netherlands, there was a strong, then-called third-world movement, that women were a part of while also being part of the feminist movement. That said, not many women were working at senior positions in the Dutch government at the time. The Mexico City UN Women's Conference had put governments under pressure to do something about it, which is why our function at the ministry was created, but we still had to do much advocacy internally. We always focused on the men who were favorable, and for the most part, those men had wives who were progressive. When I joined the Ministry of Foreign Affairs in the Netherlands, we claimed that within the context of the Ministry for Development Cooperation we were imposing Western images of men and women, with the husband earning the money and the wife being the housewife—which is of course not at all true, especially not in Africa. There, women are earners, not housewives. So we pleaded very much and tried to convince them to address this problem and change their approach. We managed to make the case for greater local participation and ownership of development projects, based on a study that had exposed how the Dutch development aid didn't reach women, or in some instances even made things worse for them. Between women in development ministries in the Netherlands, Sweden, and Norway, as well as in USAID, where Arvonne Fraser was very active, we were able to influence the way countries' development assistance was being evaluated. We focused on the evaluation forms and ensured that the impacts on women, men, and children were considered separately. Now we take such procedures for granted, but it was really very pioneering.

As coordinator of International Women's Affairs, I had a little pot of money with which I could do some innovative things all over the world. We were first approached by Women's World Banking New York to see whether we could provide grants. That was before the local WWB Netherlands branch had been established. When I first learned about WWB, I remember having a rather limited vision of it, but we were open to every initiative that would increase women's economic independence, so we gave it a good chance. At that time the ministry was very focused on poverty alleviation, and of course, WWB did that, too. It was, however, very much a battle, because while everybody in the Ministry for Development Cooperation knew what the World Bank was, with Women's World Banking, I had much explaining to do, including directly with the minister. He was an economist and had many questions about how the money was going to be distributed and how the guarantees were functioning, was it a bank or wasn't it a bank, and why especially for women.

Notwithstanding some of the questions being raised, based on Floris' interest in helping to set up the institutional framework for WWB in the Netherlands, and his advice that due to its renovation there could be a very discounted rate for a meeting at the Amstel Hotel in the historical district of Amsterdam, it seemed logical to me to hold an international meeting of the Committee to Organize in Amsterdam. Some members of the planning committee thought the first meeting should be in a developing country, but I felt strongly that we should meet where our legal registration was likely to take place.

By this point there was some tension brewing in the committee. I remember a phone conversation with Margaret (Peg) Snyder one Sunday when I was in Washington; Peg suggested that Caroline Pezzullo and I should co-manage the committee. We had been discussing whether WWB should be part of the UN system. I felt strongly that to be regarded as legitimate in the world of finance we had to find a banker to be the managing officer. Virginia, Peg and I finally agreed that Anne Sheffield, who had worked with International Planned Parenthood Federation (IPPF) and Battelle Human Affairs Research Centers, and was going to be traveling to Latin America and Africa, could be a consultant to help plan the first meeting and might ultimately assume leadership.

Anne became frustrated by the lack of resources available and the lack of clarity in WWB plans. In a letter of July 16, 1978, she stated:

> It has been increasingly apparent that there are serious tensions and disagreements within the committee as to how WWB should develop…I have also found both disagreement and fuzziness as to how WWB can best achieve its goals, particularly when the movement comes to focus on the details of implementation rather than the overarching concept. The array of documents describing WWB is a case in point, as is the difficulty in coming to closure. I am not wedded to the traditional concepts of management and organization, but as yet WWB does not seem to have replaced them with something else that works.

This quotation demonstrates that we did not have a preset notion of how to operate; we were hoping it would emerge from the international meeting. From the outset, our goal was to build a movement. We did not want a top-down process. We created WWB as an organization that would support and service that movement. This tension between the openness of allowing the movement to develop and the efficiency of a top-down management approach has continued through my entire association with WWB. I continue to hold to this view, and I believe it was the reason for WWB's success. Launching such a dramatically new idea takes new thinking. Looking back, I would keep the tensions, because dissent keeps things alive. We were trying to start something new and raise money for it—step by step by step—with no road map or "business plan" for "scaling-up," which would now be the norm for start-ups. Everything was a subject of debate.

During my 2011 interview, Bill Dietel had vivid memories of how new and surprising this all was.

Bill Dietel

This is where I think we circle back to what you were trying to get at originally. At the end of the day, it's people. It isn't money, and it isn't really even ideas. Ideas are always out there. The money is always out there somewhere. But nothing happens until a person grabs the idea, gets the money and makes it go. Who would have chosen you? You chose yourself and said, "I'm going to do this!"

After working in Washington, I returned to New York, where I was given an office at RBF for six months to work on WWB. Then Carole Hyatt, a pioneer in youth markets and head of the Children's Research Service, generously offered WWB two rooms in her office on 48th Street at an extremely generous rate, and I moved out of the RBF offices. Lilia Clemente put me in touch with Ada Molinelli, who had just retired from Chase Bank. She came to work and was like a godmother to me for the next five years. My sister Mary came to New York to help manage the office, as I was frequently traveling to raise money for WWB. As is the case with most new entrepreneurial enterprises, we survived with overworked and underpaid part-time staff and numerous summer interns, as well as generous volunteer help for several years.

Over the next few years, we moved offices from 48th Street to the basement of a brownstone on East 82nd Street, to the Spanish Institute on Park Avenue. Finally we signed a lease for an office on East 40th Street.

I am forever grateful for the hard work and fun and support that the devoted staff, volunteers, consultants, summer interns, friends, and family contributed so enthusiastically during those early days. To Lee Chase, our part-time bookkeeper from day one; Anne Hartwell, for her good humor and generosity of time; Tony Sheldon, for his advice and friendship; Kim Pollack; David Ralston; Diana Clavel; Paula Hays; Amy Davidsen; Fern Mele; Michele Burger; Barbara Luton (deceased 2007); and Catherine Ruckelshaus—thank you for your wonderful team spirit. To those of you who are not mentioned in this history and to many of you whom I was unable to track down—I will not forget you.

During my Washington tenure, I had met Beatrice Harretche, head of Technical Cooperation at the Inter-American Development Bank (IDB) at the recommendation of John Hammock (the executive director of Accion) and others, and I frequently visited her offices to get her suggestions and advice about Latin American projects, always hoping she could suggest good people in the IDB and throughout Latin America. Beatrice invited me to an IDB meeting in Buenos Aires in 1978 to discuss issues about women in development in Latin America, where I met Queenie de Vivo and Margarita Guzmán. I thought Beatrice might help identify someone as a candidate for executive director, or that she might take the helm of SWWB when she retired. She attended the 1980 meeting in Amsterdam, became one of the first trustees and was the second chair of the WWB Board.

When Sara McCue and I interviewed Beatrice in early 2009 (she died in January 2011), Sara asked what her IDB colleagues thought of her relationship with me and the ideas for WWB. Without the slightest hesitation, Beatrice responded, *"They thought I was crazy."* Asked why she was interested in our ideas at WWB, despite the skepticism of the IDB, she said it was the first time she had seen an initiative that could bring skills and professional opportunity to grassroots women, something she cared about deeply, having provided funding from the IDB for projects that supported women's work, including the founding of Manos del Uruguay, a global retail organization. Beatrice was the first person I knew who truly understood and taught me the significant impact that making money and skills available to grassroots women could have on the evolution of traditional village economics. Her description of the shift in dynamics in local village life that occurred when Manos del Uruguay would take yarn from sheep ranchers to the mountains, and pay indigenous women to knit the beautiful sweaters that Manos would then market worldwide, often came up as an example of future opportunities and challenges for WWB.

Many people stepped up to help in this early period. One of the most important, for me personally and for the realization of our idea, was Bradford Morse, whom I had met several times through our mutual friend Martha Stuart. Brad had recently moved to New York to take a job as administrator of the United Nations Development Program (UNDP). Virginia and Peg had met with several people within the UNDP about financial assistance. Virginia, whose judgment I had learned to trust, suggested we meet with Brad to formally request a grant from UNDP.

Virginia and I met with Brad, Arthur Brown (associate administrator of UNDP), Tim Rothermel (chief of the Executive Office of the UNDP administrator), and William T. Mashler (senior director, UNDP Division for Global and Inter-regional Projects) in 1978. (Brad later said to me, "The best thing I ever did was to give you Arthur Brown.") There was some confusion about whether we could get a grant without first having approval from the UN member states. I made up my mind that I wasn't going to leave that meeting without some kind of commitment from UNDP. After nearly an hour of conversation, Brad suggested that UNDP could provide up to $250,000 in seed funding for us to hold meetings in five regions of the world to determine interest and potential use for our concept of bringing women into the financial system. (I remember thinking that there was no doubt in my mind that the concept was doable.) It was after this meeting, when I had argued so

Status of Governments' Reactions on
the Women's World Banking Project
as of 1 December 1980

Bureau	Endorsed	Interested	Not Interested
Africa (RAF/79/029)	Kenya Liberia Senegal Tanzania Zambia	Benin Botswana Cameroon Central African Republic Gabon Gambia Ghana Ivory Coast Lesotho Nigeria Seychelles Togo	
Arab States (RAB/79/003)	Jordan Morocco Sudan Iraq ²/ıı/81	Egypt Tunisia	Bahrain Djibouti Lebanon Qatar
Asia and the Pacific (RAS/80/005)	India Philippines Sri Lanka Thailand	India Philippines Sri Lanka Thailand	Brunei Malaysia Singapore
Latin America (RLA/79/072)	Bolivia Chile Costa Rica Guatemala Guyana Honduras St. Vincent Jamaica Paraguay Trinidad and Tobago	Argentina Cuba El Salvador	Ecuador Panama

strongly for our idea, that I decided to put more of my own personal energy and commitment into the effort.

In retrospect, I believe that my association with the RBF helped the UNDP and others to be willing to take a risk on this project. I came to treasure Brad Morse as a unique public servant who loved people and life, and was not afraid to take risks by putting his own neck on the line if he believed it might help make life better for others.

Tim Rothermel commented on the factors that led UNDP to be supportive of WWB.

Tim Rothermel

A group of around four people at UNDP were working strictly on women's issues. Apart from that, Brad Morse had already been aware of programs that used small loans as a tool for poverty alleviation and was quite interested in the potential of that concept. When I first started working with him in

Congress in 1968, Brad was a ranking member of the subcommittee on Latin America, and one of the first people who came to visit him was Samuel Greene, the head of The Penny Foundation, or Fundación del Centavo, an organization that he had started in Guatemala in 1963, with donations of pennies from churches, clubs, Boy Scouts, Girl Scouts, you name it. . . . Sometimes they collected quarters, dollars, or even thousand-dollar checks, but the idea was that these direct loans to low-income peasants, mostly indigenous people, could accomplish what official development spending could not. For one thing, most of the loans went to women; second, the repayment record was extremely high in general and even better from the women than from the men. Brad had also been an author of Title IX of the Foreign Assistance Act, which mandated popular participation in development—i.e., tailoring programs to the communities' needs—and that was the philosophy of UNDP in those days. Brad as an individual was committed to assuring that funds were getting into the hands of people in poverty who were unserved by their own governments, rather than seeing money turned over to a government agency, and this was before the concept of getting to "the poorest of the poor" had become fashionable. (In development, there are fads, sometimes led by an individual, sometimes by a group of countries; and, looking back, there was a general momentum at the time to support this "micro" approach to poverty alleviation, with the Scandinavians and the Dutch; A.H. Khan in Pakistan; the Grameen Bank, which was approaching the Ford Foundation; etc.)

It's also not surprising that Brad would be attracted to something new like Women's World Banking, rather than a well-established institution, because he saw it as something that was designed to empower the poor, and, the fact that the poor were women was an added benefit. This mindset was also informed by the human-development report, and the notion that there are many factors that go into poverty alleviation beyond dollars and cents, one of which is the ability to make choices that will vary from one community to another. [Tim died February 6, 2012.]

As I continued to work on our project, I continued to find new people who were ready to pitch in. Mary Houghton introduced me to her former Johns Hopkins graduate school classmate Gretchen Maynes. Like so many young women at the time, she was looking for part-time consultancies to balance her life (which included two babies) and her desire to remain a professional. We hired Gretchen to do the administrative organization for the Amsterdam meeting. She helped us identify additional financial support—from the Canadian International Development Agency (CIDA), the Ford Foundation, and others—and identify new participants. Her background with the State Department and the Overseas Education Fund of the League of Women Voters in Washington, D.C., and her knowledge about development and organizational skills played a major role in making the Amsterdam meeting memorable.

Gretchen Maynes

We were trying to identify women leaders in banking and finance in the larger world, in as many countries as we could, and in as many different kinds of economies as we could. We had a concept that we wanted to present to them, but the purpose of the meeting was to get the ideas of women in banking and finance, and entrepreneurship, from various places in the world. . . . To get their ideas or their views of what our original concept was, because while we thought we had a good idea (or we wouldn't have gone to the effort) we also knew that it had to be validated by people who worked at the grassroots level or close to the grassroots level in these different countries.

I really note there were a lot of things I didn't think I could do, like get on a telephone and talk to someone in USAID or someone in the Canadian CIDA; each of them called me to tell me why they weren't going to give me the last fifteen thousand dollars or twenty thousand dollars we needed for the conference. I never would have thought I would have—it was desperation really, not so much courage—but I just told them, No, no, this answer was not acceptable, we had to have this money, if we did not have this money and if we did not have it right now, this might be cancelled because we just couldn't go ahead and borrow money to do this.

During my interview with Gretchen, she reminded me about the argument we had, because she felt it should be a very large meeting. I had a long-standing belief that if we wanted to make something happen and have a real discussion, we could not have more than thirty participants. We ended up with thirty-seven participants and twenty-five advisers from twenty-seven countries. Gretchen added that as time passed, she grew to understand the advantage of working with smaller groups.

The same topic came up in a conversation with Tim Rothermel a month or so before the meeting. I was at the US Congressional Office of Technology Assessment one afternoon when the phone rang—"Mr. Rothermel from UNDP" was calling regarding the planned meeting at the Amstel Hotel. *"There seems to be some question about the invitation list,"* he said. I gulped. *"We have had a request from a 'King' in Africa to send an observer."* I replied, *"Mr. Rothermel, at this point we have had many requests from the UN for sending observers. If we say yes to all there will be more observers than actual participants." "Is there any way to make an exception?"* he countered. *"If we say yes to one we have to say yes to all,"* I responded. *"I believe we are supporting this meeting,"* he noted. *"Yes, as an independent organization, we're extremely grateful for your generosity and support. If you would like us to return the money, we will be happy to do that,"* I said.

To this day, I don't know where this response came from. It was as though my lips moved without my control. He said, *"Oh, no, that won't be necessary,"* we then exchanged pleasantries and hung up. I was shaking. It was a turning point in my own life, in terms of believing in something so strongly that it took on a life of its own—a moment of transition from fear to empowerment.

To identify the participants, we all reached out to friends and people we trusted and asked for help in finding people who could really make a contribution. One recommendation led to another. Lilia Clemente helped identify someone from the Philippines; I had worked with Ann Roberts at RBF; Gretchen Maynes contacted a banker in Canada who identified Deanna Rosenswig; Beatrice Harretche helped identify Marlene Fernandez and Margaret (Gee) Hagen. The criterion for participants was that they understood local business and banking services and had an interest in providing financial services for women. We were seeking an international representation. (See our invitation letter, p. 211.)

I wrote a letter (dated November 15, 1979) to Robert McNamara, president of the World Bank, to invite him to attend the Amsterdam meeting, by then scheduled for 1980. August (Gus) Schumacher, who was at the World Bank, advised me to state in the letter that if McNamara could

---

COMMITTEE TO ORGANIZE

WOMEN'S WORLD BANKING

PO BOX 1691
GRAND CENTRAL STATION
NEW YORK NY 10017

TEL 212-247-8135

November 15, 1979

Mr. Robert McNamara
President
The World Bank
1818 H Street, N.W.
Washington, D.C. 20433

Dear Mr. McNamara:

I am writing to invite you to deliver the opening address at the International Workshop of Women Leaders in Banking and Finance to be held in Amsterdam March 12 - 15, 1980. The Workshop is sponsored by the Committee to Organize Women's World Banking, and participants will include prominent women in banking, finance, government ministries, and small business from 40 countries. Your participation would help to focus attention on the critical issues this Workshop will address, namely those relating to women's access to, and effective use of, the financial institutions of their economies.

As you know, a significant component of successful development is the extent to which individuals, men and women, are able to approach full economic participation. It is now recognized that the contributions of women are critical to development, particularly in view of the roles, largely unrecognized, that they play in their economies. Women's World Banking has been established to help address this need.

By way of brief introduction, the idea of Women's World Banking developed out of the 1975 International Women's Year Conference in Mexico City. A small group of women, composed of government leaders, development professionals, and individuals from the fields of banking, business, and education began to explore how best to implement the mandates from that Conference and the subsequent resolutions passed by the U.N. General Assembly urging the extension of credit to women. Since 1977, when this seminal group was enlarged and reconstituted as the Committee to Organize Women's World Banking, organizing efforts have focused on a commitment to work with existing financial institutions to encourage the extension of banking services to enterprising women and their families. In May, 1979, Women's World Banking was incorporated as a Dutch Stichting. Enclosed is the Women's World Banking Statement of Purpose which outlines our long-term goals, our first program efforts including a loan guarantee mechanism, and the rationale behind the formation of this kind of organization at this time.

(continued)

Also enclosed is a proposal for the International Workshop of Women Leaders in Banking & Finance, including a draft agenda and the initial participants list. Participants are expected to make a valuable contribution to the development of strategies for implementing the Women's World Banking program, and they will be asked to present to the World Conference of the U.N. Decade for Women (Copenhagen, July, 1980) recommendations for substantially strengthening the role of women in national economies and the contribution they can make to the development process.

The success of this first effort to bring women bankers, financial experts, and small business entrepreneurs into a dialogue on this range of issues is vitally important to Women's World Banking's objectives both in the long and short term. We believe it is of equal importance to those who share our goals. It is our hope that you would be willing to address our meeting and thereby help us in this effort. Although we are mindful of the many demands on your schedule, we are hopeful that you would be able to stop in Amsterdam enroute to or from one of your previously scheduled meetings. If, because of circumstance, you will not be available to join us, it has been suggested that your senior advisor, Mr. J. Burke Knapp, might be able to participate in your stead.

I would like the occasion to speak with you about our Workshop and about Women's World Banking in further detail. I will telephone your office next week to ask for an appointment.

Sincerely,

Michaela Walsh
Chairperson

encls: a) Women's World Banking Statement of Purpose
       b) Proposal for an International Workshop of Women Leaders
          in Banking & Finance

SPEAKING INVITATION TO THE WORLD BANK, 1979

not attend, would he designate J. Burke Knapp, executive vice president, in his stead. We had been told that Burke had been at the World Bank since its founding and was regarded with great respect by most ministers of finance around the world. If he came it would be a real coup. In those days Wall Street and Washington were very different worlds, and the number of relationships between finance and government were few. And the idea of an invitation to a global meeting of women in finance and banking was a new phenomenon for sure! We crossed our fingers and hoped!

A week or so later I had a phone call from J. Burke Knapp's office, inviting me to have lunch with him at the World Bank. I think he had real reservations about what we were doing until he realized how serious we were. And he seemed to have a genuine interest in the ideas around local loan programs for development. Before the end of the luncheon, he accepted the invitation to address the meeting and asked if he could bring his wife, Iris, as well. They both came to Amsterdam. He later agreed to become a member of the Board of Trustees, as he was in the process of stepping down from his official World Bank position and becoming a special adviser to President McNamara. When I met with Burke in August 2009 (he died in November 2009), he explained how impressed he had been with the women he had met at that meeting, and while he could not remember their names, he did remember "*the Barclays banker from Africa, the little businesswoman from Ghana, and the woman from the Philippines; what a sense of energy and intelligence.*"

Women's World Banking was determined to fill a very specific gap, but it wasn't developing in a vacuum. While there were village credit initiatives sprouting in different parts of the world, they were operating independently of one another and were generally not geared toward women. I had met Muhammad Yunus when he came to the United States at the invitation of the Ford Foundation to promote the Grameen Bank. I had known about A.H. Khan (the Ramon Magsaysay awardee), an Indian in the British Service assigned to East Pakistan (now Bangladesh) who in 1959 helped local villagers to create a credit project by combining their own assets. During those years I was a member of the Citizen's Advisory Council to USAID. I met the founders of FINCA and Trickle-Up, and members of Partners for Productivity, Catholic Relief Services, and BRAC. All these groups were starting new "micro" programs sponsored by USAID.

I knew about Accion because RBF had funded some of their programs, and I knew John Hammock, Accion's executive director. When John left Accion, he agreed to work with me as a technical adviser and helped draft a business plan for WWB. (John continued to work with WWB until 1984.) He also agreed to participate in the Amsterdam meeting, where he would share his experience with local lending, based on Accion's work in Brazil, beginning in the early '70s. He summarized Accion's entry into local lending.

John Hammock

Accion started with two guys playing tennis in Latin America on a State Department tour. They were in Venezuela, saw the slums, talked to Exxon, and asked them for funding to do something about it. It was 1961; Kennedy had just been inaugurated and had initiated the Peace Corps. People were worried about Fidel Castro. It was actually called Accion Venezuela for a while and only became Accion International in 1965 when it moved to New York and decided to have a more global focus. In 1968, Accion had projects in Brazil, Colombia, Venezuela, Peru, and Costa Rica, where I was invited to work as a consultant by Terry Holcomb, a guy I had known in grad school and who had become executive director of Accion International at the age of twenty-four. There were six of us in total, all guys. Our micro (the term "micro-business" was being used in the '70s) work began in Brazil with Bruce Tippet, who had teamed up with a Brazilian guy to do micro[credit] business where there were many people working on the sidewalks, repairing cars, cooking food, etc. Those people already had loan sharks giving them money, and we were just better lenders.

At first it was one hundred loans a year, but we didn't want to give the loans ourselves. We had to convince the private-sector banks to offer them. Banks in that period were not interested in investing in poor people at all. They saw them as a bad credit risk, and thought that if they weren't willing to go into the bank, why should the bank go out and find them. . . . Bankers were incredibly against this. If you're a banker offering a one hundred-dollar loan and you have to go through the same paperwork you would need for a fifty thousand-dollar loan, what's the point? So we had to cover the cost of the paperwork. All of the transactional costs were covered by the nonprofits, and the expenses were covered by a guarantee fund, so the bank didn't have to do anything but put up the money. In 1973, Terry left, and I took over as executive director. Because we had a private-sector board, we were considered a private-sector organization—even though most of us were lefty—and were accused of being "neo-fascist capitalist rip-offs" by the community-development types, who said that we were exploiting the poor because we were charging interest rates. UNICEF thought we shouldn't charge more than three percent. I don't remember if we were charging twelve percent or sixteen percent, but to the borrowers, it was laughable; they thought it was fantastic, compared to their other options.

Back then, microcredit was not a big deal. Our little project in Brazil wasn't really going anywhere with two hundred loans, but the only reason we were raising any money in the US were those two hundred loans, and for five years we used the same two hundred loans to finance Accion. In 1975, the organization almost went bankrupt, but then, two years later, in 1977, we got a grant from USAID called the Pisces Project, to see if our Brazilian microcredit program was replicable in other regions. That's when we found out about solidarity group lending that was working well in the Philippines and that was very attractive for banks, as it would reduce the transactional cost of checking up on each individual's ability to pay back loans, because the beneficiaries were taking on the responsibility of the selection process.

Even though Accion still had five or six different types of projects, it was very clear by 1979 that microcredit had won the day. I saw the potential for growth and didn't want to run a microcredit organization, so I left and began working as a consultant on a variety of projects. When I started working with Michaela in 1979, she had a great idea, but no programs. I took a risk, not knowing if she'd have the money to pay me, but I like to help start things. . . . Accion had never focused on women. WWB came along and focused on women, and that had a double-barreled action, which not only changed banks, but also empowered women. WWB's model also allowed different groups to do their own thing— it was never cookie-cutter. The American psyche is shaped by the book The Little Engine That Could— *every American has read it and absorbed its message of "You've got a problem? I'll fix it for you!" That's been our attitude overseas—when in fact we can never do it better than locals can.*

To ensure we were not imposing an American or Western approach, we invited the international participants to prepare background papers that explained the circumstances in their country with regard to women-run businesses and lending, and successful initiatives. These inputs offered views into the economic and social realities in countries as diverse as Brazil, India, Jamaica, Pakistan, and Thailand, among other countries, and helped form the basis of the informed discussions we would have in Amsterdam at our meeting.

A letter I sent in November of 1979 to the Ministry of Foreign Affairs in the Netherlands, requesting financial assistance for the workshop, sums up where WWB was as the critical meeting approached. After referring to the October 1979 Statement of Purpose and the Progress Report, my letter continues:

> I believe it is made clear that the loan guarantee is a mechanism for sharing risk with local banking institutions; that the mechanism operates directly between Women's World Banking and the local bank; and that the development and delivery of technical and managerial assistance is a process that Women's World Banking will initiate within the context of the national economy with which it is dealing. Women's World Banking will make every effort to share risk and to share cost at the local level. This should help make failures—as well as successes—readily apparent and allow for early termination of non-effective approaches.
>
> Also enclosed is a copy of the Charter of the Stichting Women's World Banking and its 1st year budget. Now that the incorporation in Amsterdam is complete, a temporary board has been conducting a search for an Executive Director and soliciting nominations for candidates for the permanent Board of Trustees.
>
> We should note that we are conducting an informal search for a prominent woman banker to serve as the Executive Director of Women's World Banking. Ideally, she should have a responsible position in the World Bank, an international development bank, or in the international side of a commercial bank. Preferably, she will be from a developing country. . . .

After four years of work, we were all excited about our plans for the International Workshop of Women Leaders in Banking and Finance.

3

AMSTERDAM 1980
WOMEN'S WORLD BANKING TAKES SHAPE

"'It will happen,' you said, and it did."

A TRANSFORMATIVE POINT in the evolution of our movement came during four days in the Netherlands in 1980. The scene was the International Workshop of Women Leaders in Banking and Finance at the Amstel Hotel in Amsterdam from March 12 to 15. It is remembered by many of the WWB leaders who gathered there as the moment when the organization jelled. After the enthusiasm of Mexico City, years of formal discussions and research, and hours and months of informal conversations, women gathered to make crucial decisions. Some participants had been involved since Mexico City. Some were new to the process and the idea. How were the concepts to be put into practice? Who would make each decision? What about resources? An intense four days transformed Women's World Banking from a hope to a reality. Those four days included substantive work, passionate disagreements, and allowing all voices to be heard. They also included personal connections, learning about other cultures, dancing and singing together, and a special luncheon cruise through the canals of old Amsterdam. These elements—the cerebral and the personal—are always essential for any attempt to create trusting relationships and successful partnerships!

The framework of the meeting was set in a background paper prepared by Patricia Cloherty. Pat was a friend and we both served as trustees of Alternative Technology International, a USAID-sponsored program. After revisiting the history and basic objectives, Pat analyzed the key issues and assumptions. She paraphrases:

"At the heart of the WWB concept is the belief (a) that capital can be placed effectively in the spectrum of economic activities in which women are engaged, given appropriate identification of commercial opportunities and assistance to entrepreneurs; and (b) that undertaking the effort to provide these services will enhance long-term prospects for income generation and capital formation in developing countries. WWB faces certain practical considerations; many are the issues that face any effort to begin funding of any sort, but there is the added dimension of serving women who have not dealt with financial institutions. This means that, in addition to conventional economic and financial analysis,

WWB *must assess what any given project accomplishes for women, as well as the likely financial outcome."* (See her background paper at the end of this chapter.)

One of the New York Committee members, Martha Stuart, agreed to videotape all the discussions and edited a forty-minute video of the meeting. The portions of the video that we were able to locate reveal the profound hopes and questions that each of us carried. As participants of the group sat around with glasses of wine the evening before the formal meeting, Martha began by asking, *"What happened in us that turned us into change agents? How did we get that way and how can we encourage new ways of reinforcing women?"*

Mary Houghton responded. *"I think the big word is care and love, and that's very basic. I think you have to care about people, and you have to care about what you're doing, and you have to care if you want to see change."*

Lourdes Lontok Cruz took a turn. *"Men never talk that way. They never associate money with love. They always say money is beautiful. I think only women can say that."*

Caroline Pezzullo spoke next. *"Love doesn't seem to be material, but it seems to be the motor behind a strategy to bring about change. . . . We haven't talked about. . . . why we want these economic opportunities, or why we want access to advantages of the economy. I think that's an important issue that we need to cover more in depth. It's a system-logic issue, an underlying philosophy, or religion, or a set of values by which we are motivated. Do we want just the power that we envy now or access to that to do something different?"*

Margaret (Gee) Hagen had ideas about the motivation question. *"I think we are looking for something lost rather than for new gains. . . . When we move into modernizing society, women's economic participation is taken away. . . . Development has hurt women and it has hurt them in the sense that they are no longer the vital economic unit that they were in more traditional eyes. We are talking about a capital and emotional venture."*

Beatrice Harretche spoke of her own efforts, and how they influenced her family. *"When my son was eleven, I was promoted. I went home very happy and told him and my husband. He immediately looked at me and said, 'Mother, are you going to get more money? Are you going to increase my allowance?' I said, 'Well, I have to think about this, because everything in life is according to the effort you have done. You see the effort I have done, but what have you done?' He looked at me and said, 'Mother, you think I have done little? I have contributed a mother.'"*

Many tears had been shed by this point.

Modupe Ibiayo summed up the feelings well. *"I would like to go back to the point about why we are here. Is it because we are professionals and. . . want to be identified as women leaders? Is it because we feel for the people? And if we feel for them, are we ready to do what would make them happy, and are we willing to strike a balance between this making of money and increasing the quality of life? . . . Joyful activity, I would call it, but at the same time, they must be able to carry around these two components with them; otherwise they will have money but lose what's even more important."*

The participants and observers of the meeting were leaders in business, banking and development from twenty-seven countries. The participants became the Advisory Associates of WWB, our international network. Representatives of international organizations underscored the importance of WWB as part of the larger development community. The crucial product was the *International Workshop of Women Leaders in Banking and Finance Report*. Credited to the Committee to Organize Women's World Banking, the report conveys the complexity as well as the sophistication of the discussion.

The participants ultimately agreed on seven recommendations that would characterize WWB operations:

- Support enterprising women in new and existing ventures in both urban and rural areas, in all productive sectors of the economy, with particular attention to small- and medium-scale businesses;
- Focus financial intervention on those small-scale ventures with a chance "to make a difference;"
- Require that beneficiaries have a sufficient equity stake in the venture to be motivated to succeed;
- Gear technical cooperation to match the scale of enterprises owned by women;
- Use local public and private intermediaries to help design and provide management and skills training of a type that can be withdrawn after an initial period;
- Operate on a self-supporting basis by establishing a scale of operations that can be wholly funded by earnings from a capital/guarantee fund;
- Select a "lean staff" to
  −outline basic operating policies for Board consideration;
  −identify initial projects, urban and rural, and allocate two years to their development; and
  −raise capital.

Joan Shapiro worked for South Shore Bank for twenty years. She and Gretchen Maynes were co-authors of the 1980 workshop report, *First International Workshop for Women in Banking and Finance*, and Joan vividly remembered her time in Amsterdam. *"WWB was ahead of its time and* *set in motion an initiative that has become. . . a new way of doing banking. Women's strength was apparent and women had skills to bring to a new field for low-income entrepreneurial women."* (See the report, p. 213.)

When Joan was asked in 2011 for her comments, she said that she felt *"a genuine excitement in recalling the wonder of this unusual and bold idea, and knowing that no one knew what it would become."*

Chita Tanchoco-Subido (now Jarvis), another participant, Executive Director of the Philippine Technical Board for Agricultural Credit, had strong views.

I felt dubious initially about the scope and ambition of the undertaking, but was so impressed with the remarkable vision, talent, and determination of the women from around the world that I knew it was going to succeed. I had no idea at that time (in Amsterdam) that we were witnessing the start of a movement that would touch the lives of millions around the globe.

It was at the Amsterdam meeting that I came to a new understanding of what I might do. At that time the idea that I would lead an international, global banking organization never occurred to me. But I realized that the goal was powerful, that the women had wonderful enthusiasm, valuable experience, and great differences in point of view. I could literally be an honest broker, helping bring ideas and people together to accomplish a goal.

Of the people who were there—participants hailed from countries including Belgium, Bolivia, Botswana, Brazil, Canada, France, Gabon, India, Indonesia, Israel, the Ivory Coast, Jamaica, Jordan, Kenya, Liberia, the Netherlands, Nigeria, Pakistan, the Philippines, Saint Vincent and the Grenadines, Thailand, Tunisia, the United Kingdom, the United States, and Uruguay—I would estimate that seventy-five per cent were really committed. Two observers showed up uninvited; one filed her fingernails the entire time and never said a word. To this day, I have never been able to identify who they were.

Esther Ocloo reported her experience in *A History of Women's World Banking*, a document requested at the 1985 Board of Trustees meeting and presented by Esther at the 1986 meeting.

The first International Workshop organized in March 1980 for Women in Finance and Business was the highlight of the inaugural ceremony to showcase the "Mexican WWB baby" and mark the incorporation of WWB as a stichting in the Netherlands. The Netherlands government was one of the first governments to hail the WWB concept and, apart from donating to the fund, allowed the WWB to be incorporated in the Netherlands and also hosted the first workshop. . . . After the opening ceremony, the WWB concept and the mechanism were introduced to the participants. . . . Questionnaires designed to collect information from the participants regarding socioeconomic activities of women, existing credit facilities, etc., were distributed. On the second day, John Hammock was asked to share his experience with the participants regarding the activities of women in Latin America. One of the moving and educative talks was given by Lilia Clemente on investments. . . . Participants expressed the desire to form themselves into "associates" who would go out as ambassadors and form a network for preaching the WWB concept throughout the world and help in promoting its progress.

Mary Okelo, the first African woman to be made manager of any Barclays Bank, and **Christine Hayanga**, a lawyer with the Agricultural Finance Corporation in Nairobi (both of whom I had met with Margaret (Peg) Snyder when I attended a 1977 environmental conference in Nairobi), tell the story about how on the way home from the Amsterdam meeting, speaking to each other, they agreed, *"Men will say we're crazy when we talk about starting a global financial institution for women."*

Mary Houghton had her own impression of the conference. *"My first connection to the women's movement was in 1969 when I was still at Hyde Park Bank and had become active in the Hyde Park Community Center, which had created a Women's Rights Committee. But I had never traveled outside the US. On the morning that I was supposed to leave for the Netherlands, I realized that I didn't have a passport. I remember the fancy hotel and most of the women who became the founders. I remember thinking it was emotional and frustrating, a little messy."*

Most participants had not had any previous international exposure, and had never worked with women from other cultures. Deanna Rosenswig, from the Bank of Montreal, recounted her experience.

Deanna Rosenswig

For me, it was my first time abroad by myself. I arrived in Amsterdam, at this meeting. There was a room of maybe fifty women, all of whom were trying to make something happen for women in developing countries. While I knew little about developing countries, I knew a lot about credit— corporate credit, not small loans—and had begun to understand what we are now calling "microcredit" and how that would give underprivileged women access to their economies. If women had access to their economies, they would become more powerful, would earn a living, build self-confidence, and feed their children. The challenge was the need to reach so many people with small amounts of money. I used to write loans with many, many zeros—it's much easier to do that, truthfully, than it is to do millions of one hundred-dollar loans, which is what micro is all about. What made WWB work is that there was no prescribed formula—it was never assumed that what was working in Africa would automatically work elsewhere. While some places required individual lending, in others it was group lending that was most effective. . . . One common approach, however, was that small amounts of money were always accompanied by large amounts of technical assistance and confidence-building, and that the priorities were determined by the women themselves.

I was blown away by the experience. Maybe today I'd say "blown away;" then I said "overwhelmed." It really did change my life. It was the first time I had ever seen strong women in a group. I have a BSc and MBA from McGill University, and had always been among men. I almost didn't get into MBA School because they said, "Oh, you wouldn't want to be the only woman in your class dear, now would you?" The year 1980 was the same year, or the year after, I had become a vice president of the Bank of Montreal. So for me to see so many strong women who were senior leaders in their fields was overwhelming. Plus they were all lovely; they were worth talking to and listening to. I don't think I slept that whole time; I just couldn't get enough of these people. I don't know if I was a feminist before, but I was certainly a feminist after 1980. After that, I had connections in the world. I didn't feel isolated in Canada anymore. I was connected.

The Martha Stuart Communications video of the last day in Amsterdam shows the members of the Planning Committee discussing what their expectations had been since the meeting in Mexico City in 1975 and what they felt about the meeting. Everyone looks completely exhausted. We were thrilled with the progress and thinking of how much work lay ahead. We each had learned even more about what all these women and all these cultures had to offer.

Caroline Pezzullo noted, *"What I found working with all of the women here is a new kind of support system that I have not found in the development process. It is finding a new source of energy in working with women who are looking at old development processes of their own countries, their own communities, and the world community from another perspective."*

Leslie Sederlund commented, *"What meant a lot to me as we worked is the discussion of different organizational forms that would need a relatively flexible structure. To watch everyone who participates in this workshop leave with a feeling that there was something that they can begin to do in their own countries, and that there was not a fear of the different regulations within each country that might put any restraint on the program. . . but all would work in their own different ways and yet, at the same time, consider themselves part of one united effort. . . ."*

Martha Stuart talked about working in Java with village women who were brilliant and very aware of what was going on, despite their isolation. When Martha described a women's conference to the female leader of the village, she said, *"I want you to tell everybody that women need their own money."*

Margaret (Peg) Snyder pointed out that in her experience, *"So many of the women in the villages say to me that what they need with community development is 'regular income for ourselves and our children.' That was from north and south, east to west."*

Esther Ocloo agreed. *"We had a national workshop to determine what women really needed. They planned to start with literacy. The women said 'No, no, no, we want money in our pockets.' . . . We do feel concerned about the question of teaching reading and writing, but you see if they are still poor and have nothing to eat for that day; if you tell them to bring their book and learn how to read and write, nobody will come."*

I repeated a similar story told to me by Ela Bhatt, about the early days of SEWA. She began teaching her partners about bookkeeping through a reading process, and they refused to learn. Ela designed a program to teach them with graphics, figures, and charts.

Looking back at this video, I can see that I was already articulating what came to be a mantra for me, and a key to the way WWB developed. I said this then:

I think what we have created is not so much an institution but an access to the capital resources of the world for the potential access for women everywhere. One of the unique things of this process for me is the potential that can come from women from different economic bases, different cultures, in terms of their attitudes toward control of capital and control of resources of their own culture. It is important to integrate those attitudes and those values about the use of money at whatever level we can, and those attitudes are different throughout the world. There's a tremendous strength that can be derived by looking at something that is not totally definitive. The idea of looking at some kind of process rather than an institution, looking at new ways of defining development, a developing community as opposed to a developing country.

Out of the Amsterdam meeting came the core creativity of WWB and the beginnings of a structure for the affiliates. We were hoping for a clear understanding of how to build an organization that would be relevant and possible in every region of the world, servicing the smallest business people in any community—who were generally women! This was not to be an institution for all women; it was for low-income entrepreneurial women. Ownership over production required access to banking services. We relied on the individual leadership of the women involved.

When we interviewed Sara Stuart, who along with Jay Savulich had worked with Martha Stuart filming our 1980 meetings, she stressed the importance of successful collaboration.

Sara Stuart

I think the decision of who you work with is the most important decision of the whole project. The strengths and weaknesses of the local partner will be the strengths and weaknesses of the collaboration. Also in large organizations, middle managers are often the key to success for grassroots work. Ignoring them is a huge mistake; rather they need to buy in and decide that the collaboration will benefit and support their responsibilities as a whole.

From Amsterdam onward, selecting strong local partners remained the key to WWB's success, just as Sara suggested. The affiliates that thrived and grew reflected the invaluable contribution of strong and honest leaders.

When you start something new, every day is a risk, there are no road maps, and you trust people and figure out benchmarks that you try to follow. Basically we were taking a risk on people and on ideas every day. It was very entrepreneurial—in contrast with the mood today, when people seem to be waiting to be told what to do and how to do it.

John Hammock

What drove you was your passion and your instinct. You knew that you had to get the key women together. I kept saying that we had no money and it might be a good idea to scale back the idea of a conference that brought women together from all over the world. You would not hear it! To put it nicely, you could be quite determined. "It will happen," you said. And it did. And the energy created by the first conferences, done on a shoestring with money that somehow appeared, was crucial. You were right—the key was getting the vision and passion thing right. The details followed.

During the Committee to Organize WWB board meeting that immediately followed the Amsterdam conference, a difficult debate ensued about whether I should become acting president of WWB until the formal legal approval was in place for naming a president. (My efforts as a de facto leader had been given on a volunteer basis.) After considerable discussion, and a much needed break, it became apparent that no one was eager to take on the role, and it was agreed that I would serve as acting president until SWWB's Board was formally appointed.

Before leaving Amsterdam, we also held the first meeting of Friends of WWB/USA Inc. FWWB/USA had been formally incorporated in the state of Delaware on January 4, 1980. FWWB members were the US/New York-based members of Committee to Organize who did not go on the Board of Stichting Women's World Banking.

In a letter to new Board members dated October 14, 1981, on "Roles and Responsibilities of the Individual Board of Directors Members," I wrote that such responsibilities were to "initially. . . participate in the US effort for the WWB Capital Fund Drive and in development of an education and training program which will encourage more banking and small-business links in the United States and between the United States and other countries." In November 2011, Nancy Porter Morrill, whom I knew from the Mexico City conference, where she was representing Girl Guides and Girl Scouts, described her work with FWWB.

Nancy Porter Morrill

Michaela asked me to serve as a consultant to help give shape and form to the US affiliate of WWB. I commuted regularly from my home in Bucks County, Pennsylvania, to the WWB offices in Manhattan, where I was caught up in the excitement and challenge of creating something for women and their families around the world. The products of my efforts were Board books for both the Stichting Board and the Friends of WWB USA. . . . bylaws, policies, and procedures, and strategies for implementation of minutes, as well as helping to work with the then Board of the Friends of WWB USA affiliate, including researching possible funding sources and locales for the establishment of subgroups in the US. Heady stuff! I also enjoyed being part of the camaraderie of the office staff for the couple of years I was involved.

It was exciting to finally locate Omaymah Dahann, one of the original Board members, in Jordan in April 2012. Her memories are added below.

Omaymah Dahann

For me, Amsterdam was a very rich and meaningful experience with talented, highly motivated, well-connected women who believed in the WWB concept and shared its vision. . . . Women shared information on a global level and discussed different options for the organization.

The budget was very limited. I stayed on the board of SWWB for about 10 years. Members discussed issues concerning the application of the concept: which banks would encourage the concept and cooperate, how to offer training to women to start and run their own businesses, the role of women organizations. . . . This motivated me to develop a course about management of small businesses at the University of Jordan and to participate in the Jordanian government's economic plans, which included extending loans to men and women to further their employment. The WWB idea was adopted in many ways. In 1993, I was appointed as an adviser to the prime minister of Jordan on women's affairs, where we were working on the first strategy for women in Jordan, and access to credit was one of the points in the strategy. . . . It is like a plant—the plant started growing, informally—and I was happy to see it flourish.

WOMEN'S WORLD BANKING

BACKGROUND PAPER

Prepared By

Patricia M. Cloherty

Founder of New York Based Investment Firm

Note: Prepared for Armsterdam Meeting, 1980
but Reproduced for Manila Workshop,1982

I.   INTRODUCTION

Women's World Banking (WWB) states in its incorporating papers that the
organization's purpose is the following:

>   ...To advance and promote the direct participation
>   of women and their families in the full use of the
>   economy, particularly those women who have not generally
>   had access to the services of established financial
>   institutions...

Its Statement of Purpose, of November 1979, goes on to suggest broadly
the means to be used to accomplish this goal as follows:

>   ...(WWB) is designed to operate as a decentralized,
>   flexible mechanism for linking entrepreneurial women,
>   existing financial institutions, and technical, managerial,
>   and training resources. The role of WWB...one of
>   facilitator...

The principal tools the organization will use, we are told in the same
document, include loan guarantees, extended to women's enterprises through
existing financial institutions, and management and technical assistance
to enterprises requiring it.

Last, the preliminary operating plan conveys a strategic sense of WWB's
intention to extend capital support selectively, through qualified
intermediaries, to women entrepreneurs with viable projects, in
accordance with prevailing business practice in the area.

In short, WWB has been established as a provider of capital to women
entrepreneurs.

While the concept can be stated succinctly, it obviously rests on a
number of complex assumptions about the societies and economies of many
countries. Further, from a purely practical, operating standpoint, it
raises many issues with respect to how the program will actually function
in the "real world." The process of enterprise development takes time,
and it takes both reasonable skills and commercial concepts, in addition
to capital. WWB's resources will be small compared to the task at hand.
Maximizing results to be attained with those resources will require
additional detailed and pragmatic planning.

- 2 -

WWB is convening a meeting in Amsterdam in March, 1980, at which its basic assumptions will be examined from several viewpoints, as will its operating plan. The fact that the expected participants at the meeting represent a diversity of relevant business and professional backgrounds, as well as of nationalities, will add greatly to the discussion base. And the fact that there will be an opportunity for various of the attendees to participate in the WWB program as it evolves, and to benefit from it, will sharpen the focus of the meeting.

II. PURPOSE OF MEMORANDUM

The purpose of this memorandum is to open the dialogue expected at the Amsterdam meeting by providing a brief commentary on key underlying assumptions of WWB, and establishing a preliminary agenda of practical considerations to be addressed.

A few caveats are necessary. First the treatment of key issues here is very general. It is designed only to stimulate thinking about how the general view, or assumptions, might apply in specific areas of the world, with all the cultural and other differences that pertain in those areas.

Second, the issues raised by WWB comprise only "one slice" of a broad, complex development effort that has been underway for many years. All those dimensions are not treated in detail here. But it is important to note that the real value of WWB's proposal to assist a special group -- women entrepreneurs -- lies in their ability to contribute to overall development efforts. In that context, women become a valuable national resource, singled out for special assistance, in the view that their economic advancement is a matter of common interest to all.

While it is not discussed here, the larger development context is important, and can be taken up by those knowledgeable of their own country's development agendas, at the Amsterdam meeting.

III. KEY ISSUES/ASSUMPTIONS

Three interrelated issues form the principal underpinnings of WWB, including (a) the roles of women entrepreneurs in developing communities; (b) the availability of capital to finance their enterprises; and (c) the role of commercial banks and other financial intermediaries in linking the two, i.e. as providers of capital to women entrepreneurs.

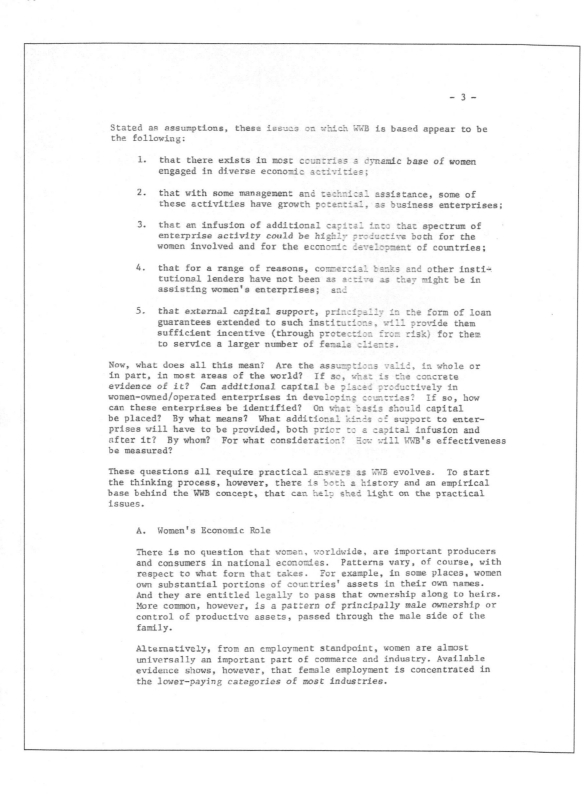

Stated as assumptions, these issues on which WWB is based appear to be
the following:

1. that there exists in most countries a dynamic base of women
    engaged in diverse economic activities;

2. that with some management and technical assistance, some of
    these activities have growth potential, as business enterprises;

3. that an infusion of additional capital into that spectrum of
    enterprise activity could be highly productive both for the
    women involved and for the economic development of countries;

4. that for a range of reasons, commercial banks and other insti-
    tutional lenders have not been as active as they might be in
    assisting women's enterprises; and

5. that external capital support, principally in the form of loan
    guarantees extended to such institutions, will provide them
    sufficient incentive (through protection from risk) for them
    to service a larger number of female clients.

Now, what does all this mean? Are the assumptions valid, in whole or
in part, in most areas of the world? If so, what is the concrete
evidence of it? Can additional capital be placed productively in
women-owned/operated enterprises in developing countries? If so, how
can these enterprises be identified? On what basis should capital
be placed? By what means? What additional kinds of support to enterprises will have to be provided, both prior to a capital infusion and
after it? By whom? For what consideration? How will WWB's effectiveness
be measured?

These questions all require practical answers as WWB evolves. To start
the thinking process, however, there is both a history and an empirical
base behind the WWB concept, that can help shed light on the practical
issues.

A. Women's Economic Role

There is no question that women, worldwide, are important producers
and consumers in national economies. Patterns vary, of course, with
respect to what form that takes. For example, in some places, women
own substantial portions of countries' assets in their own names.
And they are entitled legally to pass that ownership along to heirs.
More common, however, is a pattern of principally male ownership or
control of productive assets, passed through the male side of the
family.

Alternatively, from an employment standpoint, women are almost
universally an important part of commerce and industry. Available
evidence shows, however, that female employment is concentrated in
the lower-paying categories of most industries.

- 4 -

The picture is hardly static. In "developed" and "developing" countries, the roles of women change with conditions -- e.g., education provided; shifts in economic bases; changes in social and cultural attitudes and norms, among others. As always, whether the effects of such changes are positive or negative depends in part on one's point of view.

In the United States, over the last ten years, women have moved increasingly into entrepreneurial roles, owning and operating their own businesses. While small for the most part, and concentrated in retail and service businesses (few in manufacturing), these businesses increasingly afford women a means of making a living, of building up capital, and, often, of involving their families in the business. By owning their businesses, women are signalling a shift away from working as a paid employee for someone else. It also signals an increasing element of control over their own economic well-being. Overall, this particular trend is viewed generally as a positive trend for the country.

With specific reference to developing countries, recent studies have suggested that efforts to industrialize and to mechanize agriculture have had important negative side effects on the status of women. In oversimplified form, one argument is that industrialization processes introduced from the developing countries have tended to generate new management roles principally for men, as has the use of machinery in agriculture. As a consequence, women have lost ground in the process. And, unless they happen to be well off or highly-educated, they tend to have few occupational choices involving either upward mobility or capital accumulation.

Dr. Esther Boserup, in a seminal work on the subject, observed the following:

> Economic and social development unavoidably entails the disintegration of the division of labor among the two sexes...With modernization of agriculture and with migration to the towns, a new sex pattern of productive work must emerge, for better or worse. The obvious danger is...that women will be deprived of their productive functions, and the process of growth will...be retarded.

She goes on in case studies from Africa and Asia, to show specifically how this has occurred. Additionally, absence of educational opportunity for women in some areas, coupled with seclusion of women for religious and cultural reasons in other regions, has tended to result in differing impacts of modernization on men and women. In this formulation, then, men are more apt to be involved in the "modern" sector, and women in the traditional one.

A corollary of this proposition is that the institutions established to service modernizing industry tend not to serve women in any significant numbers, if at all. Financial institutions, in particular,

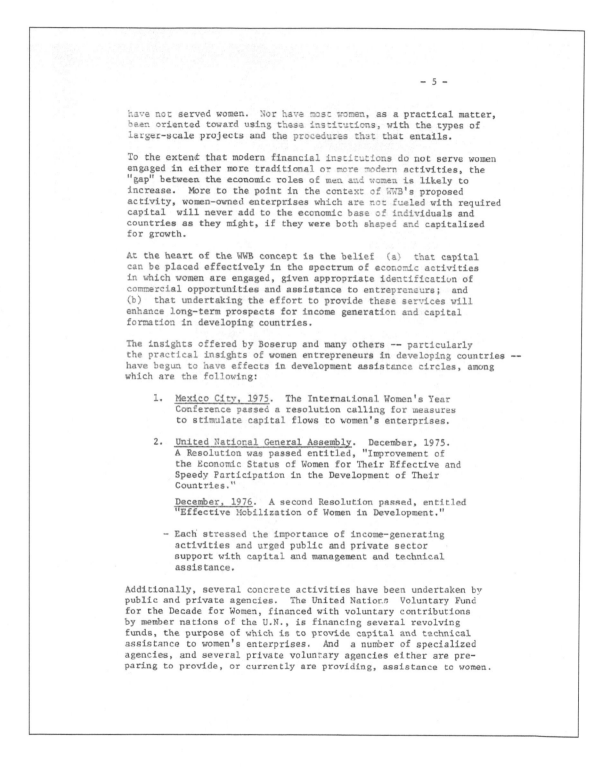

- 5 -

have not served women. Nor have most women, as a practical matter,
been oriented toward using these institutions, with the types of
larger-scale projects and the procedures that that entails.

To the extent that modern financial institutions do not serve women
engaged in either more traditional or more modern activities, the
"gap" between the economic roles of men and women is likely to
increase. More to the point in the context of WWB's proposed
activity, women-owned enterprises which are not fueled with required
capital will never add to the economic base of individuals and
countries as they might, if they were both shaped and capitalized
for growth.

At the heart of the WWB concept is the belief (a) that capital
can be placed effectively in the spectrum of economic activities
in which women are engaged, given appropriate identification of
commercial opportunities and assistance to entrepreneurs; and
(b) that undertaking the effort to provide these services will
enhance long-term prospects for income generation and capital
formation in developing countries.

The insights offered by Boserup and many others -- particularly
the practical insights of women entrepreneurs in developing countries --
have begun to have effects in development assistance circles, among
which are the following:

1. Mexico City, 1975. The International Women's Year
    Conference passed a resolution calling for measures
    to stimulate capital flows to women's enterprises.

2. United National General Assembly. December, 1975.
    A Resolution was passed entitled, "Improvement of
    the Economic Status of Women for Their Effective and
    Speedy Participation in the Development of Their
    Countries."

    December, 1976. A second Resolution passed, entitled
    "Effective Mobilization of Women in Development."

    - Each stressed the importance of income-generating
      activities and urged public and private sector
      support with capital and management and technical
      assistance.

Additionally, several concrete activities have been undertaken by
public and private agencies. The United Nations Voluntary Fund
for the Decade for Women, financed with voluntary contributions
by member nations of the U.N., is financing several revolving
funds, the purpose of which is to provide capital and technical
assistance to women's enterprises. And a number of specialized
agencies, and several private voluntary agencies either are preparing to provide, or currently are providing, assistance to women.

- 6 -

The WWB concept embodies the economic development themes first articulated clearly at the Mexico City meeting. In fact, several members of its organizing committee were involved in that meeting, and in the subsequent policy resolutions at the United Nations. They, with others, have shaped WWB as an independent entity, with the aim of achieving maximum operating flexibility as well as concrete results.

While WWB's plan, as indicated, is to piggyback existing institutions and field networks in accomplishing its goals, the fact remains that capital is its principal tool.

That being the case, attention must be given to the requirements for using capital effectively.

B. Use of Capital in Developing Enterprises

Enterprise development, particularly on a small-scale, is "in" worldwide, from a public policy standpoint, and not just for women. High levels of unemployment and inflation; declining rates of national growth; low levels of innovation and productivity; and low rates of capital investment in new plants and equipment -- all these negative factors contribute to this widespread interest.

In developing countries particularly, a premium is being placed on what is called "development of local capacity and markets." And this is happening at a time when capital reserves generally are at low ebb, in the face of mounting fuel costs, incurred mainly by the modern, industrialized sectors of national economies.

Altogether, this is a tough "macro" problem, which translates into a tough "micro" problem at the level of particular enterprises.

In interjecting its capital-providing services into what is predominantly a capital-short environment, WWB will have to develop a means of allocating the capital to those enterprises where it is apt to do the most good.

"Most good," in the context being discussed here, involves social and economic dimensions. The specific social benefits deriving from enterprise development include such goods as creation of jobs and the resulting incomes; creation of products and services for which there is a market; creation of a capital base for individuals and communities; and the development of sources of independent livlihood for families over generations.

The economic fact in placing capital, however, is that these "goods" for communities flow only from enterprises that make economic sense. For example, it would be highly inadvisable to finance a women-run handicraft center, if the market for handicrafts is not viable or is non-existent. Similarly, to finance a project producing products for $1.00, for which buyers will pay only $.50, is a formula for early failure or perpetual subsidy.

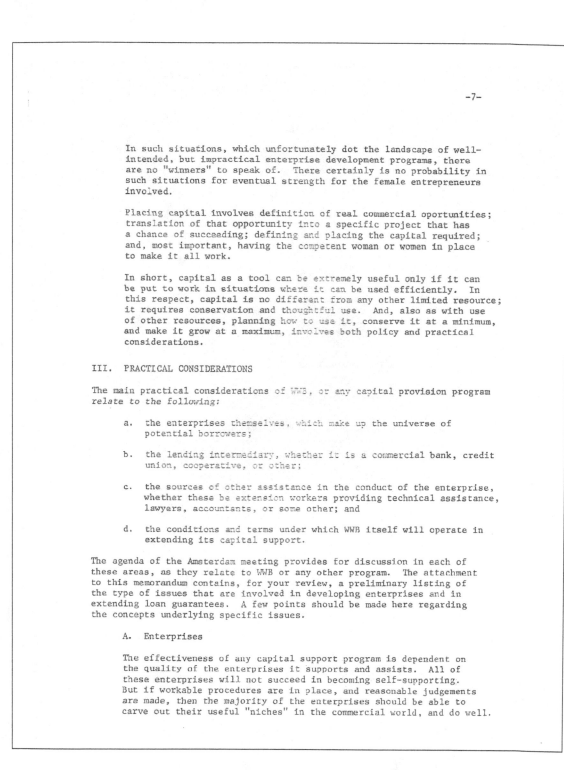

In such situations, which unfortunately dot the landscape of well-intended, but impractical enterprise development programs, there are no "winners" to speak of. There certainly is no probability in such situations for eventual strength for the female entrepreneurs involved.

Placing capital involves definition of real commercial oportunities; translation of that opportunity into a specific project that has a chance of succeeding; defining and placing the capital required; and, most important, having the competent woman or women in place to make it all work.

In short, capital as a tool can be extremely useful only if it can be put to work in situations where it can be used efficiently. In this respect, capital is no different from any other limited resource; it requires conservation and thoughtful use. And, also as with use of other resources, planning how to use it, conserve it at a minimum, and make it grow at a maximum, involves both policy and practical considerations.

III. PRACTICAL CONSIDERATIONS

The main practical considerations of WWB, or any capital provision program relate to the following:

    a. the enterprises themselves, which make up the universe of potential borrowers;

    b. the lending intermediary, whether it is a commercial bank, credit union, cooperative, or other;

    c. the sources of other assistance in the conduct of the enterprise, whether these be extension workers providing technical assistance, lawyers, accountants, or some other; and

    d. the conditions and terms under which WWB itself will operate in extending its capital support.

The agenda of the Amsterdam meeting provides for discussion in each of these areas, as they relate to WWB or any other program. The attachment to this memorandum contains, for your review, a preliminary listing of the type of issues that are involved in developing enterprises and in extending loan guarantees. A few points should be made here regarding the concepts underlying specific issues.

    A. Enterprises

The effectiveness of any capital support program is dependent on the quality of the enterprises it supports and assists. All of these enterprises will not succeed in becoming self-supporting. But if workable procedures are in place, and reasonable judgements are made, then the majority of the enterprises should be able to carve out their useful "niches" in the commercial world, and do well.

- 8 -

A first order of priority for WWB is to define what constitutes its
goal for success of enterprises overall, then to develop criteria
for selection of, and assistance to, enterprises that will be most
apt to produce that result.

The issues identified under "I. Enterprises," in the attachment
are the types of issues requiring definition for this purpose.

B. Lenders

The key issues relating to the direct lenders, whose capital will
be put up, relate to their role in making and servicing the loans;
and the amount of risk they are required to take.

In most credit guarantee programs, the financial intermediaries
which provide the capital with a guarantee from a third party,
are involved only in making a credit analysis and decision, in
monitoring collection of the loan, or in liquidating it in the
event of default.

Precisely what that role will be in the case of WWB has to be
determined. The issues spelled out in Item II, attached, begin to
define that role.

C. WWB Operations

WWB is proposed as a capital fund, with ability to cover its operating expenses, including losses for projects, from the income from
capital, and any other funds it might be able to raise.

But the nature and terms of any guarantee has to be defined in
advance of its extension, and negotiated with participating
institutions.

Illustrative questions to be thought through are contained in
Item III of the Attachment.

D. General Comment

Many of the practical considerations are universal in nature; that
is, anyone starting any fund anywhere would have to resolve them in
order to operate.

In WWB, there is an added dimension. Because women generally have
not dealt with financial institutions and all the concepts involved,
the education and training portions of the program take on added
significance, both for women entrepreneurs and for lenders. The
process of mutual education is an integral part of the program
which, while adding costs, contributes to goal achievement.

Further, because the goals of WWB are dual -- advancing women,
through economically viable projects -- the selection criteria for
projects go beyond conventional economic and financial analysis
used everywhere in the world. The critical assessment of what a
project accomplishes for women must be overlaid on the evaluative
process.

Striking the right balance between the goals, and reflecting this
balance throughout WWB's established procedures, will be the main
challenge for WWB, rather than any inherent complexity of the
issues themselves.

V. CONCLUSION

While WWB's principal focus initially will be developing countries, the
issues and assumptions it raises apply universally. And in virtually
all countries, largely as a matter of livelihood, women are engaged in
a range of economic activities which may have potential for real
entrepreneurial endeavor, with the individual and community benefits
that confers.

WWB's challenge will be to develop the approach and, over time, the
practical formula, for harnessing such creative energies productively.
Time, skill and resources will be required to accomplish WWB's goals.
And a well-thought-out plan should enhance prospects for success. The
forum provided by the Amsterdam meeting will add considerably to that
planning process.

Attachment I

Preliminary List of Operating Issues

Requiring Consideration and Decisions

I. Issues Relating to Enterprises

A. Where are the enterprises, and through what means can they be
    located?

B. What types of projects are acceptable for financing?

C. What types of financings are appropriate (e.g., fixed asset,
    working capital, debt repayment or consolidation, receivable
    and inventory financing, long-term, short-term, etc.)?

D. What does financing a particular project mean for its female
    participants over the long-term?

E. Why do particular enterprises represent good potential for
    capital placement? This must be defined in terms of such
    matters as

    - skills of women entrepreneurs involved
    - product or service offered
    - market potential
    - availability of raw material
    - appropriate pricing
    - competitive advantage in the proposed market
    - identification of the level of capital required
    - projected return on investment, given all of the above
    - provision for subsequent rounds of financing

F. What stake have the entrepreneurs in the business?

    - have they committed their own resources, however small?
    - have they records of accomplishment in related efforts?
    - what assistance will they require in conducting the business?

G. What is the nature of the ongoing assistance that will be required?

    - in production
    - in quality control
    - in cash managment and record-keeping
    - in opening new markets
    - in worker training

H. Who will analyze the business for the lender?

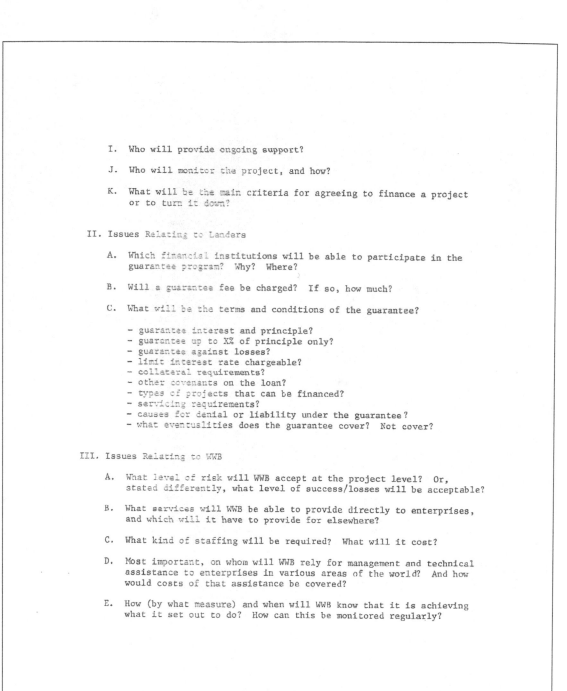

I. Who will provide ongoing support?

J. Who will monitor the project, and how?

K. What will be the main criteria for agreeing to finance a project
    or to turn it down?

II. Issues Relating to Lenders

A. Which financial institutions will be able to participate in the
    guarantee program? Why? Where?

B. Will a guarantee fee be charged? If so, how much?

C. What will be the terms and conditions of the guarantee?

    – guarantee interest and principle?
    – guarantee up to X% of principle only?
    – guarantee against losses?
    – limit interest rate chargeable?
    – collateral requirements?
    – other covenants on the loan?
    – types of projects that can be financed?
    – servicing requirements?
    – causes for denial or liability under the guarantee?
    – what eventualities does the guarantee cover? Not cover?

III. Issues Relating to WWB

A. What level of risk will WWB accept at the project level? Or,
    stated differently, what level of success/losses will be acceptable?

B. What services will WWB be able to provide directly to enterprises,
    and which will it have to provide for elsewhere?

C. What kind of staffing will be required? What will it cost?

D. Most important, on whom will WWB rely for management and technical
    assistance to enterprises in various areas of the world? And how
    would costs of that assistance be covered?

E. How (by what measure) and when will WWB know that it is achieving
    what it set out to do? How can this be monitored regularly?

4

WOMEN'S WORLD BANKING GETS DOWN TO WORK

"You're ready to do it yourself."

FOLLOWING THE AMSTERDAM meeting, our group in New York continued to work on setting up a legal entity without having any clear notion of who would run it. I had great reservations about my capacity to run an international financial institution. I continued to seek the advice and encouragement of Beatrice Harretche and in my heart of hearts I had hoped that her pending retirement from IDB might allow her to consider WWB as a bridge between her job as executive vice president of IDB and full retirement. Later on, at the SWWB Board meeting during the World Conference of the United Nations Decade for Women in Copenhagen in July 1980, Beatrice looked me straight in the eyes and told me: "*Michaela, I don't know why you're looking for someone else to run this. You're the only one who knows where it's going—you have to run it yourself.*"

By then, WWB was on the radar of the international development community. In his statement before the Copenhagen Conference, UNDP administrator **Bradford Morse** made a specific reference to WWB and urged governments to support us.

> Let me tell you about UNDP's involvement in just two of the areas which I have listed. Providing women with access to credit was a focus of considerable concern in Mexico City. A small group of women present there pursued the idea and later organized Women's World Banking, designed to expand banking services to women through existing financial institutions. Women's World Banking is a unique example of women working together to create new and better opportunities for women in our own societies. UNDP is proud to have been associated with them. They will need much more help over the next three years, as they seek to establish a core six million-dollar capital fund. I urge your encouragement and support.

We considered every possibility for where and how SWWB should be domiciled, including the idea of the organization being affiliated with UNDP. That would have required any non-US personnel to have a special visa. We also were in the process of reconsidering some initial policies, such as whether or not men could serve on the board. Floris Bannier, who was among the first men to join the board, remembers well.

Floris Bannier

In spring 1980, the first SWWB Board meeting was held in Amsterdam at the Amstel Hotel, following the first International Workshop of Women in Banking and Finance (March 12–15, 1980). I attended in my capacity as a lawyer and listened to a discussion about whether or not men could serve on the board. The vote being "no," I left the meeting and remained SWWB's lawyer. At first I thought this exclusion of men was a bit over the top, but it was their decision, and I had enough jobs and family commitments, so it was fine. In July of that year, the second UN Women's Conference (a follow-up to the 1975 Mexico City conference), was held in Copenhagen. I didn't attend, but I sent a female assistant from my firm, and when she returned, she informed me that the SWWB policy had changed and that I had been elected to the board.

We also needed to secure financing, reach out to people who were willing and able to start affiliate programs to actually bring women into the formal financial system, and organize ourselves into a functioning organization. En route home from Copenhagen, I stopped at the Norwegian Agency for Development Cooperation (NORAD) in Oslo and at the Swedish International Development Agency (SIDA) in Stockholm to determine interest in supporting a WWB Capital Fund.

During a 2011 conversation with **Dag Nissen**, the person whom I met with at NORAD and who remained a major WWB supporter (he introduced us to Professor Berit As, a future Board member), I asked him what he remembered about the day in 1980 I stopped in to ask for a favor. *"We did not do you a favor,"* he told me. *"You did us a favor. The Norwegian Parliament had just directed NORAD to start providing assistance to support women in developing countries."*

After Oslo, I traveled to Stockholm, to meet with Karin Himmelstrand, at SIDA. Karin was a friend of Margaret (Peg) Snyder. During that visit I also met with Barbro Dahlbom-Hall, a management consultant who eventually became a member of the Board.

I remember taking a train to a suburb of Stockholm to meet with Barbro. I sat waiting for her in one room of a restaurant, while she was waiting in another. What a waste of an hour, instead of conversing with someone who would become a truly valuable, loyal friend and colleague.

San Remo

We worked hard to organize the Second International Workshop of Women Leaders in Banking and Finance (co-sponsored by Accion) and our next board meeting, to be held in San Remo, Italy, in April 1981. Through Martha Stuart's colleagues at the Nobel Foundation, the foundation donated use of Nobel's home in San Remo.

John Hammock had met with Margarita Guzmán, who was working on access to credit for women in Cali, Colombia. He suggested that she come to San Remo to talk about her work, with the idea that her model might be adopted by some of the other participants who wished to create an affiliate. Her participation would lead to the establishment of the WWB Cali affiliate the following year. At the suggestion of Abe Weisblatt (director of research and training for the Agricultural Development Council), I met with Nancy Barry, a young woman serving as senior operations officer at the World Bank, with responsibility for small enterprise programs. I thought that she was a potential candidate to run WWB eventually, and I encouraged her to come to San Remo. She gave the keynote address and agreed to consider becoming a member of the SWWB Board. As we were planning the San Remo Board meeting, the Scandinavians notified us of their pending support for the capitalization of the guarantee fund. I anticipated being able to announce a major gift from Norway.

Many people who had been at the Amsterdam meeting the year before were present at San Remo. One of the entertainment highlights was the nightly fun we had at the Casino. The future success of WWB could be compared only to the success of some participants at San Remo's black-jack tables! I invited Laura, my thirteen-year-old niece, to the meeting—her first international trip. It was fun to watch her interact with women from around the world and practice her Spanish with Margarita Guzmán while jogging in the mornings. My niece Lawler was studying at the London School of Economics. She and her friend Judy drove down to the meeting and served as volunteer interns, and she still remembers all-night sessions recording the day's meetings. I think having my nieces involved helped my family understand what I was doing with Women's World Banking—and why I seemed to talk of nothing else.

Discussions went on into early mornings, with participants trying to understand exactly what a guarantee fund was, and how to incorporate a legally recognized organization that could serve women as a financial institution. As always at WWB meetings, the serious talks were part of an agenda that included lots of fun, as well as great drama. (See "Agreement Between Stichting and Its Affiliates to Promote Women's World Banking" and the Loan Guarantee Program and Private Placement Memorandums, pp. 275–282.)

One of the major points raised at San Remo (and at all future meetings), was that WWB was not in the business of paying affiliates to do what we wanted. The affiliates had to take ownership of their activities. We needed to know what they wanted to do and we would help them do it. This was a very different way of thinking from many of the international development programs and agencies, which entered countries with their own agenda and found someone to carry it out. Because we had come together as a group of women doing business, we believed that the fundamental goal was to enable women, not direct them. While we clung to this approach, it continued confusing people and more often than not—it was not a popular objective to defend.

We also introduced two totally new concepts: financial leverage and a WWB Capital Fund as the partial guarantor to local banks. For some affiliates, this concept for building access to the formal economy was never fully understood. This was a very different way of thinking for many of the international development agencies and organizations as well.

At San Remo, one of the participants from the Philippines, Lourdes Lontok Cruz, kept saying, "*Where's the beef?*" She had been at the Amsterdam meeting, and when she returned home she began promoting an affiliate, Women in Finance and Entrepreneurship (WIFE), linked to Paluwagon Ng Bayon Savings and Loan Association. She had come to San Remo believing that the Capital Fund resources would be available. Unfortunately, Lourdes's expectations were already ahead of our realities. The support I had anticipated from the Scandinavians did not materialize for four more months.

One interesting lesson I gleaned then and over the years was that the way women expressed themselves, interpreted, and debated was very different from region to region, culture to culture, and economy to economy. I learned how important the decision was to hold global meetings every two years. The meetings helped merge our different ideas for local institutions for women, and unified our voices and our thinking about how to be a global institution. I have vivid memories of Margarita Guzmán, Mercedes Canalda, and Esther Ocloo engaging in heated discussions until the wee hours of the morning about what it meant to have a global banking institution for women, women's rights, banking, etc. Esther, the marmalade queen of Ghana, would say, "*You don't understand development—give us the money and we'll do the work.*" Margarita, a banker, would counter that banking was structured very differently from nonprofits. I found that Latinas have four times as many words for every thought, while Asian women are more cautious about speaking, but are very direct when they do. . . . I found African women were initially slower in trusting other cultures. I always remember Esther Ocloo, who helped put WWB on the map, but was always cautious with me because she thought I was "*one of those Wall Street selfish types that did not understand development.*"

The questions that formed the working agenda for San Remo reflected our maturing grasp of the tasks ahead. The plenary was organized around how to improve collaboration and knowledge. The program explored several issues, including these:

How can women in banking and finance involve more of their colleagues to expand successful lending and relevant services to women business owners? How can bankers provide more assistance to small businesses? Can WWB in collaboration help finance management assistance and/or banking facilities for small businesses?

Following the plenary, working groups focused on the types of financial and economic data that would be most useful in developing programs, identifying nontraditional areas for businesswomen, and persuading more women to use their capital resources and experience to help generate financing for women's businesses. As she had helped to do for the Amsterdam gathering, Gretchen Maynes produced a significant report on the issues and discussions of the San Remo workshop. (See the report, p. 283.)

During the SWWB Board of Trustees meeting at San Remo, Floris clarified SWWB's legal structure. We decided that our strategy should include a global meeting every two years, to be followed by a board meeting. This would allow all WWB members and affiliates to get to know each other, learn from each other about the local affiliates' designs, discuss problems and policy issues, and take ownership of their views prior to trustee actions. We believed that the movement could go forward only if there was a clear, shared understanding of what we were deciding and how the decisions might affect everyone. We began to understand that we were strengthening the movement; we were creating a new global culture of women entrepreneurs. At that meeting I was elected president of Women's World Banking. (See Organizational Chart, p. 314.)

Our board meetings would often end up in tears—at least for the first ten years! I, too, cried—and still do. My view was that women had never been able to express themselves in an open global forum, so there was a long learning process for all of us, with much reiteration of strategies. It was also my view that it was better to just let it out. Sometimes we would have the same conversation ten or twelve times. Everyone had to have an opportunity to express herself and define what she needed to know. It had to be a safe space, no matter how big or small the gathering, if we were going to grow as an organization in a way that hadn't been done before. Each meeting was like a family reunion. We always seemed to forget that women had never worked together as global citizens. It was not just about numbers—we had to work on the human dimension, where the relationship-building happened. As **Beatrice Harretche** observed, prior to adjourning one of our meetings, *"WWB's unique quality is that it is not formal, but serious."*

Based on the participants' interest in Margarita's plans, we decided to hold WWB's first regional meeting outside of Western Europe in Cali, Colombia, to be hosted by Margarita and her colleagues. It was time to test our ideas on the ground.

WWB-Cali

For me, the Cali meeting was an opportunity to learn how to scale our concept so it would work for the individual borrower. We learned about many examples of local lending, such as the *Fundación Carvajal*, a foundation that had inspired Margarita's work. We had a chance to visit several of the small businesses that had received loans. Participants from all over Latin America attended—mostly women bankers, economists, lawyers, or social workers—as well as government and UN representatives. A video of this 1981 conference reflects the diversity and enthusiasm of the participants. Fortunately, John Hammock, who served as translator for me, and Susan Winer were both present to help record an understanding of the discussions that took place over the three days.

At the close of the meeting, Margarita Guzmán and her colleagues formally established a WWB affiliate, Fundación WWB-Cali, which brought together a private bank, the Corporación Financiera del Valle, and Desarrollo del Pueblo (DESAP) a management-assistance agency.

The relationship between WWB-New York and affiliates was becoming clearer, even though it would be a roller-coaster ride figuring out a new service structure as affiliates were formed, and reassessing how to help and support each of them. In the case of WWB-Cali, WWB-New York did not make a donation to WWB-Cali. Rather, WWB-New York designated a restricted fund in New York for WWB-Cali for five years and committed, in the event of default, to deliver those funds to Cali as a contribution.

Beatrice Harretche at the Inter-American Development Bank (IDB) had been involved in WWB since the early days and was eager to support our efforts in Latin America. She was the one who introduced me to Margarita Guzmán, an economist by background, who had been working on projects in Colombia in collaboration with the IDB. It was at Beatrice's suggestion that John Hammock went to Cali to meet with Margarita to explain the WWB philosophy. He urged her to attend the San Remo meeting. From there, Margarita took the initiative to organize WWB-Cali.

Margarita Guzmán

The IDB had been funding a private foundation in Cali (Fundación Carvajal or Carvajal Foundation) that was working with Accion to create a microcredit program. I had visited the Carvajal Foundation, and learned that they rejected a lot of women who were looking for loans, simply because they did not have collateral. That inspired me to gather a group of women to create a nonprofit organization that could support collateral.

Although the women who were denied loans by Fundación Carvajal lacked collateral, they had met other requirements, and had been prescreened and had received training in how to manage their finances. This helped us tremendously and we determined that if a small-business owner approached us and all she was lacking was collateral, we would sign for her.

I gathered a group of thirteen women from different backgrounds (medical doctors, lawyers, architects, etc.), who agreed to meet weekly, analyze the problem further, and think about ways to address it, including by tapping into our respective networks. One of our associates was a journalist, and her articles about our work helped people get to know us.

To build up resources for our project, we set a quota of one hundred dollars that each one would contribute. We all went around telling people about our idea; if they thought it was interesting they got involved, helped with the quota and then gave us the names of future clients, or, in some instances, were interested themselves in obtaining a loan from the foundation. Within our group, each of us took responsibility for following up with a specific borrower.

In 1980, I left my job at the Federación de Cafeteros and accepted the vice presidency of a savings-and-loans corporation at the national level. Holding an important position allowed me the freedom to take on whatever initiative I thought was appropriate, and obtain support from the contacts I had made in the finance industry. We held meetings at my office and had visibility in the financial community. Had I not assumed this work as a personal goal, it would have been very difficult to achieve the kind of results we did.

By then, I had a very clear picture in my mind: Local women have a specific need, there are businesswomen who want to help, we need an entity with resources to help. With the support of women who had economic solvency, we created the local guarantee fund so we could start operating quickly. As our group comprised women leaders in our respective fields, we had credibility, which was key in asking for help in the private sector with the development of the guarantee fund.

Eventually, we started to loan money, because we realized that by simply charging a small percentage for the collateral, we would never be a self-sufficient organization. So we presented the project to the Inter-American Development Bank (IDB) and obtained resources in the amount of three hundred thousand dollars to start lending money directly. The money was going to be disbursed to us over time, with interest close to zero. We fought a lot to obtain loans with positive interest rates, because with this model you can maintain progressive lending, as opposed to a donation, which is usually only made once.

With the guarantee program, we had close to twenty small-businesswomen as co-signers. Then as we grew, we started lending money to groups. Accion helped us with the methodology of "solidarity groups." We developed very stable relationships with the groups, and from there, we moved on to individual loans. We were always focusing on the success of the business. The idea was to preserve the jobs they had or to generate more jobs, but mainly to strengthen the business. Before WWB-Cali started lending, these women borrowed from companies that charged very high interest rates; this prevented them from saving. We wanted them to save as they progressed.

The foundation of our program was the personal relationships that we developed with the borrowers—something that isn't possible for big companies to do. We had a very strong group, and the key was not to lose energy and not to become disappointed when at times the projects we had planned failed.

We started in Cali and then set up in Medellin, Bucaramanga, Popayan, and finally Bogota, which was the hardest since it is the capital; it's easier to work in small cities where people get more involved, and the media give a new initiative more importance.

At the beginning, Popayan was part of Cali; an office there provided loans. As this office grew, the group of women (headed by a woman who was a doctor by background—often people who did not have a background in finance played an important role, as long as they had the interest and worked to acquire any knowledge or tools they lacked) decided that they wanted to be an independent affiliate. They sent a request to New York to become an official WWB affiliate. This was a great group that worked well and was fully committed. Our dream was always to become a formal bank, and after thirty years, that dream is becoming reality: Bogota and Medellin are already banks, and Cali and Popayan are in the process of becoming banks. One of the expectations of becoming a bank is lowering the interest rates. As time goes by, and the bank grows, the fear is that the bank falls into the temptation of providing major credits, which are obviously easier and cheaper. But that's not the objective. The ambivalence can always exist, but the goal is a credit mechanism that allows the beneficiaries to solidify their business.

One thing is when an idea is born locally, but when an idea is born internationally with support from a bigger network, it is easier to grow. One of the most interesting parts of working with WWB was the independence and creative freedom we had as affiliates to design and implement the program we wanted. When we became familiar with the WWB philosophy, we knew we were creating something different, but we did not know how to go about it. As the network allowed us absolute independence, local women became more interested in the creation of a new tool. Later, what the network also enabled was lateral learning, so we could learn from one another.

When I organized the WWB meeting in Cali at the very start of our work in 1981, we sent invitations to countries throughout Latin America, and each country chose their representative, but most of them were bureaucrats who really didn't connect with our efforts. Interestingly, the person who had been chosen to represent the Dominican Republic could not come, and in lieu of her, Mercedes Canalda came. She wound up being the only one of all the women who attended that meeting who actually understood the project and decided to implement it in her country, forming ADOPEM. WWB-ADOPEM has since become very successful.

I retired from my position in 1984 to dedicate all my time to Women's World Banking, and eventually co-developed the WWB training and exchange programs so the WWB network could offer a service to affiliates, get to know who was really committed and had a sound business strategy, and enable diverse affiliates to learn from one another.

Something key in our philosophy is to respect the cultures of each country. The group leader defines how the project should be implemented in her environment. For Michaela, it was hard to see how other countries worked differently. Mercedes Canalda had this saying about the WWB: "Women's World Banking is like the Sun—the farther away the better." Every country was different and had different resources, so imposing an idea would not have worked.

This diversity, along with the language barrier, made it difficult for us at times to communicate. Serving on the WWB Executive Committee, there were challenging moments with people who did not understand the Latin mentality. We are happy and enthusiastic and because of this, some thought we did not embrace the program with seriousness. As time went by, however, they realized we were achieving results, and respected our efforts.

Ana Milena Cadavid de Jaramillo, a banker from Cali who began working with Margarita Guzmán in the early days, and remains on the Cali affiliate's board, recalled her initial impressions of WWB and her experience as the organization grew.

Ana Milena Cadavid de Jaramillo

Twenty-nine or thirty years ago, Margarita had the idea of getting together a group of friends who would put together resources to help less-privileged women. At that time, women fully depended on men. The idea of creating an organization that would support these women was revolutionary to us. I was the financial manager of a big institution—a family compensation fund—that was in charge of supporting the families of workers, and so I had knowledge of the financial industry. I had also founded an institution called "Ahorra más," which, today, is a formal banking entity. When Margarita had the idea of supporting these women and providing credit to them, we knew that we would be a very essential support but we also had to loan to responsible people so as to not lose those resources. To me, "microcredit" did not exist. It was the same as loaning to X client but for a smaller amount. Our friends in the banking sector would tell us: "You guys are crazy! They are going to steal your money! In one month you guys will be asking us for help after saying you lost it all!" We didn't believe them, and we were right. It was so gratifying to see how many of the women borrowers went from feeling like nothing to feeling like businesswomen who did not have to beg their husbands for a food plate because they could now generate income and provide food for their children. This personal and entrepreneurial growth was captivating. We felt like queens of the world.

The contact with the women was important. Once we started our plan, we, the board members— there were about five or six of us—were in charge of everything: looking for the resources, identifying the micro-businesswomen, following their cases, etc. I was responsible for working with a woman who knitted jackets, hats, and gloves for babies. She dreamed of having a knitting machine. The day this woman got the money she needed, she was so excited. Whenever a woman was expecting a baby, she would be contacted for baby clothes. It was beautiful to see her growth; beyond improving her quality of life and selling to neighbors and friends, she also started selling to stores and was able to help her children finish high school.

At the beginning, we focused on Cali. Then we went to Popayan because of family connections. I was in charge of Bogota; Margarita was in charge of Medellin and Bucaramanga. Every city—except for Popayan—was able to get its own resources and board members. The result is the emergence of institutions that are the same and yet different. They are the same because they followed the philosophy of the WWB and they are different because the patrimonies were different, and the board members were independent; every region chose its own form of government and organization. We also received some donations from the Inter-American Development Bank that allowed the presidents from the five main institutions to continue working together. Eventually, Medellin and Bogota decided to join a Spanish bank and created a formal bank—Bancamía. So now only three are part of the WWB network: Popayan, Bucaramanga, and Cali.

Throughout the years, we received great support from the WWB network—not money, but a lot of knowledge from the meetings we attended. Thanks to the network, we all grew together. We did not have resources, but we had tools to fight, and that's what's important.

Portions of the video recording of aspects of the Cali meeting highlight visits to some of the first borrowers. Lucy Saavedra stands out as the first borrower and one who would remain connected to WWB-Cali for years to come. In speaking with her at the construction site of her new local in

Jamundi, in January 2010, nearly thirty years after her first loan, she emphasized how her personal and professional growth were intertwined. With many ups and downs, her business survived, transforming a small bicycle repair-shop run by her husband into a successful chain of apparel stores under her direction. Lucy shared her story.

Lucy Saavedra

My story testifies to how a simple person, without business experience, can achieve a lot by having faith, love and hope. I was the eldest of my siblings and my family faced many economic constraints. For about three years, I ate in soup kitchens. We had limited economic solvency, but we had a very strong family that gave me a lot of love. The knowledge of the Word of God was always present. I went to work at the age of twelve; I did not have any formal schooling; I only knew how to read and write; but I did love to read and the Bible became my main pillar. At fourteen, I had to change my ID to say that I was eighteen so I could start working at a factory. It was there that I met my husband, who was twenty-four. We got married two years later.

Eventually, my husband got fired from his job, and his indemnification in 1979 amounted to eighty thousand pesos). We did not know what to do. I was a housewife. The only thing that was clear to us was our faith in God. We prayed and asked what to do with this money. My husband had learned from his father how to fix bikes, but planned to become a taxi driver, when one day, due to an accident that closed off a street, he had to follow another route and stumbled on a space that was being rented at an accessible price. He liked it, talked to me, then I visited it and liked it as well, so we decided to pursue the idea of opening a bicycle-repair shop, Bicicleteria Montenegro (Montenegro being my husband's last name).

My husband and I had to learn from scratch. We needed to ask people how to manage a business. We also lost some money in the process—because people take advantage of you when you lack knowledge. At this time our children were twelve, eight, and seven years old. We started our business, and then, approximately three months later, the store was ransacked. All tools and products were gone. Luckily, at that time I was working as an arts-and-crafts teacher, which allowed us to get by. Meanwhile, my husband met with the Fundación Carvajal. They were helping small businesses by loaning money and providing training. I saw that my husband worked a lot, came home very tired, and was not making enough profit. So taking time off from my teaching activities, I decided to go for the training on his behalf and received a loan of one hundred twenty thousand pesos.

Margarita Guzmán had come to the Fundación Carvajal to make contacts with heads of households and women in charge of small businesses. We met, and she managed to get WWB-Cali to provide a five thousand-peso spot for me to showcase our bicycles at a small-business fair. This was a huge task, because we only had a small workshop, and this fair made it seem like our business produced a lot of bikes. With much effort, we produced other bikes, and we created a model for a skateboard. People were really intrigued. With the knowledge I acquired through training, we started to look for a name that would better represent us. Our eldest son unified my husband's last name and my maiden name (Montenegro and Saavedra), and that was how "Montesa" was born.

After this, WWB-Cali provided us with a loan for two hundred thousand pesos. God multiplied this number. We used some of the money to construct a workshop at our house. As time went by, I continued receiving training from WWB. Margarita and Inés Elvira, another member of WWB-Cali, helped me open accounts, referred me to people, and introduced me to a broad network that helped me grow professionally. Eventually, we were able to rent a space in a more strategic zone and also bought a small Jeep, which helped us promote our business in different areas.

"Then, we obtained bigger loans. This, of course, required me to further develop my business skills. I took night management courses at the university. As time went by and the business grew, there were some problems in the market. People were buying products from the black market and selling them at a cheaper price than our company. This was detrimental to our business. I started to default on some payments and, as a consequence, ten years later, we were ninety percent in debt and thought we would have to close the business.

Margarita fought hard to prevent the closure. She brought people who could help me with the debt. She was aware that I had not spent the money irrationally, but that the main cause of the issue was the market situation.

To get by, my husband went to Europe to find work, and my oldest son left school after a few semesters to help us out. My children and I moved to the neighboring city of Jamundi, where we arrived with nothing. We only had three machines. We managed to lower costs and get a house in which we lived and worked. We started to produce at a smaller level and offer repair services. In my years in the business, I had learned that personal contact with clients was the key to success. Since we had lowered our living expenses in Jamundi, we could pay all of our debts. I think we did it thanks to God. Some bank managers, corporations, and lawyers accepted bikes as payment. We stayed in Jamundi and managed to place our business, then called Yire, in a top position there, as opposed to Cali, where we were at the bottom. People started to appreciate us and value what we were doing.

One day, my oldest son told me about a friend of his who was selling a small shoe store. I told him that it was a hard market, but we could look into it. Since he was very good at marketing, he started promoting the shoes. The shoes were relatively expensive, and not everyone could pay the price upfront. We created a marketing plan that allowed people to buy the shoes at a forty percent down payment and pay the rest in two months without lowering the price. It was an excellent idea. We had a lot of success. We received an invitation from a business fair in Panama. My children went and met other people in the business and developed contacts, and we started importing shoes directly from Panama. These contacts even provided us with credit. Little by little, we also imported clothes. My son started traveling not only to Panama, but also to Los Angeles.

Meanwhile, my husband kept sending money from his work in Europe. With his help and our work, my youngest daughter was able to graduate from college. We then discovered more markets in places such as Santander, and also established a small business in Cali. Members of my family joined *the cause—my mother, my father, my brother—and they helped us with credit analysis. We were then able to hire accountants and established a solid business. We were also able to offer training to our employees. Today we have a chain of six stores of clothes, shoes and accessories and approximately sixty people working with us. Our company is called Simon & Company. Like our previous store, Montesa, in Cali, Simon & Company is also the union of Saavedra and Montenegro. Simon is known at the national level.*

Clara Akerman, one of the founding trustees of WWB-Cali and president since 1992, commented on the evolution of the organization during an interview at the WWB Global Meeting in 2009.

Clara Akerman

As a young professional with ideals of helping my country, I wanted to see what I could do in this movement—what could be built. Until then, my vision of poverty had been intellectual. Half of Cali's inhabitants were living on less than a dollar a day, and I hadn't had any contact with that half. We started out as a social-service institution. I remember being told to translate the bylaws of SWWB into Spanish, so I took the SWWB bylaws and the bylaws of the organization I was working with, Fundación Económica y Social (FES), and created our first WWB-Cali bylaws, based on a mix of both organizations. I was also a mentor to micro-entrepreneurs. Some of them were in prison; one was a designer. The vision of WWB was to involve women in the formal economy. Our dilemma was how to do it. We didn't have money. We didn't have a methodology. We had to develop it from scratch.

Cali was the first affiliate of WWB and the first to give a loan to a micro-entrepreneur, Lucy Saavedra, who repaired bicycles. It was amazing, because she transformed her business completely. I remember another borrower, Maria del Socorro, who sold fruit and used to go to the moneylender who would give her one hundred thousand pesos a day. She would buy fruit, sell, and then at the end of the day she had to give him back one hundred ten thousand, so she was paying ten percent interest a day. When we started to give loans at a commercial monthly rate, it was a tremendous savings compared to a ten percent daily rate! That was the marvel of WWB: the philosophy to focus on the development and improvement of quality of life. Our focus at the beginning was very expansive; it included things like child care and many social-development programs. In '86 we focused on being a financial institution lending to low-income women. We realized we couldn't do it all, and that by being an efficient financial institution that accompanied our borrowers, we were accomplishing our goal of freeing them from the moneylenders and integrating them into the formal economy. Being focused on that was our mission, making the institution sustainable and not dependent on donors, so we could guarantee our efforts over time.

Life is about phases. In the beginning we were attending to small needs of micro-entrepreneurs. . . the borrowers' businesses were often at home. . . and as the clients grew, we also grew. We started out as an NGO, but then graduated to reach more women, and so we had to change our legal structure. We're now in the process of becoming a formal bank, to be able to do savings and provide other services and products that our clients need. It's taken us a long time, because we were scared to lose the focus on poor women. We seek not only the growth of the institution, but also the growth of the client. That was always at the core of our methodology. . . and we gathered all the qualitative and quantitative information, as well as a psychological profile of the client and her paying capacity. The closeness with the client, and the long-term relationships, are what guarantee the ethics and integrity. If we continue working in that way, developing products for her needs, innovating so she grows with us, analyzing her ability to pay, not just trying to sell her products to meet our own goals, we will continue to be successful.

WWB-ADOPEM
Dominican Republic

The 1981 Cali meeting inspired others throughout Latin America. Mercedes Canalda attended the Cali meeting, and after a lengthy series of meetings, first in Cali and then at WWB-NY (where her daughter, Mecky, served as interpreter), she became determined to establish WWB-ADOPEM (Asociación Dominicana para el Desarrollo de la Mujer). John Hammock and his family moved to the Dominican Republic to help set up ADOPEM. Mercedes was a lawyer, banker, and business-woman, and she had the determination. John, who had been raised in Cuba, thought it would be wonderful to take his family to a Spanish-speaking country, so they moved and helped with the administrative structure. John was a significant influence on our understanding of how important training would be. ADOPEM continues to be a role model for many of the WWB affiliates.

Mercedes Canalda

I had already been involved in an institution that helped women in the Dominican Republic. Most women were working in the house. UNDP invited me to the WWB meeting in Cali. There I began thinking about what WWB could do for low-income women in other countries in Latin America, and I told Michaela, "This can be done in the Dominican Republic." I told her what I thought would be the best way to go about setting up WWB in the DR. She liked the idea and gave me the approval to form a group that would work towards becoming a WWB affiliate.

At that time, women needed opportunities to get loans. We started out by working with the Banco de Comercio Dominicano and giving small loans to women who were in the textile business. We focused on the center of the island—Santiago, El Guayabo—in the countryside, where there was a tradition of small businesses producing adult and children's clothing since the Second World War. For one year, we went there every Saturday and gave loans. John Hammock stayed with us for the first year, helping to organize the structure of the organization. We began with individual loans and then created a system of group loans.

In 1983, the bank gave us a bigger line of credit and said, "You're ready to do it yourself." Over time we grew, and in 2003 we shifted our management from NGO to a formal bank, while maintaining the NGO as the bank's principal investor. We have become one of the most recognized banks of the country. The NGO continues to provide financial education about savings, insurance, how to create businesses, agricultural products. We also have a youth program for our clients' children, to prepare them for work.

Being part of WWB was a great opportunity to learn about what others were doing around the world, especially through the global meetings. People were very innovative! Sometimes there were issues between the affiliates and the New York office. For example, when personnel from WWB/ New York didn't have the capacity to understand what we were doing at the country level and would approve of work plans that were difficult to implement on the ground. Sometimes they approved how success would be measured without taking into account the specifics of each country, or would contract a company that lacked experience at the country level to evaluate the affiliates' work.

When we asked about WWB's new (2011) pilot outreach initiative, Mercedes Canalda II, Mercedes' daughter and current president of ADOPEM, described the innovative soap-opera *Contra corriente*, which teaches women working from their homes about financial literacy, and offered further thoughts.

Mercedes Canalda II (Daughter)

Today we focus on how we can continue to improve on our services and reach more women. The commitment to our mission is the core of everything we do. It's internalized by the team at all levels. The focus on having a positive impact, combined with strategic planning, the development of new products, and the conviction that everyone in the organization is a leader—including at the base of the organization—are factors that enable us to excel. We constantly evaluate the quality of every aspect of our work and believe there is always room to improve.

Ricardo Canalda (Son)

When my mother started ADOPEM, she dedicated herself intensely to the organization, both her time and her resources. At first, people didn't believe in it. Then as the institution developed, my sister got involved, and then I, too, as a lawyer who had my own private practice, joined the team as a legal adviser and member of the Board of Directors, because the organization needed someone who could be trusted one hundred percent. We work together, and sometimes our Sundays are spent reviewing documents as colleagues, but the family ties have also been strengthened through our collaboration. Our mother has been our role model, reminding us to always work towards excellence and to attend to those who need opportunities—namely women, whose wise decision-making influences the well-being of the community around them. (See affiliates-agreement document, p. 275.)

5

LETTING THE FLOWERS BLOOM
A MULTITRACK STRUCTURE EVOLVES

"not a hierarchy. . . a communications hub"

We continued to solicit assistance and input from a variety of sources, including academia. Gail Harrity, now the president and chief operating officer of the Philadelphia Museum of Art, was working on her MBA at the Yale School of Management in 1981 when I visited the school to present WWB and invite the students to help design an operating plan.

Gail Harrity

I was among eight women at the Yale School of Management who interviewed Michaela to see how we could help WWB, which we viewed as an alternative business model. It was a very exciting project for me personally, because I had witnessed the entrepreneurship of women around the world, especially in places like Iran, Afghanistan, and India. Working on this project was an opportunity to apply traditional business-school skills to a new market with a clear need. Financial institutions at the time were serving a very small segment of the world population. So WWB was alternative in every respect—it was looking at alternative clients. I remember Ela Bhatt talking about how some of the smartest businesswomen were illiterate and couldn't access credit, because they couldn't work through the papers, but that didn't make them any less savvy about how to found and build a business.

Affiliates were in formation around the world. The Dutch affiliate SWWB-Netherlands, chaired by a businesswoman, Siska Pothof, decided that instead of identifying local borrowers, it would focus on helping to raise funds for the SWWB Capital Fund, along with awareness-raising activities. Siska described how she went about garnering support and developing a network of committed and well-connected people.

WWB-Netherlands

Siska Pothof

In the early '80s, I was involved in my family's business, Haaxman BV, the oldest firm in Leistein. It was rare at that time for a woman to be a managing director in a firm; men either tried to work around you or didn't take you very seriously. I had sold my business to an English firm, and so Floris Bannier, who was one of my friends, suggested that since I wouldn't have as much to do, I should help WWB get off the ground in Holland. I was very excited about the potential of WWB for generating solutions to problems of the third world. Feminine energy was beginning to grow stronger in the world, and part of the challenge was to make people conscious of it. I often found myself in situations where I had to stimulate this feminine energy and make people aware of what it represented, reminding that we shouldn't copy men's way of handling things. Most of the time, women are more practical; we don't have to talk about things—we just do them. This is especially true in developing countries, where women play such an important role in the economy. I thought that it was important to get the Dutch affiliate started, because Holland was always open to new ideas with a global perspective but for years had been pumping money into development organizations and projects where the money just disappeared. No one had any idea about the way things worked in the places where they were operating, and so the money went into the wrong pockets. WWB's small-scale approach and direct way of getting the money to where it was supposed to go appealed to me and gave me the enthusiasm to get the idea across to others and inspire them to participate.

I'm not good at participating in committees or doing a lot of talking; I was more of a catalyst. I thought the best strategy was to contact executives of banks, commercial firms, and organizations, as well people from the press for publicity. I had an intuitive way of bringing people together so they could contribute knowledge and resources from their respective fields of work to build a solid base for the organization: Rudolf Mees of the NMB Bank, because we were both interested in anthroposophy; Honey van den Horst, editor of Margriet, a women's magazine; Pauline Kruseman, the director of the Royal Tropical Institute. I also seized the opportunity of an international banking conference in 1983 to contact the conference organizers and suggest that we host a special meeting to talk to the wives who would be accompanying their husbands (the bankers) to the dinner about WWB so that they could then speak to their husbands about this exciting new venture. Fortunately, one of the conference coordinators was a woman with leadership potential who got inspired by the idea of WWB and helped make a special luncheon for wives possible. I also reached out to the secretaries of executives at important organizations, bringing them flowers and explaining what WWB meant for women, and that helped to open some doors. Then I made my house available for brainstorming sessions where people could stay and feel inspired and comfortable, thanks to the house's good energy and aesthetic and spiritual qualities.

It wasn't always easy to garner interest in WWB. During a 2010 interview at her law firm in The Hague, Marleen van den Horst recalls the initiatives that she and other members of the WWB-Netherlands team undertook at the start of the organization, as well as some of the initial responses and challenges. Marleen (the daughter of Honey van den Horst), started working with WWB-Netherlands as an intern supporting Siska's efforts, and eventually became a board member.

Marleen van den Horst

I was twenty-three and doing my PhD at the University in Amsterdam, when I was introduced to the concept of WWB. Although I liked working on my PhD, it had little social involvement, and I always wanted to do something purposeful in life as well. I had already traveled quite a bit, and lived in Sri Lanka, so I was very internationally oriented. My mother, Honey van den Horst, was editor in chief of a women's magazine, Margriet, and as a woman who had achieved a certain status in public life, she was committed to helping women develop themselves and become economically independent. She became a member of WWB's Advisory Board in the Netherlands to give greater visibility to their work and used to tell me about her activities. She and other board members enjoyed serving on the board, but having full-time jobs, they couldn't do the paperwork themselves. As there were no resources to hire staff, my mother said, "Is that not something for you?"

I was young and not yet qualified to serve on the board, but I began helping the chairperson, at the time, Siska Pothof, with administrative support. We felt that our contribution to WWB's global network shouldn't be to help women entrepreneurs in the Netherlands, where there were already opportunities for women to start their businesses, and decided to focus instead on raising funds to support the work of the WWB New York office and the SWWB Capital Fund.

We realized that in our fund-raising activities we needed to show people what WWB was about, not just talk about it, because the concept of WWB and the SWWB Capital Fund, which was there only to guarantee loans, not to provide direct support to affiliates, was rather sophisticated and needed some explanation. So I asked a photographer friend of mine, Kees Keuch, to go to Thailand and Malaysia and document the work of the women who had received loans from WWB affiliates. We created a short promotional film, Women as Entrepreneurs, Women's World Banking, and got an educational channel in the Netherlands to allocate five minutes of prime-time broadcasting for free, right before the main news at 8 p.m. We also had a color brochure printed for free and set up a direct mailing to the top companies in the Netherlands.

We were all very concrete and wanted to make real progress. I had access to Philips, a major electronics company at the time, and got them to agree to provide a computer system for the entire WWB affiliate network! They simply requested a good proposal to explain how the system would be implemented and what WWB had achieved thus far. However, to write a good proposal you need input and, in that respect, we were acting too quickly, because the New York office was not yet prepared to provide all the material we requested. It was at a stage where Michaela had opened doors remarkably well, but lacked people to support her in tying up the loose ends. So there we were with all our good intentions, telling the New York office, "We will support you and do the fund-raising here," but when we asked for information—because while Dutch people are open to new ideas, they are critical and want to know exactly how things are structured—there was no follow-up from New York. Thinking back, maybe we were also not asking New York what they needed and then putting our machinery and energy into that. . . .

The fact that WWB adopted a decentralized model with a communications hub in New York was good, because it alleviated concerns of US dominance, or that an organization based in the US would impose American ideas upon people in the Philippines, or elsewhere. . . . It was important to

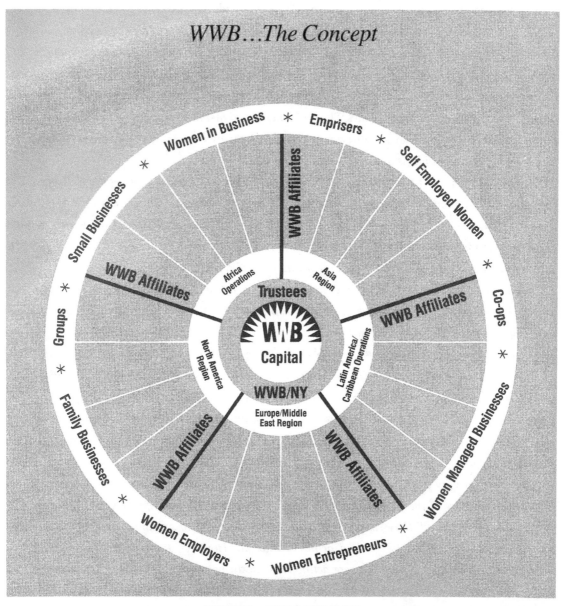

A WHEEL—NOT A PYRAMID

clarify to the affiliates involved that there was not a hierarchy, that the "communications hub" was there to connect and facilitate everyone's work, but that policy would be set out by the board, on which affiliates were represented. All of those aspects made me want to be part of the process, even though I recognized that our initiatives—though very enthusiastic and well carried out—may have been premature. It was frustrating at the time to feel that one's efforts were going to waste, but in retrospect it was part of the natural process of establishing a new organization.

The fund-raising culture in the Netherlands is quite different from the US. In the US you wouldn't be ashamed to ask for hundreds of thousands, or even millions of dollars. Here it was much more delicate, and as we were asking for considerable funds, we thought we needed to approach banks and other companies at the highest level. We had great people on our board who helped us access CEOs, so we were received and served coffee by men with handkerchiefs and the guys we talked to were the decision makers, but they didn't really hear us out. The average donation the banks were prepared to make initially was around the equivalent of $5,000, which was clearly not sufficient to run the administration and guarantee the local banks that were providing the loans. I was young and unpleasantly shocked by the arrogance we encountered. I remember leaving those meetings thinking: "These people have their heads over the clouds. Only when they wish to look down and put the clouds away, will they see the real world." No one we spoke to was familiar with the practice of what we now call "micro-credit," then small loans. The bankers were conservative, reflecting the international environment. In some circles there was the attitude, "Oh, these are feminists," or in other instances we were dismissed as "rich women."

Floris Bannier concurred.

Floris Bannier

I've been a lawyer in the biggest law firm in the Netherlands—a firm with many male lawyers—and some of them would jokingly say, "How is your women's bank?" or "How is the bank of your friends?" There are people who to this day still don't understand what WWB is about.

Marleen recalls how she used to address these perceptions.

Marleen van den Horst

I would say: "Listen. This is an organization where men and women, united, have analyzed that women especially need extra chances, in order to motivate economic development in their environment and countries. So it is not women for women; no, it is women and men jointly realizing that women can be a stronger economic power." We were very happy to have men on our board to back up that story. We felt it was necessary to stress that we were not like feminist groups, because that would not have been effective in the circles of potential donors. Eventually we dismantled WWB-Netherlands to a certain degree and gave up on approaching companies for fund-raising purposes. We kept on being supportive, doing our thing at the Ministry for Development Cooperation and stepping in whenever WWB globally needed our assistance.

Pauline Kruseman, who had been introduced to Women's World Banking by Siska Pothof in the '80s, served on the SWWB Board from 1990 to 2003. She also served on the board of WWB Netherlands, as well as on Triodos Bank's Supervisory Board.

Pauline Kruseman

When I became involved with WWB, I was working for the Royal Tropical Institute, which focuses on the relationship between the Netherlands and former Dutch colonies, like Indonesia. Women's economic empowerment wasn't an issue that I was very much aware of. I was interested in women's affairs in general and was also serving as treasurer of the board of the International Institute of Women's Archives. In the bylaws of SWWB, there was a requirement that a Dutch member should always serve on the board. In my time, it was very necessary, because as a Dutch person you were much closer to the Ministry than people in New York. I was asked to become involved with WWB because I had many relations with developing countries through my work at the Royal Tropical Institute. In '85, when the Royal Tropical Institute was celebrating its seventy-fifth anniversary, a female minister attended the celebration, and so I told her about WWB. From that point on, WWB began to receive yearly contributions from the Dutch Ministry for Development Cooperation, which was also thanks to the good work of people in the Ministry, like Geertje Lycklama, who had laid the groundwork with regard to encouraging the Ministry to support efforts to help women in developing countries with small loans. It was also Michaela's good luck that Rudolf Mees had a very broad field of interest, not only money—but also other values in life that were important to him. So from then on, the Ministry contributed quite a bit. Minister Jan Pronk was very focused on poverty, but he actually thought it wasn't a good idea to focus specifically on "poor women." Later on he became very committed to the idea of women's economic empowerment, especially for poor women, by microcredit. In his second term in the Dutch Ministry for Development Cooperation he became one of our very strong supporters. However, Minister Pronk always said, "We are not going to front you forever," and that was why he was so committed to giving extra money to the Capital Fund, because he hoped that we would become self-supporting.

Following our commitment with UNDP to meet in various regions of the world, in 1982 we held our regional meeting in Manila, the Philippines, to explore the viability of our concept in the Asia/Pacific Region. Lourdes Lontok Cruz, who had been at the Amsterdam meeting and went home to found WIFE (Women in Finance and Entrepreneurship), acted as the host. Out of that meeting, the idea of forming a WWB affiliate in Thailand emerged, although it would be another two years before WIFE got off the ground.

Lilia Clemente recounts the Manila Conference.

Lilia Clemente

The Philippines in the 1950s was one of the most prosperous countries in Southeast Asia. In the 1950s, 1960s and 1970s, the country's gross national product (GNP) grew at a rate between five to six percent per annum. However, during the early 1980s, due largely to a worldwide economic recession, growth slowed to an average of 2.3 percent per annum. Then and now, it lags behind in economic growth with half the population living in poverty. In December 1982, eight months before the country's political crisis with the assassination of Benigno Aquino, Women's World Banking selected Manila as the site of its first Asian Conference. We worked with Lourdes Lontok Cruz, a lawyer who founded and managed the Paluwagan ng Bayan Savings and Loan Association in Manila and a Trustee of WWB. We invited the Filipina Women in Banking and Finance, representing various sectors of rural banking and thrift sectors cooperatives, commercial banking and my mother, Belen F. Calderon, the first and only woman to hold a seat in the Philippine Stock Exchange. We also reached out to various organizations like the Zonta Club of Professional Women and the National Federation of Women's Clubs of the Philippines. Lending to rural low-income people, especially women, was a new concept, and outreach to very poor communities was limited.

The conference opened a Pandora's Box in terms of microcredit and role of women's entrepreneurship with the WWB. The international delegates of WWB joined the Filipina women to visit rural bankers and initially focused on microcredit. Most projects were unable to recover their costs or to reach significant numbers of poor people. Some adopted Grameen budget banking in the 1990s, which improved performance but failed to ensure sustainable and adequate outreach. Ceilings on loans and the first non-bank credit (NGOs and cooperatives for example) faced restrictions in the mobilization of savings and hindered the growth of this type of lending. The turnaround came in 1997 when the Centre for Agriculture and Rural Development (CARD)—a microfinance NGO—decided to create a rural bank: profitability soared and CARD became operationally and financially self-sufficient, and led the microfinance institutes (MFI) in the Philippines. Both CARD Bank and the Negros Women for Tomorrow Foundation have been active members of WWB since 1999. In a recent study by Economic Intelligence Unit (EIU) assessing the microfinance environment within countries, the Philippines ranked first in Asia and third overall in the microfinance index, after Peru and Bolivia. However, a substantial portion of the microfinance population remains underserved. Only approximately one-third of poor households are reached, suggesting room for growth. It took WWB to plant the seeds in the Manila Conference in December 1982, but now the dream and concept is a reality.

WWB-Philippines
Women in Finance and Entrepreneurship (WIFE)

Women in Finance and Entrepreneurship (WIFE) had been set up under the leadership of Lourdes Lontok Cruz (who died in March 2011). In her article "Friendship From Mother to Daughter," Cynthia V. Subijano, a co-founder of WIFE, reflected on how Lourdes Lontok Cruz, who had been her mother's classmate, became a mentor to her: *She awakened my social consciousness and moved me to share and give back to society.* Lourdes Lontok Cruz, Dr. Chita Tanchoco-Subido, Lilia Clemente, and Cynthia V. Subijano worked together to establish WIFE and to help women entrepreneurs in the Philippines gain access to credit. With a grant from WWB and additional funds raised locally, WWB-WIFE began extending small loans to women. Its efforts also focused on education in finance, marketing, and credit responsibility, which it transmitted one-on-one to women entrepreneurs through its Big Sister–Small Sister program. Cynthia credits the work of the organization she now directs, the Foundation for Filipino Entrepreneurship Incorporated, to inspiration from Lourdes and WIFE.

WWB-Thailand

In Asia, in addition to WIFE, the Thai program was set up as a consortium among WWB-Thailand, the Thai government, and the nongovernmental organization Zonta, with Sweden, Canada, the Netherlands, and Thailand as co-sponsors.

THE PRINCESS OF THAILAND GREETS MICHAELA WALSH

The 1987 Dutch video on WWB highlights some of the diverse enterprises that were developed with WWB-Thailand loans, guided by the conviction that *"business and idealism can be combined effectively."* Featured borrowers and businesses included a woman pushcart owner whose loan went to motorizing carrier cycles so she could increase her sales of noodles and sweets and who went on to open a restaurant after one year; a textile-factory seamstress who wanted to set up her own dressmaking business and who, three years after receiving a loan for materials, along with a bookkeeping course, was employing twelve people; a cement-block company that transformed from building blocks by hand to buying a cement press and employing three men working on the cement press and ten men in the transportation of cement pipes. The video also highlighted an instance when WWB-Thailand denied a second loan to a borrower, but helped identify alternative sources of financing.

In 2010, Alex Paulenoff, a law student who had worked at the UN during the 2006 NGO Conference that I chaired, was visiting Thailand with his partner. I enlisted him to ride his motorcycle from Chiang Mai up to the Mae Sa Valley Mountain Holiday Resort to interview Khunying Chinda Charungchareonvejj, a Thai banker and entrepreneur (vice president of the Bank of Bangkok) who started Friends of WWB-Thailand in 1984–85. Years had passed since WWB-Thailand had ceased to exist; Chinda recollected the evolution of the organization.

Chinda Charungchareonvejj

I don't recall exactly how I first came into contact with WWB. Zonta, a women's organization had sought me out ten years earlier, as they were seeking to include female executives in Thailand and other Asian countries in their network. The Zonta Club provided in-kind support, not money, to help women in different countries run projects and share training with each other. That may be how Michaela knew about my work.

When we met, I was working in the Foreign Department of the Bangkok Bank and had moved around through many departments, so I knew both the credit side as well as the domestic side of banking, and could appreciate what Michaela said about the importance of lending to women who didn't have collateral. I was able to transfer my enthusiasm and willingness to my boss to encourage him to make the loans. Even with a guarantee, the bank would not automatically make loans, but having WWB as the trusted guarantor made all the difference. At some point, Michaela said, "You have to be the president of the office in Thailand." Friends of WWB-Thailand started in 1984. We were comprised mostly of volunteers; for instance, I didn't get paid, but my director and secretary worked on very small salaries, which required that they have separate jobs as well.

With WWB, each country affiliate operates independently, based on the principle that WWB would be the guarantor for any financing. USAID [the United States Agency for International Development] was our major donor for many years, allocating funds on a monthly basis. We also received money from other international and local NGOs. The Thai government's Welfare Department also provided support, and WWB assisted with training. If any group wanted to train a leader or learn more in a specific area, we would make the arrangements and get the funds from USAID to implement the training. We were quite successful, because we managed to get many foundations to be our guarantors, complementing WWB's fifty percent guarantee.

Throughout our existence, we loaned to well over fifty thousand women, primarily in Central, Northern, and Eastern Thailand—Chiang Mai, Chiang Rai, Pai Yao, and the East. We didn't focus on the South of the country, because most of the people there were quite affluent and didn't need our assistance, or were practicing Muslims and didn't believe in charging interest. I had representatives based in each region do publicity and get in touch with people who could benefit from our work. The publicity was mostly by word of mouth. I would also talk to the magazines and women's papers, and they would write an article, which also helped bring attention to our services.

Potential borrowers who needed financial support would come to our representative and present their history; we would then analyze the data, and if we believed it was viable, we would ask the bank to grant the loan. Many of the women borrowers became successful, especially one in Lapburi, a nun who used a two hundred thousand-baht [$6,250] loan to buy a few cows and create a dairy farm. Within two to three years' time her group was able to repay the loan entirely. They now have about seven hundred cows that produce approximately four tons of milk per day.

We allowed for some flexibility. For example, if someone borrowed a smaller sum—say twenty thousand baht [$625]—they could use it as a revolving fund for another loan. Suppose they did agricultural work—growing maize, corn, or sugar cane; when the growing period was over and the crops finished—if they could pay back the capital within eight months, we would roll the loan over for them. In many cases however, there was some loan loss.

Overall, it was a great opportunity for women who were capable of doing good work, but didn't have access to funds. We were bridging the gap between the banks and the borrowers who couldn't get money from the banks because they didn't have collateral. We provided the needed backing to enable them to get the loans. WWB focused on people of least privilege; it was not meant for the rich or the middle class, so none of the other banks at the time were interested. They didn't understand the concept of "micro-credit," so they didn't make the loans. People who don't know are always scared to get involved. It was a great achievement to get so much support from the Thai government at that time, but they thought they could control the people who were borrowing from us. It was never charity; we didn't do anything for free, because we wanted the borrowers to be able to stand on their own two feet. We offered them loans so they could develop themselves and charged the lowest interest rates we could, comparable to what a good bank customer at a regular bank would be charged. With USAID, we weren't able to keep the connections alive, and the funding eventually ended. On one occasion, a senior officer at USAID whom I had mentioned our project to said, "OK, we have a certain program for underprivileged people, so why don't you just make a plan for them?" and offered us some financial support and training. But there were other expenses, like transportation for our people in Chiang Rai to communicate with the borrowers, pick up and drop off the loan, etc., and USAID wouldn't pay for all that. Most of the funding went directly to the loans.

When the USAID funding ended, we couldn't maintain our activities. By then, all the paid staff of WWB Thailand was relying on USAID money. We didn't have our own fund, and even though we were mostly volunteers, we still needed a staff of nearly ten people up in the North to function, and in Bangkok we had about five or six staff members—all of whom were also depending on USAID funds. Retrospectively, we wouldn't have been able to work for as long as we did without my connections at the bank. In Thailand, and perhaps everywhere, connections are very important. You need someone to support you.

The SWWB Board had long discussions about the role of individual board members. J. Burke Knapp offered to help identify potential supporters in Europe. One of our fund-raisers took place in London in April of 1983, hosted at 11 Downing Street by Burke's friend the Lady Elspeth Howe, the wife of the Deputy Prime Minister Sir Geoffrey Howe. Lady Howe invited representatives of the International Development Agency (IDA) and charitable organizations. We were hoping to meet London businesswomen. Surprisingly, we could identify only three women in London who owned well-known and successful businesses at that time. The numbers are very different today.

Toward 1983, John Hammock and I developed a proposal for USAID. It was our intention to have them make an investment in the Capital Fund. Someone called me from the Overseas Education Fund (OEF) and told me that the WWB project at USAID was going to be eliminated from the USAID budget before Senator Jesse Helms' Committee on Foreign Relations. Helms had said the plan was "reverse discrimination" and that he would cancel any help under any line item for WWB. I called John and told him that he had to go to Washington, because there was no point in any of us walking through that door in a skirt. He went to Washington and met with the committee for three hours; he was successful in persuading them not to cancel the investment in our debentures. Ultimately USAID gave a grant to WWB instead of making an investment in the WWB Capital Fund.

The fact that we were set up as a network that would in some cases initiate activities on the ground and in other cases support and complement existing programs, and connect them to each other, created ambiguity in how we were perceived. Similarly, to government agencies, we were trying to sell a new concept—a nonprofit organization's purpose that had as its mission the generation of profits for its members. We often ran into conflicts with those who believed all AID funds should be distributed in developing countries instead of being used as guarantees to encourage new opportunities for women and to help them gain access to the resources needed for their own production. Charlotte Bunch, who was working at the International Women's Tribune Center in the late seventies, shared her take on WWB as someone who was involved in the feminist movement.

Charlotte Bunch

I graduated from college in 1966 and was in the anti-war movement and in the civil rights movement. In the late '60s, when I became a fellow at the Institute for Policy Studies (IPS) in Washington, D.C.— a highly politicized, left-wing think tank that existed before there were so many organizations of that nature—feminism was a logical extension of my activism. Even in that environment, however, there were times when I would be in meetings and say something to which no one would respond, only to hear one of the men say the same thing 10 or 15 minutes later and elicit a response of, "Oh, what a great idea!"

When I first heard about Women's World Banking, it was around 1979, when I was doing consultancy work in advance of the 1980 women's conference in Copenhagen. At that point, I had moved from Washington to New York and joined the International Women's Tribune Center, which had been established following the 1975 Mexico City conference, because I wanted to focus more on global feminism. The women's movement that I was a part of in the US was not very globally conscious. Moreover, in terms of the recognition that economic issues were important to women, that existed in the left wing of the women's movement—in that we were aware of class and of the need to improve women's economic situation—not so much in the mainstream.

I recall having different reactions to WWB that were somewhat contradictory, but representative of the women's movement that I was a part of, in that I believed women needed this, but was also skeptical about it. First of all, I loved the name and the boldness, the concept of women asserting control in the financial arena. Secondly, I had no idea what it meant financially. I had absolutely no technical expertise, or in-depth understanding of finance or economics. I understood class, that economics matter, that money was important, and that women had no control over it. If anything, I had a socialist analysis of the solution, so I didn't even try to understand how the American, or capitalist, economy worked. I knew women needed access to credit to do business, but I was very ambivalent about that strategy. There was always the question, "Are women just going to get bought off by the system?" Those issues were part of the discourse of the day and still are. I was probably also a little intimidated, because I didn't want to reveal my limited understanding of finance, which I think was the case for other people as well. Overall, though, I was aligned with Women's World Banking's approach, because it was driven by the women in developing countries. The same was true for introducing the concept of human rights in the women's movement: that impetus also came from women in developing nations, despite the common misconception that it came from women in the West.

Kate McKee, interviewed in 2009 at her office in CGAP (Consultative Group to Assist the Poor) who was working at the Ford Foundation, developing grant-making programs to expand women's economic opportunities during WWB's founding years, described the context in which WWB was emerging from the Ford Foundation's perspective.

Kate McKee

I joined the Ford Foundation in 1978 and went off to Lagos, which was the field office for Ford Foundation across the West and Central Africa region. Ford was just starting to broaden its scope into areas including agriculture, health, and population, as well as an overall interest in civil society, NGO capacity-building, and in new topics like women's rights and economic opportunities. I came back to Ford's New York headquarters in 1981 and began to coordinate grant-making programs aimed to help people increase their income and assets. Microfinance was one of those strategies, although we were probably calling it "microbusiness" then. Ford had already begun supporting Grameen Bank, Accion, and a number of the early pioneers. I knew some of the early WWB founders, like Ela Bhatt and Mary Okelo, and was interested in the idea of an international organization that was not only focused on serving women clients, but also on being women-led and -managed. In their early days, organizations like Accion and FINCA had less of a focus on women, certainly less than Finca does now. This was kind of a new concept, one that was being developed in different ways around the world.

I met Michaela towards 1983. We had many conversations about the chicken-and-egg question: What should come first, the international support or the operations on the ground? Obviously it's not an either/or question. At the Ford Foundation, we had a strong bias towards supporting activities in the field. It was a challenge thinking about what an international network could do that would be qualitatively different from and add to the landscape of "micro-credit" that was developing around the world. It's not exactly as if at that time there was a strong body of practice that dictated exactly how microfinance was done; it was more of a "Let a thousand flowers bloom" approach. It was a time when there was growth in much of the developing world and a definite appreciation of the role the nascent private sector could play, as well as an assumption that access to finance would accelerate the private sector's development.

There was also beginning to be an appreciation for people creating their own economic destinies and of the role of the informal sector in the future of economic development. Entrepreneurship by men and women was definitely going to be a part of the overall development picture. On the women's front, it was the Decade of Women. There was a lot of preparation for the 1985 Nairobi women's conference, and all kinds of interesting collaborative programs and learning processes at Ford. We supported an organization called DAWN (Development Alternatives with Women for a New Era), which was critical of prevailing development models, such as the IMF's (International Monetary Fund's) policies on structural adjustments, and was trying to propose approaches that were more community-based and led by indigenous leadership.

There's no question that Michaela was an odd duck in the mix. The scale of microfinance was much smaller, and the key issues were figuring out the basics of how to make it work. It didn't seem that the skills you'd have from capital markets and Wall Street would be particularly relevant to the needs of micro. Obviously, now it's much clearer, but back then, it wasn't obvious. Grant making is a funny business. If I'm sitting out in Lagos or Nairobi or wherever, there's the opportunity to get to know a little more deeply what's the organizational base, what's the political economy, who are the leaders that have credibility. It's easier in that setting to be making choices and know what the consequences of those choices are. Which organizations am I going to fund? Which leaders am I going to back? It's very challenging when you are working more at a global level. We shouldn't really kid ourselves from a vantage point in New York about our ability to make a good choice about leaders. That's why at Ford, at that time, a lot of the funds were programmed through the field offices. That made it difficult to support an initiative like Women's World Banking, which was meant to be an international network. We were waiting for things to be built.

The challenge of situating a novel initiative such as WWB in the development landscape extended even to the Netherlands, despite the continued support given by the Dutch government. Geertje Lycklama explained.

Geertje Lycklama

There was resistance, because the image was, "Isn't it a little too much business?" That definitely was the perception in the development world. It wouldn't be now, because things have changed, but then the Dutch Ministry for Development was a bit allergic to anything that had to do with entrepreneurship. Another challenge from the Ministry's standpoint was that, given the emphasis on poverty alleviation, it was very clear that the money had to go directly to the third world, not to New York, so I had to fight for that, too. There was also always the risk that people who had their own interests in mind, more so than the socioeconomic dimension, would take advantage of the opportunities WWB presented. I met rich women from the Philippines who were involved, so we had some questions and many discussions with Michaela, who agreed and said, "Yes, we will produce some monsters." Second, in many cases, as soon as a project was viable and money came in, the husbands took over, so that was also something to watch out for. We were seeking money for the WWB Capital Fund, not grants for developing countries, Michaela said.

In the beginning, it was very much a struggle for survival. In the '80s, "micro-credit" for women was viewed as an isolated, "soft" practice, a view that was exacerbated by the fact that much time elapsed before results could be obtained. This changed when several evaluations showed that women were extremely good at repaying their debts. Michaela was a tremendous driving force, because she was so convinced that it should and would get off the ground, and we believed with her that it could be done, that it was important. You have to be a little bit single-minded to get something like that to succeed.

I was supportive of WWB because I thought that in order to alleviate poverty, women had to do it themselves—others couldn't do it for them. There was a spirit of optimism. We were going to change the world, and I think we did, to some extent.

Within our fast-growing network, it remained necessary to continuously explore and explain our visions and objectives to one another. This involved many informal moments of singing, dancing and ice-breaking activities—a tradition we began at our first international workshop with evenings of celebration and sharing of personal ideas and experiences. I understood that for all of us to work together, this kind of exchange was a necessity. As we knew each other more deeply, we were able to help one another—and to disagree with integrity—more effectively.

Siska Pothof's recollection encapsulated the spirit of our meetings and how it inspired curiosity among participants who wanted to learn more about each other's activities and environment as a result of their exposure. I remember Siska's house as the place where WWB took shape, between colorful parties and a board meeting that she hosted. She also has vivid memories.

Siska Pothof

I have many good memories of the people from all over the world who participated in our meetings over the years. At every meeting, someone always got up and started to sing a song from her country, and then everyone sang and danced. It was touching to experience that binding, substantial energy. Getting involved in WWB changed my life in that it opened my eyes to a more comprehensive view of what was going on in the world and how important it was to think globally. I went to the Philippines to meet with Lourdes Lontok Cruz, a banker, an exporter, and the Philippine director of Youth for Understanding, who was an initial member of WWB and launched the Philippines WWB affiliate, and to film their activities. She had an old bus and with it we traveled throughout the country to visit compounds where people were producing baskets, bags, and other articles that would then go to America to be sold in big department stores. It was moving to see what they were doing, and upon returning to the Netherlands, I contacted our minister for development cooperation, who was very interested. So, slowly the seeds were dropped and just had to be watered.

I believed that learning from one another extended to the board meetings as well. At the SWWB Board of Trustees' first biennial meeting in New York in March 1982, I pushed several people out of their comfort zones. I hired a consultant who had worked on a White House Fellows program. He led us participants in exercises to write a paragraph about ourselves, to use colored pencils to draw a portrait of ourselves, and to use modeling clay to represent our personal image of what WWB would be. Some people resisted, but eventually they went along, and the results were profound for all of us. One board member left in tears, but returned and joined in. Omaymah Dahhan, who was the head of the new Business Department at the University of Jordan in Amman, created an elaborate communications grid; Floris Bannier created a Madonna and Child. Lourdes Lontok Cruz made a collage of market women. What had begun as an exercise in getting to know each other became a way for each person to learn more about what was in her or his heart.

Nancy Barry recalls her initial skepticism upon being confronted with the activity.

Nancy Barry

At a certain point we were at a board meeting here in New York, and Michaela insisted that we do these games, sculpting WWB with clay, and then there was a star that we used to talk about the evolution of our lives. I was not really into this, but I went along with it. It turned out that a lot of stuff surfaced in terms of my own experience within the World Bank. I got very emotional in front of all these women, and a couple men, and what I remember is that from across the table came all these notes saying, "I love you, I love you, I love you." It was such a giant hug. In that moment, I internalized that you can bring your whole female person to the job. You can be courageous on issues, but you don't need to attack people's personalities or egos. So you can be both respectful and courageous and also bring humor and humanity to the job.

Barbro Dahlbom-Hall, the first woman in Sweden to specialize in executive training, who became an SWWB Board member and eventually joined the Operations Committee, reflected on the dynamics of our meetings. Her comments illustrate how the character of an entrepreneur—necessary for an organization to get off the ground—is often at odds with the qualities required for managing a growing institution and staff over time.

Barbro Dahlbom-Hall

I felt that I would never be able to grab the issues; for someone who was not a banker, it was so difficult to understand. Michaela had all the knowledge from Wall Street. She was so strong in her views and had the need to be close to people. Looking back, I can see that was one of the problems. Women's issues at that time were new and also were criticized by society, of course. Michaela brought excellent people together who were not used to working together. Michaela had a lot of excellent ideas, and ideas need to be tested and discussed. If we had other ideas, she thought it was against her. None of us were experienced enough to handle the situation. Her strong leadership would have been accepted more readily if she were a man, or if she had recruited people who were different, and could complete her, instead of recruiting people who were similar and as strong as she was. At WWB, there were many well-known people who had an interest to make a career of their own—in one way that's extremely good—but so many strong people together isn't easy. WWB opened my eyes to women's situation internationally. At that time, I was very active in Sweden. Michaela had asked me to come to New York and sit in on the Operations Committee, the Financial Committee, and also a board meeting. There were two women; one, named Ann Roberts, who asked excellent questions. At the dinner party that night, I went over to her and said, "I'm very impressed; you really asked the best questions; your questions are going to the core." She started to cry, because no one had ever said anything like that to her. She was born a Rockefeller, and I think everyone used to associate her with that heritage only.

Ann Roberts remembers that experience, which she shared during an interview in September 2011.

Ann Roberts

Barbro Dahlbom-Hall saw me, whereas many people did not. I'm not a banker; I don't have titles. What touched me the most is that, unlike many women who become professional in ways that have been defined by men, and who go into institutions that have been defined by men, the members of WWB preserved their femininity, their humanity, which made them much more powerful. I just remember how awesome they were—not because they were "important women." They weren't interested in conquering; they were interested in personal achievement.

Through my travels in Latin America with my father, I learned about justice and human rights, by being exposed to the inequalities. I came to see that all people had wisdom and value, but that our society was organized as a pyramid—if you weren't at the top you couldn't get there, and you weren't listened to. I married an Episcopal priest and went to live in the South Bronx, where I learned about cooperation and collaboration, and values and community, and got involved in the civil rights movement and in the women's movement. My family was always doing large important philanthropic things, but I was totally uninterested in sitting on a Board in the shadows of decisions that had already been made. The more I saw what was happening at the grass roots, the more I realized that you couldn't legislate democracy.

When Michaela made me president of the WWB Advisory Associates Committee, I had a unified sense of joining a global initiative, behind which were the cultural customs, belief systems, and roles that women play in their respective cultures. Very often we didn't know each other's cultural protocols, and many of the bumps and collisions in the workings of WWB emerged because of that lack of knowledge. At times, someone would be acting in a way that was appropriate from their cultural protocol, and everybody wondered what was wrong with them, because we didn't understand their process. That was a steep learning curve for all of us. Until I joined WWB, I didn't know how much I didn't know.

Ann served on the original SWWB Board of Trustees from 1980 to 1985 and was the first president of the WWB Global Advisory Associates. For a list of all who joined the board from 1980 to 1990, see p. 184.

6

BILDERBERG
BUILDING A GLOBAL NETWORK

"What I found remarkable is the searching way you talk
with one another, nobody having answers,
but putting questions."

OUR 1984 GLOBAL Meeting was held in the Netherlands, at the Bilderberg Hotel. Most of the discussions focused on the complexities we were facing in building a global network of local WWB affiliates. Each region and each country had its own unique issues.

The meeting was held in Bilderberg largely thanks to Rudolf Mees, a member of the Board of Directors of the Nederlandsche Middenstands Bank (NMB Bank), the fourth-largest bank in Holland. (Subsequent mergers of NMB and other banks created ING Group.) Siska Pothof and Rudolf Mees had met through their mutual interest in anthroposophy. Rudolf had been president of the Employers Association for the Banking Sector, and a member of the Board of Directors of Mees and Hope. He was a co-founder of the Triodos Bank (TB), which had been established in 1980 and had developed new financing techniques that proved very successful in the Netherlands. His involvement in developing the program for our 1984 meeting initiated an ongoing collaboration between WWB and Triodos Bank. Rudolf died September 29, 2010.

Rudolf Mees

At an international conference I organized for my bank to discuss the newly emerging ideas around "micro" in 1982–83, I came into contact with Michaela Walsh, who was planning her organization's 1984 Biannual Global Conference, and was hoping to host it in the Netherlands, where the organization had been registered or established as a Dutch legal entity, stichting. Even with WWB's main office in New York, the Dutch government took a decidedly positive position vis-à-vis WWB and contributed several times to its capitalization, playing a major role in getting the organization going— along with the US and the UN. Nonetheless, when Michaela came to the Netherlands to organize WWB's first international conference and sought sponsorship from the big banks, she returned empty-handed, because nobody was really aware of WWB. It was only when she reached out to Mr.

Scherpenhuizen Rom, Chairman of the Board of Directors of the NMB Bank, and a genuine strategic thinker, that he saw potential and sent the matter to me with the message to look into it further. At NMB, I was responsible for human resources and organizational policy, which included a training center that was annexed to the Bilderberg Hotel in Oosterbeek. A gap in the planning at the center had opened up, so we offered to host the WWB conference there, providing in-kind support. It was a very impressive and festive occasion, with splendidly dressed women, neatly separated in the auditorium, with English speakers to the left and French speakers to the right—a consequence of the diverse cultures involved.

The program was up for discussion. Having co-founded the Triodos Bank, I envisaged a strategic alliance between Triodos Bank, a domestic bank, and SWWB, a global banking-services movement, as organizations with kindred values. So I invited Paul MacKay, director of Triodos, to tell the conference something about TB, and introduced Michaela and Paul to each other. It was love at first sight, and Paul MacKay's presentation would mark the beginning of a long-term relationship—twenty-eight years and counting—between TB and WWB.

Paul MacKay's keynote speech had a tremendous impact on our gathering; he validated, through the Triodos Bank experience, the theory we had always espoused about linking entrepreneurial activities to positive social impact. In the *Report of the Bilderberg Workshop*, **Paul MacKay** says:

> What I found very remarkable about this workshop is the searching way you talk with one another; nobody having answers, but putting questions. . . in search of the way in which Women's World Banking is going to develop.
>
> I've heard you time and again saying, "We need a decentralized organization." If you say you need a decentralized organization, you have to know you're in a way in for trouble. Normally, one would solve this problem in a holding structure, where you have a holding and subsidiaries. A lot of papers going down the line, and you know what to do. But you have to find a way of integrating so that the totality is living in and out of the parts. By doing that, you create what I would call a "situational organization."
>
> One thing I grasped here is the quality of courage, and by courage I don't mean recklessness, or bravery, or the old type of courage, but the courage involved in being aware of being dependent on a network. Economic life can be seen as a network of interdependencies, and I think one has to be aware of being in this network—to resist the temptation of growing too fast by taking over, and becoming more and more independent. The quality of courage, then, is to remain dependent and build up a network.

In a 2010 interview, Paul reflected on what motivated him to develop a bank with a social dimension.

Paul MacKay

The collaboration between TB and WWB began when I was invited to address the WWB conference and explain the Triodos model; the response was so positive that we began to envisage a more long-term collaboration between the two organizations, especially in terms of training.

I had co-founded Triodos Bank with Rudolf Mees. We were the first new bank to be established in the Netherlands since the Second World War. In those days, only a very little equity capital—500,000 gilders—was needed, and we had twice that amount. However, from the start we were socially oriented and wanted to finance projects that would be sustainable and have a positive impact on society at large.

The human element is very important. For me the question is, "What am I here for in this world?" If that question is a living question, then I have confidence that positive things will emerge. Systems are a reflection of a way of thinking; if we think without the human element, then the system itself will lack a human sensitivity; if we include the human element in our thinking, that introduces the unpredictable, but it also enables creativity. For it to work well, you have to have confidence in the positive outcome and be willing to let go of control.

The danger of dividing finance and social impact is that we wind up creating two separate worlds; the challenge is to keep them connected. As an entrepreneur, one has to take initiative. Life is partly God-given; the rest depends on what you make of it. I'm reluctant to come up with a vision for others; I would rather kindle the inner fire within every human being and then see what develops from there. When we started out, the Netherlands Central Bank was curious and uncertain that TB would succeed, but we soon developed a strong track record.

In addition to the serious discussions, the traditional surprise entertainment was Enzo Samaritani, a multilingual ballad singer/guitarist whom I first heard sing at the Blue Bar in Rome in 1959 with Eugene Taylor, and later befriended in Beirut, when he performed at the Phoenicia Hotel. Subsequently, I visited his nightclub in Rome, L'Arciliuto (the home of Raphael), where young minstrels traveling the world still gather and communicate with each other through their music. At our event, an outdoor dinner at a castle near Bilderberg in the moonlight, he sang minstrel songs and told stories in many different languages. Everyone was convinced we were having a romance!

At one point during the 1984 SWWB Board of Trustees meeting that followed the Bilderberg Global Meeting, a trustee requested an executive session, and, as president, I was asked to leave the room, so that trustees could openly discuss their concerns about management. We were growing quickly, and there were questions about the level of staffing in the New York office and my personal management style, and also questions about management of some of the affiliates. I was completely committed to not telling the affiliates what to do, or managing from on high, and not spending money for core expenses that we did not have. But I also understood that many of the trustees' concerns were valid.

The discussions that followed clarified that each affiliate and the WWB-New York office were at different stages of development and thus had different needs. The complexity of trying to manage a fast-growing international organization meant that it was often difficult to deliver on our dreams.

Based on these challenges, and with Paul MacKay and Triodos Bank's collaboration, we committed to exploring how to design and set up a training program to strengthen the management and communications at all levels of the WWB network. The first WWB training program, conducted by Margarita Guzmán from WWB and Klaas Molenaar from Triodos Bank, was held three years later in Amsterdam.

At the Bilderberg meeting, we distributed a new brochure, designed by Charles Hollister, one of the truly remarkable designers I have ever known. Hollister was soon to retire from his work as director of communications, plans, and program for IBM. Hollister was recognized as a leader in design and intellect; he had worked closely with Ray and Charles Eames on a number of award-winning art exhibitions as well, in addition to his print work. After he left IBM, he raised three questions in considering any new projects: *Is the project important? Does it have merit? Is it generally the right thing to do?* Fortunately, WWB passed his tests with flying colors. The WWB logo he designed became recognizable around the world.

Meanwhile, in the New York office, we were grappling with the challenges of becoming an effective hub to support the network. Minutes of a September 1984 SWWB Finance Committee meeting noted that "shortfalls in revenue are possibly an endemic problem."

The WWB Operations Committee's Terms of Reference focused on improving the delegation of responsibilities and sought to "devise means to mobilize talents

REPORT OF THE
WOMEN'S WORLD BANKING
THIRD INTERNATIONAL WORKSHOP
FOR WOMEN LEADERS IN
BANKING AND FINANCE

Hotel de Bilderberg
Oosterbeek, the Netherlands
May 15-18, 1984

WWB

THE COVER OF THE BILDERBERG REPORT

and time of board members and affiliates;. . . assess needs and strengthen the New York office;. . . identify the type of people needed at headquarters, regional, and country levels; and the means of financing and methods to respond to local groups, as well as promote exchanges, apprenticeships, and exposure to successful programs within each region, [and] evaluate and provide advice on successful credit. . . and on the means of developing self-sufficiency among WWB affiliates.

As chair of the Operations Committee, Barbro Dahlbom-Hall reported to the Board after an evaluation of the New York office in 1985, stating:

> The mood in the office is one of cooperation. Everyone seems prepared to jump in and lend a hand where one is needed. . . . Much however remains to be done with respect to working conditions. A prerequisite for the growth of WWB is continuity, which, in turn, requires loyal employees. . . . Far too much is being attempted with far too few personnel. . . "like a butterfly with its wings clipped" as someone put it. . . . One of the pitfalls WWB has particularly tried to avoid is overstaffed, centralized management, but when it appears that eighty percent of working time is spent adjusting to other people's wishes there is simply not much time left over for thinking, planning or doing. . . . It was pointed out that the president is burdened with far too many roles and tasks. . . . For the first time, the president has a very capable team under her. . . . This means permitting her own actions to be brought into question, acceding to requests for more information and independence. . . . It is not easy for someone who has almost single-handedly built up an organization to realize this, let alone discuss it with her staff. "I'll have to ask Michaela," one kept hearing at the interviews.

The Reverend Sarah Lammert, director of ministries and faith development for the Unitarian Universalist Association, recalls her experience of working with me.

Sarah Lammert

My first "real" job was a position with Women's World Banking. I was hired initially as a consultant to do research for a book giving all kinds of information about banking and trade that women in the affiliates might need. I worked feverishly. I was informed by Michaela that we had to get the book out by December 1, or it would be useless. Unfortunately, when the time came to approve the layout of the book, Michaela was in Indonesia and could not be reached. I knew she wanted to approve the final draft, but her words kept reverberating in my mind. "If it's not done, it will be useless, useless, useless."

So I went ahead and approved the design for the book. Several hundred copies were printed and ready to be mailed when Michaela returned. I had completed the project, come through in the clutch, and made the executive decision required of me. I expected to bask in the glow of Michaela's approval. (Michaela had been a mentor to me and I idolized her.) But when Michaela returned and saw the stacks of books, she was infuriated. She hated the design, the paper, the binding, the font—she hated everything about how the book looked. She found it so abysmal that she wanted to throw the entire job in a trashcan. I'm surprised I still have a backside after the chewing out I received. I had wasted the precious resources of the organization, made a decision I was not authorized to make, and worst of all, Michaela told me she was disappointed in me personally. I cried my eyes out and was finally told to go home.

Imagine my surprise the next day when I came in to pack my belongings and was called in to the inner sanctum to find a smiling, delighted Michaela. "I shouldn't have been quite so hard on you, I told you to get it done or else. I've fixed it." Overnight she had had a stamp made that said "DRAFT." I was given a stamp pad and a small room, and I personally stamped "DRAFT" onto every single copy. The next year the book was updated and published in a much glossier format, but the first draft was well-accepted because the affiliates liked being asked for the input into the project, and their feedback improved the publication immensely. Even more surprising, I was offered the job as "affiliate liaison" that I had applied for. "I liked that you were willing to step up and show leadership even if it was a bad decision," Michaela said.

Our managerial issues were compounded by constraints of my determination to maintain a very low administrative overhead. This impacted both our ability to retain a larger staff and adequate office space and equipment. Ana Maria Giblen, one of our first program managers, remembers.

Ana Maria Giblen

After the whole team worked in a cramped office comprised of two rooms and a foyer in an old building, we graduated to a larger though still Spartan office at centrally located 104 East 40th Street. Shortly thereafter, we acquired three computers, and Samir Patel from India joined us and applied his computer expertise to help keep us organized while growing. . . . Leslie Wilcott-Henry joined the team as Michaela's assistant and Susie Johnson came on board to replace Julie Abrams when she decided to pursue graduate school.

Concerning staffing, my 2011 conversation with Jacqui Williams, who was hired by WWB in 1986 (and stayed until 2009), shows the hubbub and the energy of the New York environment.

Jacqui Williams

At the end of May 1986, I was in New York looking for work. The first agency I went to had gotten me a position a few years back at J. Walter Thompson. After two days, having nothing to offer me, she suggested that I visit a friend of hers at another agency. When I arrived there, the lady I was supposed to meet was on the phone; in the background, a girl with a folder in her hands called me; I went to her, and she asked me if I would be interested to work for a nonprofit organization; I was very interested, since my last job was with CARE-Haiti. She handed me an annual report of SWWB, asking me to go over it and to tell her my feelings about it. I went over it and I was surprised to find the names of some friends as members of the Board of Directors of FHAF [Fonds Haitien d'Aide à la Femme], which at the time was their affiliate in Haiti. I told her that I would be happy to meet these people. I learned then that my meeting with them would be delayed since all of them were out of town. When I went for the interview, there was only one person at the office—the president herself, Michaela Walsh. The other members of the staff were still in Rio, where they just had a global meeting. Our first meeting was very cordial; Michaela told me that I had to meet with the rest of the staff before any decision could be made. I met with them, and everybody seemed to be pleased with the interview. I was hired and started to work for WWB on June 2, 1986. It was a small office situated above the Spanish Institute on Park Avenue. We were a staff of six people, including Michaela; there was also a bookkeeper who would come once a week. There was only one computer used by all of us; each staff member had to schedule the time of the day it would be used. A few days after being hired, Michaela said that she had made a decision to keep me on, but she asked me point-blank if I would stay, or quit within a few weeks or months. I promised to stay, and I did, for nineteen years.

Soon after I joined WWB, the office relocated to 40th Street. It was a larger office, with a lot of file cabinets given to us. I thought the office was large until one day a group of people from Cameroon (they were maybe more than ten) invaded the office. They were tall and big. They all filled the whole place. Two years after I joined the organization, I participated in the preparation of a board meeting in New York. I was very amazed to see all these people from every part of the world, finding ways to change policies to help women beat the odds and create viable institutions. When I think about Women's World Banking I see diversity, variety, willpower, determination. So many people from over forty countries in Africa, Asia, Latin America, Europe, meeting together, determined to change the world by empowering women.

The office was nothing like any place I had worked before, with set schedules, signing in and out; each one of us had a voice at staff meetings and all issues were on the table to discuss. Even the logo of WWB. You could expect anything to happen: One day Michaela arrived at the office around 11 a.m. She right away told us about her experience in the subway and decided that it was a lot for us to go through every day coming to work. She felt bad about it and decided to give us the next day off.

Our bohemian office dynamics were complemented by my determination to set a new sense of financial professionalism in the nonprofit development world. From the outset, I was committed to emphasizing the importance of financial accounting. We were one of the first NGOs to publish an annual report that included the financial audits, and with covers listing all the affiliates/affiliates in formation, as a way of promoting the global nature and reach of WWB. As these reports were widely distributed, the WWB acronym gained significant recognition.

However, our name generated complications for our formal registration, both in the Netherlands and in the United States. The publicity generated at WWB's Third International

Workshop in Bilderberg in May 1984 brought WWB to the attention of Dutch Central Bank. Because of a change in Dutch banking law, a point of contention arose around the name itself, "Women's World Banking," which at that point was already being used internationally. How could an entity that was not an actual bank call itself "Women's World Banking"? Floris Bannier received a formal letter "acknowledging the illegality of WWB's name" from the Dutch Finance Ministry. He contacted Rudolf Mees. Together they visited the Central Bank and later the Ministry of Finance, where a senior civil servant, Frans en Louise Engering, who was serving as an SWWB Board member, reached a compromise to officially register the organization as "Stichting to Promote Women's World Banking." This agreement assured the Ministry that WWB would not collect deposits in the Netherlands.

Frans en Louise Engering, then serving as director of foreign financial relations at the Dutch Finance Ministry, in a correspondence from October 27, 2011, recalled his role.

Frans en Louise Engering

Far before the broader world paid attention to microcredit and women banking, WWB was created and got the support of the Dutch financial authorities. I remember that, being then the director for foreign financial relations of the Dutch Finance Ministry, I acted as a kind of advocate with my friends in the Central Bank in Amsterdam, on behalf of WWB.

I recall that Floris was delighted with the speed of the name change. I was especially pleased that, despite the legal name change from "Stichting Women's World Banking" to "Stichting to Promote Women's World Banking," that took care of several problems, we were able to continue using the initials SWWB. Most importantly, WWB would continue to be featured prominently on our logo, which was recognized worldwide.

With great relief, I reported the outcome of the negotiations to **J. Burke Knapp**, who responded, "*Well, that sounds like a reasonable compromise.*" (As for the negotiations with the Central Bank, the file on that matter was classified "under supervision," and thirty years later still cannot be accessed.)

Sylvia Chin, one of the truly dedicated members of WWB, first became involved as a junior associate at White & Case in 1979 and has remained to this day one of the guardians of legal issues in the United States for WWB. In our interview, Sylvia described some of the challenges.

Sylvia Chin

Friends of WWB/USA had been registered in the state of Delaware on January 4, 1980. WWB was to have its principal place of business in New York. In the state of New York you couldn't set up an organization that had "bank" in the name unless it was a real bank. We kept going back and forth with an attorney in the attorney general's office who wanted to know what "WWB" stood for. I insisted that it was just three letters, but he found out on his own and denied us the approval. It took about three years just to formally have an office. In the mid-'80s, they changed the law, and you could ask for permission to use the word "banking." We also had to navigate issues due to the fact that the 501(c) (3) organization in the US was Friends of WWB, which allowed donations to be tax-deductible, while the Dutch Stichting had a 501(c) (4) status in the US. SWWB was the real operating organization—we eventually moved everything over to Stichting in 1988 and 1989, which had the official office in New York, and Friends became a volunteer fund-raising board in the mid-'90s.

Despite this successful outcome on a legal basis, discussions continued about our name, which presented translation issues. **Beatrice Harretche** had remarked (in a fall 1984 Executive Committee meeting and on subsequent occasions) that *"English is the only language in which 'bank' refers to a noun as well as a verb.... The translation [of Women's World Banking] causes confusion. In Spanish, 'Banco Mundial de la Mujer' refers to WWB as a bank, not as an institution that works with and through banks."* I felt that a change of name would cause complications among members of WWB and especially with regard to fund-raising.

As WWB became more concrete, the process of developing our structure became more complex and was a constant learning process. While at the beginning, when we were starting to build the organization, we viewed everyone as a member, as we began to extend guarantees, we had to introduce restrictions. Affiliation with WWB became defined as needing (first), twenty-five thousand dollars in assets [later changed to twenty thousand]; (second), a legal structure in the country of the affiliate; (third) a management structure; and (fourth), a business plan. Some affiliates became strong, while some faded away, and others became entangled in debt.

Even for those affiliates that were successful, sometimes serious questions arose, mostly because the women weren't accustomed to working together as a team to create a new global institution. Strong personalities, culturally specific styles of management and communications, and varying levels of donor interest from country to country made for tensions and sometimes conflicts among the trustees with regard to decision-making that would affect the organization as a whole.

Nellie Tan-Wong, who headed the WWB affiliate in Malaysia, developed a concept of the "Role and Responsibilities of a WWB Trustee" (April 18, 1984), in an effort to unite us through our shared commitment:

> A WWB trustee has a very challenging role to play, as she has to be knowledgeable on the objectives of WWB; she has to be loyal, confident, and constantly open to new ways to work. . . . In an international network, one has to be able to work with others of different race, religion and custom. . . . I think one of the more positive attitudes a trustee should have is to accept her appointment, realizing that she has more to learn than to impart when working with any group.

As one of the few men on the Board, Rudolf Mees recounted his impressions of the "female culture" that characterized our meetings.

Rudolf Mees

It was an entirely female Board with three exceptions, namely the banker (myself), the accountant, and the lawyer (Floris Bannier). It was a very interesting experience for three men, all of whom came from business organizations that were comprised mostly of men, to sit on a Board of Trustees that consisted primarily of women and to find ourselves immersed in a female culture. Witnessing the differences in decision-making and policy formulation was a real adventure. One of the characteristics was that it took fairly long to reach consensus, compared to the norm for men, with much back-and forth discussion. In those instances, as a man, you really had to hold back, pause for a while, and only at the end of the journey could you say: "Madame President, if I understood it all correctly, the problem was defined as approximately this, and the approximate solution would then be that. The reply then was "Yes, yes," and a decision was made.

I found it interesting that Rudolf did not mention the emotional level and the tears that were part of every meeting during the first ten years. This was interesting to me because of Barbro Dahlbom-Hall's analysis on how women respond to female leadership and Klaas Molenaar's experience with WWB training.

7

REGIONAL LEADERSHIP GROWS STRONGER

"We may be poor of money, but we are not poor in spirit."

WWB'S DESIGN WAS to create an international institutional base that was self-supporting, with a Capital Fund made up of funds received without strings attached for the purpose of providing a partial guarantee to an affiliate and a local banking partner. Earnings from that fund would support WWB's administrative costs. It was my goal to have a network of at least ten affiliates up and running, and one guarantee program in each region of the world, at the end of ten years.

In the early stages of WWB, following its decisive 1980 Amsterdam meeting, it was very clear that the donor agencies had a particular interest in the development of women in Africa. At a November 20, 1980, meeting with the World Bank's International Finance Corporation, Margaret (Gee) Hagen, a loan officer who had attended the WWB Amsterdam gathering, remarked that "along with Colombia, India, and possibly Ghana, Kenya meets several preconditions identified by WWB and its support organization, UNDP, for start-up activities. These include the existence of a local financial institution supportive and interested in the concept of WWB and the existence of an experienced national organization with the specific project proposal they are willing to support."

Two African affiliates were WWB-Ghana, initiated by Esther Ocloo and Mrs. Justice Annie Jiagge, and Kenya Women's Finance Trust (KWFT), being set up with Mary Okelo and Barclays Bank.

WWB-Ghana

In 2010, Celeste Alexander, a PhD candidate at Princeton University who conducted some interviews in Africa during summer of 2010, interviewed Comfort Engmann, a co-founder of WWB-Ghana. As an educator, she had a very different perspective from market women and from the other women who were involved.

Comfort Engmann

When WWB took root in Ghana, there were no structures for the idea, but we went around and publicized the concept. It was formed as an NGO, and we had an uphill task. We had to submit to the regulations put forth by the Bank of Ghana. We made some mistakes. There was great interest, and we thought that one bank in Accra could cater to people everywhere. People were buying shares. We got Barclays Bank to help (they had already participated in Kenya), but there was some trouble with that. We saw that we needed training, and that became a big part of our activities. Eventually, Robert McNamara, [president of] the World Bank, came here, and Esther Ocloo, in an inspirational move, called out, "The World Bank should marry Women's World Banking!" He shouted from the podium: "I am here with my wife!" From there, he decided that the World Bank would have a Women's Desk. They gave us money to open an office in Kumasi and for our training program. Esther was very helpful, as well, in training the women to make marmalade, tie-dye, and all sorts of things. She was versatile! We started with a normal savings and took those who were attending our workshops and created "susu" groups—voluntary groups where the members guarantee each other. We had to register a separate savings-and-loans company, so that our WWB affiliate could remain an NGO.

Other people I remember from my early trips to Ghana include Barbara Fynn-Williams, who owned a trucking company that moved goods in and out of the port of Accra. I remember her as one of the cleverest entrepreneurial women I had ever met. Equally memorable are Esther Ocloo's handsome husband, in his traditional robes, and visits with her youngest son, who was a teenager in

COMFORT ENGMANN, LEFT, AND ESTHER OCLOO, LAKE NAKURU LODGE, KENYA
[PHOTO CREDIT, MARNIE MONHEIM]

the early '80s. I realized that his aspirations were not that different from those of teenagers in the United States. He led me to begin to think about how to integrate what we were doing with WWB for a younger generation. This thinking would be essential to me many years later when creating the Global Student Leadership Program. My sister Deirdre went to Africa with me one year, and she still delights me with her memories of Kenya and Ghana.

WWB-Kenya
Kenya Women's Finance Trust

Mary Okelo, the first African woman manager at Barclays Bank in Kenya, and Christine Hayanga, a lawyer at the Kenya Agricultural Finance Corporation, had attended the 1980 WWB meeting in Amsterdam and went on to found Kenya Women's Finance Trust. They recalled the behavior of banks toward women in Kenya at the time.

Mary Okelo

In Kenya, it was difficult for women to open a bank account without their husband or father's approval, let alone get access to credit. We used British Victorian law, which stipulates that women are minors under their fathers and husbands. Women were the "untouchables"—people said they borrowed very little money and weren't worth the risk. We had to fight to have laws changed. As a bank manager, I was allowed to take loans, but I refused to do so, until that right was available to other women as well. That made a big statement and people thought I was a "rebel." It was a battle of life and death. We had to challenge the status quo. Even the security guards of banks treated women poorly.

At the WWB Amsterdam meeting, people from all over the world were talking about the same issues. We were trying to address a global problem from a national perspective. We all wanted to help transform the world and were committed to changing the stuffy banks that didn't want to change their way of doing business. We learned from one another. In Kenya, Barclay's Bank, Women's World Banking, and Kenya Women's Finance Trust came together. WWB provided a guarantee. Collateral was a critical issue in getting the loans, so loans were given to groups of women who were provided with training in bookkeeping and other basics. In order to qualify, the women had to be running sustainable businesses. Understanding their situation helped us to help them; for example, if they needed to reschedule their loan, we aimed to accommodate them. . . .

At first, I was using my own funds, but eventually ran out, so I brought a group of people together in which each member contributed a minimum of two thousand shillings. About one hundred women "founder/members" contributed, and it showed the donors that we were really committed. When it came to the government, they didn't understand what we were all about. They thought we were a bank and treated us with suspicion. We had to explain that we were not a bank, but a microfinance institution helping to sensitize women to access more banking services.

Christine Hayanga

WWB could fit in everywhere, because it had to be homegrown. Attending the WWB meeting in Amsterdam helped sound out different ideas with other practitioners. My sister, Mary Okelo, was very daring and was giving loans to women who didn't even have collateral, based on her faith in the individuals' integrity. I got courage from her and helped make the case that women were bankable people who, by helping themselves, automatically help their families as well. At the beginning, we faced resistance. We made men our friends, so that they could persuade other men. We found pro-women male managers.

Kenya Women's Finance Trust (KWFT) was formally registered in 1982 and began operations in 1984. A 1986 memo from WWB-New York staffer **Julie Abrams** conveying a conversation she had with Mary Okelo reflects the challenge KWFT encountered in working with major donors:

> KWFT has received funding from several international sources, including NORAD, the Ford Foundation, and USAID. She [Mary Okelo] expressed concern that each donor agency has its own agenda and requirements, often not in sync with the objectives of KWFT. She underscored the importance of the affiliates' independence.

The issue of donor dependency became increasingly problematic for KWFT. In a 1989 letter, **Christine Hayanga** reported on the status of KWFT financing. KWFT had been probed by Ford Foundation and K-Rep (Kenya Rural Enterprise Program) Bank, which found that KWFT lacked capital and was in danger of wholly relying on donor funds:

> It is evident that the Trust has operated without sufficient funds mainly due to the fact that some of the donor agencies were not able to remit all the grant money as agreed upon. Consequently, the Trust is in deficit as shown in the accounts. . . . If the worse came to the worst, which will not happen, the law relating to bankruptcy involves lengthy proceedings, which cannot happen overnight, and we can ourselves be involved in the collection of the outstanding amount from the borrowers to ensure that we do not lose money in the transactions. In view of the foregoing, I wish to suggest that you proceed to sign the Agreement [a tripartite agreement among WWB, Barclays Bank of Kenya Limited and Kenya Women's Finance Trust] so that the Guarantee Scheme can continue in operation despite the storm that the Trust is passing through. May I add that the process of development unavoidably may lead to storms but people usually survive! We are learning how to avoid disasters, and the learning is also very important. KWFT will survive.

Despite many ups and downs, KWFT did survive and grow. We requested that the KWFT experience of having been on the brink of bankruptcy be shared with other affiliates at the WWB Global Meeting in Atlanta in 1990. Jennifer Riria, who assumed the leadership of KWFT in 1991, recalled the transition process during an interview in 2010.

Jennifer Riria

By 1991, the institution KWFT was about to close. I was working at UNDP at the time and was always interested in women's rights and economic independence, so they sought me out to help rehabilitate the organization. To head up an organization like Kenya Women was very problematic from men's standpoint. They told me to leave their wives alone, because they were getting "big heads." There was also a lot of fighting among the board members who only wanted to direct, not work. Things are different now. WWB has a lot of respect in Kenya, and we have over five hundred thousand members in the newly constituted bank. We are everywhere, even in the rural areas. Kenya Women has become a brand name. We are perceived as an entry point to reach women in this country. We developed a culture of performance and achievement along with empowerment and encouragement of the workers. We care for each other and have a good support network. The borrowers are treated like clients: If you borrow, you have to repay. We can't confuse our clients by telling them to repay their loans and then giving them charity. There is no charity. We have groups, so that if one member has a problem, the other members can provide a cushion. It's a process of positive transformation. As a group, we go beyond the money. We share in each other's joy and mourning. We also involve husbands in the businesses. We never talk about "my money," but about "our" money.

In 2011, I spoke with **Phyllis Wangiko Kibui**. Wangiko had been an accountant with K-Rep Bank when it was doing microbanking in rural areas and mentoring clients in their village huts. K-Rep was surprised to learn that 60 per cent of the clients were women. Jennifer Riria, who had been hired to reorganize KWFT, approached Wangiko to be a member of the KWFT Board in 1991. Wangiko said she was impressed with the whole concept of a global network committed to strengthening access services for low-income women, and to helping them help themselves. With a global focus on women, she was happy to see that by going into their homes, the program was designed and operated as reality—not theory. She thought what she heard was that KWFT was to be truly professional. While at first skeptical, after meeting with previous and potential donors and others, she found KWFT to be very serious. She felt there was a chance for real change. She said, "I will be in this movement."

She met Mary Okelo about a year later, when Mary returned from the African Development Bank. Wangiko was impressed that Mary had nothing negative to say about KWFT. Then when Nancy Barry came to Kenya, Wangiko saw again how serious WWB was. She ultimately came to WWB-NY, and now is at the World Bank.

In Celeste Alexander's 2010 interview with a group of KWFT borrowers who produce textiles, one of the members—a woman we know only as Ann—shared her experience.

KWFT borrower Ann

We started with thirty thousand-shilling loans and now we are getting one hundred twenty-five million, so we are growing. Within the group, we make sure that we all do our part. If anyone of us doesn't pay, it's a problem for the whole group. Once we had two members who couldn't pay, so the group paid for them. Their business went down, but they started repaying a little at a time over the course of two years. At first, my husband didn't want me to participate, but he changed his mind when he saw the business grow. Whenever I get money, he has to sign forms to acknowledge that he is aware of each step I am taking. Sometimes he works with me. The most important thing is that in the group we know and trust each other—because we all like to earn more money.

Grace Madoka, Chairman of the Board of KWFT from 2002 to 2009, reflected on the factors that make KWFT a success.

Grace Madoka

We don't do things differently from the rest of the world, but we do look at the specific issues that affect women in Kenya and apply those issues in our decisions—things like the importance of loans to help women afford access to gas and water. At first the men thought the point was to make women independent so that they could leave, but then they understood that was not the case. We keep close tabs on repayment and meet very regularly. Today, our relationship with WWB is of an advisory and training nature. Our board members are professionals who like working with each other.

WWB-Uganda

The diversity of the affiliates throughout Africa was evident from the outset.

In Uganda, the Uganda Women's Finance Trust (UWFT) was created under the leadership of **Christine (Cissy) Kwaba-Abungu**. I have vivid memories of her commitment to raising the dignity of women. The courage of Ugandan women was greater than I could have imagined. I always remember how the day after their office had been broken into and all their money was stolen, they turned around, reopened, and continued to serve their clients. Cissy's remark at one of our global meetings, during a debate about whether we should refer to "poor" or "low-income" women, stays with me to this day. She said, *"We may be poor of money, but we're not poor in spirit."* Sadly, Cissy, infected by her husband, died of AIDS in 1991.

Cissy's younger sister, Rose Tibulya, started working at Uganda Women's Finance Trust in 1987 as a stenographer and still works at the organization (now called Uganda Finance Trust). She shared her recollections of how the organization developed.

Rose Tibulya

The Uganda Women's Finance Trust was started in 1984 by a group of Ugandan women at a time when the country was politically unstable. The general objective was to help women with training for financial empowerment. Christine Aburu, the chairperson, was my elder sister. My father made sure that all of us were educated. My sister had a Bachelor of Commerce. She was a delegate at the 1985 Women's Conference in Nairobi and had considerable experience. I was still young, but she told me everything that she did, so I learned from her. The organization was set up as an affiliate of WWB. Her goal was to help women get access to assets, since they didn't have land titles. Some NGOs in Western Africa and some government officials and business people were also involved.

There were some conflicts with the government in the '80s, when the new group took over. Women had no power or security. During those days, my sister was harassed and our offices were robbed. Men thought we wouldn't succeed. Even the government despised women. But the women who wanted to start businesses or grow their businesses were motivated. First they would open an account. Then they would be trained, visited, and observed in their business. The problem with group lending was that some of the members couldn't pay, so the others would have to work harder to cover. So now there is more individual lending. I went without pay for six months when there wasn't enough money, but I didn't mind, because we were all the same and all working for the same goal.

Margaret Sajjabi began borrowing in 1989.

Margaret Sajjabi

I was selling bananas by the road. A woman who was working for UWFT thought I needed money to boost my business. I am still selling bananas, but now I have more money to do it. I was doing it wholesale. Then I started parking at the same place. She gave me one hundred fifty thousand shillings. After six months, she gave me three hundred thousand. Every six months I got a loan until I got to one million. Then she asked me if I had any security, and I said yes, so she gave me more money. After I borrowed twenty million, I opened stalls and made up a flat. My children now go to school. It was a business loan for a group, but when I reached one million, I got an individual loan. I opened a primary school and have four hundred fifty children attending. I have a big house in the village.

The challenges over the years were the times when you couldn't pay back a loan, you didn't get a profit, you needed to take your kids to school and use the loan instead of using it for the business. It happens seasonally. There was a time when I misused the money—I bought clothes for myself instead of reinvesting into the business. I found it very difficult to pay back and thought I wouldn't get another loan, but eventually I paid it back.

During a 2010 interview with Elizabeth Littlefield, formerly president of CGAP and now CEO of Overseas Private Investment Corporation (OPIC), she reminded me of her experience helping to provide training to affiliates. I asked Elizabeth to go to West Africa because a number of affiliates seemed to be having real difficulties getting started.

Elizabeth Littlefield

I originally got involved because I had gone to Michaela seeking financing for a project I was working on, and somehow came out of the meeting with a commitment to write a manual for loan officers with my newly minted credit-officer skills from being in the training program at JP Morgan. I moved to Paris shortly thereafter, and since in France you get five weeks of vacation, I offered to go work with WWB in West Africa, where two affiliates in the region had gone AWOL. I experienced the pre-professional stage of microfinance in the work that I did in all these African countries. We were still in the phase of marveling at the fact that women could pay, would pay, and that you could create a viable lending operation. We were talking about "micro-credit schemes," not institutions, and about "beneficiaries," not clients. They were getting "micro-loans" rather than financial services. The language was just beginning to shift from women being seen as a secondary beneficiary of government programs to the understanding that they can be viable clients of real institutions.

Tanzania

In Tanzania, during a 1991 USAID-sponsored workshop I conducted about launching a Tanzania bank for women, I met Khadija Simba, an entrepreneur who, with a loan from a German technology company, established one of the largest women-owned businesses in Tanzania, called Kay's Hygiene Products Ltd. Eager to use her company's assets to start a neighborhood loan program, she went on her own to Nairobi to meet with Jennifer Riria, to learn about WWB's loan-guarantee programs. I have met with Kay Simba many times and have great respect for her commitment to the empowerment of low-income women in her country. On one occasion, I went with her to meet with her borrowers who owned kiosks in their neighborhood. I wanted to know what their dreams and concerns were. One woman told me she just hoped her daughter would go to school. Another hoped for a good life for her son. It was a special moment of connection, answering a question that I had carried with me from the outset of WWB: Do women, regardless of their circumstances, carry the same dreams?

WWB-Africa Regional Office

I had gone to Nairobi for "Forum '85," the UN Decade for Women Conference and the Women's Tribune. In view of the expanding interest in WWB across the African continent, after the meeting I spent two weeks with Mary Okelo and Kenya Women's Finance Trust (KWFT), focusing on a WWB Africa Regional Office. In a trip report to the Board upon my return, I noted "a real sense of

REPORT COVERS OF THE WWB AFRICA REGIONAL SEMINARS, 1986 AND 1989

growth in WWB was evident in Nairobi," and urged that "we need to avoid a buildup of individual local power centers. While we must encourage decentralization, we need to work to strengthen links among the WWB affiliates through more effective communications." This concern validated for me the importance of regional centers, as well as the need to continue discussions about how to design exchange programs and training sessions.

Mary Okelo, who had launched and developed KWFT and helped negotiate the first guarantee agreement with Barclays Bank, Kenya, agreed to become our first part-time Africa adviser/WWB Africa regional representative to develop the WWB Africa Regional Office. To facilitate communication and learning among the WWB African affiliates, under Mary's leadership, the WWB Africa Regional Office began publishing the *WWB Africa Newsletter*. In one of the issues, **Philip Ndegwa**, governor of the Central Bank of Kenya, was interviewed and was quoted about his vision for WWB: "*WWB could research all the organisms and institutions that are linked to women's development, not to control them, but to help them find a strategic system that would complement WWB's own goals, to connect women to banking services—an organization like WWB, being apolitical, could be extremely useful. . . . We have been urging the banks to be more involved in the countryside, and I am sure that means they have got to work more closely with women.*"

Recognizing the importance of serving women in rural areas, WWB drafted a proposal in 1986 to the Dutch foundation *Stichting Steun Door Rabobanken*, which had a track record of providing financial services to low-income women farmers "for support to African women entrepreneurs in the agricultural sector."

Also in 1986, one year after the UN "Decade for Women" Conference in Nairobi, a Women's Seminar was organized for WWB African affiliates, with the goal of "putting theory into practice." Participants from about twenty countries attended, including members of the Kenyan national government; the financial community; donor agencies from Canada, Norway, the Netherlands, and the United States; the Ford Foundation; UNDP; UNICEF (represented by its regional director for Eastern and Southern Africa, Dr. Mary Racelis); Barclays Bank; and the African Development Bank. According to the seminar report, each affiliate was at a different stage of development, and participants appreciated the WWB policy of decentralization, which allowed the organization to be more responsive to women's needs at the grass roots. During that meeting, we encouraged women running affiliates to raise funds locally, so they would have control of their own destiny and grow at a pace that was appropriate for them. Similarly, Barclays Bank expressed the view that "women need to translate their potential into aggressive profit-making activities." Flexibility in choosing the model for affiliation with one's national government and with WWB was deemed valuable, and the establishment of the first regional office of WWB in Nairobi was welcomed.

The seminar report further recommended that:

> a) WWB recognize African affiliates' major constraint as being the lack of funds and respond to this need by providing some form of "seed money"; b) WWB increase information flow to the African region; c) WWB accelerate its decentralization program; d) WWB support the establishment of Regional Advisory Boards; e) WWB support regular regional seminars to strengthen both local affiliates and regional networks.

In response to the report, I sent a letter to all members of WWB (dated June 23, 1987), reporting that we had received a multiyear three-million-dollar grant from the Canadian International Development Agency (CIDA). Over a five-year period, two million Canadian dollars would go to the Capital Fund; five hundred thousand dollars would go to support Africa regional operations; three hundred thousand dollars would be allocated to affiliate training and exchanges among African affiliates; and two hundred thousand dollars would go toward an affiliate-starter program in Africa. Provided the affiliate had a business plan and a budget, a low-interest loan (one percent interest) to help cover local administrative costs for the first three years would be included.

I disagreed with the need for a regional advisory committee, and emphasized that we were committed to avoiding rules and regulations concerning communications: *"Our communication is based on the idea that everyone in our network takes responsibility for informing others and keeping informed; WWB does not provide grant money for affiliate administrative costs."* I was convinced that WWB would become stagnant if it were to be a traditional "institution," doing what outside donors' agendas would dictate and not what affiliate members wanted to do. We delivered this message over and over at all the early global meetings: "*We want to help you do what you want to do, not what we want you to do.*" It was a constant struggle to convey that WWB wasn't a donor agency, but was designed to help women come together and create something of their own.

Pursuant to many queries that came into the Africa Regional Office requesting information about how to set up and run a WWB affiliate, we provided "Guidelines" that had evolved from WWB affiliates sharing their practical experience. The guidelines state:

> We wish to emphasize that there are no cut-and-dry "official" strategies for establishing affiliates. Socioeconomic conditions as well as political and cultural factors vary from country to country; and so what is most important is that WWB promoters respond to women's economic needs in ways which are practical, appealing, appropriate, and socially relevant.

We detailed the basic profile of a "promoter," someone who: a) knows and shares WWB objectives; b) understands the economic and technical needs of women in her country; and c) has organizational skills and the ability to communicate across sectors in her country (from government officials to commercial bankers, donors, women leaders, and entrepreneurs). We also: a) recommended that a "working committee" comprise a diversity of skilled personnel including banking, social work, legal expertise, accounting, and fund-raising; b) required that affiliates conduct their own research into country laws affecting women; and c) prepared a *WWB Fund-Raising Manual for Affiliates* that involved training, promotion, and networking.

In addition to seminars that brought affiliate representatives together, the Africa Regional Office conducted country visits to provide on-site assessments and support for affiliates' progress. In an April 1987 report, **Mary Okelo** summarized her visit to sixteen countries in Africa:

> In all countries visited, we had the privilege of meeting high-ranking officials in government and in the business/banking community, women professionals and leaders of national women's organizations, women entrepreneurs both in thriving cities and rural areas. . . . We cannot overstate the value of these trips. . . . In many African countries, most NGOs require government approval to work within local communities. This is especially true for organizations with international links like WWB. Another reason why these trips have proved to be invaluable is because they have allowed us to survey the situation of African women and to see how it varies from country to country; to appreciate the diversity and cultural specificity of constraints that women face; to assess the level of their entrepreneurial activities skills development; and even to gain valuable insights into the quality and character of women's leadership at the local level. . . .

By being there in person, WWB-Africa has not only been able to ensure that our strategies, objectives, and programs are clearly understood by the women, bankers and members of government. We have also been able to pave the way for further WWB activities by local people once we have gone, by being sensitive to local politics, including those women's organizations. One instance where our presence was extremely useful in avoiding bureaucratic bottlenecks, which might have otherwise impeded a local affiliate's progress, was in Swaziland, where we went in 1985. There, the one official women's organization, specifically supported by the ruling monarchy, wields immense power to either frustrate or facilitate the development of new women's groups, depending on the way in which outsiders followed the proper protocol.

Opening the first regional office of WWB has been both a challenging and richly rewarding experience. The fact that the region includes fifty-three countries, on a continent four times the size of the US, has at times made the work seem overwhelming. . . . Compounding the problem of the size and scale of our work has been the fact that communications on the continent are poor and infrastructures still underdeveloped. The vast majority of women we would like to reach reside in rural areas, which are often outside the monetized economy, operating at subsistence standards of living. Nonetheless, the fact that it is now widely recognized that women produce, process and market up to ninety percent of the food in Africa has made governments, donors, bankers, and professional women far keener to act upon the WWB objectives.

As WWB activities in Africa increased, the need for capital remained critical. At the Africa Regional Seminar, "Strategies for Achieving Self-Sufficiency," held in Nairobi in January 1989, the participating members (from Botswana, Ghana, Lesotho, Malawi, Nigeria, Uganda, Zambia, and Zimbabwe) and a large number of donors urged increased direct support from WWB. They agreed that: "a) affiliates appeal to WWB for technical assistance; b) WWB direct the affiliates to donors; c) WWB consider giving affiliates start-up grants, in one-lump-sum payments; d) the affiliate exchange program be financed one hundred percent by WWB," among other points.

My February 27, 1989, response expressed my sentiment that we had to "explain that WWB is not a 'grant-making' institution," and resist what I perceived was a "*give*-me' attitude."

During my 2011 interview with Elizabeth Littlefield, I asked her to reflect on the relationship between WWB-New York and the affiliates in terms of expectations of receiving foreign aid.

Elizabeth Littlefield

There is nothing unusual about people wanting latitude over the way their resources are being spent. It hasn't changed that much except that when an organization gets mature enough, it knows it's going to be able to get much larger amounts of funds and grow much bigger and faster if it's got a credible plan. But, in the early days, when it's just grant money, organizations would much rather spend it their own way.

Divergent expectations between donors and receiving organizations were not uncommon. Rudolf Mees recollected an anecdote illustrating how such differences manifested, and how often misinformation and misunderstandings could erupt into false accusations.

Rudolf Mees

Serving on the WWB Board was an education in many respects. One eye-opening incident occurred in connection with a small loan in Kenya that was jointly held by the Swedish International Development Agency (SIDA), the Dutch Ministry for Development, and the UN. The Swedes had an unexpected two million kronor left over, which had to be spent before the end of the fiscal year. After much discussion, the grant was given to Women's World Banking, specifically earmarked for Africa, specifically for the Kenya Women's Finance Trust and the Africa Regional Office. Two years later, the Swedes accused Women's World Banking of corruption, so I immersed myself in the case to understand what had happened. A couple that lived in a small house in Kenya and had a tiny loan from WWB became the recipient of those funds. If you give such people two million kronor, the whole extended family gets involved. There were about fifteen family members who nestled there and who subsequently engaged themselves in the business. It was said that this reeked of corruption, but of course that was not so. Families are the social network—the traditional insurance system. I was surprised by how difficult it was to explain the situation. I would have thought that surely in the development world, people would have known how such things function.

Thinking back, Elizabeth Littlefield shared how the personal experiences of working with WWB affiliates in West Africa affected her life. Her colorful stories are typical of the unexpected and exciting circumstances many of us experienced in that early period.

Elizabeth Littlefield

There's no question that from my very first trip to Mali I fell in love with the continent, which I still describe as "home" in the biggest sense of the word, and I shifted my energy and my ambition to a path of development work. From that day on, even my days at JP Morgan were spent on emerging markets. My entire career pivoted as a result of that first trip. And I've stayed the course. If it weren't for exposure to Women's World Banking, I don't think I would have done the subsequent jobs I've done for the last 20–25 years, from CGAP to the World Bank and now OPIC.

Some of the early WWB African affiliates didn't work out very well, but they helped raise awareness about women's role in the economy, the fact that women were far more responsible stewards of financial assets than men, and that investing in women was going to translate into re-investment of income into family welfare. We were not yet at the point where people understood the need for cross-covering interest rates, or zero tolerance for defaults or late payments.

At that point, Women's World Banking itself was more of a movement than a super-organized institution. The number one factor of success was the motivation of the leader of the affiliate. In Africa, the motivation wasn't always clear. In Mali, I thought I was going to work with the women, get my hands dirty, and help them sort out their accounting, or whatever the problems were that were keeping them from successfully communicating. Somehow they got it twisted around such that when I arrived at the Bamako Airport in 1986, I learned that all the women ministers were hoping to get money out of us to earn political points. I was invited to meet the president's wife for lunch, then to the annual barefoot polo game, where I sat in the royal box. It was pretty clear that there was not a lot we could do to keep the affiliate separate from the government. So I asked how we might expand into the rural areas. We took a five-day trip to see various projects that might be funded by the affiliate once it got up and running. We went to Djenne, a beautiful place surrounded by a river, and were twenty-nine hours late in arriving. The whole village was waiting on the side of the riverbank and had a barge they pulled with rope for people to cross over. When we got there, they let off huge baskets of white doves in the air. It was an incredible way to receive us. (Michaela: I remember a similar experience in a rural village four hours outside of Bamako in the fall of 1984, when Martha Stuart was honored for her work in Mali. It was to be her last trip to Africa.)

In the Gambia, Michaela had negotiated a consultancy to help set up the Gambia Women's Finance Company, which would be funded by World Bank money. I was delighted, and thanks to Michaela's friend, A. Kendall Raine, vice president of JP Morgan, a deal was struck between the presidents of the World Bank and JPM, Barber Conable and Lewis Preston, to raise the money for the first leave of absence JPM had ever granted. But I insisted that I fly over to the Gambia first to meet the Board of the Gambia's Women's Finance Trust (GAWF), because if I was going to be working for them, I wanted them to want me. They were a little suspicious as to why they couldn't choose their own consultant, but were ultimately happy with me, and we agreed to move forward. I showed up a couple of months later. It was a complete start-up: we had no premises, no logo, no bylaws, no staff. During the course of the next year and a half, I helped set up the Gambia Women's Finance Company. People were warm and welcoming, but for some reason, they didn't know I was being paid with their money. They thought I was being offered by Women's World Banking. They woke up one morning to notice their consulting money they had hoped would carry them into the future with local consultants was all gone. It had been spent on my salary. That misunderstanding put me in an extremely awkward position.

Throughout that period (1987–88), I offered my services up to other Women's World Banking affiliates as well, and even to organizations that weren't affiliates to provide them with technical assistance. My only requirement was that they raise the money for my plane ticket. I was working with an affiliate-in-formation in Mauritania, in Rwanda where Jacqueline Novogratz had just been, and in Burundi, looking at their books and helping them to negotiate loan guarantees with the banks.

In Rwanda, I would arrive at the office in the morning, and there would be lines of hundreds of women waiting to get their loans who came back day, after day, after day. The organization was only processing four or five loans a day because they were asking for full business plans, and were doing hour-long interviews to figure out if they were worthy. They didn't have the mechanism to efficiently evaluate the proposals. They were interviewing each woman in such detail that the line was growing longer and longer and longer outside of the building. So, we set up mechanisms for triage. In Duterimbere, the women were so intent on soaking up all the knowledge they could get out of me about accounting, finance, systems for triage, etc., that after working an eight-hour day, they wanted me to do tutorials in the evening, and had me basically locked in the office until 10–10:30 at night. I felt strongly that you couldn't just say "no" to a woman that has a bad idea, or no track record, or no market for her product, or whatever wasn't proven. You had to say, "no, but." So we formed a partnership with Trickle-Up, so that the women who were rejected by the Women's World Banking affiliate were referred to Trickle-Up, which at the time was not insisting on much rigor—they were basically giving fifty-dollar grants for people to try to start up businesses. Then, if that first step proved to be viable, they would be referred back to Women's World Banking later on.

Delegating responsibility to a regional representative was important in my view, to strengthen the communication between our staff in New York and the affiliates and to help our office better understand the needs of the various affiliates in each region.

For example, the 1987 Policy Guidelines for the Latin America/Caribbean Regional Representative (RR) state that:

> The regional representative is the person in charge of establishing and maintaining the link between WWB/NY and the affiliates. In addition to evaluating and proposing WWB programs to each affiliate in the region, the guidelines also made the RR jointly responsible with WWB/NY for raising the financial resources needed to operate Regional Operations, and requested that the RR: a) provide monthly progress reports to WWB/NY; b) assist affiliates in drafting loans guarantee contracts and completing annual self-assessments; c) publish a regional newsletter; d) arrange regional meetings and seminars; and e) contact people and organizations interested in developing a WWB program.

> The guidelines were adapted for each regional representative, and the appointed representatives tried to comply with them, to the best of their capacity and with the resources they had available.

WWB-Latin America Regional Office

In Latin America, the first regional representative was Queenie de Vivo. In 2011, her daughter, Sofia, interviewed Queenie on my behalf in São Paulo. Queenie explained how she helped develop the WWB network in Latin America.

Queenie de Vivo

Beatrice Harretche was a very good friend whom I knew through the Inter-American Development Bank, as the IDB was financing Manos del Uruguay, a cooperative that I had co-founded. She called me one day to invite me to a meeting in Buenos Aires, Argentina. That's where I met Michaela Walsh and learned about WWB. From that encounter, the idea of opening a branch of WWB in Uruguay was born.

We began with the backup of people who were already involved with Manos del Uruguay. Then I invited the accountant Beatriz Migliaro to help structure the organization according to the WWB criteria. Each member contributed one hundred US dollars as initial capital. With that we went knocking at the door of the Banco de la República and Banco Central, and with their loan for the WWB Capital Fund, we reached one hundred thousand US dollars. Banco de la Republica also allowed us to use their space as our headquarters until we could manage on our own.

The initiative grew in scope and dimension. In 1985, while I was accompanying my husband, who was ambassador of Uruguay in Brazil, I helped sponsor the founding of WWB there. Already in 1979, at the WWB meeting in Amsterdam, one of the participants, Marlene Fernandes, a Brazilian economist, was so enthused by the meeting that she brought the idea back home. We reconnected when I went to Brazil, and I also involved contacts and friends I knew through my work at the Ministry of Labor, in a UNDP program for the improvement and marketing of handicrafts. Ana Lucia Sartorial Maia, a member of the Business Council of Executive Women, whose husband was the president of the Commercial Association of Rio de Janeiro, took a great interest at the local level; unfortunately, she left us too soon, a victim of leukemia. However, it was thanks to the work of the Council and the Commercial Association, along with a small group of ladies who worked like crazy, that Banco da Mulher was approved.

Learning from each other and providing technical support was a service that we all benefited from and contributed to at different points. I recall how the 1981 meeting in Colombia was an enormous help in terms of our efforts in Uruguay, because at that point we were still beginners. Later on, when we had meetings in Africa, it was our turn to give support to the affiliates there, and we maintained a close bond. We also provided technical support to the women in Bangladesh, and I personally had the chance to spend some time in Paraguay, providing technical assistance to help them establish WWB there.

Working with Manos del Uruguay and WWB gave me the chance to meet astonishing people, like Ruth Dayan, one of the early founders of Israel and a consultant to the IDB, and Enrique Iglesias from the IDB, who would become valuable references in my life. Michaela Walsh and I developed a solid workaholic friendship! I have very good memories of WWB meetings around the world, and what it meant to have the opportunity to share, along with so many fantastic women, the feeling that we were making a difference, effecting changes that were bringing low-income women closer to a better life.

Given Queenie's tremendous energy and commitment to WWB, appointing a successor following her retirement from the role of regional representative required that we clarify the terms of the job. One of the lessons learned was that it was important to hire people who, in addition to possessing management skills, were also familiar with the experiences and efforts of the affiliates in the region and felt connected to the broader vision of WWB. From our perspective, we also had to understand that people did their best with the resources they had available. This applied to all regions.

Because we were working around the world, some issues were common to all regions, but each region was unique.

WWB-North America Regional Office

In North America, plans for a regional office were initiated by Chris Weiss, who had set up a WWB affiliate in West Virginia.

Chris Weiss

In 1980, I had started an organization, Women and Employment, in Charleston, West Virginia, to get women and minorities placed in the construction industry. We went on to look at employment issues more generally and decided to advocate for women in small business. I remember that even in 1983, laws in the state were restrictive for women, requiring that they have a father or husband's signature to get a loan, and there were no credit unions available to rural women. My organization was getting funding from the Ford Foundation. Kate McKee, who was working at Ford, suggested that I meet with Michaela Walsh and talk about the problems we were having in getting access to credit. Michaela came to West Virginia in late '83 and we decided to create a local WWB affiliate. I remember thinking that if the approach could work in India, it could work in West Virginia. We had no role model, as it was the first time anyone had ever done anything in rural West Virginia. In 1984, I attended a WWB meeting in the Netherlands; it was my first trip outside of the US. The West Virginia affiliate eventually dissolved because we didn't have the capacity to provide the oversight and training that the borrowers needed. However, I continued to work with WWB, and was appointed Regional Coordinator for North America. The affiliates in the US and Canada were already established community organizations that were expanding their existing activities to include lending to micro-enterprises. One of the most successful affiliates was in Cape Breton, where there was a close alignment between the affiliate and a strong community-development organization. It wasn't until the mid '90s, however, that the understanding of micro-lending practices really began to blossom, and standards were adopted to the point where WWB's mission to be an advocate and provider for access to credit for women was realized.

As Chris mentioned, unlike the setup in the other regions of the world, most of the "affiliates" in the United States were sponsored by community organizers, as part of their local organizations. The structure of the economy in the United States presented WWB with different issues, including the size of support needed for the Capital Fund earmarked for North American guarantees.

In the December 1989 edition of *North America News* (the North America-WWB newsletter), affiliate updates indicated that affiliates were up and running in the United States in West Virginia, Philadelphia, and Ohio; and in Canada in Cape Breton. Several affiliates were "in development" in Vancouver, British Columbia; Toronto, Ontario; Fredericton, New Brunswick; Knoxville, Tennessee; San Antonio, Texas; Bozeman, Montana; and Augusta, Maine. The same newsletter states:

> In North America alone, the amount of capital owned by affiliates amounts to over one hundred thousand dollars. When these affiliates sign loan guarantee agreements with WWB, the amount will expand considerably. This figure does not take into account operating income, only those funds that WWB affiliates can utilize to their own advantage, either for guaranteeing loans or for direct lending, or for the beginning of a capital pool generating income for their operations.

Susan Winer, a founder of NABOW (National Association of Business Owner Women), had helped me build a marketing plan to define Women's World Banking in 1980–81. She went to the 1981 Cali meeting to help with translations. She and her company, RWA Associates, had prepared *A Marketing Strategy for Friends of WWB, Inc.* (March 19, 1982). In 1987, it was time for an updated strategy for WWB, so we invited her to work with us once again and attend our 1987 Executive Committee meeting in The Hague. During a 2009 interview, Susan recalled how stunned she was to learn that WWB was active in North America.

Susan Winer

I remember being in The Hague with Michaela and learning for the first time that WWB had an affiliate in Appalachia, an underdeveloped part of the United States. Because WWB was worldwide, they couldn't leave the US out of it. I found that fascinating, and understood that the root cause for economic disabilities in the US, India, or on the African continent, is pretty much the same when it comes down to low-income women—they don't have access to opportunities to get money. WWB is the bridge between access to money and access to opportunity.

WWB-Europe

In Europe, in addition to the ongoing activities of WWB-Netherlands, a WWB-inspired program was launched in France by Monique Halpern, who had been France's representative to the Organization for Economic Cooperation and Development (OECD). She also helped support the efforts of other nascent European WWB affiliates.

Monique Halpern

I was working with the French government as a representative to the OECD and was able to convince the OECD to hold its first international conference of women entrepreneurs, in May of 1985, after the Nairobi Conference. It was the first time we had disaggregated statistics. I don't remember how I knew about WWB, but I requested that Michaela Walsh be invited to that meeting. From there, we endeavored to start up a WWB affiliate in France, and began working as an NGO. Then, in 1986, Michaela came to Paris with Ela Bhatt to attend a meeting at SOFINCO, and we succeeded in getting two additional banks to work with us on the local loan-guarantee fund. It was fantastic to get all the members of the financial community in Paris to come to a meeting. It was unheard-of. . . . The idea did get picked up in France and received the attention it deserved. There was FGIF—"Fond de garantie, initiative de femme." We even had a meeting at the Senate, presided by Simone Veil. WWB was a fantastic force, a drive that things could be made possible. It swept us upwards, and gave us the possibility to start something.

Our work was being noticed by the state, so after five years of our working as an NGO, the state set up a loan-guarantee fund and ran it their way. That's a French government process, to look at what civil society is doing, and if the government likes it, to take it up and do it at the state level. We stayed involved, keeping track of the way the state program was being run, conducting studies for them and accompanying the process, although we were no longer doing it ourselves.

We supported the activities of affiliates-in-formation in other European countries. I recall attending a WWB meeting in Amsterdam along with the president of ADIEF—'87 or '88; and going to Spain to help a Swedish woman living in Madrid. . . . I remember being at a meeting years later where many of the women representing the affiliates felt sorry that big funders would give money to WWB instead of financing them directly. Some of these organizations, for example, the affiliate in Rwanda, said they would have gotten help from Norway or the Netherlands, but it went to WWB, which would then decide how to direct it—that was problematic and became an important issue to address. To this day, I don't know how that systemic issue was resolved.

WWB-Italy

Maria Grazia Randi of Milan, a member of the Board of Directors of the Bank of Italy (Consiglio di Reggenz della Banca d'Italia), and President of the World Federation of Women Entrepreneurs, played a major role in WWB-Europe. My memory of her enormous energy and integrity was reinforced in my recent (2011) conversation with her daughter, Paola Randi. Paola filled in the background as to how and why her mother became involved in WWB.

Paola Randi

In 1986, my mother organized a meeting at Mariza Pinzo's house. Its purpose was to learn about the work of Women's World Banking and WWB affiliates. My mother was connected to very impressive women entrepreneurs because of her presidency and long-term work in the World Federation of Women Entrepreneurs, and she was open to different kinds of approaches; she was also a pioneer. . . . She realized that in Italy, it was impossible for a nonprofit organization to have financial activities and give small loans of $500, which would have been an average loan for a WWB affiliate. To start a business in Italy, the amount of money you needed was much more than $500. Moreover, there was a problem of lack of trust in women who wanted to become businesswomen. In our country, everybody trusts a woman to raise children, but nobody trusts a woman to start a business.

What my mother did was to concentrate first on education and training. She basically invented the first training courses for women entrepreneurs in Italy who had been unemployed or wanted to re-enter the working world after pregnancy. She devised a formula working with the European community, major institutions, the Bank of Italy, other financial institutions, and important schools like Bacconi that provided teachers, as well as free business plans. Following the courses, there was an assessment of the companies' viability, and the women had the opportunity to get in touch directly with the people they would interact with once their business was launched. The women who participated in the training courses generally lacked financial resources for many reasons, so the training course was free, and in certain instances, the pupil even received a sort of salary to attend the course. The first course was in 1988. I participated in order to be trained as a tutor and then actually opened up an organization myself. . . . A few months ago I was contacted by a lady who had taken the course and went on to become a successful businesswoman, producing and selling wine.

Another innovative aspect of her work was to focus on ethical entrepreneurship. She contended that if a woman is the one who has to raise children and lead the family, her way of doing business can't help but be ethical. In her capacity as a Women's World Banking representative, she co-founded Banca Etica (Ethical Bank) which supports ethical business. It was a joint venture between several banking and financial institutions. She shared the WWB vision that women's way of doing business can be revolutionary and can change the world. As president of the World Federation of Women Entrepreneurs (FCEM—Femmes Chefs d'Entreprises Mondiales), she changed the organization's philosophy from purely focusing on business, to creating an international lobby with a presence at the

United Nations and different task forces that advocated for governments to develop and implement policies in support of women in business.

My mother's work changed the dominant mentality in Italy; it was revolutionary. . . .

Not only did it pave the way for the development of many training courses for women entrepreneurs in Italy, but her efforts also resulted in the establishment of a special law that is still in effect, and which utilizes public funds to give special loans to women who want to start a business in Italy. She did not work alone—Paola Barbieri Nardome, also an entrepreneur, was my mother's right arm; together they pressed the major Italian banks to start up a special credit line for women. They also worked with Silvia Costa, a politician, to promote the law.

My mother was able to connect to so many different institutions and people in order to bring about positive actions for women. Her concept that business run by women equals business with equity and ethics was really radical. I learned from her how to make something grow. If I'm half as strong as my mother was, it's more than enough. . . .

I recall that she had a wonderful experience of cooperation with WWB International. (By the time she died, in the year 2000, the international policy of WWB was much more concentrated on women entrepreneurs in developing countries.) I tried to have Paola Barbieri become the new president of WWB-Italy, but it didn't work out, so WWB-Italy is no longer there.

One of the truly remarkable businesswomen I had the good fortune to meet in Europe was Rosmarie Michel, who at the time was president of her family's company, as well as president of the Association of Business and Professional Women. Rosmarie's involvement with WWB brought great professional thinking for building Women's World Banking. When I interviewed Rosmarie in Zurich in 2010, my admiration for her commitment to women's leadership and her amazing capacity for laughter and dancing was reinforced by several of her comments.

Rosmarie Michel

I was at the 1985 UN Conference on Women in Nairobi when a young woman approached me, saying that I looked like an entrepreneur. She told me how she had started a business to enable handicapped people to make shoes thanks to a small grant through one of WWB's affiliates. Two years later, I met Michaela Walsh in New Zealand, where I was chairing a conference. She invited me to the Netherlands to participate in a board meeting. I thought organizations in Switzerland could support WWB and set out to meet with a Swiss institution that was investing in developing countries. The director, Mr. Faust, invited me for lunch in Bern and told me he would "try to help." I said, "I'm sorry, but we don't need help. We need investment. We are business people and you are business people. If you are looking for a secure investment, I can assure you that investing in women is very secure." From that point on, he and I became good friends. I was glad to be able to interfere with the patronizing attitude that was so predominant in industrial countries; when you think you are "helping," it puts you on a higher level— it's not a partnership. With WWB, it was equal partnership, and investing is also about partnership, because you can't invest if you don't trust your partner.

We spent considerable time trying to identify a potential representative for the **Middle East**, but because of the constraints of legal systems in the region at that time, we were unable to move forward prior to 1990.

The identification of a regional representative for **Asia** would be a major issue during the planning of our 1988 Board meeting in Kuala Lumpur.

The evolution of WWB and affiliates was always intertwined with the socioeconomic and political environment—ranging from economic turmoil, to natural disaster, to political uprisings—in the countries where we operated. In response to a questionnaire sent to affiliates to evaluate their progress, **Lourdes Lontok Cruz** from the Philippines responded: *"We were in a state of crisis during most of last year (1985) and up to March 1986. . . . You should have seen our struggle; it is hardly believable in modern history. We need a more stable economy to encourage women to do and strive more."*

In a memo to the Board, I asked all to *"pray for our friends in Haiti and the Philippines. During the past few weeks, as citizens, they have certainly been outstanding examples for us all in courage, integrity, love of country and trust in each other."*

The question, "Why be part of Women's World Banking?" as opposed to just building a strong identity within one's own country, was often raised by individual affiliate leaders. Trustees and management were struggling with issues as well. To be a truly global organization, we had to honor our diversity at all levels, from the Board to the composition of our staff. There was an ongoing debate among Board members about the importance of maintaining an international mix of staff members coming from diverse sectors. Beatrice Harretche, in particular, used to urge that fifty percent of the personnel in the New York office be from the development field. She also urged that special efforts be made to allow people from countries other than the United States to apply. Some of the American Board members were concerned that people from other countries would have "only the framework of their own country" and argued against "regionalism"—a view that is not uncommon in the United States, where we often forget that we are as much a product of our own cultural framework, as are people from elsewhere.

8

COMING TO MATURITY

"Affiliates learn from each other"

DURING THE FIRST five years of WWB, we were placing emphasis on identifying our colleagues and leadership, creating structure, and sorting out what WWB could be. The second half of the decade was dedicated to agreeing on management policies, achieving a balance between capital development and fund-raising, building unified trust among all members of a fast-growing movement and institution, and praying that we could become self-supporting. Obviously this process created real tensions. As we moved forward, and worked out solutions to unexpected problems and misunderstood issues, many of us gained increasing trust in, and commitment to, a future for Women's World Banking.

We always were aware of the need for new and changing tools that would help support the affiliates directly. To avoid becoming overly dependent on donors, some members explored possible directions that were available to WWB, namely a profit-generating component. In terms of fund-raising, at a 1984 Finance Committee Meeting, we had decided to focus on "attracting big donors and substantial gifts, because the cost of small fund-raising (five thousand to ten thousand dollars) is prohibitive and does not justify the results." However, fund-raising from major donors made the notion of "independence" become increasingly important. We drafted a "self-reliance policy statement" to clarify and solidify the philosophy, function, and raison d'être of WWB, and to serve "as a guideline for everyone in the WWB movement so that in presenting our organization to both potential donors and beneficiaries we express a common vision and a coherent, shared understanding of WWB's purpose."

We were developing the idea of Women's World Enterprise (WWE) as a commercial entity (sometimes referred as a program-related investment or a social enterprise) to: a) provide services and training to a wider range of businesses which could benefit from a broader service product. . . ; b) enlarge on the objectives and potential of WWB as it currently exists; c) differentiate WWB from other similar not-for-profit and public sector entities, which appear to serve the same markets as WWB; and d) provide an additional source of revenue to move WWB towards self-sufficiency. . . [as well as] training tools, including a handbook on international trade, a basic business handbook, and a compilation of stories with case studies of grass-roots entrepreneurs, their problems and successes.

These discussions sparked concern among some of the Board members about the impact of undertaking any for-profit activity, and created what I continue to regard as a healthy tension between the need to keep the focus on low-income women entrepreneurs while also creating a viable organization to support our efforts. In minutes from a January 1986 Executive Committee meeting, **Geertje Lycklama** stressed *"the need to protect the quality of SWWB and not allow it to be corrupted with commercial activities."*

By 1986, there were twenty-seven WWB affiliates worldwide, and the Capital Fund had more than three million dollars. There were different levels of government and corporate support, often earmarked for specific affiliates and regions. So balancing these technical and financial issues was a constant challenge. The advent of new technologies added yet another level of need for training and expertise across the organization. For example, one company donated small-business technology and new computers to affiliates in the Dominican Republic and Haiti and to the Africa Regional Office, which, of course, raised new concerns about how to do the same for other members of the network.

When we met with Ela Bhatt in 2011, she described an experience of the apprehension with which new technology was sometimes received.

Ela Bhatt

In the fall of 1984 Martha Stuart came with a great many suitcases. The local people did not know the best agricultural methods, and Martha believed she could use video to train them. I thought this new technology was not going to work very well. But Martha went ahead and, as the women watched the videos, I could see that they were learning. So technology could help these women, who had little education. But later, when I learned that Martha had taken a lot of videos and was going to edit them down, I became very upset. I thought, "This will not be the truth," because whoever does the edit decides what is shown. Martha told me not to worry. "It's like the difference between a butcher and a surgeon; whoever holds the knife determines the truth."

One of the FWWB (Friends of Women's World Banking) women who could not read or write became the filmmaker whose final product was presented in the Upper House of the Indian government. (Martha died in 1985.)

WWB's rapid growth required new tools for management and communications. To make sure we were all on the same page, we needed to hear from the affiliates more regularly. That proved to be a challenge, based on the workload of the staff and the irregular completion and transmission of status reports.

In advance of our 1986 Global Meeting in Rio de Janeiro, Ramesh Bhatt spent six weeks with WWB in New York to help develop a self-assessment survey. We hoped that this survey would provide the basis for an open and honest discussion about our strengths, weaknesses, and needs at our Rio meeting, where we were also introducing a draft affiliation agreement for the first time.

In a letter to participants prior to the Rio meeting, I wrote, "I pray it will help us know each other better, trust each other more and understand better how to help ourselves and our colleagues move ahead in our effort to create more local empowerment and control over our own productive energies and benefits."

Many Rio participants felt we achieved our goals. **Chris Weiss**, of our West Virginia affiliate, noted in her meeting evaluation that "*the exchange with affiliates was especially valuable, and I feel strengthened in my sense of community with other women of the world. . . and would like to visit the affiliates.*" For some affiliates however, there was dismay that not all had a chance to present their work. One of the participants lamented the lack of time for affiliate presentations.

In addition to our formal meetings in Rio, we visited the favellas (settlements of shacks), the banks, and also the beach! I invited my nephew James to accompany me to Rio as a volunteer intern. He was stunned when we stepped off the plane to be met and interviewed by the Brazilian press. Throughout the week, he became so enthusiastic about WWB that he later went on to help publish the memorable book, *Women at Work—Unity in Diversity*, for our 1990 Global Meeting in Atlanta. (I cannot describe the loss I felt over James's death in April 2011.)

As we left Rio, I felt conflicted: On one hand, I felt renewed enthusiasm about my commitment to organize WWB as an institution in support of a movement, not a "top-down" directorate. On the other, I had real concerns about how to meet our management and capital needs. The sense of urgency stemming from the Global Meeting and the Trustees' meeting in Rio motivated us to assure that the staffing of WWB would be strengthened and that training and learning, based on the varied stages of growth and experience within our network, would be implemented at the soonest.

With regard to training, we contracted Klaas Molenaar, who was with Triodos Bank, to work with Margarita Guzmán representing WWB. We had a clear concept of what the training would do and how it would operate initially.

> The pilot Management Training Institute is designed for the affiliates with programs to learn and to produce management tools at the same time. This will not be a standard textbook training, but will be tailor-made to fit the needs of WWB affiliates. Each affiliate attending the course will do a case study before the course in order to bring their collective experience to the training. The affiliates chosen have active programs and have been through many stages of development. The idea is to build examples out of their experiences, while strengthening areas of weakness (such as strategic planning.)

> The Initial training course will run for three weeks. At the end of a five–six month period following the course, there will be a follow-up visit to each participant.

After all the visits are complete, the entire groups will come back together and finalize a syllabus based on the lessons learned.

Klaas Molenaar

I had presented a proposal for organizational development based on personal development, and Michaela said she loved the idea. There were twenty-two women on average in every program and typically one man (me).

The idea behind the training sessions was that the affiliates would learn from each other—from their peers, and then move on as they advanced. It was important to build confidence and learn how to transfer authority. We managed to put the examples in a broader perspective and favored an open way of learning by discussion. People like Paul Mackay explained the philosophy behind Triodos Bank and how TB had been able to implement it in the Netherlands. The sessions were also a very important lifeline for WWB, because if the network of WWB wanted to survive it had to render service to its members. The affiliates appreciated that the WWB hub was offering something that was useful—their initial attitude was often that WWB wasn't offering them enough. . . . It also enabled them to learn from other affiliates. We conducted the program in different languages: English in the Netherlands, Spanish in Chile, and "Portuñol" in Brazil.

Working with only female participants, I witnessed how in some instances they help each other out more than in a male group, but in other cases they can be ruthless in telling each other to deal with any problems they had. Some of the younger participants experienced cultural shock. I remember a lady from Uganda who had never been abroad before and whose luggage didn't arrive. The Latin American participants took her to buy new dresses and makeup—when she came back to the workshop, she looked like she had transformed into a mature woman—there were small things like that, that you never expect to happen. It was a personal development process, as well as a professional learning process. In terms of the outcome, we frequently met resistance from Board members of affiliates who didn't want the managers to have their own ideas and become more independent as a result of the exposure they received through the programs. The training program also had a broader impact, in that it inspired Triodos Bank to get into micro. Rudolf Mees had really understood the importance of it, if TB wanted to gain an international reach.

It also impacted my own career. Facet, my company, never would have been created had it not been for my work with WWB. TB is also now a major shareholder of Facet. Because of those training sessions, I let go of my other work, and got to see how the WWB network became stronger.

All of the courses had moments of creativity or fun to break up the seriousness. We would go out to eat after the day's work, and a participant from Guadeloupe ordered the biggest ice cream the restaurant had—so the waiter came with ice cream in a vase, and she actually finished it!

On one occasion, one of the Indian participants representing SEWA, who had never been abroad before, suggested that Peter Blom and I do a dance in sarongs! On another occasion, I had to do a male striptease behind a white curtain. Margarita and I did all the training sessions together, three times in the Netherlands in 1987, once in Chile in 1988. We visited all the affiliates—they were crazy trips—with Margarita Guzmán, Ann Duval, myself, and Peter Blom visiting five or six countries in two weeks, as far away as Thailand, Ghana, Guadeloupe, the US, etc. In Ghana, Ann Duval wanted to pay with a credit card in the hotel, and the hotel had never seen a credit card.

There was a moment when I decided to stop the program, because we had been successful, and they could run it themselves. I never regretted that decision. We had grown too close to each other; the contact was too easy; it became too much fun—that wasn't the purpose of the exercise. I changed a lot in training style. I started to look differently at women and also learned that I would never allow a board to be comprised only of women. Women are more open, but there are always fights going on; they don't know how to say "sorry," drink a beer, and forget it.

During our interview with Margarita Guzmán, she agreed with Klaas's assessment and elaborated further.

Margarita Guzmán

The idea was to generate a mechanism that would allow the participants to work together for three weeks and gain the tools to do follow-up on their own, implementing what they had learned from each other. There were participants from all continents. Out of it emerged people who would be very important for the future of the network, such as Jennifer Riria. We got to see who was really committed and tried to help give them the support they needed to succeed. Many of the participants had never traveled before, and it was a cultural shock for them to leave their countries and be exposed to foreign countries. I remember a young woman from India who was engaged in an arranged marriage and who was amazed to be in a society where people chose their husbands or wives for emotional reasons. There were some challenges, such as language barriers (there were some Honduran participants at the first session in the Netherlands who didn't speak English, so we had to stay up late to translate the day's proceedings to them), or emotional issues that came up—being Dutch, Klaas didn't always understand the way in which women from other regions reacted to certain circumstances. We always maintained a coherent methodology, no matter where the sessions were held. Eventually we felt we could run the program ourselves.

In our 2009 interview with Peter Blom, executive director of Triodos Bank, he described his role in this training.

Peter Blom

WWB asked us to organize training for their affiliates, as we had been through the phase of creating a bank in a professional way and could provide that experience and know-how. In those days, I traveled to many affiliates around the world, contributing to this training course. The affiliates were very motivated, and I was impressed by their dedication to the cause of making it possible for women to have access to credit and build their own lives. It was much broader than just banking; it was really about helping women to develop.

However, one challenge that struck me was that in many countries, as soon as someone became a more professional woman in banking, she would get a nice job in another bank, and WWB was at times like a training center for other banks. At first I thought, "Why are those women doing that?" and then I understood, traveling around, that their families were highly dependent and as professional women, it wasn't just their children they had to provide income for, but also for their large extended family. So they were not always able to commit to the lesser pay they would receive at one of the WWB affiliates. Consequently, the affiliates were in a constant search for new women—I think that has changed now. There was an upside, because they appreciated what they learned through WWB and were inclined to bring that learning to their work in other banks, helping those institutions that were traditionally more conservative become more sensitive to this new group of clients, including women. Indirectly, we also helped many of the communities that these women came from, by enabling the women to become generators of good jobs for others.

Training and exchange have remained an intrinsic part of WWB since 1986. In a 2011 correspondence, Ana-Maria Giblen, a sociologist and WWB program officer from 1986 to 1988 who first learned about WWB in her hometown of Lima, Peru, recalled her experiences visiting affiliates in Latin America.

Ana-Maria Giblen

My job was to organize and develop affiliates to assist them to make maximum impact in helping their respective societies. Before I stepped foot in a plane, I had to immerse myself in the history and culture of each country and affiliate organization. This meant reading the complete files covering the past seven-plus years, supplemented by many phone calls, though this was sometimes tricky, given the extremely rural locations in some countries. With this knowledge, I then sought to forge an intimate relationship with each affiliate and affiliate-in-formation. This demanding prep work paid off nicely for WWB, I believe. Ultimately, I felt I had first-rate colleagues, as well as special friends, all over the world.

My first trip was to the Dominican Republic (DR) and Haiti in December 1987. ADOPEM in the DR had early success and attracted the funding interest of the progressive governments. However, there was a tendency, which we had to combat, of growing too quickly and "force-feeding" loans and expansion on entrepreneurs before they could manage it. This potential pitfall was to become a pivotal challenge of microfinancing everywhere, as the concept and sponsoring entities expanded. More successful than many later microfinance entities, we did it right by building the right foundations and building gradually from the grass roots in a manner properly attuned to the culture.

So, for example, the special long-distance friendship I forged with ADOPEM's Mercedes Canalda prior to our meetings enabled us to function quite effectively during my limited stay. [In one instance, she convinced the affiliate about the importance of working together with other affiliates to build a global institution.] *The DR's neighbor Haiti represents a very different culture and language, yet my visit there accomplished the desired results because of thorough preparation. In a 1988 trip to Latin America, my knowledge of the affiliates and their different cultures—in this case aided by my having grown up in Peru and other South American countries—allowed me to surmount long and hard obstacles and get the affiliates on a healthy growth path. As a representative of WWB, I was honored to be given Keys to the City for Santa Cruz, Bolivia, the second-largest city in the nation.*

Ela Dec ran a WWB-inspired program in Poland, Women in Rural Enterprise Development. Ela shared her experience with training during a 2010 interview.

Ela Dec

I was working at the Foundation for the Development of Agriculture, which had been started by David Rockefeller in late '80s. My director gave me three options of programs I could develop, and one was a micro-lending operation for women. I said, "Why not?" Michaela came a month later. It was 1991, and women in Poland, especially in the rural areas, were going through a difficult process. The economy was upside-down and women were usually the first to lose their jobs. Women in general were much better-educated than men and were always more eager to do things, but there were no laws to protect them. Our program was designed to provide micro loans and technical assistance, training, and advisory services to rural women to help them start and develop their small businesses.

There were no examples within the region, so I was sent to the US, then to Cali, Colombia, to sit with Margarita Guzmán and visit micro-lending programs there. It was very helpful. I learned a great deal and realized that if you look at a micro-entrepreneur in Poland and a micro-entrepreneur in Colombia, India, or in the US, their education might not be the same, but they know how to count, they know what profit they're going to make if they borrow a certain amount of money, they know what the risks are and how to develop their business. They're the same people in different clothes. Based on that exposure, I had a slight idea of what I would do, but still, it was developed on the spot, and I learned as I went along. As a city person working in the rural areas, I had to think twice about what I should tell the women, how should I dress and behave. I had to build a level of trust.

I organized a conference to introduce women in Poland to the idea of entrepreneurship and access to credit. Michaela and Margarita helped. In general the women were ready. They came from all over Poland and were mostly community leaders. The problem was getting them to believe there was an opportunity specifically for them, because they weren't used to having a program designed for women only. As soon as they got the idea, the women became our ambassadors. It was not a huge program, but in the community it had a significant impact and it was a huge empowerment for local leaders.

I joined the SWWB Board in 1996. The program I ran was housed within an organization, and didn't fulfill the requirements of becoming a full Women's World Banking affiliate. We had a male director, most of the Board members were male, and we had other programs within the foundation. However, I became part of the WWB network, which was really beneficial, because we had access to

Women's World Banking members who came and helped us with all kinds of issues. The whole process was very interesting. It was incredible to visit the businesses that were funded by us and see them grow and meet the children who were supported as a result. . . . The program was so "sexy" that the foundation didn't want to let it go and become independent, and so I eventually decided to leave.

The personal experiences of being exposed to other cultures that came out of the global meetings and exchange programs marked participants in significant ways. Deanna Rosenswig's personal memories indicate the kind of impact that these trips had on individuals.

Deanna Rosenswig

Memorable moments at WWB were those global meetings where you had two hundred women from all over the world all dressed up to dance and sing at night. Going to meetings all day, being serious trying to fix the problems, but at night we were just people enjoying each other. I have a memory of myself dressed up in an African woman's outfit, not only was she African, but she was six feet tall— Mary Okelo. I wore her dress tied up with her pap. On another occasion, I remember going to India and going into a house, where a mother was making clothes, and of course we took off our shoes. I don't know why but I was wearing high heels; I came out and all the little girls in the village were walking around in my high heels. I remember those things, the shared experiences with other women in the world. Or standing in China, waiting for a train with Ela Bhatt. There was a Chinese woman knitting, and Ela just took the needles and started to finish knitting. Those were special times in my life.

The 1987 trip to China mentioned by Deanna was an exchange program at the invitation of the All China Women's Federation, for a twenty-member delegation of women from WWB and other women's organizations. The trip was special because of Wang Ying, our English-speaking guide, who subsequently moved to the United States and became part of the WWB network.

Wang Ying

I remember WWB and you as President and Founder were introduced to the All China Women's Federation (ACWF) by the Chinese Embassy/NY General Consulate. We sent the official invitation to you. Your delegation came.

A highlight of the trip was a dinner hosted by the chairwoman of the Central Bank at the People's Hall in Tiananmen Square. The China trip was an open door to a new culture, a new geography, lots of fun, talking, and time to think in new ways. I began to question my ability to manage an organization that had experienced such a leap in its scope and management needs, along with the persistent dilemma of "never enough money." Did WWB require more "management" than I had the energy to provide? This led me to begin thinking seriously about transitions in leadership and, specifically, how and when I would make the transition from my role as president of Women's World Banking. I had no experience in understanding the implications of a change of leadership and the impact it would have on the organization and its future. It would be two more years before I would go before the Board to present my intention not to renew my contract.

In 1988, we submitted a "Proposal for WWB Affiliates to Examine Alternative Credit Programs" to the Ford Foundation, in collaboration with the Institute for Social Studies in The Hague, where Geertje Lycklama was based. The proposal was geared to raise funds for an on-site visit for WWB affiliates to meet with founding members of the Self Employed Women's Association (SEWA) in India and the Grameen Bank in Bangladesh. SEWA and Grameen had received worldwide acclaim for their innovative approaches to meeting the credit needs of their constituencies. The proposal explained how our principles of affiliates' autonomy, coupled with learning and exchanges, underpinned our efforts. By December 1987, thirty-three affiliates were legally registered, and twenty-nine others were in various stages of formation.

The proposal stated:

> WWB functions in a noncompetitive manner and is anxious to cooperate with other intermediaries and institutions, whether they be in the government, nonprofit or private sector. . . . WWB seeks to facilitate the process of meeting the needs of women entrepreneurs while never seeking to control that process or the direct or indirect beneficiaries of that process; WWB operates only through participating local intermediaries and affiliates, which maintain their own independent ownership, autonomy, and integrity; WWB is committed to keeping the authority and decisions at the community level where people understand the financial and economic realities faced by small business in their local area. . . .
>
> Although promoting access to credit is one of the cornerstones of successful small enterprises, it is recognized that credit alone is not a panacea for development. . . . Recent socioeconomic research clearly demonstrates the linkages between direct assistance to women and the development of self-reliant national development strategies. . . . The office of WWB/New York, WWB's coordinating center, operates primarily to help affiliates organize themselves. The working methods of the office are sensitive to the needs of the affiliates; it responds to the expressed needs of the affiliates. It sees its role primarily as one of giving ideas, and arranging for the exchange of experiences through networking and improved communication. Networking has been explicitly adopted as a WWB objective. Also, care has been taken to retain the dynamics and authenticity of the process: the main watchwords are dialogue, trust, decentralization, and flexibility, and the nature of WWB/NY's support operations is continually evolving. The need for effective management is clear. Without a better understanding of business-management techniques, the impact of the

WWB-CHINA TRIP—DINNER WITH THE PRESIDENT OF CENTRAL BANK

loan programs will be reduced. However traditional business school, classroom training is not effective in the environments in which WWB operates; therefore new techniques must evolve out of local circumstances and through shared experiences of local affiliates.

We received the grant. Geertje Lycklama, representing the WWB Board of Trustees, agreed to lead the delegation of representatives from WWB-Brazil (Lucia Souza-Castro), WWB-the Gambia (Njoba Faye), WWB-Ghana (Comfort Engmann), WWB-Cali (Margarita Guzmán), WWB-Kenya (John Makyo-Swande); WWB-Uganda (Cissy Kwoba-Abungu); and WWB-New York (Ana Maria Giblen). Geertje Lycklama recalled her impressions of the visit.

Geertje Lycklama

I served on the SWWB board from '84 to '88. One of the most interesting things I did with WWB was towards the end of my term, from January to February 1988, when I went with a group of women from Africa to visit the Grameen Bank and SEWA (Self-Employed Women's Association)—both very exciting banking institutions, very different from one another, and interesting to study. . . . It was helpful that coming from the West, one wasn't there to tell the affiliates what to do, but instead to create opportunities for them to learn from each other, and from other banks, such as Grameen and SEWA, that were well-established by then. I had already encouraged that approach in my first policy paper in the ministry, suggesting that it was important to foster learning across borders within developing countries, so people could benefit from each other's experiences.

Of course, every country involved had its own history, background, and legislation. So the affiliates all developed their own forms according to what was appropriate for their environment, and the New York Board didn't have much of a grip on that, which was also very correct, because if people want economic independence, they have to find a way to attain it in their own setting.

Based on a trip report by **Comfort Engmann** of WWB-Ghana, the WWB 1988 Annual Donor Report included the following summary of participants' impressions.

> The three-day program prepared by SEWA provided an excellent opportunity to gain insight into how SEWA is conceptualized as part of the trade-union movement, the cooperative movement, and the feminist movement. Participants were most impressed by the fact that these women, who face seemingly insurmountable obstacles such as poverty, illiteracy, and lack of protective labor laws, have been able to build a bank of their own. The bank offers the unique service of visiting the members' places of employment to facilitate depositing money; the women can also easily reach SEWA's headquarters.
>
> Another unique feature of SEWA Bank is that it is a full-scale bank, owned and managed by women. All participants were very impressed with the high loan-recovery rate and believe that all the WWB affiliates can learn much from SEWA's procedures.
>
> At the Grameen Bank in Bangladesh, participants were impressed by the integrated and holistic approach taken in dealing with the target population. Although the focus is on the poor, and the whole life and work situation of the loan receiver is taken into account, the atmosphere is businesslike, and nothing is free. There is close cooperation between the bank workers and the client. An important observation was made that the approach of the Grameen Bank shows that changes can be made through local resources and without outside "experts." Saving is compulsory, and the loan-recovery rate is very high because of institutionalized mechanisms of social control and peer-group pressure.
>
> The participants agreed that this learning experience enhanced management capacity, allowed for the transfer of information and problem-solving among affiliates, and built confidence. Each participating affiliate had recently initiated or planned to initiate credit schemes. Participants gained creative insights and practical solutions to deal with planning, management, and banking issues related to serving their clients. Each representative identified concrete steps for the implementation of new programs in the area of leadership development and rural

credit access and confidence-building in their local affiliate. As one participant said, *"Now that I have seen this, I will not give up, but will continue the struggle to build credit facilities for women with the help of WWB."* Another participant stated, *"Some of the things I thought were impossible I see happening here."*

Ana-Maria Giblen, who participated in the visit, representing the New York office, recalls her impressions.

Ana-Maria Giblen

In Ahmedabad, a large city in northwest India, SEWA inspired our visiting affiliate representatives by showing how a loan as small as ten dollars had made a real difference in the life of a family and was repaid on time, with heartfelt pride. We visited women working in the outdoor markets and in their hamlets and sat with them while they spun fabric or made incense or rice to sell. Nevertheless, while proud to help women help themselves in India, so much more work remained to be done. A stark reminder of this was the airport scene in India, where an unstaffed immigration queue for "females, handicapped, and the mentally ill" kept us waiting for hours, while men were sailing through their own line.

The 1988 SWWB Board of Trustees meeting was hosted in Kuala Lumpur by Nellie Tan Wong, who had launched and managed the WWB affiliate in Malaysia, WINTRAC (Women in Trade and Commerce), since the early '80s. She had been urging us to get a regional representative in Asia, a role that she volunteered to assume. During our stay in Malaysia, we visited Malay and Chinese villages, met with the president and various members of the Central Bank in what was then emerging as a very strong economy in South-East Asia. Nellie Tan Wong wished to host a WWB-Asia Regional Meeting in Malaysia to enable greater communication among WWB affiliates in Asia. This became the subject of much correspondence and contention, as the proposed meeting was delayed to 1990. The meeting would coincide with the WWB Global Meeting, which all affiliates were invited to attend. I felt strongly that, as important as the regional meetings were, the global meetings were indispensable for keeping the worldwide movement alive. My position was perceived as undermining the region's autonomy. Respecting local/regional autonomy while staying connected to the vision of the whole required a delicate balance, and members were not always on the same page.

Ann Partlow, a trustee who joined the board at the Malaysia meeting shared her memories.

Ann Partlow

It was the first time that I met women from all over the world. I was in awe of these professional women who were so interesting and of the way WWB brought them together to help motivate small business in their respective country. I probably didn't say a word the whole meeting, and just sat there listening and taking it all in. I remember all the emotion because I think there were tears before the meeting was over. My business experience was almost entirely in the male world—there were hardly any women. To witness all these professional women with a charitable agenda was amazing. I recall how much organization was involved in preparing the meeting. Michaela's niece Katherine was very efficiently helping to get things done. The whole atmosphere was so different.

From Malaysia, Nancy Barry, my niece Katherine, and I, went on to Indonesia to visit the KUPEDES village savings-and-loan program that Richard Patten had designed with support from the World Bank. This program had proven to be one of the most (if not the most) efficient micro-lending programs on record and had a major influence on the health of Indonesia's National Agricultural Bank during the near collapse of the South-East Asian economy.

During a previous visit to Indonesia in 1984, a Ford Foundation friend introduced me to an American woman with an Indonesian name who resided in Jakarta, spoke the local language, and was studying indigenous economies. She represented, for me, one of the truly devoted development professionals that I had ever met. She later worked with WWB in the lead-up to the 1995 UN Women's Meeting in Beijing (the twenty-year review of the first UN Conference on Women). She was Ann Dunham, President Barack Obama's mother.

9

END OF AN ERA

"This was a turning point in my life."

AS MY TIME at the helm of WWB was coming to an end, we were examining the progress we had made from both social and economic perspectives. I summarized my thoughts in a May 19, 1989, letter to the trustees (see p. 131.)

In the summer of 1988, I was invited by Bradford Morse, president of the Salzburg Seminar (and former administrator of UNDP), to serve as faculty, along with professors from Harvard Business School, about entrepreneurship for developing countries programs. I invited one of my oldest friends, Kay Lawrence, to the 1989 Salzburg meeting, as she had always been one of my biggest supporters but had never been to a WWB event. It was at that meeting that I met Tony Kaminski from Warsaw, who put me in touch with Diana Medman. Several years later, Diana became the founder of WWB-Russia and an SWWB trustee.

Because 1989 would mark ten years since WWB's incorporation, Brad arranged for us to host SWWB's 1989 Board meeting at the Salzburg Seminar. I encouraged Sylvia Chin to attend the meeting, hoping that she would become interested in joining the Board. She remembers.

Sylvia Chin

Michaela asked if I'd be interested in becoming a Board member. I was honored and speechless. I said, "Yes. What does it involve?" She said, "Why don't you come to the annual meeting?" It was going to be in Salzburg. It was an amazing meeting, held at the Salzburg Institute, in the Schloss Leopoldskron, the location for filming the exterior scenes of The Sound of Music. *The only reason they didn't film the interior there was because it was small. The place was gorgeous, full of mirrors and gold chandeliers. We had dinner there after the Board meeting. Many members were there with their children. I had brought along my husband and two-year-old. We stayed at a bed and breakfast close by, since there weren't a lot of rooms. They came along for dinner. Everybody ended up singing and dancing—it was really magical. I remember it being an intense meeting with many different issues being discussed.*

From my perspective, much of it was over my head, because I didn't come from a development-policy background. There were a lot of acronyms. It was extremely interesting to see how each Board member was dedicated to reviewing financial statements. There was also great interest in discussing overall economic policy and its effect in different jurisdictions. I did not particularly realize how different an environment it would be from what I was accustomed to. It was very consensus-building, compared to more male-dominated meetings. There was a lot less grandstanding and in some cases, more passion.

It was at the Salzburg meeting that I informed the trustees that I would not seek a renewal of my contract upon its expiration on August 31, 1990. I promised to advise the Board of my choice for a successor in advance of our 1990 Global Meeting in Atlanta. Perhaps the Board didn't believe I would really step down in 1990. Some of us have different recollections about what unfolded during that transition period and how it could or should have been handled. (Over the years, I have often heard how difficult any transition in leadership is, whether in families, or in organizations, and that chaos remains until new leadership has been accepted.) In hindsight, it is clear that our failure to formalize a nomination/appointment process led to much confusion.

WWB was at a crossroads at many levels. Beyond the question of who would lead the organization going forward, there was a need to evaluate WWB's activities and determine what aspects of the organization required strengthening or modification. We were further motivated by the donors' desire for a formal evaluation that would validate their support of Women's World Banking throughout its first decade. Remembering that we started without a business plan and charted new territory, we didn't have clear benchmarks to measure our progress or a fixed notion of where the organization needed to focus for the following decade.

We hired Develop Finance Consultants, Limited (DFC) to conduct an independent analysis of WWB, including affiliates worldwide. The mandate and salient points of the assessment are worth noting, especially because the report generated controversy among our Board members. (See excerpts from the report, p. 315.)

The Board discussions based on the DFC Ten-Year Assessment brought to the fore many of the concerns that we had been grappling with from the outset.

The following quotes from our Executive Committee and European Regional Coordination meeting, which was held at the NMB Bank in Amsterdam (November 1–2, 1989), shed light on the depth of our discussions.

Michaela Walsh pointed out that she had not been interviewed by DFC, and emphasized that an important issue about the DFC report was the *"imbalance in the report between WWB as an organization and as a movement—the latter is not addressed."*

Nancy Barry drafted an overview of the assessment and identified issues for our attention. She noted a *"false dichotomy between whether WWB should focus on 'poor women,' or on 'entrepreneurial women.'"* She also pointed to *"trade-off decisions. . . . recognizing the inherent tension between deepening and broadening an organization such as WWB."*

Floris Bannier commented that, with regard to trade-off decisions, it was a question of *"principle versus organizational constraints."*

```
MEMO:     Trustees
FROM:     Michaela Walsh
DATE:     May 19, 1989
SUBJ:     GROUP DISCUSSION - LEADERSHIP
```

I think it is accurate to say that WWB has grown way beyond any of our dreams. Since 1975, it has maintained: a steady growth with no major failures; an honest and clean financial history; an increasing sense of institutional identity; and, a continued development of a management system that struggles to be efficient with a minimal budget and staff. It has done this without compromising our cornerstone - to be a global financial intermediary, functioning through a decentralized non-hierarchical management structure.

It is essential that WWB begin to define (in more specific terms) the criteria it applies in its selection of Leadership - for Trustees and for its President. It is also important that we understand the difficult process of change. Due to its phenomenal growth and unique mission, WWB has been experiencing real change during the past two years, and most probably, this trend will continue for the next two years. As we move from an idea to a viable global institution, I see this as a major opportunity for all of us.

The Assessment and Partners' Review of WWB (which is still <u>in process)</u> will determine WWB's viability as a financial institute. This assessment should also shed some wisdom on WWB's future choices and direction, and its ability to influence the type of leadership WWB will want for the future.

The level of enthusiasm of the WWB Network has accelerated during the past year, and I believe this will continue throughout the Tenth Anniversary 1990 celebration. I expect this will create greater expectations from our member affiliates, more growth in our core businesses, and new opportunities for collaboration with others.

Last year, a large number of the original Trustees and Founders of WWB left the Board (1/3 of the Trustees' terms expired). Next year, another 1/3 of that group will also terminate their terms of office. This means that a new generation of Trustee Leadership will begin.

It is clear to me that the Board is facing some major issues, which need to be openly addressed in its discussion:

1) The WWB/NY office has always been maintained by a minimum staff and budget. Part of this may have been possible because of my own entrepeneural style and energy.

BOT/89/IX.1

MEMO FROM MICHAELA WALSH TO WWB TRUSTEES, MAY 19, 1989

However, as I take on new roles and relinquish responsibility for the management of WWB/NY, it has become very clear to me that one person cannot "do it all." The potential for "burn-out" by anyone in the WWB/NY environment, as it is currently designed, is a very real issue. WWB/NY simply needs to be more efficient -which means more people, more space, more equipment - a larger budget.

2)   The new Regional Coordination Committee will be a major contribution to WWB. I feel strongly that once it is functioning, it will be the basis of WWB's future growth. However, the implications of identifying management and supervisory staff for these locations need to be understood by the Trustees and their ideas shared with WWB/NY and the Coordinators.

In August, 1990, my five-year contract as President is set to expire. This means that WWB has had the full-time leadership of one of its founders for ten years. I am proud of our accomplishments but I also recognize that the management of an institution and the development of an institution requires different skills, talents, and perceived priorities. Prior to the termination or renewal of my contract, I feel very strongly that the Trustees should consider the criteria they feel is important for any leader.

These are all fundamental changes, which will continue to influence WWB's development. During the next few years, new opportunities and new problems will continue to surface. However, as I see it, the major fundamental change is that we have been and will continue moving from a Dictatorship into a Democracy at least throughout my term of office. To that end, the issue that needs to be addressed is how do we develop a procedure which will assure that:

1)   The Trustees sets criteria for the selection of their own membership.

2)   The Trustees begin to define the criteria for the type of leadership they want from a President.

Once we begin to define the skills we need; we can begin to clarify the criteria for the people we need to create a strong leadership team to guide WWB during the next six years.

BOT/89/IX.1

Ann Duval, who had been working with WWB as an assistant administrator and later as a vice president, and worked closely with DFC, found the report useful and noted that *"without a strong institutional base, the movement will not continue to grow."* She was not in favor of *"letting a thousand flowers bloom"* when there were challenges surfacing within the existing network.

Margarita Guzmán stated, *"DFC has ignored the regional management aspect of WWB and has not dealt with affiliates as independent institutions with their own assets."*

Margarita's insight underscored a common misconception about WWB. This perception was reinforced by some of the affiliates as well. As **Deanna Rosenswig** pointed out, many of the affiliates saw WWB *"as a donor organization and see themselves as the recipients of services rather than part of the organization."*

A missing element in the report, as Margarita noted, was that it did not give *"an indication of how the clients themselves perceive WWB."* **Mary Okelo** agreed, and noted that *"DFC has used a different yardstick than what women themselves use."* **Nancy Barry** concurred, noticing that *"even after the Executive Committee wrote to DFC about this, they refused to comment on the qualitative side of WWB."* This, too, was characteristic of a trend—whereas in the early days there was space for qualitative measures of success, by the end of the 1980s, donors had become clearly focused on numbers.

The DFC observed that

> The Loan Guarantee program, which WWB initiated in 1982, was a unique approach to opening up women's access to credit and allowed WWB to differentiate itself among the funded organizations. Over time, however, similar credit schemes have become widely accepted as an integral part of development-assistance programs. The fact that the WWB approach is no longer unique has meant greater competition for donor funds. . . .

Michaela noted that it should be recalled that the Loan Guarantee Program was designed as a tool to educate and provide access—*not* to be *the* credit program or to generate income.

Whoever would lead WWB going forward required the skills to navigate in an increasingly competitive environment. Strong leadership and the ability to secure funding were matters of survival. Our efforts to be self-sustaining by developing a for-profit component of WWB hadn't yet taken off.

Early in 1990, based on a commitment to advise the trustees of my recommendation for a successor, I went to Washington, D.C., to meet with Nancy Barry and ask her if she would agree to be the nominee. My recollection is that Nancy replied that she wasn't yet ready to leave the World Bank. Nancy does not recall my asking her whether she was interested in assuming the presidency. Recent conversations with four of the trustees confirm that each of them knew that I had approached Nancy Barry prior to approaching Mary Okelo, who was then at the African Development Bank (ADB).

In a recent interview with Mary, she also remembered my telling her that I had approached Nancy, who was not available for the role. As special adviser to the president of the African Development Bank, Mary informed her boss, Babacar N'Diaye, about her nomination. He was enthusiastic about what Mary's leadership of WWB would represent for Africa.

At the March Executive Committee meeting in New York before our 1990 Atlanta Global Meeting, I circulated a memo recommending Mary Okelo for the presidency. Then Nancy Barry said she, too, was prepared to stand. It was an awkward situation.

Following the Executive Committee meeting, I was trying to delegate more responsibility to management and staff in New York and in the regional offices. Ann Duval, who had started out as my assistant, had been elected vice president for operations, and began assuming a stronger voice with regard to WWB programs. She and I had very different points of view about WWB's priorities vis-à-vis institutional management or network development, which, combined with the question of succession, affected the staff's strong sense of being a team. According to the input from staff members in their recent interviews, they felt this tension undermined the organization's ability to embody its ideals. Ultimately, this led to Ann Duval's resignation prior to our Global Meeting in Atlanta.

I also put energy into thinking about a new investment fund—Women's World Growth Fund—which was never launched.

Ann Partlow, who had joined the Board in 1988, remembered the environment in the office.

Ann Partlow

I remember Ann Duval complained about management issues, disorganization, and managerial process. I thought it was strange that the Board took her very seriously and I thought took her side. She was creating a huge stir about how badly the place was managed. I felt I had very little knowledge of what was really going on, and I didn't know at the time that Michaela had already indicated that she wouldn't renew her contract. But almost everyone else seemed to feel that Ann Duval was right in her judgment that there was a need for change. It appeared that she wanted to position herself for the presidency but somehow others decided she was not the one.

I personally focused more and more energy on the planning, which started in Salzburg, for our 1990 Global Meeting. It was to be a major celebration—ten years since the initial meeting in Amsterdam—as well as a significant transition of leadership for WWB. This, combined with coping with my own process of departure from a position in which I had invested all of my dreams, time, and energy for so long, clearly had me functioning on emotional overdrive.

Once we determined to hold the 1990 meeting in Atlanta, we contracted Zuzu Tabatabai to act as coordinator. She and her colleagues named the meeting "Give Women Credit," and were successful in arranging for Atlanta Mayor Andrew Young, who had previously been US ambassador to the UN, to be the keynote speaker at the opening-night dinner. German artist Ursula Schulz-Dornburg designed a beautiful poster for the event titled "Eternal Wheat," which symbolized the fruition of what we had planted a decade before.

Jacqui Williams of the New York office staff remembers the Atlanta meeting.

Jacqui Williams
Preparing the tenth anniversary of WWB was a real challenge, between staff members, consultants and temporary help (mostly young, intelligent relatives of Michaela, friends of Michaela), all of us dedicated and committed to succeed. . . . I can say that our efforts paid off in making the meeting a real success. I had the opportunity to meet all these women from all over the world; some of them I had to help with my knowledge of the French language.

This was a turning point in the life of WWB.

Talk about variety! While in Atlanta, "Madame Sall" from Senegal suffered an accident, and I was asked to accompany her to the hospital, which I did. I had to translate to her whatever the doctor was saying. Her ankle was broken. The shock to her was when the doctor said he was going to put a pink cast on her foot. I thought he was joking until I saw the lady with a pink foot. "What are my children going to say when they see my pink foot?" This is just to say that at Women's World Banking, variety is always present.

Many of my old friends and supporters came to celebrate with me, including Dorothy Lyddon, Kay Lawrence, Genevieve Maxwell, Joan Dunlop, Myrtle Haidar from Beirut and Linda Dietel. My sister Sarah still talks about how sharing a room with Lourdes Lontok Cruz was a lifetime experience for her!

Aside from the "roasting Michaela," some of the highlights for me were John Hammock's acting as emcee; the presence of Marilyn Waring, notable feminist and newly elected MP from New Zealand; Peggy Dulany's luncheon speech; and the moving story of the honorary first borrower of WWB from Cali. I attribute my scattered memories of that meeting to the strong (and sometimes traumatic) emotions I was experiencing, which are apparent to me as I revisit videos of that gathering.

The vision that we shared at the start of WWB, as I had articulated in one of the conversations during our first International Workshop in 1980 in Amsterdam, continued to be realized.

"ETERNAL WHEAT" TENTH ANNIVERSARY POSTER, 1990

At the 1990 meeting, many creative and committed people articulated the power of WWB and what WWB had meant over the decade to individuals, to local organizations, and to women around the world. The following quotes have been selected from four videos, randomly chosen from more than fifty tapes made at the 1990 Give Women Credit Global Meeting, and from the video report of the meeting done by Sara Stuart, who with her mother had filmed the first WWB meeting in 1980.

Michaela Walsh

We have created not so much an institution but access to the capital resources of the world. The last three days show the potential that can come from different economic bases, different cultures, different attitudes, and financial resources. It is important to integrate different attitudes and values. We are looking at something that is not totally definitive. . . some kind of a process, not an institution, breaking down some of the traditional barriers. This is our greatest potential.

Floris Bannier

The strength of Women's World Banking and the strength of each participant is a very fortunate combination of inspiration and common sense. And that makes Women's World Banking very different from a number of other organizations where either the inspiration or the common sense prevails.

Deanna Rosenswig

I didn't know what I was going to in 1980. I was there as a representative of Canada. The meeting opened my eyes to microcredit and the plight of women. I saw this vision of all these women and was awed by its power and intensity. Then Michaela took me under her wing, as she did for many of us. I was transformed. I'm part of an institution or movement that really works, and we can measure it in terms of bottom line achievement, but also through the network. WWB provides a vehicle for successful businesses. Banks can learn a lot from that, as they themselves are seeking different ways of reaching smaller businesses.

You can measure it in terms of true bottom line achievement but much more importantly, we can measure it in terms of the reach. We've created a network of people all around the world who share not only being women, but share the desire and commitment to build this world into a better place, not only for women, but for everyone.

Cissy Kwoba-Abungu

We have a motto which now we call, "never give up." Because we have made the commitment to ourselves, and we wanted it to succeed. Being professionals, we thought there was no reason why we shouldn't pick up this idea, because it had worked elsewhere. It had worked in Canada, in Italy. . . .

Our dream is that after five years, ten years from today, we don't want to be depending on the donors. We don't want to be just a bridge between the poor women and the banks; we think that over time, the women we are supporting are going to become the members, the owners, the directors of the organization.

Sarah Mangli

We have mainly three types of clients: we have those who are dealing in cultivation, we have those who are dealing in livestock keeping, and we have those who are venturing in cottage industries, like food processing and weaving. We provide training, which has turned out to be a very important aspect of our program, because they are low-income women, and need training to implement credit successfully. We have technical assistance, we assist the women in providing feasibility studies and business plans, so we have training, technical assistance, credit, and savings. Even women who have not benefited from us, who have not received any loans, are very much interested in saving with us, because we explain to them in the local language. They don't have to adjust to the official commercial bank atmosphere. Many women can't speak in English. It's difficult to define who is the poorest of the poor. It's better to go to the woman who has already been in business, however small, rather than starting up a business for somebody who has not been in business, because we are not dishing out money, we are in business, and we want our money back with interest.

Nora de Martinez

The secret of our success has been to keep our costs low by having efficient personnel who can manage a considerable number of clients and by carefully selecting women for our program who have strong businesses. This way, there haven't been losses.

Margarita Guzmán

Our education has been structured such that someone tells us what to do. So we are educated to be employees, not entrepreneurs. So if the group that forms the affiliate does not have this innate entrepreneurial spirit, they will fail, because they will feel, "Oh, I can't go to the bank. I can't borrow money, I can't pay interest." But these are all lies. They can go to the bank, yes there is money, yes there are resources in the country, and yes we have talent. We just haven't had a chance to discover it yet.

Nancy Barry

The biggest input as a catalyst that WWB has to offer is giving people concrete visions about how others went through similar stages. There is more in common amongst successful programs than there are differences. Everybody doesn't have to make the same mistakes; we can learn from each other's experiences.

Sylvia Fletcher

In Latin America, we have a very strong regional identification. We have a lot of diversity, yet there are so many ties that link us together and make us feel and act regionally. One might ask, isn't it more propitious for us to have a strong regional organization like the major development banks have, rather than worrying about developing a worldwide global network? I think that when we get together with affiliates from other countries, that question is answered. The diversity, the feeling, the identification we get of women across the world is so overwhelming that we couldn't possibly think ourselves into a little corner regionally again once we have seen the benefits of a global network.

The exposure to all the other third world countries in Africa, in South America, and Asian countries have made us realize that the problem of poverty is global, and therefore we have to help each other find the solutions to these problems.

Agnes Ntamabyariro

Microenterprise is not at all developed in Rwanda. In any case, we are behind. The Women's World Banking program of exchange among the affiliates can help us find new ideas, ideas for developing small businesses.

Mary Okelo

A seed has been planted. Now we have got to nurture it, and we have to see it grow and continue to empower women, continue to ensure that women have access to resources. We have just started, so we have got to increase the momentum, and we have got to educate the policy makers. We have to influence them. We have to make them realize the importance of including everybody in the process of development. I see Women's World Banking becoming one of the strongest movements that is going to transform the world.

Ela Bhatt

We have come a long way. . . . It was a very difficult struggle and we have made it. Michaela has brought us all together and taken us in a direction as a movement. The future of my country is in the hands of women. Those who are marginalized have to be brought into the mainstream. Credit is only one tool. Technical assistance is equally important. We have to increase women's income, employment and assets. More and more families are female-headed households. WWB is one of the organizations of women helping them to understand themselves, improve their skills, and make their presence felt in world affairs. The most important goal is that women gain political visibility, and make a dent in the revision of policies and create policies.

Michaela Walsh

I think that women are going in that direction generally. I think that one of the things that Women's World Banking has done is to put a focus on the impact of that movement. Unless we begin with an understanding that women need to take ownership over the decisions of their own lives, and the control of the resources that affect their lives, then all the political power and influence in the world is not going to make that much difference. It's not so much the financial institutions as it is the caring, understanding, and sharing of the needs of other people, and taking ownership over that.

I would wish that over the next ten years whatever we do to expand the impact of Women's World Banking, there is that constant awareness that the real objective is the ownership by the individual woman who's borrowing for her business or the management of the affiliate or the ownership of those resources, because that is how one makes decisions; it is on the basis of that ownership. If we fail to hang on to that bottom line, then the whole mission of Women's World Banking will be skewed.

Esther Ocloo

It's very special to me, I feel thrilled and happy and as I look back, I couldn't have believed this would happen. Without dreams, the people perish. And this dream was dreamt some fifteen years ago. We never realized it could grow into a thing like this. But it has materialized simply because those who were the original dreamers all got involved, they cooperated, and they worked together. The idea came because we were thinking of the suffering of women. There were two problems militating against women: education and lack of money in the pocket of the average woman. I have always said if this world is to be saved, it will be saved by women. So give credit to women, give economic power to women, and the world will be free, the world will have peace, because women build the world.

J. Burke Knapp

I came to Amsterdam in a little different capacity. I came as an outside speaker, yet I got so caught up with the spirit of the thing that I became an insider. I came already persuaded that women were the great underutilized resource in development, but there was always the problem of how do you mobilize them? How do you bring their talents to bear? This (WWB) struck me as a practical idea. It struck me that the leadership had not only a lot of idealism, but also a lot of sense about how this problem could be attacked. In other words, Michaela converted me. I thought it was a wonderful meeting, it launched a wonderful enterprise, it's been a great adventure, and it's now still at the very beginning. "This is not the beginning of the end, but just the end of the beginning."

Christine Hayanga

I think not so much of myself as an individual, but of what has happened to women—knowing that now women can go to the banks and be seen, knowing that the government can now support women as people, people who are important, people who are playing an important role in the economic development of their countries.

Nancy Barry

From the outset, there has been a very strong sense of not only self-sufficiency, but self-determination at the local level. Women's World Banking, the global superstructure, is really not a superstructure at all, it is a network of services that are made available to people at the local level as they try to build lending services, technical and marketing services, and the other types of empowering economic services at their local level. . . . I think that relates directly to why WWB is a network; what we have seen more and more is we are not talking about the expert model. We are talking about lateral sharing, where systems for making small loans, mobilizing savings for people with little savings have been built.

These systems are quite different from traditional banking systems; WWB provides the extension so that there is access for people who normally wouldn't have it. . . . WWB is a financial institution; it is a network; it is a movement; and increasingly, it is a way of life.

J. Burke Knapp

I think the secret of the Women's World Banking way of life, as we've come to talk about it, is the intimacy of the relationship between the people in the affiliates who are trying to help the small-enterprise women entrepreneurs and the women themselves, and I think there's some danger in, for example, aspiring to make larger loans to bigger enterprises. There's always going to be a place for the smaller enterprise, and this is where this style of lending and this style of assistance are particularly relevant and appropriate. I'm a little worried when people talk about financial institutions as if that's the objective. Financial aspects are very important, but financial institutions could also mean a departure from this intimacy of relationships that from the outset I have mentioned is very important. It's the provision of credit accompanied by a caring attitude and a follow-up in terms of technical assistance and management. There's no substitute for that in the massive financial institutions.

Michaela Walsh

I think that my own interest in WWB has been to try and create an institutional framework in which people, particularly women, have the right to access resources, particularly limited resources, and one of those is money. In most societies, one does not have access to resources without money, and therefore I saw money—credit, capital, management, markets—as the point of access to some kind of right to those elements of the world. My own vision went one step further in that the issue of WWB is not an institution—you cannot build an institution without confidence and trust in the people involved in the institution. Therefore, the idea of calling this WWB had very significant relevance to the point of entry for any woman. Unless they had the confidence to gain and use access to the resources, then there's no purpose to the institution. The name and purpose encompassed a whole dimension of trust in terms of how you build partnership.

It's a very encircling, non-hierarchical environment in which I really try to encourage confidence in people wherever in the economy they function, and figure out how to make those services and facilities and help available in whatever step they are on. Hopefully WWB will be able to adapt to women's needs on a global level, and then it becomes a movement. It's a movement with more than just experts and bureaucrats and politicians, because you won't have a movement unless you have a massive number of people who decide what that movement is from their own environment, their own location. I think over the next ten years there is an opportunity to focus more on influence from a public perspective—with easy access to technology, the decisions at the political level will be made on a very local level. And that's where most women function. If we can help build a bridge in understanding between that local perception and a more global or centralized perception, then you will have an institution and you will have a movement without any need to build a building.

Mary Okelo

Right now a number of countries—and let me speak for Africa—Africa is in a crisis. Part of that is due to the policies; the strategies that have been applied have not worked. But WWB—by insisting on women's participation in decision-making, and having access to resources, and being able also to participate—is helping change or transform economies and making them economically efficient. When you empower women economically, the standards of living go up, not just for an individual, but for the whole family. If you educate a woman, you educate a nation. That transformation that WWB is doing is such a strong miracle, and I can see the movement growing stronger and stronger and bringing about more and more positive change. I don't think any country can afford to exclude women from the mainstream, because they are the main actors, the main participants in development and this is really what WWB is doing—to reinforce them, to enable them to open doors that were previously closed to them. We owe this to the founders, particularly to Michaela, who has sacrificed so much; she has enabled us to transform our lives, to create confidence in us, to give us a voice and be able to look to a better future.

The 1990 SWWB Board meeting following the Global Meeting was held at the Martin Luther King Jr. Center in Atlanta. The tension and miscommunication that had been building culminated there.

Expecting Mary Okelo to be named WWB president, the president of the African Development Bank (ADB) dispatched a representative as his proxy to accompany Mary to the Global Meeting and the Board meeting.

Rudolf Mees requested that non-voting members leave the room so the Board could reach a decision. The Board agreed that Nancy Barry was the ideal candidate, and unanimously elected her president, with Mary Okelo as executive vice president. It is clear to me that this decision reflected Nancy's experience at the World Bank and with WWB, as well as her profound commitment to the global affiliate network. She had what WWB most needed.

The ADB representative questioned the Board's decision, adding to the awkwardness of the situation for everyone involved.

Mary Okelo, in our recent interview, said that she experienced the news as a *"bombshell,"* but she also said she felt that at that time WWB was an evolving institution with no system for succession in place, and that until we had worked through the transition, we didn't know what systems were needed. She added, *"WWB transformed me and many of the people involved—you mentored me to be myself. It was a big vision, but we all were carrying our own baggage."*

In our tenth year, WWB was featured on *CNN* and *NBC's Today* show and in *TIME Magazine*, (see p. 144).

Women's World Banking

Asociación Dominicana para el Desarrollo de la Mujer: ADOPEM
Association of Women Entrepreneurs of Karnataka: AWAKE (India)
Association pour le Developpement des Initiatives Economiques par les Femmes: ADIEF (France)
Association pour l'Integration de la Femme dans L'Economie Malienne
Association pour la Promotion Economique de la Femme (Burundi)
Associazione per la Women's World Banking in Italia
Banco da Mulher - Associacao Brasileira para o Desenvolvimento da Mulher
Basali Boitjarong (Lesotho)
Corporacion Mundial de la Mujer - Medellin
Corporacion Femenina Ecuatoriana
Corporacion Mundial de la Mujer - Colombia (Bogota)
Corporacion WWB Filial Chilena WWB - Chile
Credimujer (Costa Rica)
DUTERIMBERE - Rwanda
Femin'Autres (France)
Femmes et Initiatives pour le Developpement Economique de la Guadeloupe
Fonds Haitien d'Aide à la Femme: FHAF
Friends of WWB Association in Thailand
Friends of Women's World Banking Ghana, Ltd.
Friends of WWB - India
Friends of Women's World Banking - Jamaica, Ltd.
Friends of WWB/USA, Inc.
Fundación Mundial de la Mujer - Bucaramanga (Colombia)
Fundación Boliviana para el Desarrollo de la Mujer
Fundación Hondureña para el Desarrollo de la Mujer: FUNHDEMU
Fundación Laboral WWB en España
Fundación Mundo Mujer - Popayan (Colombia)
Fundación Uruguaya de Ayuda y Asistencia a la Mujer
Fundación WWB - Colombia (Cali)
Kenya Women Finance Trust, Ltd.: KWFT
National Association for Resource Improvement: NARI (Bangladesh)
Société Senegalaise de Garantie d'Assistance et de Credit: SOSEGAF
Stichting WWB Nederland
The Gambia Women's Finance Company: GWFC
The Uganda Women's Finance and Credit Trust, Ltd.
Women Entrepreneurs Resource Development Agency: WERDAN (New Delhi)
Women in Finance and Entrepreneurship: WIFE (The Philippines)
Women in Trade and Commerce, Sdn, Bhd.: WINTRAC (WWB/Malaysia)
WWB/Miami Valley Affiliate of Women's World Banking (Yellow Springs, Ohio)
Women's Association for Women's Alternatives (Pennsylvania)
Women's Entrepreneurial Growth Organization: WEGO (Akron, Ohio)
Women's Trust of Zambia, Ltd.
Women's World Banking, West Virginia Affiliate, Inc.
Women's World Finance/Cape Breton Association - Canada
Zimbabwe Women's Finance Trust

WOMEN'S WORLD BANKING AFFILIATES AND AFFILIATES-IN-FORMATION AS OF 1990.

EXCLUSIVE INTERVIEW

Vol. 135, No. 23   JUNE 4, 1990

TIME

Women Start Taking Credit

An unusual institution helps Third World entrepreneurs

Melba Lucy Montenegro was poor but ambitious. The 29-year-old mother of three dreamed of opening a bicycle factory in her hometown of Cali, Colombia. But when she asked several regional banks for a loan, they refused her request because she lacked any collateral. Then she heard about a group called Women's World Banking, which studied her business plan and agreed to guarantee up to 75% of any loan she received. With the group's backing, Montenegro found an institution that was willing to lend her $3,125. Eight years later, she owns three bicycle-repair shops and employs 18 people. "The world has enough workers," says Montenegro. "What I wanted to do was create more jobs."

Women's World Banking, which celebrated its tenth anniversary in April, is unlike any other financial institution. At a time when governments are raising billions to revive the economies of Eastern Europe, the group, which has its headquarters in New York City and 47 affiliate chapters on six continents, arranges for women who have no collateral to receive commercial loans that typically run from $150 to $600. One of its smaller loans, for $50, went to a woman in India who used the money to build an oven so she could sell chapati, or flat bread. One of the largest helped raise $1 million to start a dairy cooperative in Thailand. "Our goal is to reach women who have been bypassed by the traditional banking system and to bring them into the economic mainstream," says Ela Bhatt of Ahmedabad, India, the current W.W.B. chairman.

Under the loan-guarantee program,

In Cali, Melba Lucy Montenegro talks with a customer at one of her bicycle-repair shops

"The world has enough workers. What I wanted to do was create more jobs."

the international organization of W.W.B. promises to be responsible for 50% of a loan, while the local chapter takes on an additional 25%. But many of the loans are so small that most banks would not consider them worth the paperwork. In those cases, the local chapters raise money on their own, then lend it directly to clients.

W.W.B. is run on a tight budget but has a sterling record. With nearly $12 million in loan guarantees outstanding, W.W.B. has suffered only $35,000 in losses. That translates into a repayment rate of better than 99%. "We're not a charity organization. We require that the individuals who come to us take on some of the financial risk themselves," says Michaela Walsh, a former partner in a Wall Street financial firm, who founded W.W.B. with six other businesswomen from around the world.

By helping women achieve greater economic independence, the organization has prompted political change as well. The Ke-

nya branch of London-based Barclays Bank, which works closely with the local W.W.B. group, no longer requires a husband's signature when a woman takes out a loan. W.W.B.'s formula for economic emancipation works so well that affiliate groups have formed in North America (in Nova Scotia, Ohio and Texas) and may soon get started in Eastern Europe. A group of Polish women have approached W.W.B. about raising money to start a chicken hatchery in their village.

W.W.B. plans to offer still more financial services. Says Nancy Barry, who will become the next president of the group in September: "In the past ten years we have focused on access to credit. In the next ten years we will be helping women find investors for their businesses, helping them get more training and developing larger markets." Not bad for a bunch of women who used to find themselves laughed out of the bank. **—By Christine Gorman**

TIME MAGAZINE ARTICLE ABOUT WOMEN'S WORLD BANKING, JUNE 4, 1990

10

GETTING THERE FROM NOWHERE

"It was the best of times, it was the worst of times."

by Lilia C. Clemente

Michaela Walsh asked Lilia Clemente, who led the financial strategy of Women's World Banking during its formative years, to write WWB's early financial history and assemble the reports for 1980 to 1990.

Financing WWB's Start-Up, 1977 to 1982

It was the best of times, it was the worst of times, it was the age of wisdom, and the age of foolishness, it was the season of light and the season of darkness, it was the spring of hope and the winter of despair.

This classic quotation from Charles Dickens' *A Tale of Two Cities* describes the birth and survival of Women's World Banking from seed-planting in 1975 to blooming in the global gardens from 1976 to 1982. An analogy can be drawn between a plant's roots and globalization and the whole world system. As a plant's roots quietly and powerfully grow and dig deeply, those roots break concrete and clay pots to get their way. The human species has been constantly harnessing and releasing its innate powers to break out of national, cultural, and other boxes. The telephone lines, fiber optics, computers, satellites, radio, and television are women and men extending themselves to interact with a larger world and to dig more deeply and draw more nourishment from within and without.

Like a good seed in a good soil, WWB grew through the extraordinary, creative energy of women from diverse cultures, determined and confident in their vision and mission to make things happy despite the somber mood in the most turbulent period in modern economic history. Led by the visionary founder, Michaela Walsh, who believed in the paradigm of women as agents of change in development and growth, the success of WWB can be attributed to the founder's understanding of the value of responsibility and decision making at the grassroots level. In shaping WWB, there was no centralized bureaucracy to institutionalize control, nor paternalistic dogma. Empowered entrepreneurial women in any country joined together as WWB affiliates and took responsibility and authority for their own local programs.

The Big Picture

During the go-go years of the 1960s, a performance orientation and the youthful culture energized Wall Street with a belief in the "new economics." John Brooks writes in *The Go-Go Years* that there was a belief that only someone under forty could understand the growth of fast-moving economies. A remark of one University of California student—"Don't trust anyone over 30"—became the rallying cry of the student movement. One could argue that the shape of American society, influenced by the prolonged war in Vietnam, the civil rights movement, and the women's liberation movement, reflected our growing social concern. The economic backdrop was favorable for the equity markets. A carefully orchestrated tax cut set off the longest expansion in the postwar period. Although resources were strained, in part from the soaring costs of Vietnam War, we would not feel the pain until the 1970s became problematic and concerns shifted from social movements to basic survival, as inflation eroded economic prosperity. We worried about the future as never before, and we had good reason, driven by a welter of conflicting events and purposes. The "movement decade" of the 1960s had given way to the "me decade" of the 1970s.

The world suffered boom-and-bust scenarios as serious recessions and unemployment hovering around 8 percent alternated with inflation. Consumer-price rise averaged 2.2 percent annually in the 1950s and 2.3 percent in the 1960s. Throughout these two decades, investors secured above-average real returns from equities. The 1970s saw inflation averaging 7.1 percent, while 1974–82 was a period of further volatility, false harbors, and poor returns, as conflicts erupted in the Middle East, and the nation was traumatized by the Watergate affair and two oil shocks. The first began in October 1973, when the Organization of the Petroleum Exporting Countries (OPEC) embargo caused the price of oil to rise from $3.12 a barrel in October 1973 to $11.63 in December. This resulted in annual inflation surging to 12.5 percent by December 1974—up from 2.9 percent in August 1972. The second oil crisis was caused by the decline in oil exports from Iran following the revolution in January 1979. By year end, the oil price had risen 150 percent. The term "stagflation," a combination of low growth and high inflation, became Wall Street jargon to describe the economy—which was bad news for investors.

WWB's Roots

During this period of malaise and uncertainty, Women's World Banking put down its first tiny roots in 1975 as the First International Conference for Women took place in Mexico City. The 1975 conference marked the beginning of the United Nations Decade of Women. It stressed the huge economic cost of discriminatory practices—legal, financial, cultural, and educational—that prevented women's active participation in the economic mainstream. The conference closely examined women's economic role, beginning with this startling fact: Women performed 65 percent of the world's work, yet they earned only 10 percent of the income and owned less than 1 percent of the world's property.

Given this dramatic disparity, how could women achieve economic self-sufficiency? A small group of women from diverse cultures decided to create a tangible response to that question. They resolved to provide a global support network for women who possessed entrepreneurial qualities but who lacked the capital, management skills, and confidence to start and manage viable businesses. The WWB women visionaries concluded that the most effective course of action was to improve women's access to credit and financial services in their local economies, by establishing a mechanism that would enable them to use their skills, talents, and capital more productively. Thus, the proposed activities of WWB were new and experimental. By April 1977, the Committee to Organize WWB started with contributions from its members of $1,703.33, which was deposited with South Shore Bank. In March 1979, Accion, a Boston-based nonprofit organization led by John Hammock, who worked with us in the conceptual and feasibility stage, provided $3,000 to cover the costs of the incorporation of the Stichting Women's World Banking, a Netherlands foundation formed in May 1979 under Netherlands law. Women's World Banking was up and running.

Breaking Out, 1979–1980

WWB received a confirmation on June 19, 1978, from the United Nations Development Program (UNDP), of a pledge of $175,000 toward the organization's seed capital. From April 1, 1977, through December 31, 1980, WWB received a total of $180,652 in grants, led by UNDP ($68,380); the Swedish International Development Authority, SIDA ($35,000); the Ford Foundation ($20,000); the Netherlands Ministry for Development ($8,000); the United Methodist Church Women's Division ($20,000); with the balance from individual WWB member contributions. WWB disbursed its funds prudently; total spending was $111,049, out of which $71,731 was allocated to costs of the First International Workshop for Women in Banking and Finance in Amsterdam, while personnel costs were marginal, with only $11,110 and legal and accounting fees of $10,029. WWB ended the three-year start-up period with a Fund balance of $69,663 for the year ended December 31, 1980.

That the initial start-up costs of $180,652 kept WWB alive can be attributed to the sacrifice and sweat equity of Michaela Walsh and her lean team of volunteers. WWB founders decided to disburse the money over three years and made vigorous efforts to raise funds beyond the initial sources, to broaden the support base. Under the leadership of Michaela Walsh, WWB survived as the staff donated their sweat equity and prioritized the program development for loan guarantees. For the six months that ended June 1981, restricted cash of $58,106 guilders ($21,860) represented a contribution from the Netherlands Minister for Development and was used for specific loans for India for the Self Employed Women's Association (SEWA). The UNDP Country Specific Program Development costs during the same six-month period in June 1981 designated $19,447 for these countries: Columbia, $16,924; India, $1,523; and Kenya, $1,000.

By 1981, the concept of WWB became a reality and faced the challenge of taking off in the decade of 1980s.

Investment Environment in the 1980s

In March 1980, Michaela Walsh and the Committee to Organize WWB presented a Discussion Paper on the issues involved in launching a WWB Capital Fund to the International Workshop in Amsterdam.

In my Discussion Paper in Amsterdam on WWB Capital Funds, I presented the following several fundamental changes in the institutional and economic structure under way, making it appropriate for Women's World Banking to pursue a balanced diversified Capital Fund—one that preserves capital yet has potential to generate income sufficient to offset the rate of inflation.

- **Shape of the Market and Economic Environment.** The multiplicity of changes in the world economic and political relationships and priorities leads us to believe that the world will not return to the type of economic and financial markets that existed in the 1950s and 1960s.
- **The Process of Investment Management: A Need for Broader Skills.** The changing requirements, priorities and interrelationship of the economic system and our expectations for liquidity managers over the next several years have broad significance for the scope and modus operandi of the investment manager and analyst's task.
- **Changes Affecting Securities Community.** The legal and regulatory investment environment within the US is under constant reexamination and change. For purposes of multinational investment, money managers must understand the applicable rules and regulations of other governments.
- **Changes in Portfolio Risk/Return Expectations.** The unique advantages of international diversification can be demonstrated both theoretically and empirically. The basic premise can be stated that because international security prices and bond yields are not perfectly correlated from country to country, international diversification reduces the volatility of a portfolio; at least it maintains the rate of return and thereby creates a more efficient portfolio.

Moreover, Women's World Banking was designed to work worldwide. Therefore, in line with the objectives of the organization, it was a natural move for a fund to be internationally diversified.

Because of the difficult environment, concentration upon selection should be focused, beyond usual management abilities, on people whose combined understanding, skills, and tendencies permit usage of the most appropriate mix of investment vehicles for the prevailing environment.

Women's World Banking Financial Timeline

1977	1978	1979	1981	1982
Committee to Organize WWB Funding: $1,703.78	June 19, UNDP pledged $175,000 toward seed capital	$3,000 Costs of incorporation Stichting WWB	Approval of Stichting WWB Executive Committee of $10 million, 8% debenture issuance, September 9,1981	AID pledge $120,000 for 3 years

March 1984	1981 to 1986	1990
$153,397 invested in October 1983	$145,288 increased to $2,876,748 on March 31, 1986	Out of $2.9 million, $1.6 million represented the Capital Fund

For more details, please see WWB Financial Spreadsheets, p. 326.

Financial Metamorphosis,1980–1990

After WWB survived its first three years (1977 through 1980) with a modest budget of $180,652, how did WWB make the big leap and take off with capital to grow and attain self-sufficiency during its first decade?

To meet this daunting challenge under Michaela's leadership, we organized the WWB Finance Committee. This committee would be responsible for the financial activities and investments, as well as budget review, strategies, and guidelines for investment. We assembled the best talent available from our collective networks with these criteria:

- Members who will commit their time
- Constituents of the finance and investment team
- Open-minded thinkers who resist micromanaging staff decisions
- Commitment to the mission and vision of WWB
- Support by the full Board of Trustees

We agreed that the financial committee should remain small—five to six members at most— and should meet formally four or five times a year and communicate as needed. I became the first Chairperson of WWB's Finance Committee and a member of the Executive Committee from 1980 to 1983. I was supported and surrounded by the seven distinguished and multidisciplined members; J. Burke Knapp (World Bank), G. Arthur Brown (UNDP), A. Kendall Raine (JP Morgan), Joyce Sohl (CIO, Women's Division, United Methodist Church), and Michaela Walsh (WWB president). To preserve the commitment and goodwill of the original funders, our Finance Committee focused on developing a strategic and tactical financial plan. Any start-up organization or company confronts three issues: clarify, define, and confirm the concept to make it clear to investors and the public. Our options were:

- Is SWWB a charitable organization with plans to exist mostly on grants?
- Is SWWB an endowment with plans to exist mostly on earnings from donated capital?
- Is SWWB a business with plans to finance day-to-day operations with secure fees and commercial loans?

Understanding the purpose of accumulating capital and assets represents the first step in formulating a strategic financial plan. Other important factors we considered were:

- Expectations for a capital base as a source of support, near-term and long-term
- Organization's appeal and image to regulators, donors, and recipients
- Legal requirements (such as taxes)
- Characteristics of WWB organization programs
- Specific limitations imposed by donors

The Finance Committee referred to the various discussions of WWB trustees and materials from the International Workshops held in Amsterdam (1980) and San Remo in making policy decisions. Women's World Banking (WWB) states in its incorporating papers that the organization's purpose is the following:

> [WWB] is designed to operate as a decentralized, flexible mechanism for linking entrepreneurial women, and training resources. The role of WWB. . . is one of facilitator. . . .
>
> The principal tools the organization will use include loan guarantees extended to women's enterprises through existing financial institutions, and management and technical assistance to enterprises requiring it.
>
> Last, the preliminary operating plan conveyed a strategic sense of WWB's intention to extend capital support selectively, through qualified intermediaries, to women entrepreneurs with viable projects, in accordance with prevailing business practice in the area. This principle was noted by Patricia Cloherty in her background paper at the International Workshop of Women Leaders in Banking and Finance in 1980.
>
> In short, WWB was established as a provider of capital to women entrepreneurs.

While the concept can be stated succinctly, it obviously rests on a number of complex assumptions about the societies and economies of countries. Further, from a purely practical, operating standpoint, it raises many issues with respect to how the program will actually function in the "real world." The process of enterprise development takes time, and it takes both reasonable skills and commercial concepts, in addition to capital. WWB's resources were small compared to the task at hand. Maximizing results would require detailed and pragmatic planning.

Three intricate issues formed the principal underpinnings of WWB.

- The roles of women entrepreneurs in the development community
- The availability of capital to finance their enterprises
- The role of commercial banks and other financial intermediaries in linking the two, i.e., as providers to women entrepreneurs

While WWB's plan was to piggyback on institutions and develop field networks to accomplish its goals, it was always clear that provision of capital was the principal objective.

We prepared and implemented our strategic financial plan for WWB with an active fund-raising campaign and the private placement offering of Stitching Women's World Banking 8 percent debenture intended to support SWWB's operations with its interest earnings and to collateralize guarantees to affiliates. Our Financial Committee also prepared its statement of Investment Polices and Guidelines. It was important for WWB to adopt governance practices and an investment process that included socially responsible practices consistent with the people involved and with the goals of WWB. Our Finance Committee members believed that a thorough and rigorous application of asset-allocation policy with risk-reward parameters was a major driver of the professionalism and growth.

We adopted the following statement of WWB Investment Policies and Guidelines:

1. Investment Goals and Objectives

    The investments shall be managed and investment decisions shall be made so as to achieve long-term financial stability for Women's World Banking and to sustain and strengthen its capacity as a not-for-profit organization dedicated to fostering the direct participation of women in the full use of the economy, particularly those women who have not generally had access to the services of established financial institutions.

    a. producing income to support Women's World Banking's core-program development and administrative functions;

    b. preserving the purchasing power of Women's World Banking's assets by achieving growth adequate to offset the effects of inflation from year to year;

    c. achieving modest growth in the capital value of the investments when the above-listed priority objectives have been met and when market and economic conditions so warrant.

    The investment portfolio shall be reappraised on a continuing basis in order to respond to changing circumstances in the economy and in Women's World Banking's organization and financial operations.

2. Investment Guidelines

    a. Women's World Banking's investments shall be limited to publicly traded securities.

b.   The Finance Committee shall have the authority to retain one or more independent and qualified investment managers to manage Women's World Banking's investment portfolio to reflect Women's World Banking's financial and ethical concerns as outlined in the investment policies and guidelines. The Committee shall monitor the performance of such investment managers on a regular basis to determine that the polices and guidelines are being followed.

c.   The appointed investment managers, under supervision of the Women's World Banking Finance Committee, shall be responsible for maintaining a mix of domestic and international equities, corporate and government bonds, and short-term investments. Asset mix may be adjusted to a maximum of 25 percent equity securities, subject to periodic review.

3. Policy Constraints of Investments

Women's World Banking Investment Managers Shall Avoid Securities:

a.   Of any issuer doing business with South Africa considered an inappropriate investment by virtue of refusal to subscribe to and actively implement the Sullivan Principles or the EEC Code of fair employment practices.

b.   Of any issuer having its principal place of business in the Republic of South Africa and South-West Africa/Namibia.

c.   Of companies doing business with countries which have consistent records of human rights violations.

d.   Of US companies listed among the 10 leading military contractors for the previous year or which derived more than 25 percent of their previous year's sales from military contracts.

e.   Of companies that are direct contributors to nuclear weapons research and development, the production of key components for nuclear warheads, or the management and construction of nuclear weapons facilities, bases, and installations.

f.   Of companies engaged in research or manufacture of products for chemical, biological or germ warfare.

Where did WWB raise funds for capital?

To build upon the initial fund-raising, WWB identified potential funding sources from three groups:

- WWB's constituency of individual women worldwide.
- The private sector, such as corporations, foundations, national church groups, banks, and institutions that could consider WWB as a program-related investment

(PRI) with the promise of a monetary and social return.

- The public sector, including regional, national, and international organizations such as the UNDP, the US Agency for International Development (USAID), the Canadian International Development Authority (CIDA), and the Scandinavian countries.

Without the resources to hire a fund-raising professional, the fund-raising efforts during the first five years from 1980 to 1985 fell heavily on WWB's financial committee, led by and approved by the Board.

Since 1981, WWB has solicited and received grants or donations from governments and individuals. The circumstances surrounding the gifts vary from case to case. For example, sometimes WWB entered into an agreement where the donors and gifts were documented only by informal letters. Other donors have specific purposes for which grants are to be received and WWB has expressly agreed to the commitment.

After an intense study and discussion among the WWB Finance Committee and its trustees, we explored options to set up a WWB Capital Fund in the middle of a bad economic recession and with interest rates reaching historic highs (in excess of 15 percent).

On September 9, 1981, WWB authorized and approved a Private-Placement Memorandum (PPM) offering to solicit subscriptions for a $10 million issue at an 8 percent interest rate, due on January 1, 1990. Upon approval, we set up a task-force group composed of myself; Michaela; John Hammock of Accion; Tom Hunter, WWB's accountant; and Robert Lessor, a Swiss American citizen and respected bank analyst, to write a draft of the PPM offering. We had the indispensable help of WWB Dutch-based legal counsel Floris Bannier and US-based legal counsel Lester Nurick of Wilmer Cutler Pickering.

WWB will forever be grateful to Lester Nurick, our securities counsel, for putting together the final private placement memorandum for the WWB Debenture offering and other associated relevant documents, acts, and literature. Most of all, we benefitted from his wise counsel and his generosity with time and commitment. Memories linger of the task-force team's hard work. I recall working until 3 a.m. in my office at One World Trade Center when we finished the draft of the PPM. We finally stopped because Michaela had to catch the train with a copy of the draft for discussion with J. Burke Knapp of the World Bank and the counsel, Lester Nurick.

Notable features of SWWB Debentures included:

- Stitching WWB was organized in May 1979 under the not-for-profit laws of the Netherlands and enjoys an exemption from Netherlands income tax. The US Internal Revenue Service (IRS) ruled in April 1982 that SWWB meets the legal requirements for exemption from federal income tax as an organization whose purpose is to promote social welfare.
- Friends of Women's World Banking (FWWB) was formed in December 1979 as a Delaware corporation and has been qualified to carry on activities in New York. Its corporate purposes are closely related to those of the Stitching WWB and include

providing financial support for SWWB on a selective basis. On March 1981 the IRS recognized Friends' exempt status as a charitable organization under the laws governing US federal income tax and said that contributions to Friends are deductible by US taxpayers as charitable contributions.

- The SWWB decided to build a Capital Fund that may be used in part to support its guarantee programs. Friends may make funds available to the Stitching for this purpose but only on condition that those funds and any interest earned may be used ultimately for activities that Friends have specifically approved.
- Proceeds from WWB's Debenture offering were placed in the Capital Fund and grants received by WWB may also go into the Capital Fund. The proceeds of the Fund will be developed to cases which will be selected not only for their economic viability, but also for their social impact.
- According to the offering, the Capital Fund to the extent practicable will be kept intact and will invest in high-grade obligations as well as existing investments.
- The offering memorandum states that "investment income from the Capital Fund, after the payment of interest and charges on the debentures and costs of administrating WWB's investment portfolio, will be retained in the Capital Fund. The offering further states that payments for WWB's administrative expenses, working capital, and guarantees will come from the Fund's accumulated net investment income.
- The rate of return proposed for the debentures at 8 percent is substantially below market rates of 15 percent when it was launched.
- The Bank America Trust Company of New York was the authenticating agent, registrar, and fiscal agent.

The years 1982–83 focused on the sales of the SWWB debentures by coping with these issues:
- Clarify tax implications to US investors
- Examine the advantages of selling debentures
- Identify the target audience
- Set up goals in terms of total sales over a given period

The Private Placement Memorandum was redrafted in November 22, 1983, to include the expansion of WWB program, growth in the number of affiliates, and updated financial statements of WWB. The period from 1982 to 1986 represented the "bull market," or higher returns from investments in bonds compared with stocks and bills. The WWB Financial Committee believed that providing an 8 percent return along with the investor's psychic income (or the impact of social return) represented potential for good returns. As reflected in the chart below, substantially different return opportunities were available from stocks, bonds, and cash in any given year.

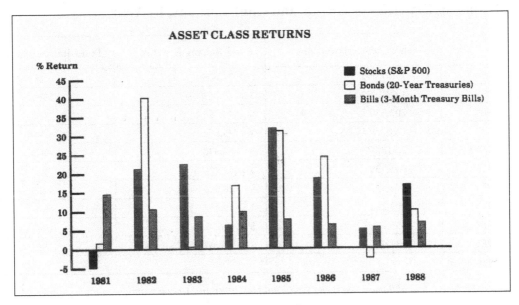

Source: Data Stream, Reuters

WWB Support Received in 1984

Royal Norwegian Ministry of Development Cooperation	$ 253,522.00
Swedish International	$ 119,517.00
US Agency for International Development	$ 108,147.00
United Methodist Church	$ 31,000.00
Friends of WWB/USA, Inc.	$ 30,930.00
Canadian International Development Agency	$ 23,319.00
Netherlands Ministry for Development Cooperation Program	$ 8,000.00

WWB Support Received in 1986

Canadian International Development Agency	$ 1,001,059.00
Netherlands Ministry for Development Cooperation Program	$ 885,079.00
Royal Norwegian Ministry of Development Corporation	$ 421,882.00
United Nations Development Program	$ 50,000.00
Friends of WWB/USA, Inc.	$ 24,500.00
US Agency for International Development	$ 17,865.00
Swedish International Development Authority	$ 10,000.00
Sundry Contributors	$ 688.00

Fund-Raising Expenses to Grants and Contributions, by Year

	Grants and Contributions	Fund-Raising Expense	Fund-Raising Ratio
1990	$ 1,401,093	$ 37,609	3%
1989	$ 1,691,970	$ 46,242	3%
1988	$ 703,530	$ 47,753	7%
1987	$ 1,782,965	$ 44,856	3%
1986	$ 2,418,073	$ 54,340	2%
1985	$ 605,935	$ 44,930	7%
1984	$ 574,435	$ 48,024	8%
1983	$ 993,224	$ 39,434	4%
1982	$ 453,276	$ 4,610	10%
1981	$ 137,981	$ 14,663	11%
1980			

Source: 1980 by Statement of Purpose Women's World Banking, 1981 and 1982 by (only unaudited from Peat, Marwick, Mitchell & Co. through March '82), 1983 to 1986 by SWWB Annual Report, 1987 to 1990 by KPMG.

From its asset base of $111,521 in 1980 to 1990, WWB enjoyed a phenomenal growth of 5,636 percent when it ended the year with an asset base of $6.4 million (see Balance Sheet).

Balance Sheet

Total Assets (Asset Account)		% Incr. (Decrease) in Value with 1980 as Base Year
1990	$ 6,397,798	5636%
1989	$ 7,660,044	6768%
1988	$ 5,949,614	5235%
1987	$ 5,723,893	5032%
1986	$ 4,657,145	4076%
1985	$ 2,763,666	2378%
1984	$ 2,348,613	2006%
1983	$ 1,909,454	1612%
1982	$ 406,313	264%
1981	$ 29,887	(73)%
1980	$ 111,521	

In 1990, the sizeable growth in the balance sheet (asset account) can be attributed to WWB's outstanding performance during this decade.

Operating activities as reflected on net assets grew from $75,088 budget to $1 million in 1990.

Operating Activities

	Increase (Decrease) in Net Assets
1990	$ (1,107,719.00)
1989	$ 1,623,736.00
1988	$ 233,773.00
1987	$ 1,245,071.00
1986	$ 1,939,657.00
1985	$ 262,511.00
1984	$ 260,604.00
1983	$ 732,712.00
1982	$ 382,366.00
1981	$ 75,088.00
1980	

Total expenses of managing WWB, including its general administration, loan programs, workshops, regional coordination program, and development and education, are reflected in this chart:

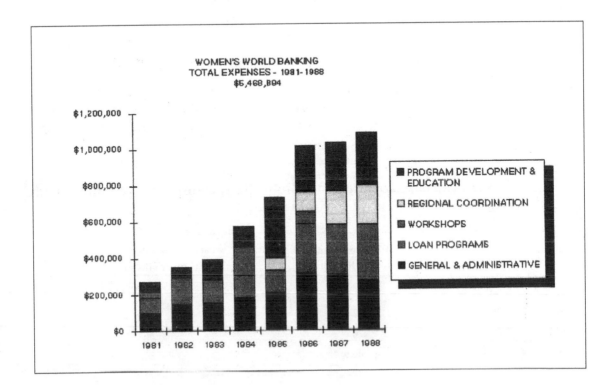

Implementing WWB's Investment Mandate

WWB's trustees decided to select complementary external investment managers in the area of equities, bonds, and money markets.

In 1983, Clemente Capital Inc., of which I am founder and CEO, entered into a joint venture with Mitchell Hutchins Asset Management (a subsidiary of Paine Webber Inc.) to provide our expertise in setting up the firm's global funds. We launched the Clemente Global Partnership LP and an open public mutual fund, Paine Webber Atlas Global Fund. I was confident that our company could produce good performance for WWB. I therefore made a case to be selected as one of its external investment managers and resigned from being a WWB trustee and the chairwoman of its Finance Committee. WWB's Board of Trustees accepted my proposal in October 1983 with an investment of $153,000 (the minimum amount of investment allowed in the Clemente Global Partnership LP).

Global investing has made the world my base of operations. It's a world big enough for one to get lost in but small enough to find one's home. By home, I mean a state of mind where one sees connections between cultures, people and events, reasons and interests, the past, present, and future—connections that make picking stocks, bonds, and companies, and working and playing together in the global garden great fun. Seeing the global web of markets spun full circle is a delight that outweighs the jet lags and the world roller-coaster rides that characterize a global investor's life. In a web whose center shifts from "me" to "we" as the world becomes more interdependent, time and space no longer are the barriers to beat. It's walking through cultural walls, keeping one's head around a market crash, and keeping one's bearing on a freeway of market value.

I had my share of success in the '80s as I managed the $153,000 of WWB's global portfolio and made it grow to $2.4 million, or an annualized return of 45.6 percent. The other external manager had an 11 percent annualized return on his domestic portfolio.

WWB Investment (managed by Clemente Global Partnership LP), from the Fourth Quarter of 1983 to 1989

Date	WWB Investment (% Annual Returns)	Performance Benchmark (Lipper Global) %
1983	4.8	1.6
1984	-2.1	-3.5
1985	70.6	36.2
1986	46.9	30.8
1987	9.1	-3.4
1988	14.7	17.5
1989	39.9	21.5

Source: WWB Annual Reports and Clemente Global Investors Price Waterhouse Audited Statements, 1983–1989.

WWB's survival can be attributed to three factors:

- WWB's staffing was very thin; funds were not available to beef it up. The small staff kept pressure on to allocate and control resources carefully.
- Frugal management of the organization by living within its means and active volunteerism by its WWB members and networks.
- WWB achieved its goal of self-sufficiency with a prudent, consistent management of its investment funds through its election of external managers who produced exceptional performance in equities, bonds, and money markets.

By the end of the 1980s, the trustees decided that with interest rates and economic growth soaring to levels not seen in a new generation, with the dawn of a new era where globalization was going to bring prosperity to the whole new world, the world was no longer divided on ideological grounds but centered on modern American-style capitalism, with its technological change and increased rate of productivity. Therefore, in the roaring '90s, the WWB's 8 percent debenture was no longer attractive as a fund-raising tool. The past ten years of the 1980s had been devoted to testing WWB's objectives and to completing the first phase of its long-term organizational plan. This phase was intended to test the marketing of WWB as a financial intermediary for low-income women and to establish a network of independent affiliates to provide the mechanics for completing programs on a local level.

WWB's effectiveness in acting as a financial intermediary has been substantial, judging by the number of loans successfully guaranteed. The increasing demand for affiliate programs in additional countries confirms the cultural and economic role that the affiliates play in local enterprise development. WWB's success in the end is measured by how many businesses are being helped by WWB and, more subjectively, by the cultural, social, and economic impact of WWB's Loan Guarantee Program and other programs. Its thirty-three year existence and performance record speak for themselves.

Today, the United States and the world are confronting extraordinary policy uncertainties. The current fiscal deficit has no precedent. The Euro Zone debt crisis and possible bankruptcies are creating uncertainties and adversely affecting business and consumer confidence, and the allocation of resources.

As we find ourselves still in the midst of the journey, we can feel lost amid the assault of changes. The words from painter William Blake should come in handy:

Do not let yourself be intimidated by the horrors of the world. Everything is ordered and correct and must fulfill its destiny in order to attain perfection. Seek this path and you will attain from your own Soul an even deeper perception of the eternal beauty of creation. You will attain an ever-increasing release from that which now seems so sad and terrible.

In the end, we find comfort and refuge in our core, the values that worked, whenever, wherever. Alexis de Tocqueville wrote, "Crisis is America's nature, and it manages to overcome it." Making it through this crisis is possible in America, one country with the most colorful collection of people from all over the planet. We learn *E Pluribus Unum,* meaning one formed from many. Our American life is a tapestry composed of the strengths and characteristics of a great many diverse cultures. As part of the immigrant Diaspora, I feel a deep love and gratitude for this nation and culture, which made possible a movement like WWB. And if you get down to it, you find the same basis of family, friendship, and truth as the glue that holds us together. Only this time, we're called upon to have and give it a larger, deeper measure, like connecting and reaching out to the underserved through the WWB movement.

The new world is here. Women's World Banking continues to reach out. The great cultural task at hand is to use our nurturing powers in the home, in the workplace, to see the growth of women's entrepreneurship, especially in underserved markets, and be true global citizens in every way we can, beginning with ourselves.

"The past is but the beginning of a beginning." —*H.G. Wells*

We took many roads to get to America and make the connection with WWB. My own trip began in the Philippines and brought me to America in June 1960, first to study and then to be part of the changes in the world. The youth in America were at their idealist best. If President John Kennedy's sights were on the moon, the youth set their sights on nirvana. My dreams were big, but none of them prepared me for the long road my life would take. Had I been able to catch a glimpse of myself in a crystal ball, I might have laughed in disbelief at the images of my determined self. Going up against giants in the highly competitive world of international finance, managing $6 billion of assets for mutual funds and institutional investors, and listing two closed-end funds on the New York Stock Exchange. I never imagined that I would help to plant WWB's capital seeds and nurture its investment growth from 1980 to 1990, the critical first decade. Three decades later, WWB is an established movement that has achieved its mission.

Filipino Americans think big, and I was as bold and brassy as they come, and, like many of my fellow immigrants, I accepted with gratitude the sometimes surprising turns in my life. After finishing our studies in Chicago, my husband and I relocated to New York City in 1969. The future is indeed a storehouse of surprises. From my first job as an investment analyst/portfolio manager at CNA Financial Corporation in Chicago, the Ford Foundation gave me a big break in 1969, when at age 28 I was given authority and responsibility as the director of investment research and assistant treasurer, to help co-manage the $3 billion investment portfolio. Toward the end of the '60s, McGeorge Bundy, Ford Foundation president, became concerned about the rising cost of higher education. He began to study the management of endowment assets to determine whether they could be managed more productively and help to slow the cost increases. Bundy was not concerned only about the management of education endowment, but also about the Ford Foundation's ability to manage its assets and meet its commitment to education.

The year 1969 was notable in US history. Neil Armstrong walked on the moon. The New York Mets won the World Series, and two seminal reports commissioned by the Ford Foundation were published. *The Law and the Lore Endowment Funds*, by William L. Cary and Craig B. Bright, addressed the legal thinking that governed endowment investing. *Managing Educational Endowments*, by Robert Barker, analyzed investment thinking and recommended improved investment processes and policies. The IRS established Code Section 4944 to discourage investments that would jeopardize the charitable purpose of the Foundation, and to reform reporting and payout.

Since I greened and bloomed at the Ford Foundation, the experience and exposure I had to sophisticated talent and to building increasingly complex and diversified investment portfolios with a global approach was a big help as we launched WWB. The other pioneering action of the Ford Foundation was its decision to go global, with its asset allocation to international securities in 1971. Besides the Ford Foundation, the two other international firms investing globally were TIAA-CREF and JP Morgan Asset Management. Buying foreign stocks then was like ordering an unknown exotic dish. Today, the cross-border flow of capital and technology is breaking down barriers across markets, cultures, minds, and hearts. The more barriers break down, the more people of diverse origins connect in tackling problems of global dimension. Time and distance continually shrink, and today a person perched on the Colorado mountaintop can buy stocks in Singapore, Moscow, or Frankfurt with a phone call or an electronic trading network. Yet not long ago, Wall Street was indeed a "Walled Street" that kept women out. After 175 years, the New York Stock Exchange became coed when Muriel Siebert purchased a seat for $445,000 on December 28, 1967. Then many comments were made about the absence of ladies on the Stock Exchange Floor.

Another big break in my life was the day in 1977 when I met Michaela Walsh. Senator Leticia Ramos Shahani, a dear friend, was a member of the Committee to Organize WWB. She served twelve years in the Philippines Senate and was an outstanding diplomat, educator, and leader of women in economic development. She also served as United Nations Secretary General and Secretary General of the UN Third World Conference in 1985. She arranged for me to meet Michaela and made sure our paths crossed. Memories of our meeting linger on as we discovered the many "coincidences" in our lives. Michaela belonged to a family of five siblings, while I am the oldest of seven children, and we were fortunate to have parents who emphasized education and public service. Both of us were raised by Catholic nuns. It was my privilege to have the influence of the American Maryknoll nuns, while Michaela was educated at Notre Dame High School and Manhattanville College. Discipline and traditional values of respect for elders and hard work were emphasized.

The "coincidence" we found so striking was that we had both taken "the road less traveled." Michaela took off for Beirut to open Merrill Lynch's office in the early 1960s. As part of my work at CNA and the Ford Foundation, I spent time in Tokyo and learned how to invest and do business in the male-oriented society when their stock market opened to foreigners in the '60s. So Michaela and I swapped notes on our unique experiences in the for-profit and nonprofit worlds and working internationally. The "coincidence" that topped them all was the path we both had taken into the nonprofit world of foundations—Michaela worked for the Rockefeller Brothers Fund (RBF), while I was at the Ford Foundation when we met. We both were risk takers. Michaela resigned from her job at RBF to launch WWB, while I resigned from the Ford Foundation to become an entrepreneur. My parents, both entrepreneurs, would tell me, "When you have achieved a measure of experience, business contacts, and prestige, cut the umbilical cord and be on your own." I took their advice and founded Clemente Capital in 1977 as a boutique investment management firm.

As a new entrepreneur, I decided during our meeting that Michaela's mission of launching Women's World Banking was simply my cup of tea. We were both prepared to get it done with our experience and our access to a network of men and women. Our backgrounds perfectly prepared us to link with women entrepreneurs around the world and help women play a role in their respective economies.

Now I know why the 4Gs (Genes, Global, Grunt Work, and God) are my favorite words. The word "genes" because it represents a natural rush to go on, mutate, and make a way for a better breed of species. The word "global" because it suggests a way of life that cures my claustrophobia and makes one walk through walls that only seem there but are not really. The words "grunt work" represent the "passion quotient" to work hard to achieve one's goal and commitment, and thank God for the wisdom of the popular saying, "Today is the first day of the rest of your life." Thank you for making things happen—for Leticia Ramos Shahani, for meeting Michaela Walsh and making my connection to WWB possible, and for my field of global investing that provides me with access to the world that gives connections between cultures, between people and events, between reason and intention, between the past, the present, and the future. There was never a doubt in my mind that WWB would be a successful movement.

11

REFLECTIONS

"Change can come from the center,
and it also comes from the fringes."

THE TIME of WWB's inception, the 1975 Conference on Women in Mexico City, gave way to an unprecedented global recognition of the force of women's voices and the importance of their being at the design table of any project. This enthusiasm led to significant new support for "women in development" and created space for innovation and new institutional directions for the international-development world. It was in that environment that I began working with women at the UN to help create what is now known as Women's World Banking.

Although beyond the purview of the first decade of WWB's existence, many of our interviews shed light on some of the dynamic changes that have taken place since 1990. These commentaries offer perspectives that connect the WWB history to the present day. In retrospect, there were many signs, up to DFC's warnings in its 1989 assessment, that we could have or should have paid attention to in WWB's early years. Perhaps, had technology been more sophisticated then, we could have foreseen certain challenges and taken measures accordingly—focusing on sustainable regional management structures, defining more specific restrictions regarding the use of the Capital Fund, and having clearer policies about the management of WWB's investments. But many times, I believe WWB has fulfilled its mission "beyond my wildest dreams," namely, when I think about the numerous independent women-run financial institutions around the world that emerged through the WWB original network of affiliates and that continue to deliver on their mission in support of entrepreneurial women at the local level. Mariama Ashcroft spoke to this in my recent interview with her about WWB-Gambia.

Mariama Ashcroft

GAWFA [Gambia Women's Finance Association] has served as a lamppost for the Gambian microfinance industry for a very long time, because it has remained true to its mission of serving low-income women, especially in rural areas, and has pioneered the introduction of practices and systems that mirror international best-practice standards. For this reason, it has enjoyed the goodwill of the government and regulators who have protected it from failure.

When asked what I would do differently, I can't answer that question. There are so *many* possible answers I don't know where to begin. We could have done everything differently. Each person would have her/his own take on that. During my interviews, the most profound answer to that question for me came from **Beatrice Harretche**. Just as she had confronted me in the early days by telling me I had to run WWB, in 2009, when I asked about what she considered to be the biggest mistake I made during my leadership of WWB, she responded: "*Concentration of power; a mistake most every human makes. When you have people who don't understand what you are saying or trying to do, it is inevitable.*" Her remark struck me because it went to the core challenge that I personally confronted as president of WWB. Thinking about Beatrice's comments, I wonder, does strong leadership imply concentrating power or imposing one's vision? Not either, necessarily. Based on my personality as an entrepreneur, and my firm belief in decentralization, I functioned in the only way I knew in order to make our pioneering vision a reality.

Byron Kennard

It's very bad for humans to get in over their heads, and that's what large-scale does. That's why dictatorships are bad. No one individual can expect to exercise arbitrary power over others, because they don't know enough. So we have to have respect for self-organizing systems, which means we can't impose expectations on it so much as we can try to understand and see where it's headed and make that compatible with what our social needs are. Scale also has to do with the freedom of the entrepreneur. Freedom of those people who have new ideas and know how to make them happen. It boils down to the capacity of people and what their imaginations allow them to see. People in charge are generally unable to envision the power and creativity of decentralization. They're prohibited from it, because without centralization, they wouldn't be at the top. Today, a hermit in a cave can be connected to a computer and through it, to the entire world.

Decentralization—technologically, economically, and socially—represents a superior organizational system because it's self-organizing. Earth Day in 1970 put Environmental Protection on the agenda, but all that the Earth Day organizers knew was that "big business was poisoning the planet;" that was more or less the message of Earth Day. We woke up the day after to discover that we had acquired power within the Congress. Senators were calling up and asking what we wanted. So we had to figure out very quickly how to talk about things like tax policy, science and technology policy, agricultural policy, housing policy, and we didn't really have the expertise and knowledge. We had to form organizations and institutions that would step in and change things. Hazel Henderson and I started a thing called the Public Interest Economic Center with Allen Ferguson to try to transform the discipline of economics and to make it relevant to the new environmental revolution. It was in this context that I ran across a book called Small Is Beautiful *by E.F. Schumacher, which became my Bible and turned me on to the notion of scale. It's interesting—Earth Day, which created the environmental movement, not only in this country, but worldwide—was one of the most powerful grassroots demonstrations in all human history. It was local; it was free; it was creative; it was voluntary. People did what they wanted to do, wherever they were. And twenty million people did that on their own, with really no control and very little guidance. All the central office did was pick the date and raise the banner. The accumulated impact was huge.*

Byron, Hazel, and I, from different points of the universe, still have in common the commitment to reach out beyond the conventional and form connections and collaborations—an approach that requires letting go of control and allowing each partner to bring ideas forward.

Recently, I talked to Ron Léger, now retired and living in the French Alps. A program officer at the Canadian International Development Agency (CIDA) when WWB was founded, he became one of WWB's early and very enthusiastic supporters and commented on the principle of decentralization from the perspective of a donor in his 2011 interview.

Ron Léger

We (CIDA) were, I think, one of the very first contributors to WWB. I was very, very proud that Michaela early on started setting up the Capital Fund to be more independent, and proud to see that grow. We were absolutely forceful to encourage autonomy, because, for example, the way you would create Women's World Banking in Kenya will not be the same as in the Dominican Republic, or in Bangladesh, or in India. Some international NGOs literally forced what I call "photocopies." That was something that Michaela, who had already had international experience, knew was impossible. For WWB, the unifying strategy was to encourage each country to find its own way, with the right team of local women to set it up. I had the pleasure to meet some of the women who were the initial co-founders, like Mary Okelo, Ela Bhatt, Mercedes Canalda, and other very strong, independent, and rooted women with good connections. That strength gave spring to the organization and gave me the confidence to support it in the early days.

Many international NGOs become so dependent on donors like our own government, that the donors wound up dictating policies and sometimes the actual projects of those organizations— something that I view as a total disaster.

Toward the latter part of the '80s and early '90s, the requirements for reporting back to donors began to be more elaborate. The "let a thousand flowers bloom" approach was becoming a thing of the past; organizations had to show results in quantifiable terms, and the emphasis on success in numbers began to trump other areas of focus. Russell Phillips, who was vice president of Rockefeller Brothers Fund when I began working on WWB, commented on the changes in the development world that he witnessed throughout his career.

Russell Phillips

As vice president, I had oversight of the entire grant program. We didn't have a whole lot of money to work with; typically, we were making $15,000 grants; most were done on a repeat basis annually. At that time, for some reason, the NGO sector took off. I'll never forget sitting in front of the president's desk when he said, "When I got started in this field in 1937, you could count the NGOs in New York City on your fingers. . . . When you went to a dinner party, the guests were always trustees of each other's organizations." In the '60s, the sector just exploded; everyone wanted to create an NGO, and foundations were being created by the week. Through the mid-'80s when we were active, you checked out the person, the capacity, the viability of the idea, and if you determined it was worth doing, you wrote a check and, said, "Go do it and tell me sometime how it came out." Fast-forward to the '90s; there was too much money and too many organizations. I think what has happened in the foundation field is that foundations are increasingly being run like businesses. So if you're a trustee responsible for grant-making programs, what you want to see during the time you're a trustee is return on the money you've been responsible for granting. That puts a premium on what recipient organizations are doing that didn't exist earlier on. Nowadays program officers take fewer risks, because they have to justify their decisions to their board—so they assume more and more control of what's being done with the money, and recipient organizations have less and less space to be innovative. It takes a long time for grants to show results. By having to account for money, instead of for people and other hard to measure areas of impact, a climate of more control developed. I imagine that if Michaela were to appear today with the same kind of context, she would have a hard time getting funding, because she wouldn't be able to show quantitative results in eighteen months' time.

Validating that point, Marilou van Golstein from Triodos Bank, who is the Dutch representative trustee on the SWWB Board, recalled how useful unrestricted grants from the Netherlands were for WWB.

Marilou van Golstein

The fact that the Dutch Ministry of Development Cooperation became a major supporter of WWB, especially under Jan Pronk, was due less to the emphasis on women than to the interest in development overall. Exceptionally, the Dutch never gave orders regarding how the funding should be allocated, it was unrestricted—something that would be far more difficult to obtain today—and that helped WWB enormously. Of course, there were yearly updates and assessments of results. There was faith in the organization and in the responsibility and accountability of the people involved, so it was really up to WWB to mark its own path. As I recall, Michaela's vision was that WWB would be entrepreneurial; it was not about giving handouts to women, but about empowering them to take care of themselves and their families, and to develop their potential. WWB was never intended to operate like a traditional bank, but rather to integrate financial services with the whole concept of women's empowerment. It wasn't like she had a very clear business plan. The vision was the starting point and then she had to figure out what would be the best form to make it real.

I always believed and promoted the idea that change had to come from the edges. When I asked William (Bill) Dietel what he thought about it, as someone who had spent his career working within established institutional frameworks, his response added nuance to my conviction and resonated with me.

Bill Dietel

My experience is that change comes from both places. It can come from the center, and it also comes from the fringes. With modern technology, we are much more aware of what happens on the fringes now than we were in the '70s and '80s. . . .

Microfinance was pioneering in an intellectual sense: It was the idea that growth and change may be most efficacious when decentralized, as opposed to the historic tendency to centralize, to aggregate. . . . That happened elsewhere in the culture, but it started on the financial side, of all places.

I don't understand why some people are just naturally attracted to the new, the different, and the high-risk. I can't explain that, but I happen to be one of those people: a risk-taker. What you end up doing is betting on people. But it isn't just a gut reaction; there's got to be some evidence somewhere that somebody can really pull off what they're hoping to do. There's something really immensely attractive about a person who really has a dream, and obviously is beginning to generate some passion and wants to try it. There are people like myself who by accident, not by virtue of anything I did, end up in a position where we can help them make something happen. We're not the ones who make things happen, but we help these individuals. And that gets done often in my experience with just a positive reaction. The next thing you know, you are helping to provide start-up money and contacts that can give the person a fighting chance at getting started.

By the end of the first decade of WWB's existence, the changes in the development world affected the field of "micro," which by then had gained momentum and had begun to be viewed as a viable instrument for poverty alleviation. John Hammock, who, after directing Accion and working with WWB, went on to become the head of Oxfam-USA, shared his reflections.

John Hammock

In 1970, nobody thought any of these "poor people" could pay back loans. But Accion, WWB, and others disproved them all. We've proved that banks can give loans to the poor and not only not lose money, but actually make money. It only took twenty years. . . . The problem is that when the spread gets bigger and suddenly the organizations become banks, the social reasoning starts to become privatized. It's a real dilemma, because as the loan size gets bigger, you stop reaching certain people. Accion never reached the poorest of the poor. People who are destitute cannot pay back a loan. Accion was only reaching people who could pay back a loan. All we're doing with micro is lowering the pyramid; we're not reaching the bottom. However, it's only inevitable to grow with your borrowers, if the organization loses sight of its goals. The tendency is to hire private-sector types who do not value the social bottom line. There's been a big split in the microcredit community from day one. The Accions of the world saw it as a private-sector thing—we have to charge interest rates and live off the spread. Then there's always been the other strong camp saying, "You're exploiting the poor. The goal is social, and microcredit is just a tool to get into the community; we don't have to be repaid." Personally I think that's unethical, because if you give someone a loan and charge little or no interest and then you leave, they still have to get money from somewhere, and unless they have the cost of money in their business from day one, they're going to get screwed. . . . WWB falls into the business-category side. It's a social business, but you still have to repay your loans. Another problem these days is that donors have a lot of power in the development model—and there is more funding going to nonprofits and less to governments. This feeds into the Reagan philosophy of getting government out of the way, which at the end of the day is wrong, because a government is still responsible for its people. It's great for nonprofits, but it doesn't do much in terms of long-term viability. For instance, if there is a clinic in Rwanda and one in Burundi, and USAID decides they're not going to give you the ten million dollars this year that they gave you last year, now you have to close down one of those clinics. If the government had that clinic, it would hang around. Or say you're in a community for three years, I guarantee you'll leave thinking that the community's major issue is whatever you were working on, because the community knows what you've got money for from the beginning, even before you get there, and they'll make you think that's their priority. The best model of development is not for Americans to do it, but for local people to do it. That's what WWB did in setting up local organizations. WWB-New York is not going to do it. Each affiliate does it their way. The question is how do you keep creating space for change? We know what works. I'm convinced that change is possible.

Elizabeth Littlefield, who was appointed director of the Overseas Private Investment Corporation (OPIC) in June 2010, conveyed her thoughts about the impact of the WWB movement and "micro."

Elizabeth Littlefield

Women's World Banking was like the Pied Piper in Africa, and everyone saw the movement beginning and wanted to join. It was a very powerful movement, but the notion of financial disciplines had not yet been absorbed. As WWB evolved, it transformed from a movement into something that was a very effective and powerful network of individual institutions providing ever more sophisticated and demand-responsive products over time.

I have very strong feelings that the overpromising and the hype that was accompanied by this turning into not just a movement in the developing countries, but a movement in the West, was very damaging. It was the worst thing that ever happened. We were quietly building financial systems in poor countries that served the majority of the population of that country, and that required long-term technical financial support. And suddenly, it's swept up in this maelstrom of excitement, and rock stars, and movie stars, and it just set us back many, many years in terms of professionalizing this very serious business. Building financial systems for poor people is very serious business, and it became unserious, or unprofessional—more like charity and more like a cause, rather than a profession. That was very problematic, and drew the attention of so many that wanted to make money. It points directly to what's going on now, where the hype got far ahead of the reality.

Christine Bindert, having worked in major institutions such as the IMF and Lehman Brothers and served on the board of WWB, also offered her thoughts on the evolution of "micro."

Christine Bindert

I believe that microcredit as a concept is a very good one. But I do not believe that a big institution— like a bank—can do it from the standpoint of basic shareholder return. Bigger banks cannot get involved in microcredit; it's a complete absurdity; it doesn't work. Banks have to make a living; they have shareholders, right? Even if it's the state. And by definition, they are so inefficient in terms of cost that they cannot give a loan for $50—it's impossible. So I think that's a complete misnomer. Perhaps they are doing it for PR, or it's the flavor of the day.

Peter Blom, director of Triodos Bank, explored the question of "micro" from the standpoint of the values behind banking more broadly.

Peter Blom

There is no better example of people working in a real economy than microfinance. Banking should serve those people who put their skills into the economic process, make products, and provide services. However, microfinance is not the solution for getting people out of poverty. That requires a much broader development picture in which money is a very important tool, but it's also about education, governance, and many other aspects. We still have a long way to go in learning that it is not our investments in developing countries that are key, but rather that those countries take over their own social and economic development. So I am really critical of Wall Street and London City investment companies who think this is the new sector and that they can make a lot of money on it. There has to be a shift of thinking on the part of economists so that the market fundamentalism—which is very strong in our part of the world— can be replaced by maximizing sustainability instead of maximizing profits. It is much more important for these countries to strike a balance between people, profit, and planet, or it will be just about profit again. We in the West try to export too much of our model to those countries, and the model has failed. We should be more humble about what we can do and really support, not dictate. What is good about the financial crisis is that it makes clear that the business model of the big banks is not sustainable. Getting bigger is not the answer. Probably the answer is getting smaller again, but very much interconnected through networks—not the old village bank with no connection whatsoever. Banks are about relationships, not about transactions. But we started to earn more money with transactions and therefore we didn't serve the relationships anymore, and now we are paying a very high price for that. For banking to go back to relationships means there has to be an adequate size where those relationships can really be nurtured.

Klaas Molenaar, who was exposed to microfinance at the country level through the training sessions for WWB affiliates that he had developed with Margarita Guzmán, shared his perspective.

Klaas Molenaar

You've been pulled into microfinance too much—at the beginning it was about small entrepreneurs. You have to be strong about maintaining diversity. There are very different views from Latin America to Asia to Africa, completely different cultural settings in which the affiliates operate. Large affiliates with thousands of members can be part of the same network as smaller programs. The diversity strengthens the ability to seek solutions. If you don't treat WWB as a movement, it will not survive. If you create it as an institution it will not survive: You start competing against your members.

Klaas's point raised another question I have had from the outset, and still grapple with: Does a movement die upon becoming represented by organizations? How can we ensure that external circumstances and bureaucratic and funding prerogatives don't overtake the initial mission for which organizations are created?

At a SWWB Board of Trustees meeting in 1989, in connection to a discussion about whether to maintain WWB's regional offices, **Geertje Lycklama** said, *"WWB is part of the larger women's movement, and somebody needs to watch this."*

For WWB, maintaining our commitment to our mission meant we had to trust that each member of the WWB network (New York Management, Board of Trustees, and each affiliate) would evolve at its own rhythm; that WWB's unique structure would successfully build up its management experience over time; and that our trust in each other would determine our future. These principles remain critical in the present day, as affiliates continue to draw attention to key questions like, "Historically, what stake did network members have in WWB? Who owns WWB as a network?"

Pauline Kruseman (former director of the Royal Tropical Museum and the Amsterdam Museum) was introduced to WWB by Siska Pothof in the 1980s. She served on the SWWB Board from 1990 to 2003, and remains a major enthusiast. She also served on the Board of WWB-Netherlands as well as the Triodos Bank's Supervisory Board. She recollected how the balance between the WWB "movement" and institutional structure was addressed.

Pauline Kruseman

*As the organization grew, most of us on the board were much more focused on management, the budget, the finances and our reports to the Ministry. **Ela Bhatt** was always very quiet, even as a chairperson, and then would say, "Nobody talks about poverty and women. Is that perhaps an issue we can talk about?" It was fantastic, because that was the issue, but sometimes you had to talk about budgets and reports and requests from the Ministry, but it was great that at least once every meeting, she reminded us what we were really there for.*

One issue that always drew attention however was that not all of the affiliates were really growing, so some of the affiliates stayed small. And it raised the question, "Is that because it is all women?" "Why are Grameen or the other one in Indonesia growing enormously and have many, many participants?" That was also a question from the Dutch Ministry—that WWB was not growing enough. So that was quite often a heated discussion in the Board—how is everybody performing? All the affiliates are, of course, independent organizations, so you always had to be a little bit careful not to be imposing too much.

Nicki Armacost, who joined WWB in 1990, shared her take on how the values of the movement were carried throughout WWB's institutional evolution.

Nicki Armacost

We always used to check in with affiliate members on new policies. Decisions weren't made in New York and pushed outward; they were made together in a communal context; endorsement was always sought through the membership structure. That was enabled by the fact that the affiliate leaders were always members of the Board of Directors, so the ultimate decision-making body of the organization had members of the network embedded in it. They always understood that it was their duty to represent the entire network in their deliberations. You can't have everyone on a Board of Directors, or you would have an organization like the UN's General Assembly. On our Board, it was understood that members were representative of the broader network, and that mutual accountability for results (meaning that we were each accountable to one another for our results), and commitment to maintaining WWB as a women-centered organization, were central to our ethos even as we continued to grow. That made this network different from some of the other microfinance networks that were out there; it was very much a participatory network that relied on members' views, deliberation, and discussion. We were never afraid to have discussions at Women's World Banking; some of them were quite passionate; we didn't always agree.

I think of WWB as a web, where we are all interconnected, no matter where we are. It's really important to stay connected to the values, even as each generation copes with challenges that are specific to its time. The '70s were very different times; to talk about women as entrepreneurs was radical then. People wanted to talk about women as victims, but Michaela and the founders kept communicating with people who weren't really that interested in listening and eventually charmed them into giving money to the nascent organization and growing it into what it is today, which is actually a real powerhouse for change. What poor women need twenty years from now may be different from what they need today, and the organization will have to adapt, but the organization's vision is what will keep the staff and affiliate members mobilized, namely that the affiliate network is a touchstone for the values of the organization.

When we met with Nancy Barry, who was president of Women's World Banking from 1990 to 2006 and who had served on the WWB Board since 1982 while working at the World Bank, she offered her views on local ownership, as well as the growth of WWB as an institution.

Nancy Barry

When I first became involved in WWB, I was at the World Bank, leading a lot of the World Bank's work on small enterprise, exports, and industrial competitiveness. At the same time I was learning a very different way of working by being part of WWB. There was no real concept of microcredit in the 1980s, no real notion of what was and was not working in terms of financing the poor. My role in the '80s was about building the small-enterprise lending portfolio, and those were mainly loans of about one thousand dollars for projects all over Asia, Latin America, and Africa. It was interesting to juxtapose that with the original and what I consider "evolved" vision of WWB. The underlying principles of WWB, which ended up making it very unique, and make it unique to this day, were:

- *One, that local leaders know best. That in itself was revolutionary; the entire principle of development aid is that the money and the know-how exist in the North, and all you have to do is transplant it to the South.*

- *Two, lateral learning. Local leaders working in the Dominican Republic, Colombia, India, and Kenya, communicating what they are doing, what's working, what's not working; building a set of common principles, standards, and ways of working together. It means each leader is a change agent, but a change agent that does not feel alone.*

If you look at the document that was created during the first meeting (the 1980 International Workshop of Women Leaders in Banking and Finance), the core principles were all there. And not just on the primacy of poor women as economic- and social-change agents, but the whole notion of the structure of WWB—which was completely without precedent—building a lateral organization was present. In some ways it was good, because it shook out the serious from the non-serious and allowed for natural leaders to emerge in the network, and those subsequently became the members of the Board. If it had been super efficient and top-down, it would have had more passive types, and the wrong ones would have been supported.

In terms of local ownership, however, you cannot presume that by not telling affiliates what to do, they will always opt for the most responsive approach to poor women, especially if they get funded by external actors that may be pushing their own agenda. Particularly in places like Africa, there was a real tendency to be donor-driven. I remember in one of my early regional meetings with the African affiliates, I challenged them to spend one hour without mentioning the word "donor." It was tough. That self-confidence has shifted, and the recognition that they can call the shots grew over time.

Another core principle of WWB from the beginning was to employ business approaches to economic and social change. It had to be sustainable, not charity. By insisting that every affiliate establish a small capital fund of twenty thousand dollars, it allowed us to separate those that were serious about building local organizations from those that were just interested in having a few women they could speak about at cocktail parties. That happened in 1986 at a crazy meeting that took place in Brazil, although there was a big fight. (I remember a Bangladeshi woman saying, "We're a poor country. We can't afford twenty thousand dollars!" and then watched her spend twenty thousand dollars on jewelry in Brazil. . . . She did not last as part of the WWB network.) We needed to have a transformational agenda. It's not enough to make one loan, or a million loans, to your own clients. You need to take that leadership and shape the movement—not the industry but the movement—by sharing what you know with others, impacting policy makers, getting mainstream banks involved in microfinance, really using your leadership as a woman to create systemic access for low-income women.

Some women-led affiliates grew at a very rapid clip, and their vision and the depth of their connection with low-income women made it possible to create an ethos within the industry that was very, very different than a male-led ethos.

Mary Ellen Iskenderian, president of Women's World Banking since 2006, shared her insights on what drew her to WWB and on the future of the organization and microfinance more broadly.

Mary Ellen Iskenderian

I first heard about WWB towards 1985–86, when I was getting my MBA at the Yale School of Management. WWB raised the consciousness around the difficulty that women entrepreneurs had to obtain funding and presented a practical, market-based solution to the problem that was intriguing (and is what students today still find attractive). From Yale I went to Lehman Brothers and worked in investment banking for four years. Eventually, I felt that the work I was doing was getting further away from my values—I had an undergraduate degree in development economics—and so I applied to the Young Professionals program at the World Bank. I was accepted and assigned to the IFC (the World Bank Group's International Finance Corporation), where I worked on identifying private-sector solutions to poverty alleviation. Around that time, the Berlin Wall fell and I had the opportunity to work in the former Soviet Union as countries were opening up. It was there that I witnessed microfinance at work firsthand and understood the progress it could bring for people who had no faith in the financial system, but had hopes to become entrepreneurs.

Leaving the IFC and joining WWB in 2006 was incredibly refreshing—it's an organization that is much smaller and more nimble than what I was used to, where you can make changes and respond to changes. It was exciting to get to be in an organization with a majority of women—very different from the IFC and Lehman Brothers. However, I was struck by how far away from the women-focused mission the organization had drifted since its inception. WWB had become centered on building strong institutions on the ground that had an unswerving focus on women, but in terms of the New York-based team, the commitment to women's economic empowerment wasn't so alive.

I've endeavored to bring it back to the roots with an explicit focus on women's economic empowerment. We work with a three-year strategic planning process. WWB continues to be strong in innovation. The bigger job we've taken on is continuing to make the business case for why it makes sense for financial institutions to focus on women and serve women's needs. It's remarkable how many don't realize the power women have around financial decisions—even in very conservative cultures— being the saver of household money is a very important role.

There are real concerns about larger institutions getting involved in the credit process, as they invariably turn microfinance into consumer finance and have an understanding of risk-assessment that is very different from the way you need to analyze risk for women working in the informal sector. For example, in Paraguay, a mainstream bank in rural areas was doing market research, going to household after household where women were bringing three times more revenue to the house than the husband who was doing cash crops, but because the bank understood cash crops, it was willing to finance him. . . even if neither one owned land titles. . . the mainstream banks were more ready to lend to him. Fortunately, some financial institutions are open to this education process.

"Micro" is no longer limited to credit only. There is a broader dialogue under way, and an opportunity to think about the range of products that you can offer in partnership with larger institutions.

Sylvia Chin, who joined the board of WWB in 1989 and whose firm has continued to provide the indispensable (and often pro bono) long-term legal counsel throughout WWB's existence, also commented.

Sylvia Chin

I hope that the organization will maintain a pre-eminent leadership role in microfinance and particularly as a development voice against those who would view the field as just a profit-making venture. It took a lot of persuasion to get people to appreciate the value that extending credit and other types of support to local entrepreneurs can have—even though it's difficult to measure except for individual anecdotes. . . . The disadvantage is that microfinance has become a buzzword. Young people come and say, "I would just love to work in project finance," but they don't have understanding of what that is. We're now seeing abuses, because people jumped on the bandwagon without evaluating the overall scheme, thinking it was a magical elixir.

Living with the Future Now

Lilia Clemente

One basic attitude we try to embody in our WWB work is a distrust of grandiose schemes. As the old song goes, "little things mean a lot." While WWB as an institution is built of solid blocks on which we can stand, networks, diversity, and developing relationships worldwide provide a context in which individuals can safely grow, learn, and change.

I believe that the higher the rate of change, the more we need to have a firm grasp of our WWB roots planted in 1979, not to cling to them, but to assure the continuity of things worth bringing into the future—and in the end, we find comfort and refuge in our core, that bag of values that worked whenever and wherever. Only this time, we are called upon to have and give it in a deeper, larger measure. As the Russian poet Andrei Voznesensky said, "We need a revolution of the mind." Shock and confusion are often associated with accelerated change. Women and WWB can thrive in the midst of chaos by seeing order and openness to change. Whatever it may require, I say it's all worth it, because the future is, indeed, not what it used to be.

Helen Junz

For me, seeing the coming into being of what many would have thought to be but a dream, is the tremendous achievement of that small group of women who started it all in Mexico City. What must not be lost is the recognition of how innovative the concept of WWB was, and how difficult its implementation is, and how successful it is in the end, as most would consider WWB in its middle age to be part of the mainstream of what today is called microfinance—provision of full financial services to microbusinesses. I consider it a privilege to have been associated, albeit only at the edges, in this achievement.

Part of my motivation for this history is to show the complexities behind and beyond the trends, and encourage people to tap into their creativity and pursue their dreams.

Personal passion for social change combined with the unpredictable has always guided me toward new pathways. After 1990, I pursued many initiatives; I was privileged to chair the Board of Synergos Institute, a nonprofit founded by Peggy Dulany to reduce poverty around the world by bringing together communities, governments, civil society, and philanthropists. I wanted to work with younger women to help them understand the importance of cultural diversity and the development of leadership skills. I am grateful to Manhattanville College's former president, Richard Berman, for making that opportunity possible. Susan Stehlik, who refers to it as the most creative work she had done up to that point, and I co-designed Global Student Leadership (GSL)—a summer program for female undergraduate students from developing countries. Of approximately 125 GSL students from around the world, many have now launched local leadership and ethics programs in their own countries. With that program, as with WWB, the commitment of women working together; learning and gaining strength, courage, and hope from each other creates ripple effects that are changing the way the world works, person by person. The work of many individuals has been a beacon for me.

In closing, it's important to stress that WWB's innovative approach for finance and women was based on concepts that are not unique to WWB. Cooperation, community-driven solutions, and shared ownership and responsibility are often critical to survival. For me, no one understood that better than Wangari Maathai.

Wangari was a forceful inspiration for many of us. Her vision of the human relationship to nature—as echoed in her own words read at her memorial service—puts all of our work on this earth into perspective.

WOMEN'S WORLD BANKING

August 21, 1990

Michaela Walsh
President

Dear Friends & Colleagues:

As many of you know, on August 31st I am resigning as President of Women's World Banking. Nancy Barry, a long time member of WWB a Trustee since 1983 and Vice-Chairman of the Board since 1987, will become the new President of Women's World Banking on September 1st. Mary Okelo, also a Trustee since 1982 and a Director of the Afican Development Bank, will become the Executive Vice President and is expected to join WWB later this year.

This transition has been under discussion among the Trustees and myself for over two years. Without exception we are convinced that their creative energy, talents, commitment to the integrity of WWB and its future, and Nancy's long experience as one of the women leaders at the World Bank will guide WWB to new levels of respect and opportunity.

During the past few months many people have asked me, "Why are you leaving WWB?" I have assured them that I do not see this change as my departure from WWB or from my original dream and I shall continue to support the new management as a Trustee. WWB has become a way of life. WWB is more than a global financial institution, an affiliate network, a movement, a commitment of individual members sharing a dream.

As I traveled through the 1980's helping to build WWB, the real joy I experienced was finding so many women and men who shared similar concerns about building new business opportunities for women. Many of us, from diverse backgrounds with individual skills and regional relationships, began working as a team, to build a new type of financial institution: a global institution designed and managed by women, who are committed to seeing women take our places as partners in management and decision making in a newly emerging sustainable economy.

Our efforts together have been honest and open. I have operated under the theory that: "Decisions about the future based on less than truly honest assessment and understanding of the past, will be to our disadvantage and inadequate." We have learned to respect each other. We have learned to suffer temporary conflicts, and misunderstandings of style. Together we have learned that our strength rests in taking individual responsibility for working together and trusting our common dream. Together we have built a global network of nearly 50 local affiliates in over 40 countries; a global capital base of $10 million including over $3 million in local capital funds; a total loan portfolio of over 56,000 loans, or $11.5 million in new money to women running small and micro businesses;

Stichting to Promote Women's World Banking
104 East 40th Street New York, NY 10016 (212) 953-2390 WOMBANKING TELEX 5101012670 WWB

MICHAELA'S RESIGNATION LETTER

a loan loss rate of less than 1.5%; a new Management Institute; a series of management tools including an Affiliate Exchange program, a Start-Up Loan program, "How To Manuals" a World Trade Atlas; and a global newsletter WWBNEWS. Together we have created WWB and we have laid the foundation for a movement to build business partnerships among women around the globe.

As we begin the 1990's, my dream is to see WWB's major strength continue to be its people and to see an ever-expanding network of women in business working together towards our shared goals. Reality requires ever-changing and expanding talent, experience and commitment. I am confident that WWB's future depends on its capacity to deepen and expand its own management and services, expand its resources and strengthen its global network. Nancy Barry is the best person I know to lead WWB at this time. Because of the confidence I have in Nancy and Mary as a team, I am leaving with great joy and confidence — and with a sense of pride in my own tenure. But most important, I also leave with enormous gratitude to each and every person who has had the patience to tolerate my doggedness, the understanding and kindness to support my efforts and the loyalty and trust of friendship I so deeply needed. I could not wish them more.

My own priorities continue to focus on finding new business and banking opportunities for women by encouraging a broader public understanding of WWB and by encouraging greater investment opportunity into the hands of women. Before the end of 1990 I expect to launch a new WWB affiliate. Women's World Growth Fund will be an investment fund for women, which I have been working toward in an ad hoc way for many years. I trust you will join me with your enthusiastic support.

This week, WWB/NY moved to new offices, which will be shared with another organization and a former Trustee.

        WOMEN'S WORLD BANKING
        8 WEST 40TH STREET, 10th FLOOR
        NEW YORK, NEW YORK   10018
        TEL. (212) 768-8513
        FAX. (212) 768-8519

It is wonderful space that serves to confirm WWB's goal to build partnerships and to serve as a communication center. Together new leadership and new space reaffirm that WWB is not just a credit project. WWB is a real financial institution owned by women who are GIVING WOMEN CREDIT!

                        Sincerely,

                        Michaela Walsh
                        President

We are all part of nature. . . . There is a pattern that we are very much a part of, but that we really don't control. I'm very aware that I cannot live without the green trees. I'm humbled by the understanding that they can do very well without me! I'm also humbled by the fact that they sustain me, and not the other way around.

—Wangari Maathai (1940–2011)
Founder, Greenbelt Movement

Photo Martha Stuart Communications

Photo Doug Goodman

Photo Sherith Jarkosh

NOTES

1. Frank P. Walsh was chair of the National Industrial Relations Commission, 1913–15, appointed by President Wilson; joint chair of the War Labor Board, 1917–18, with former President Taft; chair of the Saint Lawrence Waterway Authority, 1930–31, under President Franklin D. Roosevelt. The Waterway Authority became the New York State Power Authority, to which Walsh was reappointed by Governor Herbert Lehman and on which he served until his death, in 1939.

2. Boserup, Ester, *Women's Role in Economic Development,* New York: St. Martin's Press, 1965.

3. On December 15, 1975, the United Nations General Assembly adopted Resolution 3522 (XXX), "Improvement of the economic status of women for their effective and speedy participation in the development of their countries." It states:

   > The General Assembly 1. Urges Governments, governmental and non-governmental organizations to support more vigorously official and private efforts to extend to women the facilities now being offered only to men by financial and lending institutions; 2. Requests Governments to encourage all efforts by women's organizations, cooperatives and lending institutions which will enable women at the lowest level in rural and urban areas to obtain credit and loans to improve their economic activities and integration in national development; 3. Urges Governments and the organizations of the United Nations development system, including specialized agencies and non-governmental organizations to incorporate in their programs, workshops and seminars, courses designed to improve the efficiency of women in business and financial management.

   Additional references appear in UNGA Resolution 3520 of 30 January, 1976, and Resolution A/RES/31/175 of December 21, 1976, "Effective Mobilization of Women in Development." (See the resolution, p. 192.)

4. Leticia Shahani's essay "The UN, Women, and Development: The World Conferences on Women" is published in *Developing Power: How Women Transformed International Development*, edited by Arvonne S. Fraser and Irene Tinker, New York: The Feminist Press, City University of New York, 2004.

AIDS AND DOCUMENTS

SWWB Organizing Committees and Working Groups, 1975–1980   181

SWWB Global and Trustees Meetings, 1980–1990   182

SWWB Trustees, 1980–1990   184

SWWB Consultants, Volunteers, Staff, and Interns, 1980–1990   187

SWWB Affiliates and Affiliates in Formation, 1975–1990   188

Key to Acronyms, by Chapter   190

United Nations General Assembly Resolution 3520 of January 30, 1976, and Resolution A/RES/31/175 of December 21, 1976, "Effective Mobilization of Women in Development"   192

SWWB Charter   198

SWWB Bylaws   205

Letter of Invitation to 1980 Amsterdam Workshop   211

Report on the First International Workshop of Women Leaders in Banking and Finance, Amsterdam, The Netherlands, March 1980   213

Agreement Between Stichting and Its Affiliates to Promote Women's World Banking   275

Loan Guarantee Program and Private Placement Memorandums   280

Report on the Second International Workshop of Women Leaders in Banking and Finance (co-sponsored by Accion), San Remo, Italy, April 1981   283

SWWB/WWB Organizational Chart   314

Executive Summary of 1990 Ten-year DFC Evaluation and Table of Affiliate Status   315

Financials   326

SWWB ORGANIZING COMMITTEES AND WORKING GROUPS, 1975–1980

MEXICO CITY STEERING COMMITTEE 1975

Hamamsy, Gasbia (Egypt)

Martinez-Garza, Bertha Beatriz (Mexico)

Rha, ChoKyun (Professor) (Republic of Korea)

Ocloo, Esther (Ghana)

Saurwein, Virginia (USA)

Snyder, Margaret (Peg) (USA)

UNITED NATIONS AND NEW YORK WORKING GROUP 1977

Mair, Lucille (Jamaica)

Pezzullo, Caroline (USA)

Saurwein, Virginia (USA)

Sederlund, Leslie (USA)

Shahani, Leticia Ramos (Philippines)

Snyder, Margaret (Peg) (USA)

Stuart, Martha (USA)

Walsh, Michaela (USA)

COMMITTEE TO ORGANIZE WOMEN'S WORLD BANKING 1980

Bulengo, Martha (Sierra Leone)

Cloherty, Patricia (USA)

Hamamsy, Gasbia El (Egypt)

Jiagge, Mrs. Justice Annie (Ghana)

Mair, Lucilla (Jamaica)

Martinez-Garza, Bertha Beatriz (Mexico)

Ocloo, Esther (Ghana)

Pezzullo, Caroline (USA)

Saurwein, Virginia (USA)

Sederlund, Leslie (Iran)

Shahani, Leticia Ramos (Philippines)

Snyder, Margaret (Peg) (USA)

Stuart, Martha (USA)

Tabatabai, Zohreh (Iran)

Walsh, Michaela (USA)

SWWB GLOBAL AND TRUSTEES MEETINGS, 1980–1990

1980
March 15–16
Amstel Hotel
Amsterdam, The Netherlands

July 15 & 17—Trustees only
UN Conference Hall
Copenhagen, Denmark

1981
March 30–April 3
Nobel Foundation
San Remo, Italy

1982—Trustees only
March 21–24
Equitable Life Board Room
New York, NY

November 17
Extraordinary Meeting of the Board of Trustees
Manila Hotel
Manila, Philippines

1983—Trustees only
March
Alma Matthews House
New York, NY

1984
May 13–15
DeBilderberg Hotel
Oosterbeek, Netherlands
1985—Trustees only

May 24–26
WWB-NY office and Alma Matthews House
New York, NY

1986
May 24–25
Sheraton Hotel
Rio de Janeiro, Brazil

1987—Trustees only
May 22–23
Private Apartment in Radio City Music Hall
New York, NY

1988
May 26–28
Hosted by Nellie Tan-Wong
Kuala Lumpur, Malaysia

1989—Trustees only
June 10–11
Schloss Leopoldskron
Salzburg, Austria

1990
April 21–28
"GIVE WOMEN CREDIT"
Martin Luther King Center
Atlanta, GA

EXECUTIVE AND/OR FINANCE COMMITTEE MEETINGS
(where information was available)

1981
July 22—Executive
September 9—Executive
October 25—Executive

1982
May 17—Finance
September 8—Executive & Finance
December 17—Finance

1983
January 13—Executive
March 13 & 17—Executive and Finance
May 31—Executive & Finance
July 27—Executive
October 7—Finance
July 27—Executive

1984
February 14—Finance
April 18—Investment Sub-Committee
July 18—Executive
September 5—Finance
September 20—Executive
November 20—Finance

1985
January 10—Executive & Finance
March 4—Finance
September 12—Executive
November 21—Executive & Finance\
Banca de la Provencie de
Buenos Aires Office, NYC

1986
January 25   Home of Siska Potof
Blaricum, The Netherlands
November 25—Finance (Conf. Call)

1987
January 17–18—Executive
Seidenhof Hotel
Zurich, Switzerland
May 22—Executive & Finance

1988
March 11–13—Executive and Finance
May 12—Finance
Harrison Conf. Center
Glen Cove, NY
Sept 9–10—Executive

1989
March 9–11—Executive
Cos Club, NYC
November 2—Executive & Region
Coordination Committee
NMB Bank
Amsterdam Netherlands
December 20—Executive Conference Call
WWB-NY Office

1990
March 23–24—Executive
Bedford Hotel, NYC
August
White & Case Offices

SWWB TRUSTEES, 1980–1990

Sashia Holleman Nauta Van Haesolte	Netherlands	1983
J. Burke Knapp World Bank	USA	1986 Deceased 1985
Rudolf S.H. Mees Nederlansche Middenstandsbank, N.V.	Netherlands	1990 Deceased 2010
Martha Stuart Martha Stuart Communications, Inc.	USA	1985 Deceased 1985
1982		
Barbro Dahlbom-Hall Management Training and Development Specialist	Sweden	1988
Mary Okelo Barclay's Bank, Nairobi	Kenya	1982
1983		
Manilla Chaneton de Vivo Latin American Regional Rep.	Uruguay	1988
Engering, Frans Ministry of Finance	Netherlands	1983
Lourdes Lontok Cruz Paluwagan Ng Bayan Savings & Loan Assoc.	Philippines	1988 Deceased 2011
Modupe Ibiayo Okojie Finance Consultants, Ltd.	Nigeria	1983
1984		
Geertje Lycklama Women and Development Programme Institute of Social Studies	Netherlands	1988
Nellie S.L. Tan-Wong Wintrac (WWB/Malaysia) Sdn. Bhd.	Malaysia	1990
1985		
Maria Margarita Guzman WWB – Cali	Colombia	1988
Helen B. O'Bannon University of Pennsylvania	USA	1988 Deceased 1988
Deanna Rosenswig Bank of Montreal	Canada	1992
1986		
Christine Bogdarnowicz-Bindert Lehman Cooperation	Germany	1992

Rosmarie Michel Confiserie Schurter AG	Switzerland	1998
Babacar N'Diaye African Development Bank	Ivory Coast	1992
1987		
David Sambar Sambar International Investments, Ltd.	UK	1993
1988		
Do Sung Chang Cho Hung Bank	Korea	1994
Chinda Charungcharoenvejj FWWB Association in Thailandia	Thailand	1994
Sylvia Fletcher WWB – Credimujer	Costa Rica	1994
Barbara Fynn-Williams Bajata Agencies	Ghana	1994 Deceased
Margaret Catley-Carlson Dept. of National Health and Welfare	Canada	1996
Ann Partlow Rockefeller & Co.	USA	1994
Berit Aas University of Oslo Institute of Psychology	Norway	1994/1995
1990		
Mercedes Canalda Asociacion Dominican Para el Desarrollo de la Mujer (ADOPEM)	Dominican Republic	2004
Sylvia Fung Chin White & Case	USA	Legal Adviser
Pauline Kruseman Stichting WWB Nederland	Netherlands	2002
Elizabeth Littlefield Morgan Guaranty Trust Company	UK	2000
Yoshio Terasawa Multilateral Investment Guarantee Agency	Japan	1996

*See ex-officio members.

SWWB CONSULTANTS, VOLUNTEERS, STAFF, AND INTERNS, 1980–1990

CONSULTANTS AND VOLUNTEERS

Chase, Lee (Bookkeeper)

Hammock, John (Programs)

Hartwell, Anne (Fund Raising)

Hollister, Chas C. (Brochure Design)

Hunter, Tom (CPA)

Luton, Barbara (Office Admin)

Maynes, Gretchen (Global Meeting)

Monheim, Marnie (Africa Newsletter)

Morrill, Nancy (Friends of WWB/USA)

Novogratz, Jacqueline (Africa Program)

Shapiro, Joan (Global Meeting)

Sheldon, Tony (Advisor)

Winer, Susan (Marketing)

STAFF AND SUMMER INTERNS

Abrams, Julie

Burger, Michelle

Case, Nancy

Clavel, Diana

Davidsen, Amy

Duval, Ann

Hayes, Paula

Horwood, Joanne

Giblen, Ana Maria (Peru)

Lammert, Sarah

Lopez, Hector

McClanahan, Chris and Laura

Mele, Ferne (Italy)

Mollinaro, Ada

Patel, Samir (India)

Pollock, Kim

Rafi, Shazia (Pakistan)

Ralston, David

Robinson, Sharon

Ruckelshaus, Catherine

Wilcott-Henrie, Leslie

Williams, Jacqueline (Haiti)

SWWB AFFILIATES AND AFFILIATES-IN-FORMATION, 1975–1990

AFRICA

Burundi
Assoc. pour la Promotion Econ. de la Femme (APEF) (1988)

Gambia
The Gambia Women's Finance Company (GWFC) (1988)

Ghana
Friends of Women's World Banking Ghana, Ltd. (WWB-GHANA) (1982)

Kenya
Kenya Women's Finance Trust (KWFT) (1982)

Lesotho
Basali Boitjarong (Women for Self Reliance) (1982)

Mali
Assoc. pour l'Integr. de la Femme dans l'Economie Malienne (AIFEM) (WWB-Mali) (1988)

Rwanda
Duterimbere (WWB-Rwanda) (1982)

Senegal
Societe Senegalise de Garantie d'Assist. et de Credit (SOSEGAF) (1988)

Uganda
Uganda Women's Finance and Credit Trust (UWFCT) (1982)

Zambia
Women's Trust of Zambia, Ltd. (WFTZ) (1982)

Zimbabwe
Zimbabwe Women's Finance Trust (ZWFT) (1988)

LATIN AMERICA

Bolivia
Fundacion Boliviana para el Desarrollo de la Mujer (WWB-Bolivia) (1982)

Brazil
Banca da Mulher-Assoc. Brasil para o Desenvolvimento da Mulher (WWB-Brazil) (1982)

Chile
Corporacion WWB Filial Chilena (WWB-Chile) (1988)

Colombia
Corporacion Mundial de la Mujer-Medellin (1982)
Fundacion Mundo Mujer-Popayan (1982)
Fundacion Mundial de la Mujer-Bucaramanga (1982)
Fundacion WWB-Cali (1982)
Corporacion Mundial de la Mujer-Bogota (1988)

Costa Rica
Credimujer (1982)

Dominican Republic
Asoc. Dominicana para el Desarrollo de la Mujer (ADOPEM) (1982)

Ecuador
Corporacion Feminina Ecuatoriana (1982)

Guadeloupe
Femmes et Initiati. pour le Dev. Econ. de la Guadeloupe (FIDEG) (1982)

Haiti
Fonds Haiti en d'Aide à la Femme (FHAF) (1982)

Honduras

Fund. Hondurena para el Desarrollo de la Mujer (FUNDHDEMU) (1982)

Jamaica

Friends of Women's World Banking Jamaica, Ltd. (1982)

Uruguay

Fundacion Uruguaya de Ayuda Asistencia a la Mujer (FUAAM) (1982)

ASIA

Bangladesh

National Assoc. for Resource Improvements (NARI) (1982)

Friends of WWB-Bangladesh

India

Friends of WWB-India, Ahmedabad (1982)

Assoc. of Women Entrepreneurs in Karnataka (AWAKE), Bangalore (1982)

Women Entrepreneurs Resource Dev. Agency (WERDAN), New Delhi (1988)

Malaysia

Women in Trade and Commerce, Sdn. Bhd. (WINTRAC) (WWB-Malaysia) (1982)

Japan

WWB-Japan

Philippines

Women in Finance and Entrepreneurship (WIFE) (1982)

Thailand

Friends of WWB Association in Thailand (WWB-Thailand) (1982)

EUROPE

France

Assoc. pour le Dev. Des Initiative Eco. Par les Femmes (ADIEF) (1982)

Italy

Associazione per la Women's World Banking in Italia (WWB-Italy) (1982)

Netherlands

Stichting WWB Nederland (1982)

Spain

Fundacion Laboral WWB En Espana (WWB-Spain) (1988)

NORTH AMERICA

Canada

Women's World Finance/Cape Breton Association (1988)

USA

WWB-NY Office

Friends of WWB-USA, Inc. (1980)

WWB-West Virginia Affiliate, Inc. (1982)

Women's Association For Women's Alternatives (1982)

Women's Economic Assistance Ventures (WEAV) (1988)

Women's Entrepreneurial Growth Organization (WEGO) (1982)

KEY TO ACRONYMS, BY CHAPTER

About This Book
- WWB – Women's World Banking
- SWWB – Stichting Women's World Banking (1979), Stichting to Promote Women's World Banking (1985)
- RBF – Rockefeller Brothers Fund
- SEWA – Self-Employed Women's Association

Chapter 1
- NYSE – New York Stock Exchange
- FIG – Foreign International Group
- PTAs – Parent-Teacher Associations
- MIT – Massachusetts Institute of Technology
- UN – United Nations
- NGO – Non-Governmental Organization
- AAAS – American Association for the Advancement of Science
- UNITAR – United Nations Institute for Training and Research
- UNDP – United Nations Development Program
- WID – Women in Development
- ECOSOC – Economic and Social Council
- UNGA – United Nations General Assembly
- UNIFEM – United Nations Fund for Women
- INSTRAW – The International Training and Research Center for the Advancement of Women
- SIACO – Trade Union of Swedish Academics
- UNCTAD – United Nations Conference on Trade and Development

Chapter 2
- CPA – Certified Public Accountant
- OTA – Congressional Office of Technology Assessment
- USAID – United States Agency for International Development
- IPPF – International Planned Parenthood Foundation
- IDB – Inter-American Development Bank

- CIDA – Canadian International Development Agency
- FINCA – Foundation for International Community Assistance
- UNICEF – United Nations Children's Fund
- USAID – United States Agency for International Development

Chapter 3
- BSc– Bachelor of Science
- MBA – Master of Business Administration
- FWWB/USA – Friends of Women's World Banking USA

Chapter 4
- SIDA – Swedish International Development Agency
- NORAD – Norwegian Agency for Development Cooperation
- WIFE – Women in Finance and Entrepreneurship
- DESAP – Desarrollo del Pueblo
- ADOPEM – Asociación Dominicana para el Desarrollo de la Mujer

Chapter 5
- GNP – Gross National Product
- CARD – Centre for Agriculture and Rural Development
- MFIs – Micofinance Institutions
- EIU – Economic Intelligence Unit
- OEF – League of Women Voters Overseas Education Fund
- IPS – Institute for Policy Studies
- CGAP – Consultative Group to Assist the Poor
- DAWN – Development Alternatives with Women for a New Era

Chapter 6
- NMB Bank – Nederlandsche Middenstands Bank

- TB – Triodos Bank
- FHAF – Fonds Haitien d'Aide à la Femme

Chapter 7

- KWFT – Kenya Women's Finance Trust
- K-REP – Kenya Rural Enterprise Program
- UWFT – Uganda Women's Finance Trust
- OPIC – Overseas Private Investment Corporation
- CIDA – Canadian International Development Agency
- CGAP – Consultative Group to Assist the Poor
- GAWF – Gambia Women's Finance Trust GAWFA (Chapter 10)
- JPM – JP Morgan
- RR – Regional Representative
- NABOW – National Association of Business Owner Women
- OECD – Organization for Economic Cooperation and Development
- ADIEF – Assoc. pour le Dev. Des Inltiative Eco.Parles Femmes
- FCEM – Femmes Chefs d'Entreprises Mondiales

Chapter 8

- WWE – Women's World Enterprise
- ACWF – All-China Women's Federation
- WINTRAC – Women in Trade and Commerce

Chapter 9

- DFC – Development Finance Consultants, Ltd.
- ADB – African Development Bank

Chapter 10

- OPEC – Organization of Petroleum Export Countries
- EEC – European Economic Community
- PRI – Program Related Investment
- PPM – Private-Placement Memorandum
- EIU – Economic Intelligence Unit

Chapter 11

- IFC – the World Bank Group's International Finance Corporation
- GSL – Global Student Leadership

UNITED NATIONS

GENERAL

ASSEMBLY

Distr.
GENERAL

A/RES/3520 (XXX)
30 January 1976

Thirtieth session
Agenda items 75 and 76

RESOLUTION ADOPTED BY THE GENERAL ASSEMBLY

/on the report of the Third Committee (A/10474)7

3520 (XXX). World Conference of the International Women's Year

The General Assembly,

Recalling its resolution 3010 (XXVII) of 18 December 1972 in which it proclaimed the year 1975 International Women's Year,

Recalling also Economic and Social Council resolutions 1849 (LVI) and 1851 (LVI) of 16 May 1974 on the convening of an international conference during the International Women's Year as a focal point of the international observance of the Year,

Recalling further its resolutions 3276 (XXIX) and 3277 (XXIX) of 10 December 1974 as well as Economic and Social Council resolution 1959 (LIX) of 28 July 1975 concerning the World Conference of the International Women's Year,

Recalling the importance of the participation of women in the implementation of the decisions of the General Assembly at its sixth 1/ and seventh special sessions 2/ as well as in the implementation of the Programme of Action on the Establishment of a New International Economic Order, 3/

Having considered the report of the Conference, 4/

1/ Official Records of the General Assembly, Sixth Special Session, Supplement No. 1 (A/9559).

2/ General Assembly resolutions 3361 (S-VII) and 3362 (S-VII) and decisions taken at the 2326th and 2349th plenary meetings of the Assembly.

3/ General Assembly resolution 3202 (S-VI).

4/ E/5725 and Add.1.

76-02513

/...

Having considered also the note by the Secretary-General on the establishment of an international research and training institute for the advancement of women, 5/

Convinced that the Conference, through the adoption of the Declaration of Mexico on the Equality of Women and Their Contribution to Development and Peace, 1975, 6/ the World Plan of Action for the Implementation of the Objectives of the International Women's Year 7/ and other resolutions, has made a valuable and constructive contribution towards the achievement of the threefold objectives of the Year, namely, to promote equality between men and women, to ensure the full integration of women in the total development effort and to promote women's contribution to the development of friendly relations and co-operation among States and to the strengthening of world peace,

Considering the valuable and constructive contributions towards the implementation of the threefold objectives of the International Women's Year made by conferences and seminars held during the Year,

Convinced also that the promotion of development objectives and the solution of crucial world economic and social problems should contribute significantly to the improvement of the situation of women, in particular that of women in rural areas and in low-income groups,

Convinced further that women must play an important role in the promotion, achievement and maintenance of international peace,

Considering that the decisions and recommendations of the Conference 8/ should be translated into concrete action without delay by States, organizations of the United Nations system and intergovernmental and non-governmental organizations,

Recalling that the Conference stressed the important role of regional commissions in the implementation of the World Plan of Action and related resolutions of the Conference, 9/

Convinced that periodic and comprehensive reviews and appraisals of the progress made in meeting the goals of the World Plan of Action and related resolutions endorsed by the Conference are of crucial importance for their effective implementation and should be undertaken at regular intervals by Governments and by the organizations of the United Nations system within an agreed time frame,

---

5/ A/10340.

6/ E/5725, part one, chap. I.

7/ Ibid., chap. II, sect. A.

8/ Ibid., chap III.

9/ Ibid., resolution 4.

/...

Noting that the Conference recommended the continuing operation of the
Commission on the Status of Women or some other representative body, 9/ within
the structure of the United Nations, designed specifically to deal with matters
relating to the status of women, so as to ensure the implementation of continuing
projects designed to carry out the programmes set forth in the World Plan of Action,

1.   Takes note of the report of the World Conference of the International
Women's Year, held at Mexico City from 19 June to 2 July 1975, including the
Declaration of Mexico on the Equality of Women and Their Contribution to
Development and Peace, 1975, the World Plan of Action for the Implementation of
the Objectives of the International Women's Year, the regional plans of action
and the resolutions and other recommendations adopted by the Conference, and
endorses the action proposals contained in these documents;

2.   Proclaims the period from 1976 to 1985 United Nations Decade for Women:
Equality, Development and Peace, to be devoted to effective and sustained national,
regional and international action to implement the World Plan of Action and
related resolutions of the Conference;

3.   Calls upon Governments, as a matter of urgency, to examine the
recommendations contained in the World Plan of Action and related resolutions
of the Conference including action to be taken at the national level, such as:

(a) The establishment of short-term, medium-term and long-term targets, and
priorities to this end, taking into account the guidelines set forth in sections I
and II of the World Plan of Action, including the minimum objectives recommended
for achievement by 1980; 10/

(b) The adoption of national strategies, plans and programmes for the
implementation of the recommendations within the framework of over-all development
plans, policies and programmes;

(c) The undertaking of regular reviews and appraisals of progress made at
the national and local levels in achieving the goals and objectives of the World
Plan of Action within the framework of over-all development plans, policies
and programmes;

4.   Requests the Secretary-General to transmit to the relevant organs of
the United Nations and to the organizations of the United Nations system the
decisions and recommendations of the Conference;

5.   Invites all relevant organizations of the United Nations system concerned:

(a) To submit, within the framework of the Administrative Committee on
Co-ordination, to the Economic and Social Council at its sixty-second session their
proposals and suggestions for implementing the World Plan of Action and related
resolutions of the Conference during the United Nations Decade for Women: Equality,
Development and Peace;

10/ E/5725, para. 46.

/...

(b) To develop and implement, during the first half of the Decade, under the auspices of the Administrative Committee on Co-ordination, a joint interagency medium-term programme for the integration of women in development, which should co-ordinate and integrate activities undertaken in accordance with subparagraph (a) above, with special emphasis on technical co-operation in programmes relating to women and development;

(c) To render, in accordance with requests of Governments, sustained assistance in the formulation, design, implementation and evaluation of projects and programmes which would enable women to be integrated in national and international development;

6. Calls upon the regional commissions to develop and implement, as a matter of priority effective strategies to further the objectives of the World Plan of Action at the regional and subregional levels, bearing in mind their respective regional plans of action;

7. Urges all financial institutions and all international, regional and subregional development banks and bilateral funding agencies to accord high priority in their development assistance, in accordance with requests of Governments, to projects that would promote the integration of women in the development process, in particular women in the rural areas, as well as the achievement of the equality of women and men, priority being given to countries with limited financial means;

8. Urges non-governmental organizations, at the national and international levels, to take all possible measures to assist in the implementation of the World Plan of Action and related resolutions of the Conference within their particular areas of interest and competence;

9. Decides in principle, in accordance with resolution 26 adopted by the Conference, to establish, under the auspices of the United Nations, an International Research and Training Institute for the Advancement of Women, which would be financed through voluntary contributions and would collaborate with appropriate national, regional and international economic and social research institutes;

10. Invites the Secretary-General therefore to appoint, with due consideration to the principle of equitable geographical distribution, a Group of Experts on the Establishment of an International Research and Training Institute for the Advancement of Women, consisting of five to ten experts to draw up, in consultation with the representatives of existing regional centres and/or institutes for research and training which have similar objectives and goals, the terms of reference and structural organization of the Institute, giving special consideration to the needs of women of developing countries, and requests the Secretary-General to to report to the Economic and Social Council at its sixtieth session on the basis of the recommendations of the Group of Experts;

11. Affirms that a system-wide review and appraisal of the World Plan of Action should be undertaken biennially, and that such reviews and appraisals should

/...

constitute an input to the process of review and appraisal of progress made under the International Development Strategy for the Second United Nations Development Decade, 11/ taking into account the Programme of Action on the Establishment of a New International Economic Order and the decisions resulting from the sixth and seventh special sessions of the General Assembly;

12. Affirms that the General Assembly and other relevant bodies should also consider biennially the progress achieved in the promotion of the full equality of women with men in all spheres of life in accordance with international standards and, in particular, the participation of women in political life and in international co-operation and the strengthening of international peace;

13. Expresses the hope that the Ad Hoc Committee on the Restructuring of the Economic and Social Sectors of the United Nations System, which will consider the report of the Group of Experts on the Structure of the United Nations System entitled A New United Nations Structure for Global Economic Co-operation, 12/ will take full account of the need to implement the World Plan of Action and related resolutions of the Conference, as well as the requirements of the United Nations Decade for Women: Equality, Development and Peace, and appeals to the Ad Hoc Committee to ensure that the machinery designed to deal with questions relating to women should be strengthened, taking into account, in particular, the role of the Commission on the Status of Women and the procedures established for the system-wide review and appraisal of the World Plan of Action;

14. Decides to include in the provisional agenda of its thirty-first session an item entitled "United Nations Decade for Women: Equality, Development and Peace";

15. Invites the Secretary-General to submit a progress report to the General Assembly at its thirty-first session on the measures taken to implement the World Plan of Action and related resolutions of the Conference, and on the progress achieved in initiating the procedures for the Plan's review and appraisal by Member States, the United Nations organs, the regional commissions, the specialized agencies and other intergovernmental organizations concerned;

16. Requests the Secretary-General to ensure, if possible within existing resources, that the Secretariat unit responsible for women's questions possesses adequate personnel and budgetary resources in order to discharge its functions under the World Plan of Action in co-operation with all organizations of the United Nations system;

17. Requests further the Secretary-General, in the light of paragraph 16 above, to take into account the requirements of the World Plan of Action and related resolutions of the Conference in preparing revised estimates for 1977 and the medium-term plan for 1978-1981 and to report thereon to the General Assembly at its thirty-first session, in accordance with established procedures;

11/ General Assembly resolution 2626 (XXV).

12/ E/AC.62/9 (United Nations publication, Sales No. E.75.II.A.7).

/...

18. Urges all States, the organizations of the United Nations system and intergovernmental and non-governmental organizations concerned, as well as the mass communications media, to give widespread publicity to the achievements and significance of the Conference at the national, regional and international levels;

19. Requests the Secretary-General, as a matter of high priority, to issue within existing resources, in the official languages of the United Nations, a simplified version of the World Plan of Action as a booklet, which would highlight the targets, goals and main recommendations for action by Governments, the United Nations system and non-governmental organizations and which would explain the relevance of the implementation of the Plan to the daily lives of men and women throughout the world;

20. Decides to convene in 1980, at the mid-term of the United Nations Decade for Women: Equality, Development and Peace, a world conference of all States to review and evaluate the progress made in implementing the objectives of the International Women's Year as recommended by the World Conference of the International Women's Year and, where necessary, to readjust existing programmes in the light of new data and research available.

2441st plenary meeting
15 December 1975

CHARTER
OF
STICHTING WOMEN'S WORLD BANKING

1. <u>Name; Seat.</u>
1.1. The name of the Foundation is Stichting
Women's World Banking.
1.2. The principal office of the Foundation
shall be in Amsterdam, the Netherlands.
The Foundation may also have branch offices
or working offices elsewhere, both within
and outside of the Netherlands.

2. <u>Purpose.</u>
2.1. The purpose of the Foundation is to advance and promote the direct participation
of women and their families in the full
use of the economy, particularly those
women who have not generally had access to
the services of established financial
institutions. To that end the Foundation
shall operate as an independent financial
institution to provide loan guarentees or
other security to banks and other financial
institutions and to provide technical or
other advice and assistance to direct or
indirect beneficiaries of guarantees.

The Foundation shall also collect and make
available data relating to the aforementioned purpose. The Foundation is not
formed for the pecuniary profit or for the
financial gain of any private individual
and no part of its assets, income or profit
shall be distributed to or inure to the
benefit of any private individual except in
furtherance of the aforementioned purpose
of the Foundation, provided that reasonable
compensation may be paid for services ren-
dered to or for the Foundation in furtherance of its purpose.

A.1.1

2.2. Everything connected with or conducive to the aforementioned purpose in the broadest sense shall be part of the purpose of the Foundation.

2.3. The operations of the Foundation in pursuance of the aforementioned purpose may be described in more detail in by-laws to be drafted by the Board of Trustees.

3. Assets; financial means.
3.1. The assets of the Foundation shall consist of the capital set aside at the time of the establishment. The financial means of the Foundation shall further be provided by

- subsidies, donations and other contributions;
- interest, proceeds of investments;
- whatever the Foundation shall acquire in any other way.

The Foundation may also obtain financial means by borrowings and through other forms of obtaining credit.

4. Board of Trustees.
4.1. The Foundation shall be governed by a Board of Trustees. The Board of Trustees of the Foundation shall consist of a number of Trustees to be determined by the Board itself, provided that the number shall not be fewer than five nor more than twenty-five. Trustees shall be nominated by co-option by a simple majority of votes.

4.2. At least one Trustee must be of Dutch nationality and reside in the Netherlands.

A.1.2

4/84

4.3. On the Board of Trustees shall serve, to the extent possible, representatives of management, financial contributors, associated financial institutions, co-operating organizations, technical and other advisers, and direct and indirect beneficiaries of guarantees.

The Board shall be composed in such a manner that Trustees represent the regions of the world.

4.4. At the time of establishment of the Foundation, there shall be a temporary Board of Trustees consisting of the following persons:

1. F.Q.W. Bannier   5. Virginia Saurwein
2. Anita Kalff   6. Leticia Romos Shahani
3. Diogo de Gaspar   7. Michaela Walsh
4. Esther Ocloo

Within one year of the establishment of the Foundation, the temporary Board of Trustees will appoint the first group of Trustees constituting the permanent Board of Trustees.

4.5. At the first bi-ennial meeting of the permanent Board of Trustees, the Trustees shall be divided as equally as possible into three groups. The term of the Trustees in the first group shall end at the second bi-ennial meeting, the term of the Trustees in the second group shall end at the third bi-ennial meeting, and the term of the Trustees in the third group shall end at the fourth bi-ennial meeting, so that one third of the Trustees may be appointed every two years. With due observance of the provisions of this clause 4.5, a

A.1.3

Trustee serves for a period of six years. After expiry of half her/his period of office, a Trustee may be directly reappointed.

4.6. If additional Trustees are appointed in between bi-ennial meetings, they shall serve for the remainder of the term of the group of Trustees appointed at the previous bi-ennial meeting. If Trustees are appointed to fill vacancies on the Board of Trustees, they shall serve for the remainder of the predecessors Trustee's term, which term shall be deemed to be a full term in respect of the person filling the vacancy.

4.7. Membership of the Board of Trustees shall end by:

- death;
- mental incapacity;
- resignation, which shall take place by sending a letter to the Chairperson specifying the date of resignation (in the event no such date is mentioned, the date of receipt of the letter shall be considered the date of resignation);
- removal by the Board, which can be done by resolution adopted by a simple majority of votes.

5. Officers.

5.1. The Board of Trustees shall appoint from their members a Chairperson, a Vice-Chairperson, a Secretary and a Treasurer, which offices must be held by different persons. The board shall further appoint an Executive Director who shall be ex-officio a Trustee. The Board may appoint other

A.1.4

4/84

persons in the service of the Foundation who are not Trustees.

5.2. The Chairperson, the Vice Chairperson, the Secretary, the Treasurer, the Executive Director and any other person appointed to an office by the Board shall serve in such office at the pleasure of the Board.

5.3. The Board of Trustees may issue by-laws or regulations regarding the rights and duties of the persons in the service of the Foundation or in any other capacity acting on behalf of the Foundation.

5.4. The Foundation shall be represented by one or more persons as authorized by the Board.

6. Duties of Officers.

6.1. Apart from the provisions of by-laws or regulations issued in accordance with Article 5.3, the Executive Director, the Secretary and the Treasurer shall have the duties described in the next sections.

6.2. The Executive Director.

The Executive Director shall direct the day-to-day operations of the Foundation and shall follow instructions given by the Board of Trustees to whom she/he shall be responsible for:

- presenting an annual operating plan to the Board of Trustees, as well as any project plans and other proposals which require Board approval;

A.1.5

- providing a communications link between the Board and all Associates, potential collaborators, and the public, except when those functions may be delegated;

- everything required for the satisfactory progress of the Foundation's operations and everything the Board may delegate or instruct her/him to do.

6.3. The Secretary.

The Secretary shall be responsible for:

- the Deed of Incorporation as well as all deeds of amendment thereto, in the original or in a copy, as well as all by-laws, codes of regulations and other rules established by the Board of Trustees;

- the minutes of all ordinary and extraordinary meetings of the Board of Trustees.

The Secretary's function shall also include giving notices or information as required by this Charter, keeping the records, archives and the official documents of the Foundation; giving information about this Charter, by-laws, codes of regulations and other rules; and minutes to Trustees who make a reasonable request therefor; and all activities incident to the office of Secretary, including everything the Board of Trustees or the Executive Director may from time to time assign or delegate to the office of Secretary.

A.1.6

4/84

6.4. The Treasurer.

The Treasurer shall, upon request by the Board of Trustees, give a bond for the faithful discharge of her/his duties in the form to be decided by the Board of Trustees.

The Treasurer is charged with the control of the assets and funds of the Foundation. She/he shall follow the instructions of the Board of Trustees regarding the investment and deposit of the Foundation's funds and components of assets.

The Treasurer shall provide for adequate and correct bookkeeping and for documentation of all financial transactions, and shall respond to Trustees who make a reasonable request for information with respect thereto. The Treasurer shall distribute a full annual accounting for approval by the Board of Trustees in accordance with Article 9 of this Charter and upon request she/he shall also render a statement of the financial situation of the Foundation at Board Meetings. The Treasurer's function shall also include all duties incident to the Office of Treasurer and everything the Board of Trustees or the Executive Director may from time to time assign or delegate to the office of Treasurer.

6.5. The remuneration of the Executive Director, the Secretary and the Treasurer, as well as the other conditions under which they perform their functions, shall be determined by the Board of Trustees.

A.1.7

The conditions of employment of other persons in the service of the Foundation shall be determined by the Board of Trustees upon recommendation by the Executive Director.

7. Meetings of the Board of Trustees.

7.1. The Board of Trustees shall meet bi-ennially. The Board of Trustees may also meet when the Chairperson, the Executive Director or a majority of the Trustees deems a meeting necessary.

7.2. Meetings shall be held in the Foundation's office or at a location (which may be outside the Netherlands) designated by the Chairperson.

Meetings shall be convened by the Secretary who shall give at least 30 days notice to the Trustees. An agenda of the meeting shall accompany the convening notice.

7.3. Each Trustee has the right to attend Board meetings and to vote thereat. Each Trustee shall have one vote. The chair shall be taken by the Chairperson or in her/his absence by the Vice-Chairperson or in her/his absence by the Executive Director. If neither the Chairperson nor the Vice Chairperson nor the Executive Director is present, the Trustees attending the meeting shall elect an ad hoc Chairperson.

7.4. The Secretary shall keep minutes of the proceedings, which shall be approved at the next meeting. The minutes shall be signed by the Chairperson and the Sec-

A.1.8

retary. In the absence of or at the request of the Secretary, the Chairperson may appoint another person to keep the minutes.

7.5. In a year in which no bi-ennial meeting is held nor an extraordinary meeting during which a resolution in this respect can be passed, a resolution in writing shall be adopted as referred to in Article 8.3 to approve the annual accounts as referred to in Articles 9.2 and 9.3.

8. Adoption of Resolutions.

8.1. To constitute a quorum for the transaction of business at any meeting of the Board of Trustees, the presence, in person or by proxy, of a majority of Trustees in office at the time shall be required, disregarding any unfilled vacancies which may then exist, provided that:

a. if there are five (5) or fewer Trustees in office, the presence of all five shall be necessary, and

b. if there are fewer than five (5) Trustees in office, the remaining Trustees or Trustee shall constitute a quorum solely for the purpose of filling a vacancy or vacancies in order to have five (5) Trustees in office who may then proceed with the transaction of all business including the filling of further vacancies.

In the absence of a quorum, any meeting may be adjourned by the vote of a majority of the Trustees present, but no other

A.1.9

business may be transacted. No notice need be given at the meeting at which such adjournment is taken. At any reconvened meeting at which a quorum is present, any business may be transacted which might have been transacted at the meeting as originally noticed.

8.2. Except as otherwise provided by this Charter, resolutions shall be adopted with a simple majority of votes validly cast. Resolutions pertaining to issues shall be adopted by a show of hands. Resolutions pertaining to persons shall be adopted by closed and unsigned ballot-papers unless a resolution is carried by acclamation.

Blank votes or abstentions shall be disregarded for all purposes when determining whether a majority vote has been cast.

8.3. The Board of Trustees can, without meeting, adopt resolutions. In that event, all the Trustees shall be invited to give their opinion in writing. A resolution in these cases shall be adopted of the majority required for such resolutions by this Charter has declared in writing to be in favour of the resolution.

9. Fiscal year

9.1. The financial year of the Foundation shall coincide with the calendar year.

9.2. Annually, within five months after the closing of the Foundation's financial year, the Treasurer shall draft financial accounts (such as a balance sheet, profit and loss account and explanatory memo-

A.1.10

randum), which shall be submitted to the Board of Trustees,

9.3. The adoption without reservation of the annual accounts for the preceding financial year by the Board of Trustees at any bi-ennial meeting or by a resolution pursuant to Article 8.3 shall discharge the Treasurer with respect to the performance of her/his duties over the preceding financial year.

9.4. The Treasurer's report shall be made available to the public unless the Board of Trustees determines otherwise.

10. Associates

10.1. The Board of Trustees may grant the status of Associates to individual persons, groups of persons, and organizations.

10.2. Associates shall be subdivided into the following categories:

a. Financial Contributors

The status of Associate may be granted to persons or organizations which have undertaken to contribute to the foundation either as a member of the committee of 100 or as a Friend of Women's World Banking.

b. Financial Institutions

The status of Associate may be granted to financial institutions which have made a commitment to support women's economic development through loans,

A.1.11

4/84

advances, credit, services, etc.

c. Co-operating Organizations

The status of Associate may be granted to regional, national or local organizations which have agreed to advice and assist Women's World Banking in co-ordinating and monitoring its projects.

d. Technical and other Advisers

The status of Associate may be granted to persons or organizations giving advice or other services in the fields of administration, technical training, personnel management, etc.

e. Recipients

The status of Associate may be granted to persons, families, groups of persons or families, women's organizations or other organizations which are the direct or indirect beneficiaries of the Foundation's activities.

10.3. The role of Associate is to be determined by the Board of Trustees.

10.4. The Board of Trustees may, in its discretion, terminate the status of Associate with or without giving its reasons. Except as the Board of Trustees may otherwise determine, the status of Associate shall be terminated as soon as the Associate in question no longer meets the description of her/his category as determined by the Board.

A.1.12

11. Committees

11.1. The Board of Trustees may establish Committees consisting of Trustees or other persons, provided that each Committee shall include at least two Trustees. Committees shall report not less frequently than annually to the Executive Director who shall co-ordinate their activities.

11.2. The authority of a Committee shall be determined by the Board of Trustees, provided that the Board of Trustees may not delegate to any Committee the power to amend this Charter or to appoint Trustees, officers of the Board, Associates or the Executive Director.

12. Amendment of Charter; Dissolution of the Foundation

12.1. Resolutions to amend this Charter can only be taken by a vote of at least two-thirds of the Trustees in office.

12.1. A resolution to dissolve the Foundation can only be taken under the same provisions as made in Article 12.1 regarding amendments of this Charter.

A resolution to dissolve the Foundation shall include the appointment of liquidator or liquidators, which may be the Board of Trustees or one or more of its members.

12.2. All the assets of the Foundation remaining after the payment or other satisfaction of its liabilities shall be distributed taking into account the purpose of the Foundation and otherwise to organizations whose object is the general welfare.

A.1.13

4/84

BYLAWS
of
THE STICHTING WOMEN'S WORLD BANKING

Article 1. General Provision

1.1. In these Bylaws:

- The Stichting means: the Stichting Women's World Banking;
- the Charter means the Charter (Statuten) of the Stichting;
- a Meeting means any meeting of a body, organ or any other group of persons referred to in Article 8.3 of the Charter;
- words and expressions used or defined in the Charter shall have the same meaning in these Bylaws unless otherwise provided or inconsistent with the context;
- any reference to the feminine includes a reference to the masculine.

1.2. Relation of Charter of Bylaws.
In case of a conflict or discrepancy between the charter and the Bylaws, the charter shall prevail over the Bylaws.

1.3. Language.
In case of a conflict or discrepancy between the Dutch and the English text of the Bylaws, the Dutch text shall be considered to be the authentic one.

Article 2. Trustees

2.1. Ex-Officio Trustees

Founding trustees who shall have retired shall automatically become ex-officio trustees. Ex-Officio trustees shall

A.2.1

205

serve until resignation but in no event longer than until the bi-ennial meeting next following the date of their resignation. Ex-Officio trustees shall receive all notices and other information sent to trustees and may participate in all meetings of the trustees without vote. Committee members, appointed as ex-officio members of the Board of Trustees shall receive all notices and other information sent to trustees and may participate in all meetings of the trustees without vote.

Article 3. Corporate Action

3.1. The nominations referred to in article 5.1 of the Charter shall take place at the bi-ennial meeting and shall remain in force until the next bi-ennial meeting. Interim vacancies shall be dealt with in the next following board meeting.

Article 4. Officers

The board of trustees may, at any meeting, elect one or more additional officers as mentioned in article 5.1 of the Charter, and such officers as it may from time to time determine. The same person may be elected to more than one office, except that the same person shall not hold the offices of both President and Secretary or any two or more of the offices of Chairperson, vice Chairperson or President. A vacancy in any office may be filled by the board of trustees at any meeting. All officers shall hold office at the pleasure of the board of trustees or until their respective successors shall have been elected and shall have quali-

A.2.2

4/84

They shall receive such salaries or other compensation as may be authorized by the affirmative vote of a majority of the entire Board of Trustees.

The meeting may authorize the President to lay down the terms of employment, whether or not within previously defined limits. The meeting itself shall define the purport of the function.

Article 5. Chairperson and Vice Chairperson

The chairperson shall be the chief policy officer of the Stichting and shall have the general supervision of the activities of the Stichting and over its several officers, subject, however, to the control of the Board of Trustees. She shall preside at all board meetings of which she shall be present and shall be a member ex-officio of all committees. She shall be entitled to have notice of committee meetings and to attend and vote at such meetings, but she shall be under no obligation to attend and shall not be counted to determine the number necessary to make a quorum or to determine whether a quorum is present. Any Vice Chairperson shall discharge such functions as may be assigned by the trustees. She shall in the absence of the Chairperson preside at meetings and during the absence or disability of the Chairperson shall perform the duties of the Chairperson. In the absence or disability of the Chairperson or a Vice Chairperson specifically so empowered, another member of the Board may be appointed

A.2.3

by resolution duly adopted at any meeting to discharge the Chairperson's functions or any of them specified in the resolution.

Article 6. President

The Executive Director may bear the title of President. Without prejudice to Article 6.2 of the Charter, the President shall be the Chief Executive Officer of the Stichting and shall have general supervision over the business of the Stichting and over its several officers, subject, however, to the control of the Chair and the Board of Trustees. She shall prepare and present the business to be acted upon and shall, in the absence of the Chair or a vice Chairperson specifically so empowered, preside at all meetings at which she shall be present.

The president shall be a member Ex-Officio of all committees; she shall be entitled to have notice of committee meetings and to attend and vote at such meetings, but she shall not be counted to determine the number necessary to make a quorum or to determine whether a quorum is present.

Article 7. Corporate Action

Action taken at meeting of trustees shall be placed on record in one set of minutes.

Article 8. Meetings

The written notice of all Board meetings shall specify the place, date and hour of the meeting and, in the case of a special meeting, shall also state the

A.2.4

4/84

purpose or purposes of the meeting and indicate that the notice is being issued by or at the discretion of the person or persons calling the meeting.

All meetings shall be held both in-or outside the Netherlands, as the Board of Trustees may from time to time direct. In the absence of such direction, meetings shall be held at the office of the Stichting.

Article 9. Financial Accounts

The financial accounts, mentioned in Article 9.2. of the Charter, have to be verified by a register-accountant in the meaning of the Wet op. de Register Accountants of the Netherlands or a non Dutch auditor or firm of auditors of equivalent status. The report will have to show in appropriate detail the following:

- the assets and liabilities including any trust funds of the Stichting as of the end of a twelve months fiscal period terminating not more than six months prior to said meeting;

- the principal changes in assets and liabilities, including any trust funds, during the year immediately preceding the date of the report;

- the revenue or receipts of the Stichting both unrestricted and restricted to particular purposes for the year immediately preceding the date of the report;

A.2.5

- the expenses or disbursements of the Stichting, for both general and restricted purposes, for the year immediately preceding the date of the report.

The annual report of the Treasurer shall be filed with the records of the Stichting and either a copy or an abstract thereof entered in the minutes of the proceedings of the meeting.

Article 10. Committees

a. There shall be an Executive Committee of the Board of Trustees consisting of not less than three and not more than five persons, all of whom shall be members of the Board of Trustees and appointed by the affirmative vote of the majority of the entire Board of Trustees. A vacancy in the Executive Committee may be filled by the Board of Trustees at any meeting. A meeting of the Executive Committee may be called at any time when the Board of Trustees is not in session by any two members of the committee or by the President. A majority of the committee shall constitute a quorum for the transaction of business, and the committee may act upon the affirmative vote of the majority of those present. The Chairperson of the committee shall be a member of the Board of Trustees other than the Chairperson or the President and shall be appointed by the Board of Trustees. The Executive Committee shall serve for the period between the board meeting at which they have

been appointed and the next bi-ennial board meeting. Members of the Executive Committee may be reappointed immediately.

The Executive Committee shall have all powers of the Board when the Board is not in session and with due observance of Article 11.2 and 12.1 of the Charter. The Executive Committee shall keep regular minutes of its proceedings and shall report all actions to the Board of Trustees at the next meeting of the Board following such action.

b. There shall be a Finance Committee consisting of not less than three nor more than nine persons, at least two of whom including the Chairperson shall be a trustee of the Stichting. The members of the Committee shall be appointed by the Board of Trustees and shall serve for the period between the meeting at which they have been appointed and the next bi-ennial board meeting. Members of these committees may be reappointed immediately. A vacancy in the Finance Committee may be filled by the Board of Trustees at any meeting. The Chairperson of the committee shall be a member of the Board other than the Chairperson or the President and appointed by the Board of Trustees.

The Finance Committee shall formulate and propose investment and financial policy to the Board of Trustees and shall implement such policy as is approved by the Board. Pursuant to such policies, the Finance Committee shall establish investment guidelines and shall have the authority to exercise those powers relating to the investment management of the Stichting's assets which are conferred upon the Stichting by law and by its Charter.

If an investment manager is appointed by the Board of Trustees, the Finance Committee shall supervise the performance of such manager as provided in the contract between the Stichting and the investment manager.

The Finance Committee shall meet quarterly and keep regular minutes of its proceedings and shall report all actions to the Board of Trustees at the next meeting of the Board following such action.

c. The Board of Trustees may, by resolution, provide for additional committees and may delegate to such committees such powers as it may deem desirable with due observance of Article 11.2 of the Charter. These committees may include, but not be limited to:

An Operations Committee
A Program Committee
A development Committee
Each committee shall consist of not less than two, nor more than seven members, at least two of whom shall be a trustee of the Stichting.

Members of the committees shall be appointed by the Board of Trustees

A.2.8   4/84

and shall serve for the period between the meeting in which they have been appointed and the next bi-ennial board meeting. Members of these committees may be reappointed immediately unless the Board has decided otherwise at their appointments.

A vacancy in one of the Committees may be filled by the Board of Trustees at any meeting.

The Chairperson of each committee shall be appointed by the Board of Trustees.

The responsibility of each Committee shall be determined by the Board of Trustees prior to the appointment of its members. Each committee shall keep regular minutes of its proceedings and shall report all actions to the Board of Trustees at the next meeting of the Board following such action.

Article 11.   Associates

The Associates referred to in Article 10 of the Charter may have meetings whether jointly or per category, as referred to in Article 10.2 of the Charter.

A meeting shall be held when the Board of Trustees considers it necessary and also when at least one quarter of the Associates or, if applicable, the Associates of one category, so request. Meetings of Associates, whether for a special category or jointly, shall be convened by the Executive Director; meetings are held at a place to be indicated in the convening note. Meetings are presided over by the

A.2.9

Executive Director or by a person to be nominated for this purpose by the Board of Trustees; if no such person is present, the meeting shall appoint a Chairperson. The meeting of Associates shall advise the Board of Trustees about all questions and matters submitted to the meeting. It is also allowed to advise, at its own initiative, whenever it deems fit and proper.

Resolutions binding a category or all Associates may be taken only in meetings of the respective category or the joint meeting of all Associates.

Such resolutions can only validly be taken in a meeting at which at least half the members of the respective category are present or represented, or in case of a joint meeting of all Associates, in a meeting at which at least one third of the Associates is present or represented.

Resolutions are taken with a simple majority of votes.

Article 12. Amendments

These Bylaws may be amended by vote of the Board of Trustees at any meeting, provided that the notice of meeting shall have included a summary of the proposed amendment.

A.2.10

4/84

WOMEN'S WORLD BANKING

TEL-212-247-8195

PO BOX 1691
GRAND CENTRAL STATION
NEW YORK NY 10017

A critical financial problem for women is the inability to obtain the types of banking and financial services that would enable them to partici-pate more fully in the development of their countries. Since the 1975 International Women's Year Conference in Mexico City, a small group of women has pursued this issue with a view to developing new institutions to address this need. Their effort has been to understand more fully the role of entrepreneurial development in the development process, and specifically the role of women in that process.

You have been identified as a prominent woman with experience relevant to the problem of financing women in their own enterprises. On behalf of the Committee to Organize Women's World Banking (WWB), I am therefore writing to invite you to join in this dialogue at an International Work-shop of Women Leaders in Banking and Finance to be held March 12-15, 1980, in Amsterdam.

The purposes of this Workshop are four-fold:

- to address the critical issues involved in women's access to and effective use of credit and financial services;

- to help develop the specific components and strategies for imple-menting WWB's program at the national and local level;

- to serve as part of the core network for identifying collaborating institutions for WWB;

- to present to the World Conference of the U.N. Decade for Women (Copenhagen, July, 1980) recommendations for substantially strengthening the role of women in national economies and the contribution they can make to the development process.

Women's World Banking is an independent financial organization incorporated in the Netherlands as a Dutch Stichting. WWB is in the process of developing a program to be initiated in 1980. Workshop participants are expected to make a valuable contribution to this process. Attached is a Statement of Purpose of Women's World Banking which explains in more detail the goals and initial programs of our effort.

Workshop participants will number approximately 40, from Asia, Africa, Latin America, Europe, North America and the Middle East. We are inviting the participation of women entrepreneurs, bankers and financiers whose experience can help to insure that the programs developed at the Workshop address some of the real obstacles that stand in the way of women's access to financial services.

A questionnaire on women's use of banking services and existing encouragements/barriers to tha t use will be sent to each participant for her reply in advance of the meeting. Some will be asked, in addition, to make a formal presentation during the panel discussions on specific issues. Following the Workshop, participants will be asked to agree to address appropriate audiences in their own countries on the issues discussed at the Workshop and the plan of action of Women's World Banking.

WWB is asking each participant to cover her transportation costs to this meeting. A letter seeking financial support for your travel to the Workshop is being sent to your institution. In the event that this is not feasible, WWB is prepared to help to cover travel costs, round trip, economy class.

The Workshop will begin at 6 p.m. on Wednesday, March 12, with a reception and dinner. We have invited a Senior Director of the World Bank to join us on this occasion. Sessions will continue for two full days, concluding with a banquet on Friday evening. Participants are expected to attend all sessions.

We sincerely hope that you will be able to join us for this Workshop. If not, we would appreciate having the name of a colleague in banking from your country.

It is important that we receive a reply at your earliest convenience. Please write to the above address or cable WWB ATINT WASHDC.

Sincerely,

Michaela Walsh
Chairperson

Enclosures

INTERNATIONAL WORKSHOP
of
WOMEN LEADERS IN BANKING AND FINANCE

AMSTERDAM
March 12–15, 1980

A REPORT

COMMITTEE TO ORGANIZE

WOMEN'S WORLD BANKING

REPORT

of

INTERNATIONAL WORKSHOP

of

WOMEN LEADERS IN BANKING AND FINANCE

AMSTERDAM

March 12-15, 1980

Prepared by:

Joan E. Shapiro, Rapporteur
Gretchen S. Maynes, Consultant

Committee to Organize
  Women's World Banking
P.O. Box 1691
Grand Central Station
New York, New York 10017

ACKNOWLEDGEMENTS

The Committee to Organize Women's World Banking is indebted to many for support of the first International Workshop of Women Leaders in Banking and Finance. Individual contributors made the Committee's work possible; individual participants gave of their time and expertise. Many banks, businesses and organizations supported this effort by funding the travel and participation of their representatives. Two organizations, ACCION International and A.T. International, gave moral and logistical support, the value of which is immeasurable. Those institutions which provided major funding were:

Board of Global Ministries of the United Methodist Church

Ford Foundation

Netherlands Ministry for Development Cooperation

Swedish International Development Authority

United Nations Development Programme

United States Agency for International Development

The banks, businesses and organizations to whom we extend our appreciation are:

African American Institute
    United States

African Continental Bank
    Nigeria

Algemene Bank Nederland
    The Netherlands

American Express International
Banking Corporation
    Indonesia

Bangkok Bank, Ltd.
    Thailand

Bank Hapoalim
    Israel

Bank of Montreal
    Canada

Barclays Bank International, Ltd.
Development Fund
    England

Barclays Bank of Kenya, Ltd.
    Kenya

Caroline Pezzullo Associates, Inc.
    New York, New York, U.S.A.

Clemente Capital, Inc.
    New York, New York, U.S.A.

Danielle Hunebelle's International
Letter
    France

First State Bank
    Kansas City, Kansas, U.S.A

Inter-American Development Bank
    Washington, D.C., U.S.A.

(continued)

Martha Stuart Communications, Inc.
 New York, New York, U.S.A.

Muslim Commercial Bank
 Pakistan

PACT (Private Agencies
Collaborating Together)
 New York, New York, U.S.A.

Paluwagan Ng Bayan Savings & Loan
 Philippines

South Shore National Bank
 Chicago, Illinois, U.S.A.

Tessler-Cloherty, Inc.
 New York, New York, U.S.A.

The World Bank
 Washington, D.C., U.S.A.

On behalf of the Committee, I wish to thank them all.

Michaela Walsh, Chairperson
Committee to Organize
WOMEN'S WORLD BANKING

Members of the Committee to Organize Women's World Banking:

Martha Bulengo

Patricia Cloherty

Gasbia El Hamamsy

Annie Jiagge

Lucille Mair

Bertha Beatriz Martinez-Garza

Esther Ocloo

Caroline Pezzullo

Virginia Saurwein

Leslie Sederlund

Leticia Ramos Shahani

Margaret Snyder

Martha Stuart

Zohreh Tabatabai

Michaela Walsh

TABLE OF CONTENTS

Preface

Introduction and Summary

Opening Plenary

Workshop I   : Identifying Commercial Opportunities

Workshop II : Seeing Women as Entrepreneurs

Workshop III: Finding Sources of Assistance for People Going into Business

Workshop IV : Priorities for Assisting Women in Enterprise

Workshop V   : Designing Practical Means of Supplying Capital and Skills
                to Women's Enterprises

Program   : "The Anatomy of a Development Bank"

Workshop VI : Next Steps

Closing Plenary

Appendices: I   : Workshop Participants and Observers

             II : Operating Issues Requiring Consideration, from the
                    Workshop's Background Paper, by Patricia M. Cloherty

             III: Excerpts from the Discussion Paper, Women's World
                    Banking Capital Fund, by Lilia C. Clemente

             IV : Draft Statement to the World Conference of the
                    UN Decade for Women, Copenhagen, July, 1980

             V   : Commentary on WWB Questionnaire Findings

             VI : WWB Documents and papers offered by participants
                    to the International Workshop of Women Leaders in
                    Banking and Finance.

Photographs Courtesy of Martha Stuart Communications, Inc.

Women's World Banking (WWB) is an international, independent financial organization created to promote the direct participation of women and their families in the full use of the economy, particularly those women who have not generally had access to banking and financial services.* It is currently designing a program to redirect financial resources and technical services to these women. Its approach, initially, will be:

- to initiate a loan guarantee mechanism to generate financing for women's income-producing activities;

- to arrange for technical assistance for ventures receiving loan guarantees, as needed, in order to ensure their viability; and

- to expand and strengthen the network of women who participate in financial decision-making in their economies.

In order to test and refine its approach and to broaden the network of women well placed to assist in implementing its program, the Committee to Organize Women's World Banking brought together leading women in banking, finance and entrepreneurship from 27 countries for a workshop in Amsterdam in March 1980.

The guidance which emerged is contained in the following report. Participants offer it to the newly elected Board of Directors of Stichting Women's World Banking**, together with their commitment to work with WWB to encourage entrepreneurship, self-reliance and greater independence of women.

---

*
 Documents of Women's World Banking include:

- Statement of Purpose, which provides more detailed information on its history, rationale and approach;

- Charter of Stichting Women's World Banking; and

- Workshop Background Paper, by Patricia M. Cloherty, a relevant piece for those seeking to provide capital and skills to women entrepreneurs. Operating issues she identifies as requiring consideration by the Stichting Board are attached as Appendix II.

** Stichting Women's World Banking was incorporated in the Netherlands on May 11, 1979. On March 16, 1980, core members of the Board of Directors were elected (see list on following page).

INTRODUCTION AND SUMMARY

The purpose of the International Workshop of Women Leaders in Banking & Finance, convened March 12-15, 1980 in Amsterdam, was to:

- discuss the critical issues involved in women's access to, and effective use of, financial services including credit;

- develop strategies for implementing WWB's program at the national and local level;

- identify collaborating institutions for WWB; and

- prepare recommendations to the 1980 World Conference of the UN Decade for Women.

The participants (37) and observers (25) represented business, banking and other related professional expertise*: portfolio managers, consultants and economic analysts; an urban architect and managers of urban development corporations, owner/operators of food processing plants, craft cooperatives, independent publishers and a video producer, senior executive officers and managers of international funding agencies, private development-oriented commercial banks and women's banks. Observers came from governments, international foundations, national and international institutions for financial and technical cooperation. The fact that many of the attendees will participate in the WWB program as it evolves, and benefit from it, sharpened the focus of the meeting.

The achievements of the Workshop were as follows:

- It brought together women leaders in business and finance from 27 countries to think about ways of providing capital and know-how to enterprising women. These women will hereafter serve as Advisory Associates of WWB, a network of international advisors who will begin to identify commercial opportunities and build in their countries the indispensible links with individual and institutional intermediaries.

- As attested by the presence of key public, international financing and technical cooperation agencies**, it heightened awareness of the problem of women's exclusion from the economic mainstream and their potential contribution to small-scale enterprise development. These ideas are embodied in WWB's Statement to the World Conference of the UN Decade for Women.

---

* See Appendix I for a listing of Workshop participants and observers.

** Senior representatives of the World Bank and the United Nations Development Programme addressed the Workshop at its opening banquet.

- Participants endorsed WWB's overall intention "to extend capital support selectively, through qualified intermediaries, to women entrepreneurs with viable projects, in accordance with prevailing business practice in the area."

- A video report, "Founding Meeting, Women's World Banking," was produced in which participants discuss basic economic issues confronting women. Copies of the video were distributed to all participants and are available for viewing in many countries.*

- A commentary was written on the results of an informal questionnaire offered to Workshop participants in advance of the meeting. The questionnaire's purpose was to increase our understanding of the issues addressed at the Workshop and begin to document the need for research in this area.**

The recommendations of participants in professional positions in banking and business were that WWB should:

- support enterprising women in new and existing ventures in both urban and rural areas, in all productive sectors of the economy, with particular attention to small and medium-scale businesses;

- focus its financial intervention on those small-scale ventures with a chance to "make a difference;"

- require that beneficiaries have a sufficient equity stake in the venture to be motivated to succeed;

- gear technical cooperation to match the scale of enterprises owned by women;

- use local public and private intermediaries to help design and provide management and skills training of a type that can be withdrawn after an initial period;

- operate on a self-supporting basis by establishing a scale of operations which can be wholly funded by earnings from a capital/guarantee fund;

- select a "lean staff" to

    - outline basic operating policies for Board consideration;

    - identify initial projects, urban and rural, and allocate two years to their development; and

    - raise capital.

The report which follows is not a word-for-word recapitulation of the meeting; transcripts are on record to provide that history. Rather it is a summary of key discussions and recommendations, interspersed with a small sampling of the anecdotes and experiences which gave the Workshop its unusual content and meaning.

---

* Video report produced by Martha Stuart Communications, Inc., 66 Bank Street, New York, N.Y. 10014.

** For commentary on questionnaire findings, see Appendix V.

OPENING PLENARY

As an historic overview, members of the Committee to Organize Women's World
Banking (WWB) reviewed the genesis, rationale and assumptions of the
organization. Its overriding goal is to advance women through viable
business ventures. Its major premise was articulated at the 1975
International Women's Year Conference in Mexico City, namely, that to
participate fully in the economic development of their countries, women
need greater access to credit and other tools of the formal money economy.

The founding group of WWB organized around this need. Members of this
group spoke of their four-year commitment to launch an organization which
would:

- serve to increase women's involvement in the financial workings
  of their countries, both as entrepreneurs and as decision-makers;

- develop a global network of women in banking and business;

- establish initially a loan guarantee fund as an incentive for
  lending institutions to extend credit to women;

- create a network of cooperating institutions, or "intermediaries,"*
  in each participating country;

- develop a system flexible enough to adapt to varying national
  needs and conditions;

- offer education and training prior and/or simultaneous to the
  delivery of credit when needed;

- seek out enterprising women;

- provide small-scale credit;

- provide start-up credit as well as expand existing credit;

- select to assist enterprises which will have both an economic
  and a social impact;

- focus on income-generating activities of low-income women,
  urban and rural;

- work with cooperative endeavors and group enterprises when
  feasible; and

- cooperate with national and international agencies to broaden
  the impact.

---

* The concept of intermediaries appears frequently in background papers,
proposals and Workshop discussions. In this report, "intermediaries"
refers to the entire range of potential sources of help for WWB-supported
businesses, including lending institutions, providers of technical
cooperation and local organizations who borrow with a WWB guarantee to
re-lend. Intermediaries are individuals and institutions who know their local
economies and are qualified to intervene in their area of expertise between
WWB and the enterprise.

WORKSHOP I: IDENTIFYING COMMERCIAL OPPORTUNITIES

Criteria for WWB-Supported Enterprises

In order to establish mechanisms to identify commercial opportunities, WWB staff will develop criteria regarding profitability, size, location, type and nature of priority businesses:

- Profitability

   There was unanimity that a WWB-supported enterprise must be profitable. Where possible, it should also yield significant social benefits. Other agencies are better equipped than WWB to deal with enterprises requiring deep or indefinite subsidy.

- Size of Enterprise

   Participants favored criteria skewed to give priority to very small enterprises or, alternatively, to small enterprises with potential to evolve into medium-sized ventures. Working with small-scale business borrowers is difficult and will require greater cooperation from intermediary institutions than working with medium-scale businesses. The latter often have access, albeit limited, to the services of credit and commercial banks.

   Several bankers with extensive small business lending experience endorsed WWB's supporting entrepreneurs with potential to move from small to medium-size. They cautioned the group not to spend valuable time and talent resources on small businesses which would be unlikely to grow or make a measurable impact. Women entrepreneurs and WWB need visible success. Size, per se, therefore, should not be WWB's criteria but rather, "What will make a difference?"

- Location: Urban or Rural

   Some participants argued that since two-thirds of the women in the developing countries depend on rural economies, WWB should concentrate its activities in that sector.* Others argued that the urban poor were neglected and steadily growing; that the problems of urban squatters were serious; and job creation a critical requirement.** A concensus developed that WWB should explore the gamut of commercial opportunities in different countries and regions and diversify its activities between urban and rural enterprises.

---

*   A suggestion that WWB consider placing deposits in banks in Thailand, for re-lending to women's enterprises in rural areas at more reasonable interest rates than are currently available, was received from Mrs. Chinda Chareonvejj of Bangkok Bank, Ltd.

**   A proposal for WWB's support for the informal economic activities of low-income women in Brazil, in particular of "favelas" (squatters' settlements), was received from Marlene Fernandes of Banco Nacional de Habitacion.

- Type of Business

    All categories of business activity -- industrial, agricultural
    and commercial services -- potentially qualify for WWB support,
    but demand may vary by locality. Lending institutions favor
    industry and tend to discount small retail trade and commercial
    services due to the smaller, less controllable asset bases of
    these businesses. They also prefer financing larger loans
    which involve fixed assets to providing small working capital
    loans secured by inventory and receivables.

- New or On-Going Business Support

    Participants were divided on this question and recommended that
    WWB be flexible enough to respond to requests from both new and
    existing businesses. Many of the latter need very small advances
    (equivalent of US $100 - $1,000) so WWB should investigate low-
    cost means of helping women obtain such financing. At the same
    time, start-up operations, which are particularly difficult to
    finance conventionally since the equity portions of the
    financing are totally illiquid and are fully at risk, often
    represent opportunities for economic growth. Participants urged
    WWB to support new ventures and to try to develop innovative
    lending techniques.

Loan Terms and Conditions, Including Technical Cooperation

In terms of conventional lending procedures, participants viewed collateral requirements as major stumbling blocks for most businesswomen: small business owners have virtually no collateral; women might own a large percent of business assets world-wide, but husbands or families control them; and banks in developing countries often require 200% - 300% collateral on a loan. Most bankers agreed that collateral was over-emphasized by lenders and urged WWB to focus on other lending criteria, e.g., management capacity, business experience, business objectives, market potential of product or service, availability of technical resources, business liquidity, adequacy of cash flow, group guarantees. Some suggested that WWB should eliminate the collateral requirement for advances under a certain amount.

The founder and president of a successful savings and loan often makes "character loans." One of her customers needed money to buy a pig; there was no collateral or business plan and no way of getting them. He got the pig because she knew he'd pay her back. He did -- and now has a hog farm. She commented: "If we don't do banking business this way, we're all going to starve."

"Mrs. ..... has a small candy factory; it can hardly be called a factory because she had no capital and she and her family were the ones doing the candies. Since the Philippines hardly import candies, this business has ... potential. Her son-in-law worked with me at the bank and had introduced her to me....Of course to work without...collateral is a fear of all bankers, but I was willing to take the risk because if she did not pay I could fall back on her son-in-law. We started by giving her 5,000 pesos...about US$625....Slowly she was able to buy two jeeps...which she later mortgaged to use for 7,000 pesos, about US$875. The factory prepares candy made out of carabao's milk;...another kind is made out of tamarind fruit. Yesterday I granted her a loan of 150,000 pesos, about US$18,750 after she presented a small real estate...bought with from proceeds of her business. Even then, whatever collateral she was offering was not enough to answer for the loan, but this time we looked at her paying capacity....She is doing very well, paying almost 8,000 pesos, about US$1,000 a month. Her husband markets her candies."

Other suggestions included using sliding interest rates, building equity-generating mechanisms into loan conditions, and making small advances for unusually short-terms (30-60 days) with early, frequent repayment.

Kanta Kalu (20), a loader-unloader in the Railway Yard, learned about SEWA Bank (Women's Bank) in 1974 from her neighbor. She had to support her husband (jobless) and three children from the daily earnings of Rupees 5 (Rs. 7.50 = US$1). SEWA Bank, after proper inquiry and personal field visits lent her Rs. 50 to start a small vending stand with candies, toffies, biscuits, etc., in her neighborhood. Kanta repaid Rs.52 after three weeks, and demanded more credit. She borrowed Rs. 100, and her small business grew. Her husband attended the vending stand while she was labouring at the Railway Yard. SEWA Bank asked her to attend a three-day productivity training class. With much reluctance she joined and completed the course. Her interest in the business grew as she learned the principles of marketing and management. In the meantime her husband left her. She bought an old pushcart for Rs. 60 from her meagre resources and took a loan of Rs. 150 from SEWA Bank to vend vegetables. Since 1977 she has been increasing her sales while gradually increasing the amount of her loans -- from Rs. 150 to 400; and today a loan of Rs. 700 is outstanding on her. She also makes deposits in her saving account regularly when she comes to the Bank to repay her monthly installments.

From the daily average turnover of Rs. 150 she earns about Rs. 30-40. "Now," as she said, "I have a comfortable living in my home -- a petromax, a paved flooring in my hut, a brass pot with a brass lid and brass plates and bowls for all four of us. I also did a pilgrimage when my firstborn was sick. Above all, I have about Rs. 400 in my savings account!"

Now Kanta desires to get rid of her old pushcart and buy a new one with "Dunlop" tires to speed up her business. Her husband has come back, but is still unemployed.

Her only headache is the police demanding bribes which she refuses to give, hence harrassment from the police for "encroaching" on the vehicular traffic. There are hundreds like her in the market. SEWA, being a union of vendors and the self-employed, is leading a campaign to make the market a pedestrian zone.

227

On the question of technical assistance -- by concensus hereafter called "technical cooperation" -- participants observed that for many small enterprises, loans per se are less important than management and advisory services. New enterprises cannot succeed only with credit, and technical cooperation is often the key to success. At the same time, WWB should be aware of these caveats:

- When dealing with very small businesses, technical cooperation can be over-emphasized. The decision to provide assistance as well as the level of that assistance must be geared to the scale and complexity of the business.

- Subsidies in the form of technical cooperation should be limited, e.g., two years. WWB's goal should be to move a credit, as soon as is feasible, entirely to a commercial bank.

Major Operating Issues

As WWB designs its program and operating plan, two questions will require careful, precise definition:

- What mechanism(s) will WWB use to identify commercial opportunities? Exactly how will WWB reach women entrepreneurs?

- Once identified, what criteria will WWB use for financing these opportunities and for assisting women entrepreneurs?

Both of these questions are explored in WWB documents and in subsequent workshops. At this stage, concensus was reached on the following in regard to the first question:

- Access to information (about entrepreneurs, business opportunities, lending institutions, governmental and non-governmental intermediaries, and laws and customs of each country) is central to WWB's objective of identifying and stimulating commercial opportunities. It must develop an effective network to collect and disseminate information.

- WWB should rely as much as possible on local information and knowledge.

- WWB should seek cooperation at all levels -- local, regional and national.

- Available voluntary energy -- organized either individually or in teams -- should be mobilized to help identify commercial opportunities. It is unrealistic, however, to expect to depend upon volunteer activity in poor countries. There business identification should be conducted by paid WWB staff, nationals trained by WWB, or a technical body permanently in place. WWB should, of course, attempt to tap the existent framework of banks (commercial, development, mortgage), lawyers, accountants, businesspeople in trade associations, credit unions, etc.

- WWB should be aware of the major constraints of working with the informal sector.

- The questions of whether to finance the entrepreneur or the market -- the individual with capacity or a specific, high-growth business activity -- requires further discussion.

Discussions focused on women entrepreneurs in the countryside, in the cities, and on the role that regional support organizations can play in assisting them.

Rural Enterprises

Main entrepreneurial activities of village farmers and rural workers include food production, processing and preserving, chicken farming, and marketing; other rural enterprises are craft and artisan businesses, textile mills and garment factories.

Primary sources of credit for rural women are family members or friends; occasionally, non-governmental organizations in the area make loans from small revolving funds. Commercial banks are rarely sources of credit for rural enterprises. Participants suggested that WWB attempt to match its funds to rural development banks willing to allocate money to women, particularly for seed capital.

Opportunities exist to enlarge the pool of small businesses, particularly in food production and processing. Aside from its inherent value, growth in this area could promote links between rural businesses and urban marketing activities run by women. Practical education, training and access to relevant information are needed to help women develop management skills and entrepreneurial ability.

Principal problems are the shortage of support systems for women entrepreneurs and their lack of control over their economic activities. Participants noted that marketing is frequently the point at which women either do not participate or lose direct control. It is an area where WWB could provide information and training.

Cooperatives are a form of rural organization which, in theory, maximizes the potential market and ensures adequate compensation for the productive enterprise. Some participants cautioned that cooperatives are not the only or necessarily the best form of organization; each enterprise should be structured according to its needs and cultural traditions; and where there is no history of cooperatives, the enormous time and effort involved in organizing one may not be justified.

Linkages between groups engaged in similar or complementary business activities for the purpose of converting local and national markets into international ones should be encouraged by WWB. (Two craft groups represented at the Workshop, Artisans Cooperative, Inc., USA and Manos del Uruguay, have since begun negotiations for a collaborative marketing venture.)

Urban Enterprises

Urban women entrepreneurs include vendors, hawkers and owners of small to medium-sized enterprises. Their wide range of business activities includes commercial services, manufacturing (especially food and food processing), craft industries and construction. Strong traditions of female entrepreneurship exist in the urban areas of some countries. WWB should draw on them, where possible, and work with a variety of forms of enterprise, with women in lower and middle-income groups, the literate and the illiterate. Opportunity exists: As one participant observed, "In urban areas, if you can get out to sell, you'll do business; you don't have to stimulate demand."

Obstacles to the success of small business were familiar ground for participants. "Small is beautiful, but small is not simple." Women entrepreneurs face the problems of being small, and others as well:

- Prohibitive cost of credit

    Without access to commercial bank credit, women entrepreneurs are forced to rely on their own limited savings or those of family and friends and, once these are exhausted, on loan sharks and private money lenders who charge 10%/day to 10%/month interest. Compared to these rates, a commercial bank's 20% - 25% /year interest rate is affordable.

- Cultural prejudice and tradition

    There are natural entrepreneurs among women, particularly in some countries of Africa and Southeast Asia. This tradition of successful women in business is the exception rather than the rule. Even in such cases, women's economic independence is often perceived as threatening to spouse and others, participants felt.

    Many business opportunities are closed to women through tradition. Participants felt that WWB should encourage women to break through cultural barriers by training in non-traditional areas with non-traditional role models. To do this requires identifying personal strengths, building on past experience and estimating capability.

- Increasing complexity with growth

    As business grows, so do its problems. Female and male entrepreneurs do not differ in this regard. The small vendor's or artisan's main concern is to sell enough to pay bills and feed the family. If a business prospers, however, the owner has to begin thinking about accounting systems, personnel management and marketing.

- The law

    Legal barriers operate formally and informally. Although
    discrimination in lending is illegal in many countries,
    women's access to credit is, in fact, severely limited.
    Participants cited joint ownership of assests for married
    women (which prevents them from borrowing independently)
    and complex licensing requirements as examples of
    barriers that exist in spite of non-discriminatory laws.
    (Statistics on economic discrimination against women
    in Pakistan are included in a Workshop paper, "Potential
    of Women in the Money Economy of Pakistan" by Ms. Akram
    Khatoon.)

Trends that represent opportunities as well as risks for WWB are world-wide
inflation, which is reducing real income and moving women out of the home
to supplement family income; the high rate of unemployment, which is
encouraging women to go into business, particularly in the informal sector;
and the resurgence of small-scale enterprise in the developed world.
Participants felt that WWB's reaction to these opportunities should vary
with locality, resources and prevailing business practices.

Regional Support Organizations

A major task for WWB and its supporters world-wide will be to identify and
establish a cooperative, working relationship with a variety of
intermediary organizations at the regional and national level. The choice
of organization as well as individual women within them will be keys to
WWB's success in encouraging women in business. Such intermediaries
include chambers of commerce, business and professional associations,
legal and accounting firms, educational and voluntary citizens' organizations,
regional agricultural credit associations, social welfare boards, women's
institutes and bureaus, trade and export organizations, trade unions,
women's organizations and cooperatives.

Discussions focused on the functions these intermediaries could fulfill
in the life cycle of a loan. Specifically, regional support organizations
could:
- "sell" WWB's program to potential borrowers, support organizations
  and leaders;

- help identify businesses ripe for WWB-supported loans;

- collaborate with WWB in establishing criteria for administering
  and servicing loans;

- provide technical cooperation and managerial services; and

- monitor business progress and evaluate success, sharing what is
  learned nationally or internationally as appropriate.

Where possible, an entrepreneur should not tie herself to any one
organization, but rather seek out individuals in those organizations that
serve her specific needs.

Participants briefly described some of the more effective lending organizations
in their countries which had regional support components:

The South Shore National Bank of Chicago, Illinois, U.S.A,
America's first neighborhood development bank, is located
in what was a rapidly deteriorating urban area. The bank
has pledged to use its deposits almost exclusively for credit
within that community and provides "in-house" the technical
services (e.g., packaging of loan requests, pre and
post-loan counseling for borrowers, etc.) which WWB
would entrust to local intermediaries.

The Illinois Neighborhood Development Corporation, of
which the bank is but one operating subsidiary, is
committed to investing in the area and to working with
other collaborating institutions to help meet urgent
local economic and social needs. The lending policies
of the bank play a critical role in this integrated
approach to the area's development, and are yielding
impressive results. In six years, the bank has extended
US$30,000,000 in development loans.

SEWA (Self-Employed Women's Association) of Ahmedabad,
India has its own cooperative bank which lends to its
members and provides them with assistance to facilitate
their dealings with commercial banks. In addition, it
offers guidance in processing, storage, production,
marketing, and in accounting and legal services.

ACCION International/AITEC is currently serving as an
intermediary between a large number of micro-businesses
(those with gross receipts of less than US$100,000)
in depressed areas of the State of Maine, U.S.A. and
commercial banks in the region. They are considering
establishing a guarantee fund and/or trying to persuade the
Small Business Administration of the U.S. federal
government and the banks to work together to provide
credit for these micro-businesses.

FINDING SOURCES OF ASSISTANCE FOR PEOPLE GOING INTO BUSINESS

Discussions of the financial and technical resources available for people going into or expanding business raised a number of central operating issues for WWB:

Financial Resources

- Debt/equity ratios:

    These should not be the same for all WWB-supported businesses, since circumstances will vary widely. Participants felt, however, that borrowers must have a stake in the enterprise sufficient to motivate them to succeed.

- Types of financing:

    Fixed asset, debt repayment or consolidation, capital investment, receivable and inventory financing, working capital and the terms of loans must be analyzed on a case-by-case basis, participants felt. They made the following observations:

    - WWB should consider the comparative advantages of short-term vs. long-term financing in deciding its priorities.

    - In regard to both short-term and small-scale borrowing, WWB must be aware of local costs such as supervision, high servicing costs, special mechanisms to ensure repayment.

    - International financial institutions tend to cater to long-term financing of investments and foreign exchange costs; they do some short-term financing of trade.

    - Although a development fund might prefer fostering capital investment as a more productive use of its money, it would consider financing working capital because of its scarcity. Accounts receivable and inventory financing would also be acceptable if its purpose were to expand an existing project.

    - Participants were divided on the question of equity financing: some argued that in its pilot project, WWB should provide both the loan guarantee and equity financing; others opposed direct equity financing in any circumstances.

- Sources of financial collaboration:

    These were discussed in some detail. WWB is designed to be able to work with any financial institution, local, national or international, large or small, private or public. Its objective should be to create a "map of institutions" to build a network at the national level and work with a variety of funds at the international level.

Considering domestic financing sources, participants questioned whether WWB could persuade commercial banks to work with its guarantee fund without guarantees on both principal and interest. Assuming that these small loans (US$50 - US$200) are desirable, that commercial banks will find them impractical, and that alternative financial institutions will have to be used, how will WWB go about implementing a system that links these institutions with WWB and with small businesses?

Government guarantees and banking regulations in certain countries were cited as examples of policies which might be helpful to WWB's effort. In some Southeast Asian countries,

- private national banks are required by law to invest a percentage of their portfolio in small enterprises, generally with guarantees up to 80%;

- some governments require banks to disburse a percent of their loan portfolio to small enterprises; and

- the Central Bank provides 50% guarantees on loans.

Less encouraging are cases in which governments require banks to invest in small enterprises, but no action is taken.

Considering international sources of finance, discussion focused on the problems most of these institutions have in acting effectively at the local level. Usually they deal through local banking institutions, and too often funds committed for credit to small businesses are never actually disbursed. Participants felt that WWB might well be capable of playing a useful role here.

A concensus was reached on a number of issues related to financial resources for WWB:

- In identifying either international or domestic financing sources, WWB should work with those which, when combined with its own resources and guarantee, will have the greatest impact on local enterprises.

- In negotiating loan guarantees, WWB must ensure that the criteria of lending agencies are consonant with its own.

- WWB must try to convince banks of its intent to apply sound criteria of credit-worthiness, and banks will have to demonstrate their ability to apply reasonable credit standards in order to qualify for the guarantee. Further, a clear understanding of circumstances under which WWB's guarantee will be/will not be honored will have to be developed.

- An aggressive campaign will be required to sell banks the WWB program. Advisory Associates of WWB must be involved in the development of promotional materials and in a strategy for approaching banks in their localities.

A number of participants stressed the obstacles to small business lending. They noted that even banks receptive to such lending, those with special development lending departments, find that costs of staff time to counsel entrepreneurs, book and monitor small business loans are enormous. It would appear, therefore, that some changes in time-honored commercial lending practices will be required. A few banks world-wide have tested new methods of lending. They abolished the lengthy, costly paperwork and rely on the hunches of "street-wise" loan officers. Results from these few lending programs indicate that loans are less costly to make and no riskier than any others. In fact, it may be that the economic benefit to the borrower of being able to borrow from an institution rather than from "sharks" provides added motivation to repay and maintain a good record.

A representative of ACCION International reported on the success of a program in El Salvador to assist informal sector entrepreneurs. In two years it has achieved the following results:

Number of borrowers:	approx. 3000, half of whom have taken 2 - 4 loans
Number of women:	84%
Amount of credit advanced:	approx. US$1.5 million as of August 1979
Average loan size:	US$80-US$120 for 80% first loans
Cost per loan:	approx. US$30
Loan losses:	less than 1%
Delinquency rate:	approx. 3.4% late payments

In summary, the program works as follows: FEDECCREDITO, a credit agency, works with PRIDECO, a community development agency, to set up the loans, which include the provision for a group credit guarantee. The main problem to date has been devising a mechanism to give adequate technical assistance on a massive scale at an acceptable cost.

Other issues discussed on which there was no consensus were:

- the overall question of the operating mechanisms WWB must develop to link financing sources with women in villages and urban areas; and

- the complementary issue of how WWB as "facilitator" will make the connection and do it effectively with adequate control at the local level. The structure of the administrative unit must be spelled out by the Board of WWB, participants felt.

This same question of how the "link" will actually operate in delivering technical cooperation is raised in the following section.

Management and Technical Cooperation

Management, hereafter understood as management services, was defined as the intelligent use of resources which increases a businessperson's capacity and makes funding possible.

Technical cooperation was meant to include access to relevant information, training in necessary skills, and assistance in implementation.

Recommendations to WWB in the area of management services and technical cooperation were of a general nature: clearly, universal guidelines would be inapplicable owing to the varying size, location, type of business, experience of entrepreneur and stage of business development. Participants argued that:

- The environmental and cultural background of potential borrowers must be considered at all stages of assistance; this was especially true for new businesses.

- The notion of "thresholds" is central to deciding when to offer management and technical services. A threshold is the point at which an entrepreneur is capable of absorbing information and moving to a new stage of business development.

- The type of delivery system, as well as the information itself, must be geared to each entrepreneur and group.* A variety of communication methods -- written, oral, visual -- should be employed to make the body of knowledge useful, particularly for low-income and semi-literate women: "We must listen; start from where people are." WWB should work with select institutions, e.g., university adult learning centers, banks and others to create simple accounting systems and train locals, on site, to monitor their application and to produce basic materials on financial and banking services.

- Technical cooperation needs must be linked to size and scale of business. As the director of a successful small business program in developing countries observed:

  "An important concept is not overburdening people with too much technical assistance that they don't need. Staging is important. Maybe only credit is needed -- then leave it at that. The more technical assistance you give, the more expensive it gets."

- "Twinning" -- bringing together potential entrepreneurs with thriving ones -- should be incorporated into technical cooperation schemes whenever possible, and is preferable to bringing in outside specialists. Twinning can even occur internationally in some circumstances.

---

* "Urban Craft," a paper offered by Gloria Knight of the Urban Development Corporation, Kingston, Jamaica, provides an example of an appropriate delivery system and of an integrated approach to meeting needs of new entrepreneurs.

- Attention should be focused on women's economic activities, particularly those in the informal sector, that go largely unnoticed and unaided. What, if anything, can be done to assist these efforts?

There are hundreds of milk producer women in the villages. There are other landless women laborers, starving without work for half of the year. They wish to supplement their income by raising cattle and selling milk. They want finance to buy cattle (cows, buffaloes, goats) from the commercial bank. But the bank finds the labourers' proposal not viable for lack of proper collateral.

SEWA Bank intervened. Who would be guarantors to poor, starving women workers in the villages? When their own lives are not viable, their proposals are far from being viable! SEWA Bank deposited Rs. 50,000 as a guarantee fund in the said commercial bank, the interest proceeds of which also work as a subsidy on the loan.

Thus 18 women received Rs. 2,000 for buying cows six months ago. The monthly repayment of Rs. 50 comes regularly. In the end, Rs. 400 will be paid on the installments from the accumulated interest of the credit guarantee fund provided by SEWA Bank to the commercial bank.

The women are now members of the village women's milk cooperative which has 43 total membership.

Resources for management services and technical cooperation for Women's World Banking are public and private, individual and institutional and should be sought at the local, national and international level.* WWB will need to assess how to work with these resources most effectively. Participants stressed the need to create a broad-based membership of "stockholder" organizations in each cooperating country to maximize women's participation and contribution at the local level. Many expressed the view that WWB's success will depend on its ability to identify and engage resources at the local level.

---

* In this connection, representatives of the UNDP announced the commitment of substancial resources by their organization for a joint effort with WWB to provide for the assessment of national banking practices and structures; holding of national or regional workshops for key members of various sectors of the economy to address the issues of women in the economy; identification and development of local collaborators; and the selection of potential WWB guarantee candidates. The UNDP has also agreed to support a portion of Stichting Women's World Banking's initial three-year operational budget.

WORKSHOP IV: PRIORITIES FOR ASSISTING WOMEN IN ENTERPRISE

Participants addressed the following three questions:

What are the priority needs of women establishing or maintaining businesses?

● More credit:

> It was generally agreed that limited savings, lack of collateral, prohibitive cost of informal credit and barriers to independent borrowing effectively eliminate women's access to the regular financial system. Access to a variety of credit sources was also considered important. One participant stressed that women often have difficulty knowing when a business warrants application of capital, i.e., when that capital will cause it to expand and not be consumed by operations.

● Greater awareness of available funds, counseling and educational services:

> There are exceptions, but most women are unsophisticated about the business world; when they go into business, they tend to choose small, uncompetitive activities which are all the more difficult to finance. Knowing how to get the necessary help will give women greater confidence to enter into more competitive businesses and to borrow productively.

● Technical cooperation and managment services.

> Counseling is essential for women developing new enterprises as well as for individual entrepreneurs who wish to increase their productive capacity. Ways must be created to increase access to non-technical support (e.g., household support systems, day-care centers, time-saving devices).

● An organization to support their efforts to achieve self-reliance:

> As one participant said, "Alone women are weak; together so many things become possible."

● Assistance from intermediary organizations:

> One participant observed, "...help to small-scale businesses will be done through institutions at the local level, groups often not themselves profit- or management-oriented. An important unresolved question...is how WWB can work through groups such as these -- given their different orientation -- to accomplish its objectives." Other participants made the following observations:

>> - If women are to move out from traditional credit sources to institutions where money is available on more reasonable financial terms, they will need the help of intermediaries.

>> - There is no one ideal intermediary. WWB should investigate all options and identify strengths -- particularly institutions in which women hold strategic positions.

>> - Assistance by intermediaries should be for a limited period.

- Where possible, WWB should work first with local intermediaries and later with those at the national level.

- There may be advantages in working with private rather than
government agencies: the latter has to consider national
priorities, necessarily moves more slowly, and often
cannot act on an individual level. Where government does
assist, ensure that there is one person responsible for
working with WWB and that a local task force is created
to coordinate the effort.

- If universities or other educational institutions participate,
their work must be part of a concrete program with
measurable objectives. People from the community as well as
students should be recruited to work in the field.

- WWB should engage volunteer assistance -- "use an energy
source wherever you can find it" -- but recognize that
concrete results may be more likely with paid staff.

- Developing techniques whereby intermediaries are the conduit
for passing funds to women entrepreneurs would be valuable.*

- There is need to increase women's role in decision-making,
lending activities and management techniques. Most commercial
bank officers are men, and it is often difficult for women
to establish business and account relationships. Institutional
change will not take place until there are more women loan
officers. Participants cited women's branches in their
countries set up to meet this need.

- The capacity of the mass media to help meet the needs of
women in business was emphasized. Materials on basic
business practices are needed and must be adapted for rural
and urban needs. (A special workshop on "Video as a
Development Tool" dealt with some of these issues.

---

* Participants discussed the case in which the intermediary, or "national
cooperating association," becomes the fiduciary of a loan guarantee and
re-lends the funds to an enterprise, or group of enterprises. In some
countries, there are legal constraints to this arrangement; but frequently,
by-laws can be altered so that the intermediary legally can borrow from an
external source and re-lend to a smaller enterprise. Where no such authorization is possible, a parallel financing agency (e.g., commercial or
development banks) could be involved.

How do these priorities translate into program choices for WWB and its intermediaries?

- Regardless of an organization's focus -- educational, commercial, cooperative, developmental -- participants felt that all could become involved in developing programs, or incorporating into existing programs, five critical components:

    - business training for women, and the development of appropriate materials;

    - promotion of women to decision-making positions at all levels;

    - emphasis on entrepreneurial opportunities for women;

    - pressure on governments to focus specifically on women's economic activities; and

    - "networking" to link women in business and the professions.

- To meet the range of educational and technical needs, women must explore the gamut of training opportunities from individual counseling to formal university education. In particular, there is a need to encourage research on women's economic activities, to design courses for small business, and to support extension services which use field workers from economic and business faculties.

- Awareness of women's entrepreneurial opportunities should begin in the educational system at the primary and secondary level. Information on a variety of career choices, including entrepreneurship, should be presented.

- Women's organizations should offer programs in career orientation and basic business skills either independently, or in collaboration with business associations and schools.

- The international banking system can support this effort by promoting women within the system at the professional level, instituting reporting requirements in areas of women's economic activities (without which such activities have low priority), and putting more development funds into private banks to support women's enterprises. (The effect of this effort would be to "blend" a market with a subsidized interest rate.)

When dealing with rural enterprises, should WWB direct its resources to groups or to individual entrepreneurs?

If rural refers to "low income women geographically dispersed," then participants felt that supporting cooperative or cooperating groups might be an economical and administratively feasible approach for WWB:

- The group approach will require a careful study of local forms of operation and of existing and potential institutional support.

- WWB should work with "natural groups," or self-chosen groups. Any joining of groups or of individual entrepreneurs should be consonant with national customs and traditions.

How do these priorities translate into program choices for WWB and its intermediaries?

- Regardless of an organization's focus -- educational, commercial, cooperative, developmental -- participants felt that all could become involved in developing programs, or incorporating into existing programs, five critical components:

    - business training for women, and the development of appropriate materials;

    - promotion of women to decision-making positions at all levels;

    - emphasis on entrepreneurial opportunities for women;

    - pressure on governments to focus specifically on women's economic activities; and

    - "networking" to link women in business and the professions.

- To meet the range of educational and technical needs, women must explore the gamut of training opportunities from individual counseling to formal university education. In particular, there is a need to encourage research on women's economic activities, to design courses for small business, and to support extension services which use field workers from economic and business faculties.

- Awareness of women's entrepreneurial opportunities should begin in the educational system at the primary and secondary level. Information on a variety of career choices, including entrepreneurship, should be presented.

- Women's organizations should offer programs in career orientation and basic business skills either independently, or in collaboration with business associations and schools.

- The international banking system can support this effort by promoting women within the system at the professional level, instituting reporting requirements in areas of women's economic activities (without which such activities have low priority), and putting more development funds into private banks to support women's enterprises. (The effect of this effort would be to "blend" a market with a subsidized interest rate.)

When dealing with rural enterprises, should WWB direct its resources to groups or to individual entrepreneurs?

If rural refers to "low income women geographically dispersed," then participants felt that supporting cooperative or cooperating groups might be an economical and administratively feasible approach for WWB:

- The group approach will require a careful study of local forms of operation and of existing and potential institutional support.

- WWB should work with "natural groups," or self-chosen groups. Any joining of groups or of individual entrepreneurs should be consonant with national customs and traditions.

<u>How do these priorities translate into program choices for WWB and its</u>
<u>intermediaries?</u>

- Regardless of an organization's focus -- educational, commercial,
  cooperative, developmental -- participants felt that all could become
  involved in developing programs, or incorporating into existing
  programs, five critical components:

  - business training for women, and the development of appropriate
    materials;

  - promotion of women to decision-making positions at all levels;

  - emphasis on entrepreneurial opportunities for women;

  - pressure on governments to focus specifically on women's
    economic activities; and

  - "networking" to link women in business and the professions.

- To meet the range of educational and technical needs, women must explore
  the gamut of training opportunities from individual counseling to
  formal university education. In particular, there is a need to encourage
  research on women's economic activities, to design courses for
  small business, and to support extension services which use field
  workers from economic and business faculties.

- Awareness of women's entrepreneurial opportunities should begin in
  the educational system at the primary and secondary level. Information
  on a variety of career choices, including entrepreneurship, should
  be presented.

- Women's organizations should offer programs in career orientation and
  basic business skills either independently, or in collaboration with
  business associations and schools.

- The international banking system can support this effort by promoting
  women within the system at the professional level, instituting reporting
  requirements in areas of women's economic activities (without which such
  activities have low priority), and putting more development funds into
  private banks to support women's enterprises. (The effect of this
  effort would be to "blend" a market with a subsidized interest rate.)

<u>When dealing with rural enterprises, should WWB direct its resources to</u>
<u>groups or to individual entrepreneurs?</u>

If rural refers to "low income women geographically dispersed," then
participants felt that supporting cooperative or cooperating groups might
be an economical and administratively feasible approach for WWB:

- The group approach will require a careful study of local
  forms of operation and of existing and potential institutional
  support.

- WWB should work with "natural groups," or self-chosen groups.
  Any joining of groups or of individual entrepreneurs should be
  consonant with national customs and traditions.

- Depending on available money, WWB might also consider supporting the emergence of non-traditional associations (e.g., a rural youth club funded because of its program to encourage entrepreneurs.

- Not all countries will be receptive to the group approach. Specific examples of unsuccessful group lending were mentioned; also, bankers look to individuals in cases of default and, procedurally, would be unlikely to accept group guarantees.

- Any productive effort WWB supports in the rural sector must fit into a country's rural planning program.

- Technical cooperation often involves training people in new technologies; if these include time-saving improvements, displacement may occur. One advantage in working with a group is that it can assume the responsibility of re-training or placing the newly unemployed.

DESIGNING PRACTICAL MEANS OF SUPPLYING
CAPITAL AND SKILLS TO WOMEN'S ENTERPRISES

Criteria for Selecting Financial Institutions

In selecting financial intermediaries to work with WWB-supported projects, participants suggested the following guidelines: a financial institution should be legally empowered to borrow and to lend; socially oriented (in WWB terms, geared to women's needs); development oriented; flexible enough to adjust loan terms and conditions to borrowers' individual needs; and conveniently located to the project site. Participants recognized, however, that the selection will depend ultimately on which banks have management willing to work with WWB-supported ventures.

Criteria for Selecting Women's Enterprises

Participants agreed that the ideal, bankable enterprise for WWB would be women-owned and oriented, profitable (fulfilling a market need), and employment-generating. It would have an equity base but possess fixed assets of less than US$100,000. It would be led by a woman of integrity and of proven entrepreneurial ability. Lastly, it would be unable to get credit elsewhere.

Essential Skills for Women Entrepreneurs

Appropriate skills for women in business were mentioned earlier. Here participants added organizational training, literacy followed by formal education, technical training to up-grade the quality of products, and the formulating, writing and presenting of business proposals.

Rural women entrepreneurs, they felt, needed basic information on the selection, maintenance and raising of both livestock and food produce and knowledge about the advantages of moving personal savings from the home to financial institutions where the funds could become collateral for borrowing and for establishing a credit relationship.

What Should WWB's Role Be?

In order to serve as a catalyst to supply capital and skills to women entrepreneurs, WWB will need to:

- establish a loan guarantee fund with broad institutional and individual support;
- disseminate information and build an information network;
- create a system of support services;

- identify women in cooperating countries who would, in turn, negotiate locally with banking institutions willing to accept the guarantee scheme; identify locally-based intermediaries willing to provide low-cost technical cooperation; and help to identify potentially bankable ventures. (Advisory Associates of WWB would serve as the core group of such women.)

Discussion of WWB's financial role and the operation of the capital fund was begun here, but is incorporated with the discussion of this topic in Workshop VI.

LUNCHEON PROGRAM:

THE ANATOMY OF A DEVELOPMENT BANK

Recounting her experience with the Inter-American Development Bank,
Beatriz Harretche offered a number of recommendations to those directly
responsible for launching the WWB program. We have taken the liberty of
summarizing her comments:

- Ideas such as WWB take time to ripen, but four years is enough.

- Define with care the initial plan, taking into consideration the need for:

    - a headquarters close to where the money is, at least for
      the consolidation period;

    - a small, high-level staff of professionals with experience,
      motivation and imagination in addition to academic background.

- Begin operations in one country in each of the 3 regions of the third
  world that offers good logistical support.

- Select levels of action. A decision to promote new enterprises or to
  support existing ones will influence the choice of intermediaries and
  the nature of the operation.

- Select in each country of operation at least one commercial bank, one
  development institution and one non-governmental organization working
  in credit at the grass roots level. Each of these serves a different
  clientele, works under different terms and can provide different
  services. Sooner or later they will all be needed.

- Criteria for project selection must include economic viability. It is
  essential that the entrepreneurs be informed of the real conditions of
  the financial market and the precarious conditions of the subsidy.
  To develop sound enterprises, emphasis should be placed on training
  entrepreneurs to deal with conventional financing institutions in real terms.

- WWB must be prepared to coordinate and sometimes to finance technical
  cooperation -- either in consultancy services or training or both.
  Fortunately, WWB comes into existence at a time when technical
  cooperation has changed dramatically for the better. The coordination
  of assistance between similar enterprises in different stages of
  development is a technique I recommend.

- The resources of the guarantee fund should be kept decentralized.
  Contributors to the fund around the world will certainly prefer so.
  WWB headquarters must control the operations with norms and procedures
  and appropriate accounting systems, without transfering resources to
  a focal point.

- By no means should the WWB operation be considered non-profit in the
  sense that most foundations are. In the near future, WWB must be a banking
  operation whose profits are used to pay the administrative expenses to
  establish a reasonable reserve and to finance technical cooperation to
  the women's enterprises it serves. Only after that equilibrium is
  achieved will you be able to say that the consolidation period is over.

WORKSHOP VI: NEXT STEPS

What should WWB's financial role be? Discussion centered on the immediate
task of raising a capital fund for the loan guarantee program. The
session covered three topics: sources of the capital fund, make-up of
the fund, and strategies to begin operations.

Where Can WWB Raise Funds?

WWB has three potential funding sources: individuals, private institutions
and public institutions.

- Individual women world-wide are a first and obvious source of funds.
  Costs of a mass campaign and its possible limited return may,
  initially, present obstacles to this approach. Another option
  is to attempt to raise capital from a small number of wealthy donors.

- Funding sources in the private sector include corporations, pension
  funds, insurance companies, national church groups, foundations,
  mutual funds, brokerage firms, trade unions and banks. Such
  institutions would consider WWB a program-related investment --
  an investment tied to a specific effort which promises both a
  monetary and a social return.

- Funding sources in the public sector include regional, national
  and international organizations. Some government support is,
  in fact, earmarked for women's development programs, and WWB might
  well qualify. Acquiring support from international financial
  institutions requires the endorsement of member governments for the
  WWB program.*

How Much Public? Private?

As background to the discussion of the nature of the WWB capital fund, one
participant reviewed the basic types of institutional funds:

- a "retort" fund, with continual inflows of short-term money,
  is still highly liquid;

- a "still" fund, considered complete once it is filled,
  consists of long-term funds which rarely change;

- a "trickle still" fund combines long-term, endowment-type
  funds with regular inflows of shorter-term money.

---

* Member governments of the UNDP have endorsed WWB's plans in sufficient
numbers to allow that agency to commit funds from its regional bureaus
for this effort.

The latter was recommended for WWB. Income from the non-liquid funds would provide the initial seed capital to finance both limited staff and pilot guarantees.

There was considerable debate on the subject of a diversified fund. As one participant pointed out, WWB will be operating in what is now a capital-short environment; there is no way either to ensure that a combination of public and private resources will be possible or to determine what mix would be ideal. Another reiterated the position that once the majority of an organization's funds come from government agencies, it is difficult to attract private investment. Theory aside, one banker commented, "Money is like love -- you get it where you can find it."

Participants endorsed WWB's need to seek both public and private resources and stressed the roles each sector could play. The aim should be a balanced fund -- and self-sufficiency as soon as possible. There was concensus that if WWB were able to generate the public/private mix, it would be unique among international women's funding bodies.

Alternative Strategies

In the absence of a projected budget based on income from a capital fund of US$6 million, participants suggested ways in which WWB could begin operating while building the capital fund:

- Create smaller funds at the national level raised from individual and institutional contributors, kept on deposit locally as a guarantee fund. Deposits from individuals and women's organizations could be added to these.

  The issues of adequate control over local funds and legal questions of transferability and convertability of national funds were discussed but unresolved.

- Apply the "paper approach," e.g., make use of funds of other institutions willing to provide guarantees for WWB-identified projects.

- Build up the guarantee fund from the differential in interest rates between what WWB could borrow at (assuming a subsidy on that rate) and what it would charge to lend.

- Accept gifts and grants to support planning and start-up of critical pilot projects. Once WWB can demonstrate a successful project -- one that meets defined performance standards -- it will be in a more convincing position to approach the large public and private funding sources.

- Consider, initially, matching women entrepreneurs identified by WWB with available sources of credit, local and international.

The final session focused on the nature and management of the WWB capital
fund and on immediate program choices. There were also two presentations:

a) Margaret Snyder described the history, purposes and programs of the
Voluntary Fund of the UN Decade for Women*, an important source of
future collaboration for WWB in the area of technical cooperation; and

b) Virginia Saurwein offered a draft recommendation of Women's World
Banking to the World Conference of the UN Decade for Women
(Copenhagen, July 1980).

The latter was revised and approved by the group. (See Appendix IV.)

Lilia Clemente, an investment portfolio manager, presented an overview of

a) the investment environment of the eighties and its impact on WWB; and

b) the main issues and approaches to the investment management of a
capital fund such as WWB's.

Referring to her discussion paper on investment strategy*, she emphasized
the difficulties of both fund raising and portfolio management given the
current economic picture and recent trends in the capital market. WWB
needs a diversified, balanced fund (one that preserves capital yet has
potential to generate income sufficient to offset the rate of inflation.)
Moreover, since WWB is designed to work world-wide, it is natural for the
fund to be internationally diversified. The advantages of diversification
can be demonstrated both theoretically and empirically. Because
international security prices and bond yields are not perfectly correlated
from country to country, international diversification reduces the
volatility of a portfolio; at least it maintains the rate of return and
thereby creates a more efficient portfolio. Clemente feels that it is
imperative for WWB to seek public and private resources without predetermined
quotas and stressed that management of WWB's portfolio would be judged on its
own merits, i.e., irrespective of WWB goals. Given a homogeneous policy
(one centralized capital fund), comprehensive promotional materials and
the efforts of a full-time professional fund raiser, such a fund could
be assembled.

---

*
   The Voluntary Fund was created by the UN General Assembly following the
International Women's Year. Resources of the Fund are used to support technical
cooperation activities, regional and international programs, joint inter-
organizational programs, research, communication support and public information activities. Priority is given to the least developed, land-locked and
island countries among developing countries, and special consideration given
to programs and projects which benefit rural women and poor women in urban
areas. In June 1980, the Fund was supporting 122 projects, many of which
related to income generation. For further information, write to the Fund at:
1 UN Plaza, Room DC-1002, New York, N.Y. 10017, U.S.A.

**
   Lilia C. Clemente, "Discussion Paper, Women's World Banking Capital Fund."
See Appendix III.

Several participants submitted to the group for consideration a statement on the financial structure of the proposed WWB Capital Fund based on the investment background paper and various workshop discussions. This document, endorsed by the group, recognized the importance of the UNDP contribution to support start-up operations and made the following recommendations:

- The WWB capital fund should be self-financing, for both financial and philosophical reasons:

    - An organization managed by women which proposes to help finance women's enterprises should itself be financially independent.

    - Time is critical in meeting investment needs. Financially independent organizations can move faster.

    - Financially independent organizations are self-sustaining and not dependent on annual replenishments.

- The WWB capital fund should be one central fund; local contributions could form funds to be kept in-country. However, the majority of funds should be in hard currency and held in one central account.

- The priority task is to contract competent management and select an experienced board of directors.

The Committee to Organize Women's World Banking expressed its appreciation to the individuals and groups who have lent support to its efforts during the past four years. Special gratitude was expressed to the Workshop participants and observers alike for articulating the economic realities faced by women in their countries and for sharing their views regarding how WWB might affect those realities.

As a demonstration of their commitment to WWB, participants constituted themselves as the Advisory Associates of WWB and elected a president to represent them to the Board of Directors. The groups felt that as a separate, definable entity, it would be in a better position to mobilize for future action and to represent to their various institutions, governments and constituencies the purposes and objectives of Women's World Banking. The participants agreed that the establishment of WWB's capital fund was the first priority and launched that fund with personal contributions.

WORKSHOP PARTICIPANTS AND OBSERVERS

Participants:

WATI ABDULGANI
Assistant Vice President
American Express International
Banking Corporation
Jarkarta, INDONESIA

ELA BHATT
General Secretary
Self-Employed Women's Association
Ahmedabad, INDIA

MEVROUW BINDT DE HAAN
Vice President
Les Femmes Chefs d'Enterprises
Mondiale (F.C.E.M.)
Brussels, BELGIUM

DEIRDRE BONIFAZ
Artisans Cooperative, Inc.
Chadds Ford, Pennsylvania, U.S.A.

MARTHA BULENGO
Regional Adviser on Family
Welfare
UNICEF
Nairobi, KENYA

MANILA CHANETON DE VIVO
Vice President
Manos del Uruguay
Monte Video, URUGUAY

CHINDA CHAREONVEJJ
Vice President
Bangkok Bank Ltd.
Bangkok, THAILAND

LILIA CLEMENTE
Chairman
Clemente Capital Consultants, Inc,
New York, New York, U.S.A.

OMAYMAH DAHHAN
Assistant Professor
Faculty of Economics
University of Jordan
Amman, JORDAN

VIMLA DALAL
Deputy Manager
Foreign Department
Bank of India
Bombay, INDIA

MARLENE FERNANDES
Architect and Urban Planner
Banco Nacional de Habitacion
Rio de Janeiro, BRAZIL

BEATRIZ HARRETCHE
Chief, Technical Assistance
Division
Inter-American Development Bank
Washington, D.C., U.S.A.

MARGARET HAGEN
Loan Officer
The World Bank
Washington, D.C., U.S.A.

MARY HOUGHTON
Executive Vice President
South Shore National Bank
Chicago, Illinois, U.S.A.

DANIELLE HUNEBELLE
Publisher
International Letter
Neuilly-sur-Seine, FRANCE

MODUPE IBIAYO
Manager of Operations
African Continental Bank, Ltd.
Lagos, NIGERIA

AKRAM KHATOON
Assistant Vice President
Muslim Commercial Bank
Karachi, PAKISTAN

GLORIA KNIGHT
General Manager
Urban Development Corporation
Kingston, JAMAICA

Participants (continued)

AMENA LAZOUGHLI
    Attache de Cabinet
    Ministere des Finances
    Tunis, TUNISIA

LINDA LEWIS
    The Secretary
    Barclays Bank International
     Development Fund
    Barclays Bank International, Ltd.
    London, ENGLAND

LOURDES LONTOK CRUZ
    President
    Paluwagan Ng Bayan Savings & Loan
    Manila, THE PHILIPPINES

NOZIPHO MABE
    Research Officer
    Bank of Botswana
    Gaborone, BOTSWANA

ESTHER OCLOO
    President
    Nkulenu Industries Limited
    Medina-Legon, GHANA

MARY OKELO
    Branch Manager
    Barclays Bank of Kenya, Ltd.
    Nairobi, KENYA

CAROLINE PEZZULLO
    Caroline Pezzullo Associates
    New York, New York, U.S.A.

DEANNA ROSENSWIG
    Asst. Manager, Corporate Accounts
    Bank of Montreal
    Toronto, Ontario, CANADA

VIRGINIA SAURWEIN
    Chief, Non-Governmental
     Organizations Section
    Department of International Economic
     and Social Affairs
    United Nations
    New York, New York, U.S.A.

GLORIA SCOTT
    Adviser on Women in Development
    The World Bank
    Washington, D.C., U.S.A.

LESLIE SEDERLUND
    Office of Technology Assessment
    Congress of the United States
    Washington, D.C., U.S.A.

RUTH SMITH
    President
    First State Bank
    Kansas City, Kansas, U.S.A.

MARGARET SNYDER
    Senior Officer
    Voluntary Fund for the UN Decade
     for Women
    United Nations
    New York, New York, U.S.A.

AVA STERN
    Enterprising Women
    New York, New York, U.S.A.

MARTHA STUART
    Martha Stuart Communications, Inc.
    New York, New York, U.S.A.

CHITA TANCHOCO-SUBIDO
    Executive Director
    Presidential Committee on
     Agricultural Credit
    Manila, THE PHILIPPINES

MICHAELA WALSH
    Project Director
    Office of Technology Assessment
    Congress of the United States
    Washington, D.C., U.S.A.

RUTH WASSERZUG
    Manager, Einstein Branch
    Bank Hapoalim
    Tel-Aviv, ISRAEL

EMILY WOMACH
    President; Chair of the Board
    Women's National Bank
    Washington, D.C., U.S.A.

Observers:

SALAH AL-SHAIKHLY
  Assistant Administrator
  United Nations Development
  Programme
  New York, New York, U.S.A.

VALCINA ASH
  Senator
  Grenadines House of Assembly
  St. Vincents & The Grenadines
  WEST INDIES

F.A.W. BANNIER
  Worst & Van Haersolte
  Amsterdam, THE NETHERLANDS

MARIE CHRISTINE BOUCOM
  Ministry of Women's Affairs
  Abidjan, IVORY COAST

DEDE DAVIES
  Regional Projects Officer
  United Nations Development
  Programme
  New York, New York, U.S.A.

JO FROMAN
  Ford Foundation
  New York, New York, U.S.A.

CHRISTINA GRAF
  The German Marshall Fund
  of the U.S.A.
  Washington, D.C., U.S.A.

JOHN HAMMOCK
  ACCION International
  Cambridge, Massachusetts, U.S.A.

CHRISTINE ALICE HAYANGA
  Agricultural Finance Corporation
  Nairobi, KENYA

H.P. HREXIUS
  Algemene Bank Nederland
  Amsterdam, THE NETHERLANDS

CHRISTINA JONKER
  Swedish Embassy
  The Hague, THE NETHERLANDS

ANITA KALFF
  Worst & Van Haersolte
  Amsterdam, THE NETHERLANDS

J. BURKE KNAPP
  Senior Adviser to the President
  The World Bank
  Washington, D.C., U.S.A.

IRIS KNAPP
  Washington, D.C., U.S.A.

JAMES LIBERIA
  U.S. Embassy
  The Hague, THE NETHERLANDS

RAYMOND LLOYD
  Activist for women's advancement
  Rome, ITALY

ZOULEIKHA MELLAH
  Office of Equipment & Services
  Tunis, TUNISIA

ROSE NGOUYOU
  Counselor
  Ministry of Social Affairs
  Libreville, GABON

LILLI RAY
  Researcher
  Tessler & Cloherty
  New York, New York, U.S.A.

ANN ROBERTS
  Committee of 100
  Women's World Banking
  New York, New York, U.S.A.

KOMKOT RODLOYTUK
  Bangkok Bank Ltd.
  Bangkok, THAILAND

Observers (continued)

ELIZABETH DE SALINAS
  Banco del Estado
  La Paz, BOLIVIA

ANITA UDOMCIN TANTHANA
  Bangkok Bank Ltd.
  Bangkok, THAILAND

GEERTJE THOMAS-LYCKLAMA A NIJEHOLT
  Coordinator of International
   Women's Affairs
  Government of the Netherlands
  The Hague, THE NETHERLANDS

DANIELETTE TUCKER
  Private consultant in accounting
  Monrovia, LIBERIA

OPERATING ISSUES REQUIRING CONSIDERATION

FROM WWB'S INTERNATIONAL WORKSHOP BACKGROUND PAPER, BY PATRICIA M. CLOHERTY

I. Issues Relating to Enterprises

    A. Where are the enterprises, and through what means can they be located?

    B. What types of projects are acceptable for financing?

    C. What types of financings are appropriate (e.g., fixed asset, working capital, debt repayment or consolidation, receivable and inventory financing, long-term, short-term, etc.)?

    D. What does financing a particular project mean for its female participants over the long-term?

    E. Why do particular enterprises represent good potential for capital placement? This must be defined in terms of such matters as

        - skills of women entrepreneurs involved
        - product or service offered
        - market potential
        - availability of raw material
        - appropriate pricing
        - competitive advantage in the proposed market
        - identification of the level of capital required
        - projected return on investment, given all of the above
        - provision for subsequent rounds of financing

    F. What stake have the entrepreneurs in the business?

        - have they committed their own resources, however small?
        - have they records of accomplishment in related efforts?
        - what assistance will they require in conducting the business?

    G. What is the nature of the ongoing assistance that will be required?

        - in production
        - in quality control
        - in cash managment and record-keeping
        - in opening new markets
        - in worker training

    H. Who will analyze the business for the lender?

I. Who will provide ongoing support?

J. Who will monitor the project, and how?

K. What will be the main criteria for agreeing to finance a project or to turn it down?

II. Issues Relating to Lenders

A. Which financial institutions will be able to participate in the guarantee program? Why? Where?

B. Will a guarantee fee be charged? If so, how much?

C. What will be the terms and conditions of the guarantee?

- guarantee interest and principle?
- guarantee up to X% of principle only?
- guarantee against losses?
- limit interest rate chargeable?
- collateral requirements?
- other covenants on the loan?
- types of projects that can be financed?
- servicing requirements?
- causes for denial or liability under the guarantee?
- what eventualities does the guarantee cover? Not cover?

III. Issues Relating to WWB

A. What level of risk will WWB accept at the project level? Or, stated differently, what level of success/losses will be acceptable?

B. What services will WWB be able to provide directly to enterprises, and which will it have to provide for elsewhere?

C. What kind of staffing will be required? What will it cost?

D. Most important, on whom will WWB rely for management and technical assistance to enterprises in various areas of the world? And how would costs of that assistance be covered?

E. How (by what measure) and when will WWB know that it is achieving what it set out to do? How can this be monitored regularly?

APPENDIX III

EXCERPTS FROM

"DISCUSSION PAPER, WWB CAPITAL FUND"
by Lilia C. Clemente

PART ONE: THE PROBABLE INVESTMENT ENVIRONMENT IN THE EIGHTIES AND
            ITS IMPACT ON WOMEN'S WORLD BANKING

There are several fundamental changes in the institutional and economic
structure underway which make it appropriate for Women's World Banking
to pursue a balanced diversified endowment fund.

1. Shape of the Market and Economic Environment. The multiplicity
    of changes in the world economic and political relationships and
    priorities leads us to believe that the world will not return to
    the type of economic and financial markets that existed in the
    1950's and 1960's...

2. The Process of Investment Management: A Need for Broader Skills.
    The changing requirements, priorities and interrelationship of
    the economic system and our expectations for liquidity managers
    over the next several years have broad significance for the scope
    and modus operandi of the investment manager and analyst's task...

3. Changes affecting Securities Community. The legal and regulatory
    investment environment within the U.S. is under constant
    re-examination and change. For purposes of multinational
    investment, money managers must understand the applicable rules
    and regulations of other governments...

4. Changes in Portfolio Risk/Return Expectations. The unique
    advantages of international diversification can be demonstrated
    both theoretically and empirically. The basic premise can be
    stated that because international security prices and bond
    yields are not perfectly correlated from country to country,
    international diversification reduces the volatility of a portfolio;
    at least it maintains the rate of return and thereby creates a
    more efficient portfolio...

Moreover, Women's World Banking is designed to work world-wide. Therefore
in line with the objectives of the organization, it is a natural move for
the Fund to be internationally diversified.

266

Excerpts, "Discussion Paper, WWB Capital Fund," (continued)

PART TWO: ISSUES IN SETTING UP THE WWB FUND

Because of the environment outlined in Part One, concentration
upon selection should be focused, beyond ususal management abilities,
on people whose combined understanding, skills and tendencies permit
usage of the most appropriate mix of investment vehicles for the
prevailing environment.

Two major issued to be addressed are whether WWB should select internal
or external management and whether large or small investment organizations
are best suited to its needs. Other questions to be addressed relate
to the organization of the fund. For example, should it:

- be self managed?

- employ an overseas chain network?

- hire international portfolio managers?

- buy existing international funds?

- establish an offshore office operating from London, Geneva, etc.?

PART III: RECOMMENDED APPROACH TO WWB'S CAPITAL FUND

These recommendations are related specifically to the management of WWB's
Capital Fund, and are therefore not included in this summary.

DRAFT STATEMENT TO THE WORLD CONFERENCE OF THE UN DECADE FOR WOMEN

Copenhagen, July 1980

Development of people and societies depends on women as well as men. Yet until now, women's contributions in economic sectors have seldom been recognized and, less often, encouraged or supported. In rural areas and poor sections of metropolitan areas world-wide, money is scarce and living standards inadequate. Consequently, choices are limited and productivity is low. The poor -- especially women -- cannot increase family incomes.

With access to credit and loans -- now denied them by a harsh financial system -- women could own their own enterprises and improve their lives and those of their families.

Participants at the International Women's Year Conference in 1975 addressed this problem of societal development and the role of financial institutions in that development. They unanimously endorsed the need to support both public and private efforts to ensure greater access to credit for women in recognition of their actual and potential contributions to their countries' economies. However, there has been little progress in providing new opportunities for women, especially those at lower economic levels.

We urge governments and international and national financial institutions to reaffirm their commitment to new efforts and policies designed to ensure that enterprising women have the chance to develop and own income-producing ventures. We commend to the attention of the representatives and observers at the World Conference of the United Nations Decade for Women the need to support fully private and non-governmental efforts which promote access to credit. We note particularly the establishment of Women's World Banking, a global, private financial organization which, through its innovative loan guarantee program, will link existing national and international financial resources and local technical help with individual women and groups of women who have not fully participated in the formal money economy.

We also commend to the attention of governments the attached report of the International Workshop of Women Leaders in Banking & Finance, sponsored by Women's World Banking. The report raises key issues and suggests guidelines for mobilizing national financial resources to assist lower income women in income-producing activities. Such income generation will further their integration in the development process, in line with strategies for the new international economic order.

COMMENTARY ON WWB QUESTIONNAIRE FINDINGS

The Committee to Organize Women's World Banking composed an informal questionnaire for participants of the International Workshop of Women Leaders in Banking & Finance. Its purpose was to increase our understanding of the problems addressed at the Workshop and to begin to document the need for research in this area. Respondents were assured that their *individual responses would remain confidential.*

Introduction

Twenty-eight women participants of the Workshop responded to the WWB questionnaire. Representing a broad cross-section geographically, these women came from a wide variety of careers related to banking and business. 25 percent had been in those positions for more than ten years, while less than 1 percent had been in their positions for less than one year. The questionnaire, composed of 32 questions, was divided into three sections: small business; women in business; and women in banking and financial institutions. Each section will be discussed in the order in which it appeared.*

Section I: Small Business

There were five questions in this section which dealt with sources of managerial, technical and financial assistance for small businesses in general in the respondent's country. Two of these questions asked for general views on how well small businesses were served and their major problems. The range of answers to the first question (major sources of management and technical assistance) suggests that small businesses look everywhere for managerial assistance -- from government (50%) to business associations (46%) to family sources (43%). Throughout this section the pivotal role of the family for all kinds of assistance constantly resurfaces. The vulnerability of these small businesses is reflected in the resounding negative answers given to the question on how well small businesses are served in one's country. Some 64 percent said that small businesses were not well served in their country with either capital or other assistance. The two problems cited most frequently were shortages of capital (75%) and management skills (68%). In their written comments, respondents pointed to lending institutions favoring larger enterprises, and the perceived greater risk associated with lending to smaller enterprises. Small businesses appeared to be caught in a vicious

---

*   Percentages of replies often do not total 100. Sometimes this is the result of "rounding off" numbers; more often it is a result of our request for multiple replies (e.g., what are the three major sources...?)

The questionnaire was composed and tabulated with the assistance of the International Development Program of American University, Washington, D.C. Copies of the questionnaire are available upon request.

circle: they are small with skills in short supply; yet that which would augment size (capital and training in skills) are more difficult to attract precisely because of the smallness of the enterprise. A few respondents pointed to their government having rural development as a priority and, in view of a tendency to associate small business with urban life, less commitment to lending to small businesses. There was no mention in questionnaire replies of a principal current concern of development specialists -- local rural enterprises to generate off-farm employment. Given the percentage of women cited by participants as being involved in food production and processing, a natural area of opportunity would appear to be in small rural enterprises which focus on storage of food crops, their processing and marketing.

Section II: Women in Business

There appeared to be some uncertainty about the state and nature of data kept by the respondent's country on the employment of women in business. And that uncertainty was compounded when one moved to questions about how many women were involved in independent or informal income-generating activity. The percentage of replies of "don't know," "not applicable" or no answer were greater here than elsewhere in the survey. Nor was there much more certainty about how many women are involved in the formal labor market. Part of this uncertainty could spring from simply not having confronted that question before, lack of awareness of available data, and part from the general state of disarray in data collection, availability and retrieval in the countries themselves. In so far as part of project design and feasibilty requires such data analysis, this lack should be noted by those in the WWB network.

The assumptions about the kinds of businesses owned and operated by women reflected the regional and professional diversity of the participants themselves. Many specific kinds of business were cited, ranging from boutiques and garment trade (46%) to food processing (32%) to a variety of service activities (39%). The kinds of small businesses women have (or that respondents think they have, given the absence of other data) can be characterized as highly individualized, fragmented and decentralized. It is especially difficult to find ways to service or support these kinds of endeavors, as participants pointed out during Workshop discussions. Providing management training for entrepreneurial women who are dispersed across the market place from hairdressing to taxi driving, for example, will require particular networking skills. The very nature of these kinds of jobs also means that women could not easily take time away from them to improve their skills in order to augment their business size or its security. Women's enterprises, as described by these respondents, are quasi-informal to purely informal, and labor-intensive. This means that they are also vulnerable to those factors which directly affect labor -- health, nutrition, skills, and government code regulations. On this last point it is interesting that when asked about particular problems faced by entrepreneurs, few cited local government regulations (10%). Other research indicated that women in small-scale food processing and marketing often find that local health inspection and regulations represent hurdles. Such regulations are drafted for larger businesses and make market entry circle: they are small with skills in short supply; yet that which would augment size (capital and training in skills) are more difficult to attract precisely because of the smallness of the enterprise. A few respondents pointed to their government having rural development as a priority and, in view of a tendency to associate small business with urban life, less commitment to lending to small businesses. There was no mention in questionnaire replies of a principal current concern of development specialists -- local rural enterprises to generate off-farm employment. Given the percentage of women cited by participants as being involved in food production and processing, a natural area of opportunity would appear to be in small rural enterprises which focus on storage of food crops, their processing and marketing.

Section II: Women in Business

There appeared to be some uncertainty about the state and nature of data kept by the respondent's country on the employment of women in business. And that uncertainty was compounded when one moved to questions about how many women were involved in independent or informal income-generating activity. The percentage of replies of "don't know," "not applicable" or no answer were greater here than elsewhere in the survey. Nor was there much more certainty about how many women are involved in the formal labor market. Part of this uncertainty could spring from simply not having confronted that question before, lack of awareness of available data, and part from the general state of disarray in data collection, availability and retrieval in the countries themselves. In so far as part of project design and feasibilty requires such data analysis, this lack should be noted by those in the WWB network.

The assumptions about the kinds of businesses owned and operated by women reflected the regional and professional diversity of the participants themselves. Many specific kinds of business were cited, ranging from boutiques and garment trade (46%) to food processing (32%) to a variety of service activities (39%). The kinds of small businesses women have (or that respondents think they have, given the absence of other data) can be characterized as highly individualized, fragmented and decentralized. It is especially difficult to find ways to service or support these kinds of endeavors, as participants pointed out during Workshop discussions. Providing management training for entrepreneurial women who are dispersed across the market place from hairdressing to taxi driving, for example, will require particular networking skills. The very nature of these kinds of jobs also means that women could not easily take time away from them to improve their skills in order to augment their business size or its security. Women's enterprises, as described by these respondents, are quasi-informal to purely informal, and labor-intensive. This means that they are also vulnerable to those factors which directly affect labor -- health, nutrition, skills, and government code regulations. On this last point it is interesting that when asked about particular problems faced by entrepreneurs, few cited local government regulations (10%). Other research indicated that women in small-scale food processing and marketing often find that local health inspection and regulations represent hurdles. Such regulations are drafted for larger businesses and make market entry

When asked an open-ended question concerning the circumstances under which banks in one's country might lend more to women entrepreneurs, elements of the vicious circle were cited once again. In sum, lending might increase if:

- collateral existed or guarantees were provided

- more women entrepreneurs had records of success as managers of money and people and were demonstrably credit worthy (i.e., if their businesses were larger, established and in the formal sector, instead of the opposite.

- more women entrepreneurs had "clear objectives," "specific plans," were more "articulate," presented "strong, well-prepared proposals" and were "persistant." They need to "understand what they are doing with bank facilities" and be able to "demonstrate that their businesses are bankable."

- business proposals presented by women appeared more productive and profitable

- banks had greater confidence in women because they had access to technical and managerial help supplied and financed by others

- women's social and educational status were improved

- women's business proposals conformed to the development needs of the country

- women's contributions to the economy were more widely recognized

When asked to name the first specific steps that would be required for banks in one's country to begin to service women's enterprises, there was no real agreement among respondents. Areas of need mentioned repeatedly are listed below:

- the establishment of technical managerial training for women entrepreneurs. Suggestions on the level, form and content of the help varied. Most frequently cited was training in basic business skills: accountancy, cash flow, marketing, costing, production and credit application procedures. Also cited was the need for a more general business education. Other suggestions included extention services, the "linking" of entrepreneurs, and the development of informational materials for women in business.

- an arrangement for supervisory, monitoring services for women's businesses

- the involvement of women holding positions of influence in banks, on bank boards and in decision-making roles in government

- the choice of the target group to be served and the determination of its credit needs

- the establishment of a fund from which women could borrow

- the organization of women at the grass roots level

- an effort at better data collection on women in business

- the identification of businesses that present opportunity

- the advertisement and promotion of a program of service to women's businesses

APPENDIX VI

WWB WORKING DOCUMENTS*

1. Statement of Purpose, Women's World Banking, November, 1980

2. Charter of Stichting Women's World Banking

3. "Background Paper, International Workshop of Women Leaders in Banking
    and Finance," by Patricia M. Cloherty

4. "Discussion Paper, Women's World Banking Capital Fund," by Lilia Clemente

PAPERS OFFERED BY PARTICIPANTS*

1. Bonifaz, Deirdre and de Vivo, Manila, "Artisan's Cooperative and Manos
    del Uruguay: Cooperative Support."

2. Chareonvejj, Chinda, "Women's Economic Role in Thailand."

3. Fernandez, Marlene, "Proposal for Assistance to Women in Squatters
    Settlements in Brazil."

4. Khatoon, Akram, "Potential of Women in the Money Economy of Pakistan."

5. Knight, Gloria, "Urban Craft."

MATERIALS ON EFFORTS REFERRED TO IN THE WORKSHOP REPORT*

1. AITEC/ACCION INTERNATIONAL: El Salvador Project

2. Bhatt, Tushar, "SEWA: A Star Beckons."

WORKSHOP REPORTS*

1. Video Report, "Founding Meeting, Women's World Banking," produced by
    Martha Stuart Communications.

2. Written Report, "International Workshop of Women Leaders in Banking
    and Finance," prepared by Joan E. Shapiro and Gretchen Maynes.

---

* The Workshop Reports and other WWB documents can be obtained by making
a contribution to the WWB Capital Fund, PO Box 1691, Grand Central Station,
New York, NY 10017. Suggested contributions for the materials are listed
below:

- Video: US$100
- Written: US$25
- Other materials: US$5 each.

AGREEMENT BETWEEN STICHTING TO
PROMOTE WOMEN'S WORLD BANKING AND ITS AFFILIATES

Whereas Stichting to Promote Women's World Banking ("WWB")
has been organized to advance and promote the direct
participation of women and their families in the full use of the
economy, particularly those women who have not generally had
access to the services of established financial institutions;

Whereas, WWB has decided that it would be desirable to
establish a formal relationship with and grant the status of
"Affiliate of WWB" to organizations which have been established
with the specific purpose to further the goals of WWB in whole or
in part;

Whereas, the granting of such status will help promote the
formation, growth, and cooperation of institutions around the
world mutually devoted to each other in support of   such
objectives;

Whereas for such purposes and as more fully set forth below
(name of Affiliate and description of its legal status) proposes
to enter into such a relationship with WWB;

Now therefore WWB and (Affiliate) hereby agree as follows:

1.   (Affiliate) represents and agrees as follows:

(a)   It has been duly established in (country) as   a
legal entity (describe status, e.g. corporation, association,
foundation, cooperation society) and will maintain such status.

(b) The objective of the (Affiliate) is to advance and
promote the direct participation of women and their families in
the full use of the economy and it will use its best efforts to

carry out such objectives in accordance with the philosophy, policy, and practices of WWB and in cooperation, wherever feasible, with other Affiliates.

(c) Capital Funds of not less than the equivalent of U.S. $20,000 (such equivalent to be determined at the time of contribution) has been contributed to the Affiliate for use in its operations, provided that at least 50% has been obtained obtained from local, independent sources. The (Affiliate) will use its best efforts to obtain such additional funds from such sources that may be necessary to maintain its Capital Funds at that level.

It is the goal that at least 50% of any additional Capital Funds will be obtained from local, independent sources.

(d) The Board of Directors of (Affiliate) was and will continue to have at least one member with substantial banking experience and one member who is a lawyer with banking or business experience.

(e) (Affiliate) will furnish to WWB on a date to be agreed with WWB, the following reports and information:

(i) Reports of activities under its loan guarantee programs,

(ii) Self-Assessment Reports,

(iii) Activities Statement of Account, financial statements, annual reports, information regarding its membership, management and staff, information regarding its attendance at conferences and seminars, and such other reports and information as shall be agreed with WWB.

(F) (Affiliate) will establish and maintain a minimum schedule for membership fees, fees for services, meetings, furnishing of information, and other relevant services.

2. (a) Before the (Affiliate) shall present a written request to accept funds or borrow from sources originating, or from entities whose principal office is located, outside the Affiliate's home country or from an international organization, it shall notify WWB and shall advise WWB of the details of such proposed acceptance or borrowing of such funds.

(b) If the President, upon receipt of such information, believes that the proposed acceptance or borrowing of such funds raises an issue of policy for WWB or may be inconsistent with the fund-raising activities of WWB or another Affiliate, the President shall (i) so notify the Affiliate and (ii) consult with the Affiliate to try to resolve any difficulties regarding the proposal. Failing such agreement, either the President, or the Affiliate can bring the matter to the Board of Trustees.

(c) The Board of Trustees or the Executive Committee acting for the Board shall then examine the matter and as soon as practicable, but no later than within three (3) months of the receipt of information under paragraph (a) above, decide whether to consent to the proposed acceptance or borrowing of funds. If, after due consideration, the consent is not given, the (Affiliate) will not accept or borrow such funds.

3. WWB grants the status of "Affiliate of WWB" to (Affiliate). This status entitles (Affiliate) (a) to present

itself as such (b) to use the name, Women's World Banking, in its title, and (c) to avail itself of the support of WWB in the advancement of (Affiliate's) objectives. The rights stated in the prior sentence shall cease if this agreement is terminated under paragraph seven (7).

    4.   WWB shall provide to the (Affiliate) the following:

        a) - assistance in setting up its loan and guarantee operations;

        b) - information and assistance in evaluating loan applications and monitoring loans;

        c) - assistance in developing fund-raising strategies;

        d) - opportunities for exchanging information regarding the operations of WWB and the other affiliates and other matters of common interest;

        e) - information and assistance regarding the expansion of its loan portfolios; and

        f) - assistance in protecting its name.

    5.   Neither WWB nor (Affiliate) shall be responsible for the debts or obligations of the other.

    6.   This Agreement shall become effective when the following shall have occurred.

      (a) It shall have been signed by authorized representatives of each party;

      (b) The (Affiliate) shall have furnished to WWB evidence satisfactory to it of the accuracy of the representations made by it in Paragraph 1 above; and

      (c) WWB acting upon the instructions of the Board

of Trustees, or the Executive Committee as the case may be,
shall have notified the (Affiliate) in writing or by cable that
it is satisfied with such evidence and this Agreement is
thereupon effective.

    7. Either party can terminate this Agreement at any time by
notice in writing or by cable to the other party. Thirty days
after such notice is sent the Agreement and all rights and
obligations thereunder will be terminated.

_____   _____
      (AFFILIATE)   WOMEN'S WORLD BANKING

_____
       DATE

INTRODUCTION TO THE WOMEN'S WORLD BANKING
LOAN GUARANTEE PROGRAM

This memorandum serves as an introduction to the Women's World Banking Loan Guarantee Program and to the Model Loan Guarantee Agreement, which provides the framework for the Program.

Stichting To Promote Women's World Banking ("SWWB") is a nonprofit organization established under the laws of the Netherlands, whose purpose is the advancement of entrepreneurship by women, particularly those women who have not generally had full access to the services of established financial institutions. Through the Loan Guarantee Program, SWWB, working with Women's World Banking affiliates and banks in developing countries, provides guarantees to secure loans made by local banks to small women's businesses. SWWB and its local affiliates also arrange for managerial assistance, as needed, for the ventures receiving loan guarantees.

A Loan Guarantee Agreement, entered into by SWWB, its local affiliate in the country in question, and the local bank, provides the terms under which the Loan Guarantee Program operates. Under the Agreement, the bank agrees to make available, generally over a three-year period, funds in a specified amount for loans to eligible women's businesses. Under arrangements most commonly made, SWWB agrees to act as guarantor for 50 percent of the principal of Program loans made by the bank, and the local Women's World Banking affiliate agrees to guarantee 25 percent of the principal of Program loans made by the bank, and the local Women's World Banking affiliate agrees to guarantee 25 percent of the principal of such loans. Under special circumstances other types of arrangements can also be made.

SWWB's guarantee is secured by a standby letter of credit, which is obtained by SWWB for an amount (usually denominated in U.S. dollars) equivalent to the approximate amount of loan principal for which SWWB is liable as guarantor. The amount of the letter of credit is adjusted annually to reflect the gradual build-up of guaranteed credits extended by the bank over the term of the Agreement. The local Women's World Banking affiliate maintains deposits of funds with the bank in amounts equal to the approximate amount of loan principal for which it is liable as a guarantor, subject to the annual adjustments.

In the event of a default on principal repayments by a borrower under the Loan Guarantee Program, the bank may declare a guaranteed loss. SWWB will then provide payment to the bank for its 50 percent guarantee, either by paying the appropriate amount in local currency, or by authorizing a drawing on its letter of credit in an amount equivalent to the guaranteed loss. The local Women's World Banking affiliate will satisfy its guarantee by authorizing a drawing, in the appropriate local currency amount, from its deposit.

The Loan Guarantee Agreement also provides for guarantee fees payable by borrowers under the Program, for managerial assistance to borrowers, and for reports and evaluations. Provisions are included in the Agreement to protect SWWB against some of the exchange risks to which it is necessarily subject, and to help protect all of the parties against defaults by the others.

The Model Loan Guarantee Agreement attached to this memorandum contains the standard provisions that have been used by SWWB, its local affiliates, and participating banks in the Loan Guarantee Programs established in various countries. The Model is annotated with explanatory notes to clarify these provisions and explain their necessity. Naturally, certain provisions -- Program amounts, interest rates, and the identity of the local parties -- vary from case to case; these variables are indicated by brackets [ ], and are to be determined during the course of negotiations among the parties.

-2-

$10,000,000

STICHTING WOMEN'S WORLD BANKING

8% Debentures due January 1, 1990

INTRODUCTORY STATEMENT

This private placement memorandum solicits subscriptions to an offering of $10,000,000 of 8% debentures, due January 1, 1990, of Stichting Women's World Banking (WWB) (the Debentures), a not-for-profit foundation organized in 1979 pursuant to the laws of The Netherlands. The proceeds of this offering will be used to increase the availability of business loans to women entrepreneurs in various countries, particularly in the lesser developed countries, primarily by providing guarantees and other incentives to lenders and thus help WWB to achieve its purpose:

> . . . To advance and promote entrepreneurship by women, particularly those women who have not generally had full access to the services of established financial institutions. . . .

This offering is made in the United States and other countries to governments, international institutions, foundations, not-for-profit organizations, corporations and individuals who are interested in supporting the objectives of WWB.

WWB intends to conduct its affairs in a prudent manner; however, prospective purchasers should recognize a number of respects in which investment in the Debentures differs from a traditional offering of debt securities to investors pursuing a maximum return.

(1) The proposed activities of WWB are new and experimental. WWB will operate in a number of countries, particularly in the lesser developed countries, in which there are economic and political risks which might affect the successful operation of the projects financed by WWB. There can be no assurance that the interest and principal of the Debentures will be paid on a timely basis or at all.

(2) Certain of WWB's dollar holdings will be converted to and invested in non-dollar currencies. To the extent that such non-dollar currencies are later re-converted into dollars or other currencies, such re-conversion may result in exchange losses or may be subject to repatriation restrictions because of exchange controls.

(3) The proceeds will be devoted to uses which will be selected not only for their economic viability, but also for their social impact.

(4) The rate of return proposed for the Debentures is substantially below market rates at this time.

(5) The Debentures are not secured or subject to the customary conditions of a trust indenture administered by a trustee.

This Private Placement Memorandum is dated November 22, 1983.

SECOND INTERNATIONAL WORKSHOP

OF

WOMEN LEADERS IN BANKING AND FINANCE

Villa Nobel
Sanremo, Italy
March 31 - April 3, 1981

A REPORT

WOMEN'S WORLD BANKING

Prepared by:
Gretchen S. Maynes

"...We have seen that the function of entrepreneurs is to
reform or revolutionize the pattern of production by exploiting
an invention or, more generally, an untried technological
possibility for producing a new commodity or producing an
old one in a new way, by opening up a new source of supply
of materials or a new outlet for products, by reorganizing an
industry...To undertake such new things is difficult and
constitutes a distinct economic function, first, because
they lie outside of the routine tasks which everybody understands
and; secondly, because the environment resists in many ways
that vary, according to social conditions, from simple
refusal either to finance or to buy a new thing, to physical
attack on the man who tries to produce it. To act with
confidence beyond the range of familiar beacons and to
overcome that resistance requires aptitudes that are present
in only a small fraction of the population and that define
entrepreneurial function. This function does not essentially
consist in either inventing anything or otherwise creating
the conditions which the enterprise exploits. It consists in
getting things done."

Joseph Schumpeter, Capitalism,
Socialism and Democracy, p. 132

ACKNOWLEDGEMENTS

The Board of Directors of Women's World Banking is indebted to many for the success of the Second International Workshop of Women Leaders in Banking and Finance. ACCION International, our co-sponsor for the Workshop, and the Villa Nobel, the host for the meeting, together with our contributors and participants, made this WWB program possible.

Those institutions which provided funding were:

Board of Global Ministries of the United Methodist Church
World Division

Canadian International Development Agency
NGO Division

United Nations Development Programme

United States Agency for International Development
Women in Development Office

The banks, businesses and foundations which contributed to the Workshop by funding the travel and/or participation of their representatives were:

Banks

Agricultural Finance Corporation
Kenya

Associated Belgrade Bank
Yugoslavia

Banco Nacional de Habitacion
Brazil

Bangkok Bank Limited
Thailand

Bank Hapoalim
Israel

Bank of Montreal
Canada

Commerce Bancshares, Inc.
Kansas City, Missouri, USA

Delta International Bank
Egypt

First State Bank
Kansas City, Kansas, USA

National Bank of Hungary
Hungary

Paluwagan Ng Bayan Savings & Loan
Philippines

South Shore Bank
Chicago, Illinois

Technical Board of Agricultural Credit
Philippines

The Women's National Bank
Washington, D.C., USA

286

TABLE OF CONTENTS

Women's World Banking... 1

The Workshop: Introduction and Summary........................... 2

Opening Session.. 4

A Broad View: Economic Investment Trends
& Their Relevance to WWB.. 5
    (Based on Plenary I)

A Narrower View: WWB Programs in Colombia & India............... 6
    (Based on Plenary II)

Meeting of the Advisory Associates of WWB......................... 9

Structure of the WWB Guarantee Mechanism:
Proposed Programs for Brazil, Ghana, Philippines,
Thailand & USA.. 11
    (Based on Plenary III)

Opportunities for Women in Non-Traditional
Business Activities... 15

Elements of an Economy That Affect the Small
Business and Industry Sectors..................................... 17

Expanding Successful Lending: Guidelines for
Women in Banking & Finance.. 19
    (Based on Plenary IV & Work Groups 1,2 & 3)

Other Issues in the Context of WWB Program Development........... 21
    (Based on Work Groups 4,5 & 6)

    - Gathering essential economic and financial data

    - Promoting non-traditional areas for women's
      business development

    - Using women's capital resources productively
      to finance women's businesses

Closing Remarks... 24

Appendix: List of Participants.................................. 25

Addendum: WWB Program Development, December, 1981............... 27

Women's World Banking (WWB), is an independent, international not-for-profit organization incorporated in the Netherlands to advance and promote the entrepreneurship of women, particularly those women who have not generally had access to the services of established financial institutions.

To achieve its objectives, WWB is initiating programs to increase the productivity of women small-scale entrepreneurs by linking them to existing local financial institutions and to managerial and training resources. In its first program efforts, WWB is working with local women leaders in banking and business in ten third world countries to establish loan guarantee programs. WWB believes that it is appropriate to single out women entrepreneurs for special assistance because they are a key to leading other women to participate more actively in their economies. Many of these women, in fact, belong to the poor majority. The disadvantage they currently suffer in the competition for credit and other financial services prevents them from improving their economic base, as individuals, or that of their countries.

To finance its programs, WWB has established a Capital Fund which will consist of revenues from the sale of debentures and contributions from governments, corporations, financial institutions, foundations and individuals. The Capital Fund, to the extent practicable, will be kept intact and invested in high grade obligations and, to a limited degree, equity investments. All expenditures and debts incurred by WWB will be covered by the accumulated net investment income, proceeds of grants and, only as a last resort, from the corpus of the Capital Fund.

Support for WWB's start-up and program development activities has come from:

- Board of Global Ministries, United Methodist Church
     World Division
     Women's Division
- Ford Foundation
- Levi Strauss International
- Netherlands Ministry for Development Cooperation
- Rockefeller Brothers Fund
- Swedish International Development Authority
- United Nations Development Programme
- Individual contributors

WWB's objectives can be attained only with the participation of women with the skills and commitment to initiate, implement and evaluate WWB programs in their communities. Networking among women leaders in banking and finance is, therefore, an integral part of the WWB program. In March, 1980, WWB sponsored the first International Workshop of Women Leaders in Banking and Finance for the purpose of testing its assumptions, refining its approach and broadening the network of women with the experience to assist in implementing its programs. One year later, WWB convened a second International Workshop to undertake the more difficult tasks of examining its operating plan, reviewing its first programs and program proposals, and developing strategies for supporting these efforts.

What follows is a report of that meeting.

- 1 -

288

INTRODUCTION & SUMMARY

THE PURPOSES of the Second International Workshop of Women Leaders in Banking and Finance, convened March 31 - April 3, 1981 at the Villa Nobel, Sanremo, Italy, were:

- to present WWB's investment and operational plan, focusing on the relationships of domestic guarantee programs to the Capital Fund;

- to review, in specific terms, WWB's first programs in Colombia and India and, in broader terms, the proposals for program activity in Brazil, Ghana, the Philippines, Thailand and the United States;

- to discuss the contribution of women in banking and finance in general and WWB in particular to expanding successful lending to women small-scale entrepreneurs;

- to consider the following issues in the general context of WWB program development:

    - essential economic & financial data

    - promotion of non-traditional areas for women in business

    - productive use of women's capital resources, including savings

- to define the functions of WWB Advisory Associates.

THE PARTICIPANTS were bankers, financiers, economists, lawyers and business women active in business associations from 23 countries. Many had attended the 1980 WWB Workshop in Amsterdam and came prepared with reports of their activities on behalf of WWB. A number of others new to WWB's network came authorized to express the interest of their financial institutions and/or their governments in participating in WWB programs.

THE ACHIEVEMENTS of the Workshop were:

- a concensus that WWB's proposed investment and operational plan is workable and that its loan guarantee programs would be attractive in many developing communities;

- an exchange of information and experience by participants who have developed WWB programs in Colombia and India and those exploring program possibilities in Brazil, Ghana, Kenya, Nigeria, the Philippines, Thailand, the United States and Uruguay;

- an agreement that WWB handbooks should suggest means of

    - organizing women bankers, small business leaders and others with the skills to assist women entrepreneurs;

    - persuading bankers, government officials and the public that women entrepreneurs represent a long-term market opportunity for commercial banks;

- 2 -

289

- supporting creative financing alternatives and exercising
  flexibility in structuring loans;

- counseling women borrowers;

- evaluating the local management assistance resources available
  to small borrowers; and,

- devising methods for financing the high cost of individual
  management assistance or, alternatively, facilitating group
  training processes.

● a recommendation that WWB undertake a clearinghouse function for
  technical materials for bankers, small-scale borrowers and women
  borrowers. These would include small-business guides, materials
  on training bankers in small-business and industry lending,
  simplified loan applications, business appraisal forms and
  procedures, and statements of bank policy and operating procedures
  on small-scale lending;

● a reaffirmation of WWB's intention to support both the wide range
  of "typical" small-scale business ventures and those few whose
  proprietary competitive edge make them likely to grow substantially,
  generating jobs and capital for women and their communities; and,

● a concensus that WWB Advisory Associates should assist in raising
  the Capital Fund, assessing the potential for WWB programs in
  their communities, and identifying the local financial and
  management assistance institutions available to the small business
  woman.

OPENING SESSION

The 2nd International Workshop of Women Leaders in Banking and Finance opened
with an overview of Women's World Banking (WWB) activities. Esther Ocloo,
Ghana (Chairperson of the WWB Board), reviewed the content and recommendations
of the first WWB Workshop in Amsterdam in March, 1980. She emphasized the
timeliness of WWB's first program initiatives in view of a current world
economic environment that is adversely affecting women and underscored the
innovative character of the WWB concept.

Michaela Walsh, USA (President of WWB), listed WWB's accomplishments and
actions since the Amsterdam meeting. These include:

- preparation of a draft prospectus for the sale of debentures for
  the WWB Capital Fund;

- capital development activities;

- program initiatives in a number of countries and the development
  of policies and procedures for local program initiatives for the
  consideration of Workshop participants;

- establishment of a WWB office in New York City; and,

- approval by the US Government of tax exempt status for Friends
  of WWB/USA, Inc., an organization committed to supporting the
  activities of Women's World Banking.

She expressed the hope that after looking at WWB's overall operating plan,
at the variety of proposed country programs and at the opportunities that
exist for expanding the pool of successful women borrowers, each participant
would have a clearer idea of how she could assist WWB in serving women
in her community.

- 4 -

A BROAD VIEW: ECONOMIC INVESTMENT TRENDS
AND THEIR RELEVANCE TO WWB
(Plenary I)

A discussion of global economic trends, the international investment
environment, and its implications for WWB's Capital Fund and overall
operating plan was led by Lilia Clemente. Her presentation centered on
the following points:

- An atmosphere of economic uncertainty exists world-wide; it
  is characterized by persistent recession and inflation, sluggish
  growth, disequilibrium in financial flows and growing third
  world deficits.

- Nonetheless, excellent international investment opportunities
  exist for those with sufficient information and experience.

- In these circumstances, WWB supporters should hold a long-term
  view and proceed with realistic, energetic efforts to identify
  private and public sources of support for the WWB Capital Fund.

Participants discussed at length the considerations that should influence
WWB's investment policy. They also examined a series of cash flow
projections for WWB based on varying estimates of the following: funds
raised by WWB; proportions of equity to debt capital; losses under
WWB guarantee programs; and return on invested capital. (These projections
are part of the study, "Women's World Banking: Management Perspectives,"
prepared by a work group of the Yale School of Organization and Management.)

A NARROWER VIEW: WWB PROGRAMS IN COLOMBIA & INDIA
(Plenary II)

Colombia

WWB's first loan guarantee program began in Cali, Colombia in May, 1981.
Margarita Guzman de Garrido, local coordinator of the program, reviewed the
conditions prevailing in Cali that make it particularly suitable for a WWB
program:

- the existence of a group of organized, active women in the private
  sector who formed Friends of WWB in Cali in order to promote micro-
  enterprises owned and managed by women;

- the existence of a private, non-profit management assistance
  organization for micro-scale business, Development Program for
  Small Enterprise (DESAP);

- the existence of a financial institution to help administer the
  funds, Fundacion Para La Educacion Superior (FES);

- the interest of a local commercial bank, Corporacion Financier Del
  Valle, S.A., in providing the needed credit.

Friends of WWB/Cali, WWB and FES have established a loan guarantee fund for
the extension of commercial loans to enterprises owned/managed by women in
the Cauca Valley. WWB/Cali and FES have contributed $20,000, which is on
deposit locally; WWB's contribution of $10,000 takes the form of a letter of
credit. This guarantee fund will leverage loans up to $150,000 from the
Corporacion Financier Del Valle, S.A., i.e. $5 for every $1 in the guarantee
fund.

In the case of default, losses on loans up to $20,000 will be shared as
follows: Stichting Women's World Banking - 50%; Cali Guarantee Fund - 25%;
Corporacion Financier - 25%. Losses on loans above this amount are covered
by the Cali Guarantee Fund, up to 75% of each loan up to the amount of the
Cali Fund at any time, after which the lender is responsible for any additional
losses.

The terms of agreement between FES and WWB include the following provisions:

- Loans will be made in all sectors of the economy to businesses
  that are at least 50% women-owned and that meet the bank's
  established criteria for "bankable ventures."

- Loans will be made for terms of 1-5 years for working capital,
  capital expenditures and investment in inventories or buildings.

- The Bank will charge the borrower the government-authorized rate
  for industrial development. An additional interest will be charged
  to the borrower as a fee for use of the guarantee fund. These
  earnings will be deposited in the guarantee fund at FES.

- 75% of the loans to individual enterprises will be for US $5,000 or
  less; 75% of the loans to group enterprises will be for US $8,000.

- Women borrowers must pass the pre-loan screening process of DESAP
  and agree to receive management support services from DESAP for the

- 6 -

life of the loan.

- One-third of the interest earned by Friends of WWB/Cali on the guarantee fund will be earmarked to help cover the costs of management assistance.

- FES and DESAP agree to provide quarterly financial statements on the status of the loans under the Fund to Friends of WWB/Cali.

WWB's agreement with DESAP includes the following points:

- Assistance to entrepreneurs will cover pre-loan screening, preparation of business plans, loan document preparation and management assistance for the life of the loan.

- Women management assistance officers will be hired and trained by DESAP to work with women entrepreneurs in the program.

The diagram below illustrates the organization structure and relationships of the entities in the Cali program.

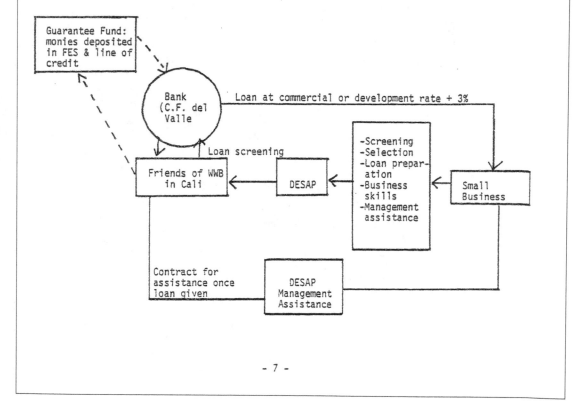

India

Ela Bhatt, General Manager of the Self Employed Women's Association (SEWA) of Ahmedabad, India, described the origins, objectives and accomplishments of her organization since its foundation in 1972. SEWA, a union of women engaged in marginal occupations, has established a cooperative bank that currently has 15,000 savings accounts and provides a wide range of services to its members. It offers cloth at mill rates to garment workers and rags to chindi workers at cost. It undertakes to redesign tools and equipment, such as hand carts and collapsible umbrellas used by women vendors. In addition, it experiments with new product designs, explores new markets and offers guidance to members in the marketing of their goods.

Women's World Banking will be involved only with the SEWA Cooperative Bank's financial and business management services. Pending approval by the Reserve Bank of India, WWB will make a direct loan of $25,000 to SEWA for a term of 6 years. Friends of WWB/Western India, independently of the SEWA Bank, will raise local counterpart funds equivalent to one fourth of the WWB loan. The SEWA Bank will use these combined funds to broaden its lending program to its constituents. Terms of the loans will not exceed two years, and the interest rates will be sufficient to cover the interest to the lender, administrative and technical services and risk reserve/ capitalization. SEWA will conduct management training sessions for loan recipients as an integral part of the WWB program. From these sessions, training materials will be developed for use in India and elsewhere.

MEETING OF ADVISORY ASSOCIATES

Advisory Associates reported on their activities on behalf of WWB and discussed the functions and responsibilities of associate groups.

- Ann Roberts, President of Advisory Associates of WWB and its representative on the WWB Board, reviewed the creation of the Advisory Associates at the WWB Workshop in Amsterdam last year and the communication via newsletter during 1980.

- Modupe Ibiayo described her efforts to organize a WWB support group in Nigeria to inform government officials, bankers, and others about the WWB program. While reception to the idea is positive, she believes that the completion of materials on WWB operating procedures, the prospectus for the Capital Fund, and the full-time commitment of a core of local personnel will be necessary to initiate a WWB program in Nigeria.

- Mary Okelo, Florence Malinda, and Christine Hayanga described the informal association known as WWB/Kenya and its success in identifying participating institutions and numerous promising women's business ventures, both rural and urban, for WWB. They reported on the visit of WWB consultant, Margaret Hagen, who met with government representatives and banking executives about cooperation with WWB. (Since the Sanremo meeting, authorization has been obtained to formalize a WWB program effort in Kenya, and plans are underway for a Kenya guarantee fund to be launched in April 1982.)

- Manila Chaneton de Vivo reported that her approach to executives at the Banco de la Republica in Montevideo resulted in a US $100,000 commitment to WWB for a loan guarantee program in Uruguay.

- Borka Vucic of Yugoslavia offered to seek endorsement for WWB from major Yugoslavian financial institutions and the government; to introduce WWB's program to financial institutions in certain of the OPEC countries; and to identify projects in Yugoslavia for WWB.

- Nadia Hafez El-Khadem expressed her own interest and that of Madame Sadat in exploring the possibility of a WWB program in Egypt. She also raised the possibility of floating a public bond issue to raise funds for the WWB Capital Fund.

The role of WWB Advisory Associates is described only in general terms in the WWB Charter. Participants agreed that the following were appropriate functions and obligations for WWB associates:

- to establish WWB in their national and local communities;

- to serve as a communications link within the global WWB network and in each country and to help establish links for WWB visitors and WWB representatives;

- to serve as a resource of information and data about a country, an economy, and specific local institutions and business practices.

WWB Associates are requested to keep WWB/New York advised on all local activities related to or of possible interest to WWB so that this information

- 9 -

can be distributed to the membership. Associates may appoint one
representative to the Board of Directors of WWB and may be invited to
serve on other Boards and Committees of WWB.

The title of Founding Associate will be given to those individuals who
attended the First International Workshop of Women Leaders in Banking and
Finance in Amsterdam and contributed to the establishment of the Capital
Fund in March, 1980 or who attended the Second International Workshop
in Sanremo and contributed $100 to the Capital Fund. (In countries
where currency exchange regulations exist, this $100 fee may be placed on
deposit in a local WWB account.) An annual Associates fee of $25 will
be charged to cover the administrative and mailing costs of the Association.
This fee has been waived for 1980 and 1981.

- 10 -

STRUCTURE OF THE WWB GUARANTEE MECHANISM: PROPOSED PROGRAMS
FOR
BRAZIL, GHANA, PHILIPPINES, THAILAND & UNITED STATES
(Plenary III)

Plenary III examined the stucture of the WWB guarantee mechanism, focusing on a set of suggested policies and procedures for the start-up of local WWB programs and several proposals for WWB program initiatives. Discussion concentrated on specific guarantee programs. Written comments on WWB's overall methodology were submitted at the end of the Workshop. The proposals are presented here in the order in which they were discussed.

<u>United States</u>

Mary Houghton, USA, proposed the creation of a guarantee fund in Chicago for the extension of US $250,000 in loans to enterprises owned by women. Key participants in the program would be: The South Shore Bank of Chicago, a private neighborhood development bank located in an economically depressed minority area; women entrepreneurs seeking commercial loans of $5,000 - $25,000; management consultants; and an organization such as the Chicago Finance Exchange (CFE), a non-profit group of women employed in a variety of finance-related areas, or an equivalent organization. The $125,000 fund would be composed of:

- $50,000 savings deposit by WWB International or Friends of WWB/USA, Inc. earning market interest rate;

- $50,000 WWB irrevocable letter of credit for a 10-year term; and

- $25,000 Chicago Finance Exchange savings deposit -- earning market rates to be deposited into Business Plan Fund.

The guarantee will cover up to 75% of each loan and the accrued interest.

With a total $125,000 guarantee fund, South Shore Bank would consider making available $250,000 in loans to qualified women's enterprises at normal commercial floating interest rates.

The uniqueness of this proposal is in the arrangment for financing management assistance:

- After the loan amount is determined, the bank will lend an additional 20% of the face amount of the loan to cover management assistance costs, regardless of whether or not the borrower has adequate equity to support the additional 20%. The South Shore Bank (SSB) will place these additional funds in an escrow account for the borrower, who will not be charged interest on these funds until they are disbursed.

- If specialized assistance is needed after loan approval, a consultant will be hired from a short list of authorized consultants with established rates agreed to by the SSB and CFE. At least one-half of these consultants will be women. The consultant's fee will come from the 20% restricted loan proceeds mentioned above.

- Where pre-loan business planning is needed, SSB will recommend such

- 11 -

assistance. One-half of this cost will be borne by the borrower; the other half will come from the special Business Plan Fund of CFE. If the loan is subsequently approved by the SSB, the cost of assistance will be added to the total amount of the loan. If the loan is not approved, neither the entrepreneur nor the CFE is repaid.

Participants were asked to identify problems the proposal might present for borrowers and lenders. Bankers questioned whether a letter of credit would be acceptable or sufficient to most local banking institutions; whether 75% of the value of the loan was a sufficient guarantee for dealing with small, inexperienced borrowers; and whether the cost of servicing the loans under this program would be too high. From the borrowers' point of view, participants objected to the rigid nature of the terms of the loan program, and to the high cost to the small borrower of this scheme. It was pointed out that the cost of doing business in Chicago would be much higher to WWB than it would be in Colombia or India. There was a general consensus that WWB should consider carefully where it used its limited funds for guarantees-- particularly in its early years.

Ghana

Esther Ocloo, Ghana, offered a written preliminary operational plan for the Ghana Chapter of WWB, one which envisions the creation of a local fund capable of bearing the majority of loan loss under a WWB guarantee program and of a local WWB/Ghana staff that would, in effect, parallel the functions of the staff of WWB International.

The legal corporation of WWB/Ghana is being designed by a Technical Committee in Accra composed of a top banker, a management consultant, a Director of the Central Bank, and two businesswomen. Significant aspects of the Ghana operation are the requirement for prior approval by WWB/Ghana staff and Board of each bank loan and the proposed close relationship of WWB/Ghana with two voluntary organizations: the National Council on Women and Development (NCWD) and the Ghana Business and Professional Women's Association (GBPWA).

The primary goal of GBPWA is to link heterogeneous groups of Ghanaian women, rural and urban, in a variety of cooperative development efforts. The following programs for Ghanaian women and girls have been initiated:

- the organization of young skilled and semi-skilled women into cooperatives for the production of school uniforms;

- the creation of a group lending scheme, supported by credit-worthy women, to assist poor rural women to organize cooperatives and to finance the purchase of vehicles to transport their produce to market and of equipment and additional labor for clearing farmland for cultivation;

- the provision of organizational, technical and financial assistance to women in the food processing trade.

The capital provided under a WWB program in Ghana would have a catalytic effect on efforts such as these.

- 12 -

Philippines

Lourdes Lontok Cruz and Chita Tanchoco-Subido, Philippines, described the
formation of Women in Finance and Entrepreneurship (WIFE), an organization
sharing the objectives of WWB. WIFE would not initially attempt to establish
a guarantee fund or other lending programs for women, since a number of
guarantee programs which target the 1.9 million self-employed women in the
Philippines are already in operation. Examples include the Industrial
Guarantee and Loan Fund of the World Bank, the Agricultural Guarantee Fund
Scheme, and the Fisheries I and Guarantee. A satisfactory level of management
assistance is provided under these programs by the Philippine Ministry of
Industry. WIFE sees its first role as that of catalyst for identifying
projects and financial institutions and for facilitating the loan process.
In addition, these participants urged WWB to consider how it could assist
women to develop investment banking and venture capital skills.

Brazil

Marlene Fernandes, Brazil, proposed a general framework for the creation of a
WWB fund and loan guarantee program in collaboration with two principal
national financial institutions: The National Housing Bank and the Center
for the Promotion of Savings and Loans. The National Housing Bank would be
a suitable partner for WWB because:

- It is a federal agency with a large network that attracts both
  public and private funds.

- Its social objectives (low income target population) are a high
  priority.

- It has experience dealing with foreign currency exchange issues.

- It has a trained, technical staff experienced in working with
  community groups.

- It has the capacity to allocate resources to WWB projects via a
  national savings and loan system.

- It can offer a lending program with unusually long terms and low
  rates.

WWB should also consider working with the Center for the Promotion of Savings
and Loans, where ten million Brazilian women have savings accounts.
Ms. Fernandes felt that a campaign could be mounted to ask these women to
forego a portion of the interest on their savings as a contribution to a
local loan guarantee fund.

Thailand

Chinda Chareonvejj, Thailand, offered the terms and constraints to the
operation of a WWB loan guarantee program with Thai commercial banks.
Thai women entrepreneurs in home industries, small business and agriculture
would apply for loans for their businesses or for the creation of
revolving funds through their local associations or non-governmental groups.
These groups would provide initial screening before referring them to the
bank. Maximum loan size would be US $10,000 in urban and $5,000 in rural
areas. Loans granted for business needs would be charged the prime rate
plus 1%; those for revolving funds, the prime rate plus 1.5%. The term of

- 13 -

the loan would be 36 - 48 months. The guarantee fund would be constituted and risk shared 50:25:25, as in the Cali, Colombia program.

Problems one might reasonably anticipate in Thailand and elsewhere include:

- some credit being utilized for other than the intended purpose -- in Thailand this is often due to the traditional role of women within the family;
- occasional disruption in repayment because of unpredictable weather patterns;
- difficulty in identifying causes of business failure, since government supported lending and training efforts frequently lack adequate follow-up and evaluation;
- unstable markets -- both domestic and international.

OPPORTUNITIES FOR WOMEN IN
NON-TRADITIONAL BUSINESS ACTIVITIES

Patricia Cloherty, USA, discussed "non-traditional" activities for women in business. The following is a summary of her remarks.

For most people, non-traditional business opportunities for women suggest their participation in trades normally reserved for men, i.e., welding, auto mechanics, plumbing. And, while this may be true in the area of jobs and employment, it is less true in the area of capital formation, which is what business development is all about.

Look at non-traditional business opportunities for women requires that you look at what is traditional, first. Women traditionally are in small businesses which have minimal growth potential and which are concentrated in service and retail sectors. Restaurants, apparel shops, personal services, trading activities--these tend to be the typical kinds of shops and businesses run by women. They serve local markets, do not have a technological base, are not capital intensive, by and large, and do not involve a high degree of proprietary know-how, including patents and rare skills.

In this framework, what is "non-traditional" for most women entrepreneurs is their entry into those businesses which have a proprietary competitive edge, have substantial growth potential, high profit margins. In the United States today, for example, such entrepreneurial opportunities can be seen in such areas as the applied biological sciences (gene splicing, or recombinant DNA technology); computer software applications and telecommunications.

Ms. Cloherty stressed that this definition of "non-traditional" requires that women look at the purely financial, fundamental aspects of business. They need to understand what constitutes a commercial opportunity and how to recognize such an opportunity when they see it.

Too often, income generation for women does not mean building up capital in a business as a result of exploiting a well-thought-through business opportunity. On the contrary, it often means that a woman works twice to three times as hard to sell products of marginal profitability. While she may earn spending money from such activity, she generally will not build up the kind of capital base that yields economic independence. While such activities are quite common and respectable, the non-traditional route for women today involves their pursuing larger prospects for financial reward. By the same token, it involves their taking more risk.

If WWB is to back women in non-traditional ventures defined in this way, its organizers will have to be clear on how to pinpoint such opportunities and how to back the right team of people to exploit them. Such opportunities can arise from the following:

- existing small businesses suitable for expansion;

- installations of major companies in various countries which need other smaller companies as suppliers to their business and to their employees;

-15-

302

- franchising opportunities; and,
- existing skill pools which can be shaped into productive, profitable activity.

When a woman undertakes a new economic venture, she must ask several fundamental questions:

- Can the product or service be sold for substantially more than it takes to be produced?
- What are the competitive trends?
- What is the regulatory environment?
- What is the projected profitability and how does it relate to industry norms?
- How can an investment be shaped which will maximize the value of the captial used?

Rigorous analysis and monitoring is essential. And WWB, through technical support, can assist its affiliates in providing the necessary know-how.

WWB will finance many "me too," or "mom and pop" small businesses of the type most women, worldwide, run. But among those, Ms. Cloherty suggested that WWB seek to finance a few non-traditional (for women) high-potential enterprises. The key lies in the know-how to identify and structure the right entrepreneurial team, backed by capital, in the right commercial opportunity.

ELEMENTS OF AN ECONOMY THAT AFFECT
THE SMALL BUSINESS & INDUSTRY SECTORS

Nancy Barry, The World Bank, described effective means of supporting small-scale enterprise development. The following is a summary of her remarks.

Backing the Winners

When developing programs for small enterprise, efforts should be focused on those product and service groups in which:

- sizeable growth potential in exports or local markets exists;

- small firms can compete, with no major advantages to large scale production;

- small industry already represents a sizeable share of industry or at least significant concentrations of small firms in the product group exist; and,

- raw materials are readily available.

While the product groups which meet these criteria will differ by country, one does find that common groups emerge in Asia, Latin America and Africa:

- organized small and medium industry, such as light engineering agro-processing, leather goods, wood products, garments and building materials; and,

- cottage and rural enterprises -- small agro-based activities, such as beekeeping, small livestock, fish ponds, small agro-processing -- and handicrafts and textiles, such as handloom products, carpets, knitwear, metal crafts and basketry.

Tapping Private Know-How .

If markets beyond the neighborhood are to be tapped, small firms face difficulties in producing the required minimum volume, making the sales, and getting products to market. Some agent must enter to organize the decentralized production base. A private agent often assumes this role, and charges a high price for his services. Government marketing organizations and cooperative systems try, often ineffectively, to substitute for the private agent.

Instead of trying to replace these private market agents, benefits can be derived from tapping their know-how and providing adequate incentives to induce them to meet development objectives.

WWB would benefit from working closely with these commercial market agents. Banks are more willing to lend to small businesses if the markets are assured; and these agents often provide technical assistance as a necessary part of their commercial system.

- 17 -

Building Small-Scale Industry Systems in Commercial Banks

To have successful lending arrangements for women entrepreneurs, the banks must have strong general small industry credit operations. Commercial banks often have strengths which can be tapped in small-scale industry lending.

At present, however, most banks are reluctant to expand credit to small-scale industries. They are fundamentally risk-averse, relying heavily on collateral rather than project viability in lending decisions, and consider small industry lending to be an insufficiently important part of their total lending to justify specially trained staff.

In spite of these biases and barriers, commercial banks often are the best vehicle for small enterprise credit operations. The following measures are important ingredients in expanding the banks' small-scale industry operations:

- specialized, trained staff for full-time work in small industry appraisal and supervision;
- incentives to banks to get them to incur the relatively higher costs of small industry lending and to reduce their perceived risks in lending to small borrowers. Attractive spreads can cover the costs and guarantees can cover part of the risks;
- management policies favoring lending on the basis of appraised project viability;
- simplified appraisal and supervision methods and application forms;
- lower costs of appraisal and supervision where banks focus lending on 5 to 10 of the more promising product groups and where lending can be concentrated in selected geographical areas; and,
- promotional and project preparation capabilities established in independent organizations that maintain good relationships to the banks.

Implications for Women's World Banking

Guarantees for commercial bank loans to women entrepreneurs could be an excellent "foot-in-the-door" for WWB. However, if general small industry lending operations are not in place, guarantees alone would not be sufficient to induce the banks to make small loans to women. Prior to launching a women's enterprise program, WWB might want to encourage the lead organization--commercial banks and promotional group--to do systematic selection of product groups for focus.

- 18 -

305

EXPANDING SUCCESSFUL LENDING: GUIDELINES FOR
WOMEN IN BANKING & FINANCE
(Plenary IV)

The questions below were first addressed in plenary, then in working groups.
The following summaries of participants' advice is intended to serve as a
basis for the development of handbooks by women in banking and business who
wish to promote successful lending to women entrepreneurs in their communities.

How can women in banking and finance involve more of their colleagues in
efforts which will expand successful lending and relevant services to
women business owners?   (Ruth Smith & Emily Womach, USA, Discussion Leaders)

Participants made the following suggestions:

- Organize women bank officers and entrepreneurs in each locale and
  country to promote small business associations. These groups can
  actively train women in preparing business plans and approaching
  banks. Through these organizations, women can enlist the help of
  others in relevant financial and trade associations.

- Persuade bankers, government officials and the public that women
  entrepreneurs are both a long-term market opportunity for commercial
  banks and a valuable community resource. Convince them that it is
  in their interests to offer counseling services and creative financing
  alternatives to meet women's needs.

- Hold seminars led by successful women business owners and promote
  the image of the successful business women in all forms of media.

- Be knowledgeable of the management assistance materials and resources
  in the community for small borrowers, what they cost and how they can
  be approached. Where resources are limited, the potential for small
  business counseling by certified accountants or polytechnical colleges
  should be considered. In some communities there are experienced,
  retired consultants in small business who provide small business
  counseling.

- Accept the obligation, as women bankers, to be helpful to women
  borrowers and to be as flexible as possible in structuring loans to
  meet their needs.

Participants felt that since first-rate small business materials are so valuable,
WWB itself might want to explore establishing a technical clearinghouse of
such materials for women entrepreneurs and bankers. Through its international
network, WWB is in a good position to be able to obtain such materials from
many parts of the world.

How can bankers provide more assistance to small business owners?
(Modupe Ibiayo, Nigeria, and Mary Okelo, Kenya, Discussion Leaders)

Participants urged women in banking and finance to influence banks to:

- Assist in marketing efforts that could benefit their small borrowers.
  (Bankers often finance both producers and consumers in a locale and
  could promote the development of international marketing groups.)

- 19 -

- Evaluate the contents and level of sophistication of management assistance materials and programs used by their small business borrowers.
- Find mechanisms to help finance the high cost of management assistance for the individual small business borrower. (In Brazil, for example, banks add 1% to the interest on the loan to pay for management assistance by an outside consultant.)
- Provide group seminars and training to offset the high cost of individual counseling.

Most participants felt that in addition to serving as a catalyst for successful lending, WWB should place emphasis on providing the means to bring women entrepreneurs to the point where they could borrow and repay loans successfully.

Can WWB, in collaboration with others, help to finance management assistance and/or banking facilities for small business? If so, how? (Chinda Chareonvejj, Thailand, Discussion Leader)

Participants proposed that WWB:

- Form a strong WWB working group of women with banking and business skills in every country where program development is envisioned, and use this group to

   - set realistic goals for the extension of credit to women locally, and update these periodically;

   - identify and engage the best management assistance available for the small business woman; and,

   - address, by whatever means are appropriate, the restrictive practices and legal constraints on women borrowers in the commercial banking system.

- Accept the reality that most banks will not pay for management assistance to small business persons and proceed to evaluate the capacity of "intermediaries" to do so, beginning with the governmental, non-governmental and women's groups. Where bureaucratic constraints are excessive or the level of performance is weak, opt for the help of banks and private management assistance groups, even if this requires raising additional funds.

- 20 -

OTHER ISSUES IN CONTEXT OF
WWB PROGRAM DEVELOPMENT
(Work Groups 4, 5, & 6)

Work Groups were formed to discuss the following three questions in relation
to WWB program development:

What kinds of financial and economic data would be most useful for developing
WWB domestic programs: (Virginia Saurwein, USA, Discussion Leader)

One of WWB's purposes is to collect and disseminate information on women's
activities as they affect women's access to credit and banking services.
Participants considered two aspects of data gathering which are currently of
primary importance: the kinds of data WWB needs to give it credibility in the
banking world, and the kinds of data needed by banks at the local level for
assessing and granting loans.

Carolyn Johnson, USA, addressed the issue of WWB credibility by describing
the uniqueness of the WWB concept:

- It seeks to readjust the financial mode to fit the person, rather
  that requiring the person to fit the mold.

- It is based on an economic model which affirms reciprocity, based
  on mutual sharing of resources, rather than on a fixed sum model
  with a win/lose proposition.

- It seeks to affirm the experience of women as women, rather than women
  only in so far as they behave like men.

In sum, she noted, WWB recognizes the strength of diversity of people and
resources, rather than the traditional view that diversity is weakness.
She believes that WWB is on the road toward developing more socially just
and productive ways of lending.

Mary Okelo commented that for most bankers, the following would be considered
important data for evaluating loan applications:

- government policy with regard to lending priorities;

- availability of capital;

- local and national government regulations;

- market assessment;

- mobility of currency;

- loan terms required; and,

- local and national economic and social development forecasts.

Participants emphasized that while WW3 should attempt to stay abreast of
the research efforts of others, its primary concern should be to document
well the WWB programs, particularly the variables leading to success or
failure in each instance. Through careful evaluation and assessment of
its programs, an initial data base could be formed to help guide the selection
and start-up of other programs.

- 21 -

How can we identify and promote non-traditional areas for women in business?
(Martha Stuart, USA, Discussion Leader)

Martha Stuart suggested that one means of developing new business opportunites
for women is through the use of video technology. Video is a communications
medium and an educational tool which warrants attention by all societies.
It has potential for facilitating communication within and between developing
countries as well as between these areas and the more industrialized countries.

Ms. Stuart described her Village Network project. She began training
villagers in Jamaica, Egypt, Indonesia and Mali in the use of video as
a part of an effort to promote literacy and family planning. Training
involved participants making tapes in which they recorded their own experience.
In each case, once training was completed, equipment was left for the
continued use of the trainees.

Such access to video in areas of the developing world opens up exciting
possibilities for direct communications between peoples on a whole range
of issues they consider important. Villagers can record their views on tape
and forward these to centers capable of distributing the video to other
groups.

WWB might contribute to this expanding video network by encouraging the
production and sharing of videos on WWB programs or the taping of what WWB
network members consider to be successful, innovative and possibly replicable
business-related experiences of women.

To demonstrate the capacity of video for direct information sharing on
development issues--most of which are linked to the issues of primary concern
to WWB--Ms. Stuart presented portions of two video projects: "Family Planning
in Mali" and "Three Generations of Javanese Women."

How can we persuade more women to use their capital resources, including
savings, to help generate financing for women's businesses? (Vimla Dalal,
India, Discussion Leader)

By its very existence, WWB is in a position to take an advocacy role in
the area of savings. Participants suggested that WWB emphasize a "savings
first" theme in all its communications about women and the effective use of
credit. Local women's banks are also positioned to do this. These
institutions could encourage school training programs in savings such as
those in India today. Participants also proposed that women's financial
institutions should accept and advocate the general acceptance of jewelry
as collateral for loans, a decision which could benefit women micro-scale
entrepreneurs.

Turning to women's savings patterns world-wide, participants asked what
is known about the relationship of what women save to what they actually
borrow in individual countries.

Agreeing that data is insufficient, they felt that sample surveys might
be a way of gathering information on some of these patterns. Participants
offered their own observations. Current savings patterns differ between
developed and developing countries. In industrialized countries, what is

- 22 -

saved relates quite directly to what is needed for investment. Today many people are salaried and not highly motivated to save. This tendency is sometimes reinforced by tax regulations that encourage people to borrow and let inflation build up equity. In countries with inadequate social security systems, however, savings are still perceived as critical and tax incentives are frequently offered to savers.

There was concensus that women, in general, are regular savers but hesitant borrowers, and could profit from training on how to borrow to finance their businesses. It was further agreed that WWB should identify and take into account the savings patterns of the women that WWB programs are designed to reach.

- 23 -

310

WORKSHOP PARTICIPANTS

JOYCE ACTON
Assistant Manager, Credit
Bank of Montreal
Toronto, Ontario, CANADA

CAMILA ARIEL
Manager, Neve Ram Branch
Bank Hapoalim, BM
Ramat-Gan, ISRAEL

KAMILLA BALAZS
Manager of Department
National Bank of Hungary
Budapest, HUNGARY

F.A.W. BANNIER*
Partner
Nauta Van Haersolte
Amsterdam, NETHERLANDS

NANCY BARRY*
Small Industry Specialist
The World Bank
Washington, D.C., USA

ELA BHATT*
General Secretary
Self Employed Women's Association
Ahmedabad, INDIA

CHINDA CHAREONVEJJ
Senior Vice President
Bangkok Bank Ltd.
Bangkok, THAILAND

LILIA CLEMENTE*
Chairman
Clemente Capital Consultants, Inc.
New York, New York, USA

PATRICIA CLOHERTY
President
Tessler & Cloherty, Inc.
New York, New York, USA

BETTY CROW
Vice President
Commerce Bancshares, Inc.
Kansas City, Missouri, USA

LOURDES LONTOK CRUZ
President & Chief Executive Officer
Paluwagan Ng Bayan Savings & Loan
  Association
Manila, PHILIPPINES

VIMLA DALAL
Manger, Walkeshwar Branch
Bank of India
Bombay, INDIA

MARLENE FERNANDES
Architect & Urban Planner
Banco Nacional de Habitacion
Rio de Janeiro, BRAZIL

JOSSELINE FETHIERE
Branch Manager
The First National Bank of Boston
Port-au-Prince, HAITI

MARIA MARGARITA DE GARRIDO
Vice President
Corporacion de A Horro y vivienda
  (AHorramas)
Cali, COLOMBIA

NADIA HAFEZ-EL KHADEM
Partner
IBET International
Cairo, ARE

JOHN HAMMOCK
Consultant on Micro Business Development
ACCION International & WWB
Boston, Massachusetts, USA

CHRISTINE HAYANGA
Lawyer
Agricultural Finance Corporation
Nairobi, KENYA

MARY HOUGHTON
Executive Vice President
South Shore Bank
Chicago, Illinois. USA

MODUPE IBIAYO
Department of Planning & Development
African Continental Bank
Lagos, NIGERIA

- 25 -

CAROLYN JOHNSON
Chair, Committee on Investment
Board of Global Ministries
  World Division
United Methodist Church
New York, New York, USA

J. BURKE KNAPP*
Senior Advisor to the President
The World Bank
Washington, D.C., USA

RAYMOND LLOYD
Activist for Women's Advancement
Rome, ITALY

FLORENCE MALINDA
Executive Officer
Kenya Institute of Bankers
Nairobi, KENYA

ESTHER OCLOO*
President
Nkulenu Industries Ltd.
Medina-Legon, GHANA

MARY OKELO
Manager, Harambee Avenue Branch
Barclays Bank of Kenya Ltd.
Nairobi, KENYA

ANN ROBERTS*
Vice President
Rockefeller Family Fund
New York, New York, USA

VIRGINIA SAURWEIN*
Chief, NGO Unit
Department of International
  Economic & Social Affiars
United Nations
New York, New York, USA

ANDREA SEHL
Yale School of Organization
  and Management
New Haven, Connecticut, USA

RUTH SMITH
President
First State Bank
Kansas City, Kansas, USA

MARTHA STUART*
President
Martha Stuart Communications, Inc.
New York, New York, USA

CHITA TANCHOCO SUBIDO
Executive Director
Technical Board of Agricultural
  Credit
Central Bank of the Philippines
Manila, PHILLIPINES

LADAVAN TANATANIT
Assistant Vice President
Bangkok Bank Ltd.
Bangkok, THAILAND

MARTHA TILAAR
Director
Sari Ayu Martha Kosmetika
  Indonesia
Jakarta, INDONESIA

MANILA CHANETON DE VIVO
Vice President
Manos del Uruguay
Montevideo, URUGUAY

BORKA VUCIC
Executive Vice President & Member
  of the Management Board
Associated Belgrade Bank
Belgrade, YUGOSLAVIA

MICHAELA WALSH*
President
Women's World Banking
New York, New York, USA

EMILY WOMACH
Chair of the Board & President
The Women's National Bank
Washington, D.C., USA

WWB WORKSHOP STAFF AT SANREMO:

JUDITH FELDSTEIN
GRETCHEN MAYNES
LESLIE SEDERLUND
JOAN SHAPIRO
LAWLER WALSH

*Member, Board of Trustees, Stichting Women's World Banking

- 26 -

312

WWB PROGRAM DEVELOPMENT, DECEMBER, 1981

The months following the Sanremo meeting were active ones for WWB and its Advisory Associates.

In Latin America, the loan guarantee program in Cali, Colombia, began. An on-site Regional Workshop sponsored by WWB, Friends of WWB/Cali and the United Nations Development Programme (UNDP) spurred WWB program development in other cities of Colombia and in the Dominican Republic, Uruguay and Haiti. Trinidad, Venezuela and Jamaica are also considering WWB programs.

In Asia, the successful completion of WWB's negotiations with the Reserve Bank of India and the registration of Friends of WWB/Western India led to the initiation of WWB's second program. The repayment of WWB's direct loan to SEWA will ultimately be used to establish a new source of capital for loans to low income women throughout India. Plans for program development in other cities of India and in Bangladesh, Thailand, Indonesia, Sri Lanka and the Philippines were advanced as a result of an Asian Regional Workshop held in Ahmedabad, India in December. Sponsors of the meeting were WWB, SEWA and the UNDP. A WWB Pacific Regional Workshop is scheduled for November, 1982 in the Philippines.

In Africa, plans are underway for an African Regional Workshop to be held in Nairobi, Kenya in April, 1982. Sponsors will be WWB, WWB/Kenya and the UNDP. WWB representatives visited Kenya, Ghana and the Ivory Coast to explore program development opportunities with local women leaders and with the African Development Bank. WWB Board member Modupe Ibiayo held a Friends of WWB/Nigeria meeting for the purpose of initiating a WWB program there.

WWB Advisory Associates and the women leaders whom they identified were most valuable participants at the regional workshops held this year.

- 27 -

Organization Chart

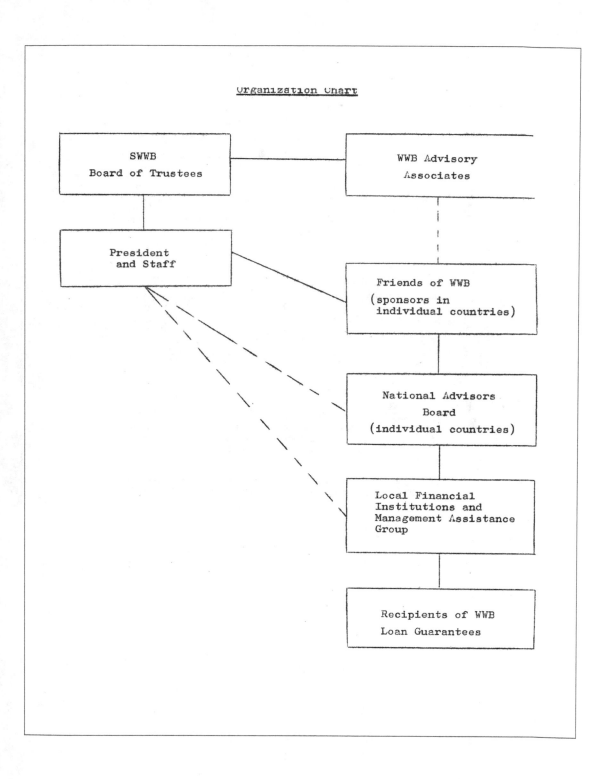

SWWB
Board of Trustees

WWB Advisory
Associates

President
and Staff

Friends of WWB
(sponsors in
individual countries)

National Advisors
Board
(individual countries)

Local Financial
Institutions and
Management Assistance
Group

Recipients of WWB
Loan Guarantees

SUMMARY

The Assignment

Women's World Banking (WWB) asked DFC to undertake a Ten-Year
Assessment of the organization. Specifically, DFC proposed to
provide answers to four questions :

1. To what extent has WWB achieved its original objectives
    and accomplished specific goals?

2. What needs to be done to give members and donors a
    better understanding of the purpose, structure,
    potential and requirements of WWB as a financial
    institution?

3. What needs to be done to improve the flow of information
    between the members of WWB, to improve WWB's continuous
    self-assessment process, and to raise awareness within
    the network for the importance of regular, systematic
    self-evaluation?

4. What, at this stage of its evolution, is required to
    render WWB a self-sustaining service institution for
    women who run small-scale enterprises?

In addition, DFC proposed to assess the first ten years' work in
terms of three specific objectives outlined in the WWB Business
Plan 1988-1991 and to recommend appropriate actions and strategies
to :

1. Strengthen affiliate network

2. Strengthen management structure

3. Achieve financial independence

The Approach

DFC used a combination of the following :

--- source documents (background files, financial and legal files, Self-Assessment Forms, etc.)

--- interviews with WWB client/participants

--- discussions with affiliate staff, management and Board of Directors

--- interviews with local donor organizations and supporting agencies, banks, and government representatives

--- on-going discussions with SWWB staff, management and Board of Trustees

In addition, DFC spoke with several global aid and development agencies and government missions, some of which are WWB supporting contributors and some of which are not.

To gather as much material as possible in the time available, DFC worked in conjunction with WWB personnel on source documents available at SWWB/NY and spent 11 weeks visiting 13 selected affiliates chosen to represent the diversity of Women's World Banking. The DFC team of consultants visited a representative range of affiliates, from the start-up stage to the most developed. We interviewed a wide range of clients and participants of WWB programs in the 13 countries to assess the effectiveness of the programs offered.

In addition, each consultant interviewed the local WWB Affiliate staff and management, the local supporting organizations and donors and the participating banks and government agencies in order to see the full picture of an affiliate's environment and operations.

The Report

The report is organised into the four sections : Objectives, Finance, Programs and Organization, preceded by a short introduction outlining the structure of Women's World Banking. Each section outlines the major achievements of WWB as well as the outstanding issues we feel need to be addressed. We close each section with our recommendations for action.

A summary of the general conclusions and recommendations is presented below.

General Conclusions

Objectives

1. WWB has created the strong identity of an independent
    institution dedicated to promoting the full participation of
    women in the global economy. After 10 years, the name
    Women's World Banking is recognized in the development
    sector and enjoys a reputation as a serious organization.

2. Moreover, WWB exerted a major influence on the donor
    community by educating the aid and development organizations
    as to the specific needs of women in development assistance
    projects. WWB is seen as one of the authorities in the field
    and continues to be asked for technical advice and assistance
    based on its experience.

3. WWB has built a distinctive global network of organized women
    dedicated to facilitating access by women and their families
    to the economic mainstream. It operates as an association of
    44 autonomous affiliates, continually striving to involve all
    of its members and supporting organizations in managing its
    evolution. The commitment to WWB ideals is extremely strong
    and continues to grow as the group resists being categorized
    as either a "development project" or a "women's program" or
    the like.

4. The lack of an easy label for WWB does highlight, however,
    the broad generality of WWB's goals. Substantially different
    interpretations remain (within the institution and among
    donors) about what should be its operational objectives and
    priorities. These differences have inhibited WWB's ability
    to develop a full range of targeted and effective programs.
    This, in turn, has hampered the institution's efforts to
    attract funding as the organization is increasingly judged,
    especially by traditional donors, by its capacity to deliver
    programs in addition to raising awareness.

5. The Loan Guarantee Program, which WWB initiated in 1982, was
    a unique approach to opening up women's access to credit and
    allowed WWB to differentiate itself among the funded
    organizations. Over time, however, similar credit schemes
    have become widely accepted as an integral part of
    development assistance programs. The fact that the WWB
    approach is no longer unique has meant greater competition
    for donor funds.

Financial

6.   Women's World Banking has succeeded in establishing itself as
      an independent financial institution with a strong capital
      base. Recognizing the short operating life of one-time
      grants, WWB took the bold step of placing the majority of its
      donations in a permanent Capital Fund. These funds have been
      prudently invested to provide interest income to contribute
      to operating expenses and to support individual guarantee
      programs managed by the WWB Affiliates. WWB also avoided the
      trap of bloating its central bureaucracy by keeping its
      budgeted expenditures within available resources; general
      administrative expenses have declined over the period as
      a proportion of total expenditures to less than 20%.

7.   However, despite the more than US$ 5 million capital base
      which has generated increasing annual investment income,
      WWB's medium-term viability is far from secure. Donor
      support has been declining over the past three years as
      priorities change and a move toward country-specific and
      project funding has taken hold; no significant new donor has
      been added since 1986. At the same time, WWB has been
      growing in scope and size. Attempts to expand its revenue
      sources via guarantee fees and interest income have had only
      limited success. Consequently, WWB faces an important
      challenge to recover and expand donor support to meet the
      needs of the present network as well as provide for future
      expansion.

Programs and Impact

8.   WWB accurately identified the main obstacles to women's
      participation in the global economy and pinpointed some of
      the key needs which require concerted action. WWB has
      devised a practical approach which centers on (1) training in
      business skills and (2) access to credit either for small
      business initiatives outside the home or for income-
      generating activities in the home, although it has yet to
      develop a programmed approach to many of the other economic,
      cultural and legal barriers to women's full participation in
      the economy.

9.   WWB pioneered the concept of granting small direct loans to
      women instead of aid monies. WWB conceived and implemented a
      Loan Guarantee Program which leveraged its capital base by
      providing guarantees to the local banks to encourage them to
      lend to women in their local communities. WWB Affiliates
      have extended the idea further with Direct Lending Programs;
      some are aiming to be small banks for the informal sector.

To ensure that women and their families have the tools they
need to gain access to the economy, many WWB Affiliates also
offer a range of counseling, training, savings and other
activities, which have, however, not been developed in as
systematic a way as the lending programs nor with as
effective support from SWWB.

10. This unique approach of loan programs is no longer unique,
having been imitated or copied by several development
programs and like-minded organizations to make it a sort of
prototype of the new approach to development assistance.
This has meant that WWB is in the position of having to
compete for donor funds even more fiercely than ever before.

11. The impact of WWB's programs can be measured firstly by their
global reach (presence in 35 countries and growing) and the
number of people reached (an estimated 38,000 loans have been
granted over the ten-year history to at least 18,000
beneficiaries, all of whom have participated in training
programs). DFC's consultants interviewed 66 clients of the
loan programs as well as graduates of the training programs
and found that, despite a general reluctance to reveal
specific increases in sales, profits etc., all but perhaps 3
have improved their skills and economic situation enough to
expand the operation or improve the working conditions or put
more food on the family table. Since the high inflation in
many of these countries distorts monetary comparisons, the
best indicator of improvement is the client's gut feeling as
to whether she and her family are living better, and on this
basis, WWB programs can be considered successful.

12. The qualitative assessment notwithstanding, there exist major
information gaps, both at the affiliate level and at SWWB/NY,
which preclude a systematic quantitative assessment of their
impact. SWWB should continue its current efforts to improve
its loan monitoring system and expand its data base to
include information on direct lending programs as well as the
guaranteed loans. Then WWB would be in a position to
undertake a comprehensive and detailed impact analysis in
order to understand better the WWB clients and the
appropriateness and effectiveness of the programs managed by
the affiliates.

Organization

13. WWB has succeeded in establishing an international structure
of sufficient flexibility to accommodate the diversity of its
activities and participants. The Stichting in the
Netherlands and Friends of WWB in the United States have

facilitated fund-raising and immediately confirmed the global intentions of the group. A large Board of Trustees comprised of committed professionals of international stature further enhanced the WWB identity, while a strong and visionary President continually attracted a talented, dedicated and enthusiastic group of women to work at all levels of the organization.

14. This strong leadership does not overpower the organization, however. The WWB concept stresses self-determination. Affiliates are encouraged to determine their own objectives and programs based on their understanding of local needs and constraints. Each affiliate has struggled to define its target market, to organize in the best structure to respond to that market and to raise the necessary operating funds to meet the needs of that market. The resulting network of WWB Affiliates is therefore comprised of very diverse groups in various stages of development and exhibiting varying degrees of confidence and competence. Of the 13 affiliates visited as part of this Assessment, 4 were experiencing serious problems in either internal management and systems or in program delivery and monitoring or both. While this represents a relatively good performance among cooperative assistance institutions, management of weaker affiliates is an area of concern.

15. As the WWB network has steadily grown in size, there are more affiliates in the start-up stage; these younger affiliates need specific assistance in managing their operations and in program development and are looking to SWWB to provide such assistance. Certain very recent initiatives such as the Management Training Institute respond to this need by involving the more experienced affiliates in the training of the younger ones, but more use can be made of the other three major SWWB offerings (the Start-Up Loan Program, the Affiliate Exchange Program and the Loan Guarantee Program) in order to strengthen the Affiliate programs and their effectiveness. SWWB needs to be actively involved in the creation, sponsorship and delivery of the training and development processes more than just overseeing them.

16. WWB has strived for clear and continuous internal communication over the years. It has established an annual self-assessment process which is intended to enable each Affiliate to evaluate its strengths and weaknesses based on its past performance, thereby enabling it to plan for the future. In addition, the process is intended to provide useful data on the impact and evolution of WWB which will enable SWWB to formulate its action plans and recommendations for the future of the entire organization. The Self-Assessment Form has

proven to be a necessary information tool to the organization, but it has been universally criticized as not being user-friendly and not providing the data needed for SWWB to assess overall results and therefore needs to be revised.

17. There is a high degree of involvement in the management of WWB at the Board of Trustees level via quarterly Executive and Finance Committee meetings as well as annual Board meetings. Affiliates are involved via international exchanges, workshops and meetings as well through as representation at the Board level (7 of the 19 Trustees are intimately involved with local affiliate operations) and through Regional Coordinators. However, WWB now needs to streamline its decision-making process and to emphasize the autonomy of a professional management structure, taking the burden of day-to-day operations off the Board, Executive Committee and Executive Director (President). It is particularly evident that the President needs to delegate more of her duties and responsibilities down the structure, not only to be more effective in strategic planning and fund-raising, but also to develop the professional skills of the SWWB staff to handle a greater part of the management of WWB and be able to pursue career paths within the organization.

18. The high degree of involvement of the various governing bodies has placed extraordinary reporting burdens on staff at Affiliates, Regional Offices and SWWB/NY which detracts significantly from their capacity to serve the growing WWB network. In addition, many initiatives to create tools and programs to ensure access to information and to ensure continued financial soundness and independence have not come to fruition due to high staff turnover, changing priorities and "too many cooks in the kitchen". WWB now needs to focus its efforts on effective program delivery and on retaining a professional staff undistracted by an excess of administration and new projects.

19. Finally, the question of the President's successor needs to be addressed. The current President has stated her intention to step down at the end of her contract in 1990 and a successor has not yet been identified. We understand that the Board of Trustees had formed a Search Committee but its progress and status are unclear at the present time. The Board needs to formulate the profile of the type of leader for the next phase of WWB's evolution as a basis for identifying candidates as soon as possible. Simultaneously, the current staffing of SWWB needs to be strengthened, both in New York and at the Regional Coordinator level, as current staffing levels are inadequate to handle the increasing responsibilities of managing and servicing the expanding organization.

Recommendations

As WWB stands at the 10-year mark, it must apply its acknowledged creativity and dedication to address what are the two crucial needs to its future success :

1. Increasing funding to ensure long-term viability

2. Strengthening program delivery to improve effectiveness

Our recommendations focus on four actions needed to address these needs in the short-term :

A. Refine and clarify operational objectives

B. Recover and increase donor support

C. Strengthen global organization and management

D. Consolidate existing affiliate network

A. Refine and clarify operational objectives. WWB suffers from the syndrome of trying to be "all things to all people". Though the desire not to be restrictive in its approach and to encourage self-determination at all levels of the organization is indeed a strength, such a large field of action has led to confusion as to the goals and priorities for its program development and the appropriateness of its funding structure. For a more efficient use of resources and greater understanding both inside and outside the organization, WWB needs to develop more specific statements of its objectives. These statements should define the priorities for its operational activities and the criteria by which to measure the achievement of its objectives.

B. Recover and increase donor support. Expanded donor support is critical to WWB's medium-term viability. WWB depends on a small group of donors for the bulk of its funding. No significant new donor has been added since 1986 and the level of unrestricted contributions has been steadily declining. WWB needs permanent fund-raising personnel to expand the donor base, to identify new sources and to push a Capital Fund Drive to solidify its financial resources and to build up the program delivery capability to enhance the institution's attractiveness to donors.

C. <u>Strengthen global organization and management</u>. WWB has avoided the top-heavy administrative structure which would have been a drain on its scarce resources during its growth period. However, the lean staffing has left gaps in key areas of management which have resulted in an overburdened staff whose service capabilities have been less effective than is expected by the affiliate network and the external community. WWB now needs to concentrate on hiring and retaining a professional staff at SWWB/NY and the Regional Coordination Centers to service adequately the needs of the existing organization.

D. <u>Consolidate existing affiliate network</u>. The unevenness in the confidence and competence of the WWB Affiliates and the programs they offer needs to be addressed before resources are used to bring new entities into the organization. This emphasizes the need for WWB to become more effective as a program delivery organization. It also means that WWB should assess the continuing "eligibility" of affiliates to maintain their affiliation, and to sanction the non-performers. While the concept of self-determination can be a source of strength, the performance of individual affiliates has a critical effect on the reputation and impact of Women's World Banking.

With these four actions, WWB would increase member and donor understanding, thereby increasing the potential support of the organization which would provide more resources to strengthen the management structure, freeing staff to improve the services and programs which strengthen the WWB Affiliates and thereby the effectiveness of Women's World Banking.

RANGE OF ACTIVITIES

Affiliate Visited	Credit		Training/Tech Assistance	Marketing	Other / Projected
	Loan Gtee	Direct			
GHANA WWBG (WWB Ghana) Ltd.	Yes	No	Yes	Yes	Savings (groups)
COLOMBIA Fundacion WWB - Cali	No	Yes	Yes	Yes	Savings
KENYA KWFT (Kenya Women Finance Trust Ltd.)	Yes	Yes	Yes	Yes	Savings
THAILAND FWBT (Friends of WWB Thailand)	Yes	Yes	Yes	Yes	
MALAYSIA WINTRAC (WWB/Malaysia) Sdn. Bhd. (Women in Trade & Commerce)	No	Yes	Yes	Yes	Investment
JAMAICA FWWBJ (Friends of WWB Jamaica)	No	Yes	Yes	No	Cooperation with local groups for educational programs
UGANDA UWFCT (Uganda Women's Finance and Credit Trust Ltd.)	No	Yes	Yes	Yes	Savings

RANGE OF ACTIVITIES

Affiliate Visited	Credit Loan Gtee	Direct	Training/Tech Assistance	Marketing	Other	Projected
COSTA RICA Asociacion Credimujer/WWB	No	Yes	Yes	Yes	Establish separate marketing company	
MALI AIFEM (Association pour l'intégration de la femme dans l'économie malienne)	No*	No	No	No		Lending
GAMBIA GWFC (Gambia Women Finance Co. Ltd.)	No*	No	No	No		Lending
RWANDA Duterimbere	No*	Yes	Yes	Yes	Savings (groups)	
BURUNDI APEF (Association pour la promotion économique de la femme)	No*	Yes	No	No		Training
INDIA WERDAN (Women Entrepreneurs Resource Development Agency)	No	No	Yes	No		

* Currently in process of negotiating Loan Guarantee Agreement with SWWB and local bank

SWWB LOAN GUARANTEE REPORT – 02/20/86

		CALI COLOMBIA		DOMINICAN REPUBLIC		HAITI		JAMAICA		THAILAND		WEST VIRGINIA	WESTERN INDIA		TOTAL
		As of 12/31/85		As of 6/30/85		As of 12/31/85		As of 12/31/85		As of 12/31/85		As of 12/31/85	As of 12/31/85		
		Local Currency (162 pesos)	U.S. Dollars $1	Local Currency (3 pesos)	U.S. Dollars $1	Local Currency (5 Goudes)	U.S. Dollars $1	Local Currency (Jam. $4)	U.S. Dollars $1	Local Currency (27.50 Bhatt)	U.S. Dollars $1	U.S. Dollars	Local Currency (12.12 Rup)	U.S. Dollars $1	
SWWB Assets	Comissory Notes	3,000	17	7,106	2,368	3,900	780			5,200	189	150	303,000	25,000	25,000
	Accounts Receivable												12,120	1,000	4,504
SWWB Liabilities	SWWB Guarantees Letters of Credit	8,000	5,000	300,000	100,000	125,000	25,000	100,000	25,000	1,833,343	66,667	25,000			246,667
	Local WWB Guarantees	405,000	2,500	50,000*	16,666*	80,010	16,002	50,000	12,500	916,658	33,333	12,500			93,501
	Local Bank Guarantees	405,000	2,500	150,000	50,000	62,500	12,500	50,000	12,500	916,658	33,333	12,500			123,333
	Total Available for program adjustments	1,602,000	10,000	500,000	166,666	267,510	53,502	200,000	50,000	3,666,659	133,333	50,000	152,094(303,000-150,906)	12,549(25,000-12,451)	476,050
LOANS	Total Disbursed	3,970,700	24,510	710,677	236,892	389,750	77,950	No Loans have been made		3,921,000	142,582	7,500	416,450	34,361	523,795
	Number of Loans	35		280		49				74		2	106		546
	Total Payments Made	3,780,673	23,337	412,194	137,398	183,195	36,639			464,730	17,081	0	170,152	14,039	228,494
	Balance due on Loans	190,027	1,173	298,483	99,494	206,555	41,311			3,438,970	125,053	7,500	246,298	20,322	294,853
	Balance Available	1,429,973	8,827	201,517	67,172	60,955	12,191			227,689	8,260	42,500	377,573	34,152	170,102

*We are in the process of renegotiating contract with D.R. due to fact that D.R. did not increase its deposit to maintain 25% liability when person was

LOAN GUARANTEE REPORT - As of 12/31/85

	CALI COLOMBIA As of 12/31/85		DOMINICAN REPUBLIC As of 6/30/85		HAITI As of 12/31/85		JAMAICA As of 12/31/85		THAILAND As of 12/31/85		EST VERGIN As of 12/31/8	WESTERN INDIA As of 12/31/85		TOTAL
	Local Currency (162 pesos)	U.S. Dollars U.S. $1	Local Currency (3 pesos)	U.S. Dollars U.S. $1	Local Currency (5 Goudes)	U.S. Dollars U.S. $1	Local Currency (Jam. $4)	U.S. Dollars U.S. $1	Local Currency (27.50 Bhatt)	U.S. Dollars U.S. $1	U.S. Dollars	Local Currency (12.12 Rup)	U.S. Dollars U.S. $1	U.S. Dollars
SWWB Asse[ts] Comissory Notes												303,000	25,000	25,000
Account Recei[v]	3,000	17	7,106	2,368	3,900	780			5,200	189	150	12,120	1,000	4,504
SWWB Liabi[l] SWWB Guarantees Letters of Credit	810,000	5,000	300,000	100,000	125,000	25,000	100,000	25,000	1,833,343	66,667	25,000			246,667
Local WWB Gu	405,000	2,500	50,000*	16,656*	80,010	16,002	50,000	12,500	916,658	33,333	12,500			93,501
Local Bank Gur	405,000	2,500	150,000	50,000	62,500	12,500	50,000	12,500	916,658	33,333	12,500	152,094 (303,000-150,906)	12,549 (25,000-12,451)	123,333
Total Available for programs adjustments	1,620,000	10,000	500,000	166,666	267,510	53,502	200,000	50,000	3,666,659	133,333	50,000			476,050
LOANS Total Disbursed	3,970,700	24,510	710,677	236,892	389,750	77,950	No Loans have been		3,921,000	142,582	7,500	416,450	34,361	523,795
Number of Loa	35		280		49		made		74		2	106		546
Total Payment	3,780,673	23,337	412,194	137,398	183,195	36,639			464,730	17,081	0	170,152	14,039	228,494
Balance due o	190,027	1,173	298,483	99,494	206,555	41,311			3,438,970	125,053	7,500	246,298	20,322	294,853
Balance Availa	1,429,973	8,827	201,517	67,172	60,955	12,191			227,689	8,260	42,500	377,573	34,152	170,102

* We are in the process of renegotiating contract with D.R. due to fact that D.R. did not increase its deposit to maintain 25% liability when peson was.....

SWWB Assets and Liabilities 1981 - 1989

	1981	1982	1983	1984	1985	1986	1987	1988	1989
Assets & Investments									
Bank of America			$1,435,845		$328,500			$2,488,081	
Irving Trust Company									
Intl Investor's Fund(Clemente Capital)			$150,000	$142,859	$162,500	$394,293	$1,000,000	$500,000	$500,000
Debenture (Sold)				$165,000					$40,000
Great Barrington Savings Bank, MA					$50,000				
Bear Sterns						$900,000			
Bank of Montreal						$124,000		$1,000,000	
Citizens & Southern WWB Investments		$190,000				$944,494	$1,300,000	$500,000	$500,000
Misc. Investments (Source unclear)					$571,863		$1,750,000	$3,000,000	
Prov Fund (Specific for Capital Fund)									
Dutch Government	$250,000								$1,500,000
CIDA			$50,000			####			
USAID			$500,000		$100,000				
UNDP					$75,000				
Norwegian Government (RNMDC)							$215,000		
Grants & Donations									
Swedish Government	????								
Norwegian Government(RNMDC)	????				$277,000	$421,822	$215,000	$400,000	$350,000
USAID		$120,000	$120,000	$120,000	$125,000	$160,000			
CIDA				$41,666	$41,667	$41,667			
Rockefeller Brothers Fund					$100,000				
Noyse Foundation									
Ford Foundation								$25,000	
Other Misc. Contributions					$30,000			$3,000,000	$75,000
Total Available to Capital Fund		$310,000	$670,000	$161,666	$1,320,530	####	$4,480,000	$10,913,081	
Total Assets	$250,000	$310,000	$2,255,845	$469,525	$1,861,530	####	$4,480,000	$10,913,081	$2,965,000
Loans Outstanding									
Bank America Intl Letters of Credit				$150,000	$150,000				
Fund Balances	$50,000	$55,000	$80,000	$81,000			$228,898	$529,964	
Loan Guarantees								$29,000	$620,012
Debenture	####	####	####	####	$1,370,000	####	$15,868,743	$17,138,243	$18,509,302
Expenditures									
Administrative/Bus.Expenses/Consulting	$35,657	$270,000							
Office Space/Rent			$30,000	$36,000					
Legal Fees	????	????	????	????	????			????	
Salaries/Pensions	????	????	????	????	????	$11,115			
Misc. Expenditures									$200,0000
Total Expenses	$35,657	$270,000	$30,000	$36,000	####	$11,115	$1,150,000	$	$200,000
Total Liabilities	####	####	####	####	####	####	$15,868,743	$17,697,207	$19,558,212

Stichting To Promote Women's World Banking - Balance Sheet

	1980	1981	1982	1983	1984	1985	1986	1987	1988	1989	1990	1990 (unaudited)
Assets												
Cash (including cash equivalents of $1,443,461 in 1988 and $3,115,731 in 1987)	$81,521	$20,196	$344,865	$333,911	$729,965	$222,969	$133,011	$3,276,029	$1,801,462	$2,645,466	$885,379	$679,298
Investments				1,402,396	1,475,668	2,249,524	4,453,134	2,244,803	3,761,362	4,554,772	4,991,331	5,718,147
Grants receivable				-----	39,202	201,625	12,548	8,207	-----	N/A	133,790	170,504
Due from Friends of WWB/USA, Inc.					34,934			136,912	217,281	138,706	185,668	92,001
Pledges receivable				124,900								
Program loan				24,713	24,713	24,713	24,713	24,713	24,713	24,713	39,713	24,713
Accrued interest				14,284	30,731	62,285	10,729	18,326	41,485	58,441	9,766	
Guaranty deposit	30,300											200,000
Furniture & equipment, net of accumulated depreciation												47,686
Other assets (money mkt fund)		9,691	61,448	9,250	13,400	2,550	-----	14,903	105,311	199,946	152,151	25,000
Deposits												
Total assets	$111,521	$29,887	$406,313	$1,909,454	$2,348,613	$2,763,666	$4,657,145	$5,723,893	$5,949,614	$7,660,044	$6,397,798	$6,909,663
Liabilities and Fund Balances												
Accounts payable and accrued expenses	20,168			52,910	75,829	33,111	47,351	-----	15,800	22,000	22,000	24,675
Debentures payable				79,000	165,000	186,000	186,000	46,808	42,691	133,253	130,093	300,277
Loans payable				150,000	361,000	372,198	362,205	136,000	138,000	136,000	1,000	300,277
Provisions for loan losses				6,464		45,527	102,637	337,262	317,327	307,259	290,892	17,364
Due to Friends of WWB/USA, Inc												
Contributions designated for future periods				124,900	-----	107,535	-----					
Total liabilities								519,870	511,818	598,512	443,985	342,316
Fund balances												
Restricted: Fund balances / Capital fund	91,353		336,849	1,243,628	1,641,667	1,641,667	3,225,124	4,187,135	4,150,645	4,665,033	4,958,073	4,665,033
Program loans and other (specific purpose grants)				69,113	49,174	74,558	184,898	207,210	242,908	554,719	392,010	654,979
Grants												24,713
Total restricted	25,667		360,546	1,312,741	1,690,841	1,716,225	3,410,022	4,394,345	4,393,553	5,219,752	5,350,083	5,344,725
Unrestricted: Designated for capital purposes			334,141	334,141	334,141	611,149	1,033,031	1,246,332	1,486,932	1,837,682	2,218,682	2,218,682
Undesignated	3,425			-150,702	-268,198	-308,079	-484,101	436,664	442,689	4,098	1,614,952	-998,060
Total unrestricted	5,425		16,395	183,439	65,943	303,070	548,930	809,678	1,044,243	1,841,780	603,730	1,222,622
Total fund balances		23,092	376,941					5,204,023	5,437,796	7,061,632	5,953,813	6,567,347
Total liabilities and fund balances	$111,521	$29,887	$406,313	$1,909,454	$2,348,613	$2,763,666	$4,657,145	$5,723,893	$5,949,614	$7,660,044	$6,397,798	$6,909,663

Note#1:
"Source from 1980 by STATEMENT OF PURPOSE WOMEN'S WORLD BANKING
"Source from 1981, 1982 (only unaudit from Peat, Marwick, Mitchell&Co though March 82')
"Source from 1983 to 1986 by SWWB Annual Report
"Source from 1987 to 1990 by KPMG

SWWB Sponsors 1980-1990

Sponsors	1980	1981	1982	1983	1984	1985	1986	1987	1988	1989	1990
Norwegian Royal Ministry			$334,141(from Jan 1, '82 to Mar '83)		$253,522	$277,008					
Royal Norwegian Min. of Dev. Cooperation							$421,882	$429,900			
Swedish International Dev. Authority	35,000(workshop)		$163,199(capital fund)	$126,693(capital fund)	$119,517(capital fund)		7,000				
U.S. Agency for International Dev.	$5,000		$500,000(15 yr loan)		$108,147	$160,779	$17,865				
United Methodist Church					$31,000						
United Methodist Church Board of Global Ministries							$10,000				
Women's Division of the United Methodist Church	$10,777										
Ford Foundation	$20,000		1990- $24,500 for expenses incurred in the West Africa regional meeting. $2,000 for expenses incurred for general operating purposes								
Friends of WWB/USA, Inc.			$68,095(from Jan 1, '82 to Mar 31, '82)		$30,930		$24,500	$305,212			
Canadian International Development Agency					$23,319	$92,806	$1,001,059	$933,750			
Netherlands Ministry for Development Cooperation	$33,000		$250,000		$8,000		$885,079				
Ministrie van Buitenlandse Zaken						$47,307					
United Nations Development Programme	$68,380		$48,540(from Jan 1, '82 to Mar 31, '82)				$50,000	$15,000			
UNICEF						$25,000					
Friedrich Naumann Foundation						$2,500					
Sundry Contributions	$3,386						$688	$2,735			
World Bank						$535		$17,725			
Association per la WWB in Italia, Milan, Italy								$500			
Pew Memorial Trust, Philadelphia, PA								$30,000			
Rockefeller Bros. Fund, New York, NY			1987- $25,000 and 1990- $15,000(for expenses incurred in the Affiliate Exchange Program), $10,000(for expenses incurred in the Self-Assessment)								
Bank of America			1990- $5,000 for expense incurred in 1990 Atlanta Conference								
Stuart Communications			1990- $1,120 for expenses incurred in the 1990 Atlanta Conference								
Individual Contributors											
M. Tillar			$2,500								
Mrs. Esther W. Hymer, Shrewsbury, NJ								$500			
Committee of 100	$9,000										
Interest	$1,095										
Total Support	**$205,638**		**$435,276**		**$574,435**	**$605,935**	**$2,418,073**	**$1,782,965**			

Source: 1980 by STATEMENT OF PURPOSE WOMEN'S WORLD BANKING
Source: 1982 by Peat, Marwick, Mitchell & Co
Source: 1984, 1985, 1986, 1987 by SWWB Annual Report
Missing Source 1981, 1983, 1988, 1989, 1990

Stiching To Promote Women's World Banking - Statement of Support, Revenue, Expenses and Changes in Fund Balances

	1980	1981	1982	1983	1984	1985	1986	1987	1988	1989	1990
Support & Revenue											
Gift, grants & individual contributions		$137,981	$453,276	$993,224	$574,435	$605,935	$2,418,073	$1,782,965	$703,530	$1,691,970	$1,401,093
Interest income		7,247	1,096	136,468	212,255	204,903	229,987	454,104	591,261	355,771	212,514
Investment income						100,811	209,547	64,669	15,590	753,661	826,006
Unrealized losses on investments											
Total support & revenue		$145,228	$454,372	$1,129,692	$786,690	$911,649	$2,857,607	$2,172,400	$1,279,201	$2,801,402	$787,601
Expenses											
Program costs:											
Local loan program and regional coordination		122,108	28,068	128,735	279,137	190,440	450,352	461,964	563,674	651,030	1,254,634
Program development and education		45,582	13,097	104,034	100,495	285,952	196,596	209,888	238,506	170,901	348,899
Total program costs		167,690	41,165	232,769	379,632	476,392	646,948	671,852	802,180	821,931	1,603,533
Fund raising		14,663	4,610	39,434	48,024	44,930	54,340	44,856	47,753	46,242	37,609
Administrative & general		37,963	26,231	64,777	98,430	127,816	216,662	210,621	195,495	309,493	254,178
Total expenses		220,316	72,006	336,980	526,086	649,133	917,950	927,329	1,045,428	1,177,666	1,895,320
Excess (deficiency) of support and revenue over expenses		75,088	382,366	792,712	260,604	262,511	1,939,657	1,245,071	233,773	1,623,736	(1,107,719)
Fund balances Beginning of year		69,663	5,425		1,496,180	N/A	2,019,295	3,958,952	5,204,023	5,437,796	7,061,532
Total fund balances End of year		$5,425	$376,941		$1,756,784	N/A	$3,958,952	$5,204,023	$5,437,796	$7,061,532	$5,953,813

ource from 1980 by STATEMENT OF PURPOSE WOMEN'S WORLD BANKING
ource from 1981, 1982 (only unaudit from Peat, Marwick, Mitchell&Co though March 82')
ource from 1983 to 1986 by SWWB Annual Report
ource from 1987 to 1990 by KPMG

Stiching To Promote Women's World Banking - Statement of Functional Expenses

	1980	1981	1982	1983	1984	1985	1986	1987	1988	1989	1990
Personnel costs	$17,660	$56,233	$14,225	$111,478	$131,201	$172,051	$209,122	$216,886	$295,118	$315,930	$434,528
Consultants' fee		60,268	9,764	89,800	115,527	248,494	352,579	398,915	382,589	445,479	580,623
Legal and Accounting	1,206	32,283	11,331	40,229	53,232	33,957	47,767	50,286	53,442	62,740	58,971
Travel & Meetings	1,335	26,956	17,954	23,001	89,667	48,828	124,380	63,088	94,307	79,174	73,664
Printing & production		19,657	9,695	8,249	18,116	17,559	23,386	48,577	25,828	4,432	5,000
Rent	800	9,780	3,079	21,814	26,943	30,600	32,104	36,554	47,448	57,456	56,760
Telphone & cables	1,386	5,808	1,584	10,682	15,709	13,991	16,246	14,986	21,695	19,704	26,689
Supplies and duplicating	622	5,215	2,064	10,868	16,174	21,764	28,203	23,778	44,217	39,065	71,913
Interest				16,196	46,546	55,613	58,204	40,943	39,191	34,728	21,503
Provision for loan losses				----------	----------	----------	----------	----------	----------	15,003	6,772
Management training institute				----------	----------	----------	----------	----------	36,490	71,704	245,511
Postage and Delivery	180										
Sundry	10										
Other		4,116	2,310	4,663	12,971	6,281	25,959	33,316	5,103	32,251	313,386
International Workshop in 1980											
Conference Facilities	$25,235	----------	----------	----------	----------	----------	----------	----------	----------	----------	----------
Travel	24,954	----------	----------	----------	----------	----------	----------	----------	----------	----------	----------
Personnel costs	13,275	----------	----------	----------	----------	----------	----------	----------	----------	----------	----------
Legal and Accounting	6,985	----------	----------	----------	----------	----------	----------	----------	----------	----------	----------
Printing, Program Information	4,488	----------	----------	----------	----------	----------	----------	----------	----------	----------	----------
Postage and Delivery	1,750	----------	----------	----------	----------	----------	----------	----------	----------	----------	----------
Telephone and Telegraph	1,141	----------	----------	----------	----------	----------	----------	----------	----------	----------	----------
Sundry	1,376	----------	----------	----------	----------	----------	----------	----------	----------	----------	----------
Total expenses	$114,285	$220,316	$72,006	$336,980	$526,086	$649,138	$917,950	$927,329	$1,045,428	$1,177,666	$1,895,320

International Workshop in Amsterdam in 1980

*Source from 1980 by STATEMENT OF PURPOSE WOMEN'S WORLD BANKING

*Source from 1981, 1982 (only unaudit from Peat, Marwick, Mitchell&Co though March 82)

*Source from 1983 to 1986 by SWWB Annual Report

*Source from 1987 to 1990 by KPMG

Stiching To Promote Women's World Banking - Debenture Sheet

(Unaudited)

	1980	1981	1982	1983	1984	1985	1986	1987	1988	1989	1990	1990
Debentures payable				79,000	165,000	186,000	186,000	46,608	42,691	133,253	130,093	300,277
Merry Youe												
Central Bank of Uruguay						5,000						
Drothy Lyddon						30,000						
Kit McKeterick						25,000						
Sister Mary Assunta Stang						5,000						
Setton Enablement Fund						25,000						
Alma Soto de Elorza						1,000						
Anne Roberts						25,000						
Victoria P. Oshiro						4,000						
Gertrude & Richard Braun						5,000						
Vedanta Centre						10,000						
Lois Barber						1,000						
Anne Hartwell						50,000						

Debentures payable note

1981: On September 9, 198~ WWB authorized, and thereafter solicited, subscriptions to an issue of 8% debentures of 1981 due in 1990 in the principal amount of $10,000,000. An aggregage principal amount of $79,000 has been sold. WWB has decided to continue such solicitation.

1982: $180,000 from USAID, band $500,000 pledge ($150,000 & 200,000 pledge) 1982.SWW B is making arrangemen ts for an issue of debentures. It is anticipated that the expenses thereof be paid from the proceeds realized on the sale of debentures. However, in the event that the sale of debentures is

1983: $150,000 is the AID/PRE loan from AID in 1983; and $29,000 is for the sale of debentures in 1983. The additional $50,000 in debentures was received in 1982. The AID figure you mentioned "in the prior table" is a grant from AID/WID toward AID/WID Administration Funds. The "base line" comment in Irving Friedman's piece to read: " WWB has been able to use its resources to expand its catalytic role in an increasing number of countires. It charges fees for giving guarantees and for arranging management assistance, usually at a rate of 3%. It can increase this fee, if necessary, on new operations."

1984: $1,000 Sisters of Mercy (Interest) Annual Report. As of December 31, 1984, SWWB had issued a total of $165,000 of 8% debentures due in 1990. A total of $10 million debentures are authorized and it is expected that additional subscriptions will be received during 1985.

1985: As of December 31, 1985, WWB had issued a total of $186,000 of 8% debentures due in 1990. A total of $10 million debentures are authorized.

1986: As of December 31, 1986, WWB had issued a total of $186,000 of 8% debentures due in 1990.

1987: As of December 31, 1937, WWB had issued a total of $136,000 of 8% debentures due in 1990. A total cf $186,200 of debenture s is authorized.

1988: As of December 31, 1988, WWB had issuec a total of $136,000 of 8% debentures due ir 1990. A total of $186,200 of debentures is authorized.

1989: As of December 31, 1989, WWB had issued a total of $136,000 of 8% debentures due in 199C. A total of $186,000 of debentures is authorized.

1990: During 1990, a total of $136,000 of 8% debentures payable became due. As of December 31, 1990, $185,000 of debentures had been redeemed.

Note#1:

*Source from 1980 by STATEMENT OF PURPOSE WOMEN'S WORLD BANKING
*Source from 1981, 1982 (only unaudit from Peat, Marwick, Mitchell&Co though March 82')
*Source from 1983 to 1986 by SWWB Annual Report
*Source from 1987 to 1990 by KPMG

INDEX

A

AAAS. *See* American Association for the Advancement of Science (AAAS)
Abrams, Julie, 89, 97
Aburu, Christine, 100
Abzug, Bella, 9
Accion, 29–31, 55–57, 147
acronyms, key to, 190–91
ACWF. *See* All China Women's Federation (ACWF)
ADIEF, 112
ADOPEM. *See* WWB-ADOPEM
 affiliates. *See also specific affiliate*
 affiliates-in-formation as of 1990, 143
 1990, as of, 143
 overview, 116–28
 "Proposal for WWB Affiliates to Examine Alternative Credit Programs," 124–25
 Stichting Women's World Banking (SWWB), 188–89
Africa. *See* WWB-Africa regional office; *specific country*
African Development Bank, 98, 103
African Training Research Center for Women in Addis Ababa, 10
Agricultural Development Council, 55
Agricultural Finance Corporation in Nairobi, 36
aids and documents, 180
Akerman, Clara, 64–65
Alexander, Celeste, 94, 99
Allan, Virginia, 11
All China Women's Federation (ACWF), 123
Alternative Technology International, 32
American Association for the Advancement of Science (AAAS), 7–8, 11
Amsterdam 1980 meeting, 32–53, 172
 and financial history of WWB, 147–48, 150
 McNamara, Robert, invitation to speak, 27–28
 Women's World Banking Background Paper (Cloherty), 41–52
"Ann" (surname unknown) of WWB-Kenya, 99
Annual Donor Report (1988), 126–27
apartheid, 10
Appalachia, 111
Armacost, Nicki, 171–72
Armstrong, Neil, 161

As, Berit, 54
Ashcroft, Mariama, 163–64
Asia Regional Meeting, 127
Asia, regional representative, 115
Assessment of Technology for Local Development, 19
asset class returns, *155*
Atlanta Global Meeting (1990), 130, 134–42
 "Eternal Wheat" poster, 135, *136*
 SWWB Board meeting following, 142
Atlanta Meeting (1990), 98
At the Edge of History (Thompson), 5

B

balance sheet, *156*
Bank of England, 3
Bank of Italy, 113
Bannier, Floris
 Atlanta Global Meeting (1990), 137
 Bilderberg Hotel (Netherlands, 1984) meeting, 93
 Committee to Organize Women's World Banking, 16, 19–21
 Copenhagen Conference (1980), 54
 Private Placement Memorandum (PPM), 153
 Salzburg Seminar (1989), 131
 San Remo Conference (1981), 57
 WWB-Netherlands, 71
Barclays Banks, 36
 Ghana, 94–95
 Kenya, 96–97, 102
 WWB-Nairobi, 103
Barker, Robert, 161
Barry, Nancy
 and affiliates, 128
 Atlanta Global Meeting (1990), 138, 140–41
 on DFC, 133
 personal reflections, 172–73
 Salzburg Seminar (1989), 130
 San Remo Conference (1981), 55
 as successor to Guzmén, 133–34, 142
 WWB-Kenya, 98
 WWB-Thailand, 81–82
Batelle Human Affairs Research Centers, 21
Beirut, 2–4
Berman, Richard, 175

Bhatt, Ela
    and affiliates, 117–19, 123
    Atlanta Global Meeting (1990), 139
    and evolution of WWB, 67
    meetings with, reflection on, 165
    Mexico City Conference, 5, 8
    Women at Work-Unity in Diversity, 118
    WWB-Europe, 112
Bhatt, Ramesh, 117–18
Bilderberg Hotel (Netherlands, 1984) meeting, 84–93
Bindert, Christine, 169
Blom, Peter, 16–17, 119–21, 169–70
Bogota, 59, 61
Boserup, Ester, 6–7
Bouttcher & Company, 4
Bright, Craig B., 161
Brooks, John, 145
Brown, G. Arthur, 23, 149
Bruce, Judith, 7
Bucaramanga, 61
Bucharest World Population Conference, 5
Bunch, Charlotte, 77–78
Bundy, McGeorge, 160
Burger, Michele, 22

C
Calderon, Belen F., 73
Cali, Columbia Conference (1981), 57–65
Canadian International Development Agency (CIDA),
    103, 153
Canalda, Mercedes
    and affiliates, 121–22
    Cali, Columbia Conference (1981), 57–60
    Dominican Republic, establishment of WWB-
    ADOPEM, 65–66
    meetings with, reflection on, 165
    San Remo Conference (1981), 56
Canalda, Mercedes II (daughter), 66
Canalda, Ricardo (son), 66
Capital Fund
    affiliates, 117
    and Canadian International Development Agency
    (CIDA), 103
    fundraising for, 67
    launching of, 148, 154
    purpose of, 69
    restrictions on use of, 163–64
    San Remo Conference, 56
    setting up of, 165
    WWB-North America Regional Office, 110
    WWB-Thailand, 77, 80
CARD. *See* Centre for Agriculture and Rural
    Development (CARD)
Cary, William L., 161
Centre for Agriculture and Rural Development
    (CARD), 73

Chase, Lee, 22
Children's Research Service, 22
China trip (1987), 123–25, *125*
Chinda Charungchareconvejj, 75–77
Chin, Sylvia, 91, 129–30, 174
CIDA. *See* Canadian International Development Agency
    (CIDA)
City Associates, 4
civil rights movement, 146
Clavel, Diana, 22
Clemente Capital Inc., 158
Clemente Global Partnership LP, 158
    investment management implemented by, *158*
Clemente, Lilia
    Amsterdam 1980 meeting, 36
    Committee to Organize Women's World Banking,
    22, 26
    Finance Committee, 149
    on financial history of WWB, 145–62
    Manila Conference (1982), 73
    Mexico City Conference, 4
    personal reflections, 160–62, 174–75
    Private Placement Memorandum (PPM), 153
    and Women in Finance and Entrepreneurship
    (WIFE), 74
Cloherty, Patricia, 32–33, 41–52
Club of Rome, 6, 19
Committee to Organize Women's World Banking,
    14–31, 33, 161
    Amsterdam meeting, 27–28
    board meeting, 39
    and financial history, 147, 149
    Status of Governments' Reactions on the Women's
    World Banking Protect as of 1 December 1980, *24*
Conable, Barber, 107
Copenhagen Conference (1980), 53–54
Corporación Financiera del Valle, 58
Costa, Silvia, 114
Cruz, Lourdes Lontok
    Amsterdam 1980 meeting, 33
    Asia, identification of regional representative, 115
    "Friendship From Mother to Daughter," 74
    Manila Conference (1982), 73–74, 81
    San Remo Conference (1981), 56
    WWB-Netherlands, 72

D
Dahann, Omaymah, 40
Dahlbom-Hall, Barbro
    Bilderberg Hotel (Netherlands, 1984) meeting, 88
    Copenhagen Conference (1980), 54
    Mexico City Conference, 12–13
    WWB-Thailand, 82
The Daily Star, 3
Davidsen, Amy, 22

Davis, Milton, 17–18
DAWN (Development Alternatives with Women for a New Era), 79
Dayan, Ruth, 109
Dec, Ela, 122–23
decentralization, 164
DESAP. *See* Desarrollo del Pueblo (DESAP)
Desarrollo del Pueblo (DESAP), 58
Develop Finance Consultants, Limited (DFC), 130, 133, 163
Developing Power (Shahani), 11
DFC. *See* Develop Finance Consultants, Limited (DFC)
Dickens, Charles, 145
Dietel, Linda, 135
Dietel, William (Bill)
    Committee to Organize Women's World Banking, 22–24
    Mexico City Conference, 4–6
    personal reflections, 167
documents, 180
Dominican Republic, establishment of WWB-ADOPEM, 65–66
Dulany, Peggy, 135
Dunham, Ann, 128
Dunlop, Joan, 5, 6–7, 9, 135
Dutch Ministry for Development, 80
Dutch Ministry of Development Cooperation, 166
Dutch Ministry of Foreign Affairs, 20, 30
Duterimbere, 108
Duval, Ann, 120, 133, 134

E
Eames, Charles, 87
Eames, Ray, 87
Earth Day (1970), 164
Economic Intelligence Unit (EIU), 73
ECOSOC, 14
Eddy, Jane Lee, 4
EIU. *See* Economic Intelligence Unit (EIU)
Engering, Frans en Louise, 91
Engmann, Comfort
    Grameen Bank visit, 126–27
    Mexico City Conference, 12
    WWB-Ghana, 94–96, 95, 125
"Eternal Wheat" poster, 135, *136*
Europe. *See* WWB-Europe
evolution of WWB, 67–68
Executive Committee, 149
    meetings, 117, 183

F
Faye, Njoba, 125
FCEM. *See* World Federation of Women Entrepreneurs (FCEM)

Ferguson, Allen, 164
Fernandez, Marlene, 26
FES. *See Fundación Económica y Social* (FES)
FIG. *See* Financial International Group (FIG)
    Finance Committee, 149–53
    investment mandate, implementing, 158
    Investment Policies and Guidelines of WWB, 151–52
    meetings, 183
    Private Placement Memorandum (PPM), 153–54
Finance Committee Meeting (1984), 116
financial history of WWB, 145–62
    asset class returns, *155*
    balance sheet, *156*
    Debenture, 153–54
    Finance Committee, 149–53
    finances, start-up (1977 to 1982), 145
    fund-raising expenses received in grants and contributions, *156*
    investment environment in 1980s, 148
    investment mandate, implementing, 158–60
    Investment Policies and Guidelines of WWB, 151–52
    1980-1990, 149–57
    operating activities, 156, *157*
    pledges received (1979-1980), 147–48
    Private Placement Memorandum (PPM), 153–54
    roots of WWB, 146–47
    timeline, *149*
    total expenses, *157*
    world support received, 1984 and 1986, *155*
Financial International Group (FIG), 4
Financial Women's Association, 4
First International Workshop for Women in Banking and Finance. *See* Amsterdam 1980 meeting
Fletcher, Jim, 17, 18
Fletcher, Sylvia, 138–39
Flynn-Williams, Barbara, 95
Ford Foundation, 4, 25, 128
    global activities, 161
    Grameen bank, promotion of, 29
    and KWFT, 97
    The Law and the Lore Endowment Fund (Cary and Bright), 161
    Managing Educational Endowments (Barker), 161
    pledge from, 147
    president, 160
    scope of, 78–79
Foreign Assistance Act, 25
Forrester, Jay, 6
Fraser, Arvonne, 5, 20
Fraser, Don, 5
"Friendship From Mother to Daughter" (Cruz), 74
Friends of Women's World Banking (FWWB), 153–54
Friends of WWB-Thailand, 75
Fundación Carvajal, 58, 62

Fundación Económica y Social (FES), 64
Fundación WWB-Cali, 57–58
fund-raising expenses received in grants and
    contributions, *156*
Fundraising Manual for Affiliates, 104
FWWB. *See* Friends of Women's World Banking
    (FWWB)

G

Gambia Women's Finance Association (GAWFA), 163
Gambia Women's Finance Company, 107
Garza, Bertha Martinez, 8
GAWFA. *See* Gambia Women's Finance Association
    (GAWFA)
Germain, Adrienne, 5, 7
Ghana. *See* WWB-Ghana
Giblen, Ana Maria
    and affiliates, 121–22
    Bilderberg Hotel (Netherlands, 1984) meeting, 89
    India, visit to, 127
    WNB-New York, 125
Give Women Credit Global Meeting. *See* Atlanta Global
    Meeting (1990)
The Go-Go Years (Brooks), 146
Golstein, Marilou van, 166–67
Grameen Bank, 25
    Bangladesh, 125–27
    Indonesia, 171
    promotion of, 29
grants, *156*
Greene, Samuel, 25
Grzywinski, Ron, 16–18, 17
Guzmán, Margarita
    and affiliates, 118, 120, 122
    Atlanta Global Meeting (1990), 138
    Bilderberg Hotel (Netherlands, 1984) meeting, 87
    Cali, Columbia Conference (1981), 57–62, 125
    Committee to Organize Women's World Banking,
    23
    on DFC, 133
    San Remo Conference (1981), 55–57
    successor, recommendations for, 133–34

H

Haaxman BV, 68
Hagen, Margaret (Gee), 26, 33, 94
Haidar, Myrtle, 3, 135
Halpern, Monique, 112
Hamamamsy, Gashia, 8
Hammock, John
    and Accion, 147
    Amsterdam 1980 meeting, 36, 39
    Atlanta Global Meeting (1990), 135
    Cali, Columbia Conference (1981), 57

Committee to Organize Women's World Banking,
    23, 29–31
Dominican Republic, establishment of WWB-
    ADOPEM, 65
personal reflections, 167–68
Private Placement Memorandum (PPM), 153
"Roles and Responsibilities of the Individual Board
    of Directors Members," 39
San Remo Conference (1981), 55
WWB-Thailand, 77
Harretsche, Beatrice
    Amsterdam 1980 meeting, 33
    Asia, identification of regional representative, 115
    Bilderberg Hotel (Netherlands, 1984) meeting, 92
    comments by, 164
    Committee to Organize Women's World Banking,
    23, 26
    Copenhagen Conference (1980), 53
    San Remo Conference (1981), 57
Harris, Rosaline, 7
Harrity, Gail, 67
Hartwell, Anne, 22
Hayanga, Christine
    Amsterdam 1980 meeting, 36
    Atlanta Global Meeting (1990), 140
    WWB-Kenya, 97–98
Hays, Paula, 22
Helms, Jesse, 77
Henderson, Hazel, 19, 164–65
Himmelstrand, Karin, 54
A History of Women's World Banking (Ocloo), 35
Holcomb, Terry, 29–30
Hollister, Charles, 87
Horst, Honey van den, 68, 69
Horst, Marleen van den, 69–72
Hossein, Hamida, 5
Houghton, Mary, 16–18, 25, 36
Howe, Elspeth, 77
Howe, Geoffrey, 77
How to Buy Stocks (Merrill Lynch), 3
How to Read a Financial Report (Merrill Lynch), 3
Hunter, Tom, 16, 153
Hutar, Patricia, 11
Hyatt, Carol, 22

I

Ibiayo, Modupe, 34
IDB. *See* Inter-American Development Bank (IDB)
IMF. *See* International Monetary Fund (IMF)
incorporating papers of WWB, 150
India
    affiliates, 119–20
    Self-Employed Women's Association (SEWA), 8,
    127, 147
Indonesia's National Bank, 128

INSTRAW. *See* International Research and Training Institute for the Advancement of Women (INSTRAW)
Inter-American Development Bank (IDB), 58–59
International Decade for Women, 6
International Monetary Fund (IMF), 79, 169
International Planned Parenthood Federation (IPFF), 21
International Research and Training Institute for the Advancement of Women (INSTRAW), 11
International Women's Tribune Center, 11, 78
International Women's Year Tribune (IWY), 7
International Workshop in 1980, 135
International Workshop of Women Leaders in Banking and Finance, 31. *See also* Amsterdam 1980 meeting
    Committee to Organize Women's World Banking, 33
investment mandate, implementing, 158–60
Investment Policies and Guidelines of WWB, 151–52
IPFF. *See* International Planned Parenthood Federation (IPFF)
Iranian Mission to the United Nations, 8
Iskenderian, Mary Ellen, 173–74
Italy. *See* WWB-Italy
IWY. *See* International Women's Year Tribune (IWY)

J

Jahan, Rounaq, 5, 7
Jain, Devaki, 5, 7
Jaramillo, Ana Milena Cadavid de, 60–62
Jiagge, Mrs. Justice Annie, 11, 94
Johnston, Charlie, 16
Joly, Charles, 16
JP Morgan Asset Management, 161
Junz, Helen, 175
J. Walter Thompson, 89

K

Kalff, Anita, 19
Kay's Hygiene Products, Ltd., 101
Kennard, Byron, 164–65
Kennedy, John F., 29, 160
Kenya. *See* WWB-Kenya
Kenya Rural Enterprise Program, 97
Kenya Women's Finance Trust Company (KWFT), 94, 96–99, 101–2, 106
Keuch, Kees, 69
Khan, A.H., 25, 29
Kibui, Phyllis Wangiko, 98
Knapp, J. Burke
    Atlanta Global Meeting (1990), 140, 141
    Bilderberg Hotel (Netherlands, 1984) meeting, 91
    Committee to Organize Women's World Banking, 28–29
    Finance Committee, 149
    Private Placement Memorandum (PPM), 153

Kruseman, Pauline, 68, 72–73, 170–71
Kuala Lumper (1988 board meeting), 115, 127
KUPEDES village savings, 128
KWFT. *See* Kenya Women's Finance Trust Company (KWFT)
Kwoba-Abungu, Christine (Cissy)
    Atlanta Global Meeting (1990), 137
    WWB-Uganda, 99, 125

L

Lake Nakuru Lodge, 95
Lammert, Sarah, 88–89
Latin America. *See* WWB-Latin America Regional Office
The Law and the Lore Endowment Fund (Cary and Bright), 161
Lawrence, Kay, 129, 135
Léger, Ron, 165
Lehman Brothers, 169
Lessor, Robert, 153
Lindisfarne Association, 5
Littlefield, Elizabeth
    Mali, trip to, 106–7
    personal reflections, 168–69
    WWB-Africa regional office, 105–8
    WWB-Uganda, 100–101
Loan Guarantee Program, 133
London, 2–3
London School of Economics, 55
Lower East Side (New York City), 4
Luton, Barbara, 22
Lycklama, Geertje
Committee to Organize Women's World Banking, 20–22
    Executive Committee Meeting (1986), 117
    Grameen Bank visit, 125–27
    SWWB Board of Trustees meeting (1989), 170
    WWB-Netherlands, 72
    WWB-Thailand, 80–81
Lyddon, Dorothy, 135

M

Maathai, Wangari, 175, 178
MacKay, Paul, 85–88, 119
Madoka, Grace, 99
Mair, Lucille, 11, 14
Management Training Institute, 118–19
Mangli, Sarah, 138
Manhattanville College, 175
Manila Conference (1982), 73–74
Manos del Uruguay, 23, 109
Margriet magazine, 69
Martha Stuart Communications Video, 37
Martinez, Nora de, 138
Mashler, William T., 23

Massachusetts Institute of Technology, 5
Maxwell, Genevieve, 3, 135
Mayko-Swande, John, 125
Maynes, Gretchen, 25–29, 57
McCue, Sara, 23
McKee, Kate, 78–80, 110
McNamara, Robert, 27–28, 95
Mead, Margaret, 14
Medellin, 59, 61
Mees, Rudolf
    Bilderberg Hotel (Netherlands, 1984) meeting,
      84–86, 91, 93
    WWB-Africa regional office, 105
    WWB-Netherlands, 72
Mele, Fern, 22
Merrill Lynch, 2–3
Merrill Lynch International, 2–4
Mexico City Conference, 20, 32, 146, 163
    description of by attendees, 6–12
    photograph of attendees, 5, 6–9
Michel, Rosmarie, 114–15
microfinance, 167
Miller, Jean Baker, 15
Ministry for Development Cooperation, 21
Molenaar, Klaas, 87, 118–20, 170
Molinelli, Ada, 22
Montesa, 63
Morrill, Nancy Porter, 39–40
Morse, Bradford, 23–24, 53–54, 129

N

Nairobi Conference (1985), 100–103, 112, 114
Nairobi Seminar (1989), 105
Nardome, Paola Barbieri, 114
National Council of Women and Development
    (UNCTAD), 12, 13
Ndegwa, Philip, 102
Nederlandsche Middenstands Bank (NMB Bank), 84
Netherlands. *See also* WWB-Netherlands
    Bilderberg meeting. *See* Bilderberg Hotel
      (Netherlands, 1984) meeting
    feminist movement, 20–22
    Ministry of Foreign Affairs, 20, 30
Netherlands Central Bank, 86
Netherlands Ministry for Development, 147
New Alchemy Institute, 1
"The New Old-Fashioned Banking" (Grzywinski), 17
New York Institute of Finance, 2
New York Mets, 161
New York Stock Exchange (NYSE), 3
    women, seats purchased by, 161
NGO Forum for International Women's ear, 7
NGOs, 12
1960s and 1970s, world events, 146, 161
Nissen, Dag, 54

Nixon, Richard, 6
NMB Bank. *See* Nederlandsche Middenstands Bank
    (NMB Bank)
Nobel Foundation, 55
NORAD. *See* Norwegian Agency for Development
    Cooperation (NORAD)
North America. *See* WWB-North America Regional
    Office
North America News, 110
Norwegian Agency for Development Cooperation
    (NORAD), 54, 97
Novogratz, Jacqueline, 108
Ntamabyariro, Agnes, 139
Nurick, Lester, 153
NYSE. *See* New York Stock Exchange (NYSE)

O

Obama, Barack, 128
O'Brien, Donal, 15
Ocloo, Esther
    Amsterdam 1980 meeting, 35–36, 38
    Atlanta Global Meeting (1990), 140
    A History of Women's World Banking, 35
    Mexico City Conference, 8, 11
    San Remo Conference (1981), 56
    WWB-Ghana, 94–96, *95*
OECD. *See* Organization for Economic Cooperation
    and Development (OECD)
Office of Technology Assessment (OTA), 19
oil prices, 146
Okelo, Mary
    and affiliates, 123
    Amsterdam 1980 meeting, 36
    appointment as WWB executive vice president, 142
    Atlanta Global Meeting (1990), 139, 142
    on DFC, 133
    meetings with, reflection on, 165
    as successor to Guzmén, 134
    WWB-Africa regional office, 104–5
    WWB-Ghana, 94
    WWB-Kenya, 96–98, 101–2
OPEC. *See* Organization of the Petroleum Exporting
    Countries (OPEC)
operating activities, 156, *157*
OPIC. *See* Overseas Private Investment Corporation
    (OPIC)
Organization for Economic Cooperation and
    Development (OECD), 112
Organization of the Petroleum Exporting Countries
    (OPEC), 146
OTA. *See* Office of Technology Assessment (OTA)
Overseas Private Investment Corporation (OPIC),
    100–101
Oxfam, 167

P

Pahlavi, Ashraf ul-Mulki, 6
Paluwagon Ng Bayon Savings and Loan Association, 56, 73
Parent-Teacher Associations (PTAs), 4
Partlow, Ann, 127–28, 134–35
Patel, Samir, 89
Patten, Richard, 128
Peace Corps, 29
Persinger, Mildred, 7
Peterson, Russell, 19
Pezzullo, Caroline, 14, 21, 33, 37
Philippines, 160–62
    Manila Conference (1982), 73–74
    Philippine Technical Board for Agricultural Credit, 35
    WWB-Philippines, 73–74
Philippine Technical Board for Agricultural Credit, 35
Phillips, Russell, 15–16, 165–66
Pinzo, Mariza, 113
Pisces Project, 30
Policy Guidelines for the Latin America/Caribbean Regional Representative (RR), 108–9
Pollack, Kim, 22
Popayan, 59, 61
Postel, Els, 13
Postma, G.J.S., 15–16
Pothof, Siska, 67–69, 81
PPM. *See* Private Placement Memorandum (PPM)
Preston, Lewis, 107
Private Placement Memorandum (PPM), 153–54
Pronk, Jan, 13
Pronk, Minister, 72
"Proposal for WWB Affiliates to Examine Alternative Credit Programs," 124–25
PTAs. *See* Parent-Teacher Associations (PTAs)
Public Interest Economic Center, 164

R

Racelis, Mary, 103
Raine, A. Kendall, 107, 149
Ralston, David, 22
Randi, Maria Grazia, 113–14
Randi, Paola, 113–14
RBF. *See* Rockefeller Brothers Fund (RBF)
regional leadership, 94–115
    Asia, 115
    Policy Guidelines for the Latin America/Caribbean Regional Representative (RR), 108–9
    regional advisory committee, 103–4
    Tanzania, 101
    WWB-Africa regional office, 101–8
    WWB-Europe, 112
    WWB-Ghana, 94–96

    WWB-Italy, 113–15
    WWB-Kenya, 96–99
    WWB-Latin America Regional Office, 108–10
    WWB-North America Regional Office, 110–11
    WWB-Uganda, 99–101
Reid, Elizabeth, 8
Report of the Bilderberg Workshop (MacKay), 85–86, *87*
Resolution 3520, 179n3
Resolution 3522 (XXX), 179n3
Rha, Chokyun, 8, 10
Riria, Jennifer, 98–99, 101, 120
Roberts, Ann, 26, 82–83
Rockefeller Brothers Fund (RBF), 4, 5, 14–15, 162, 165
Rockefeller Center employee ID card, *2*
Rockefeller, David, 122
Rockefeller Family and Associates, 15
Rockefeller Family Fund, 4
Rockefeller, John D. 3rd, 5
"Role and Responsibilities of a WWB Trustee" (Tan-Wong), 92–93
"Roles and Responsibilities of the Individual Board of Directors Members" (letter by John Hammock), 39
Rom, Scherpenhuizen, 85
roots of WWB, 146–47
Rosenswig, Deanna
    Amsterdam 1980 meeting, 36–37
    Atlanta Global Meeting (1990), 137
    China trip (1987), 123
    Committee to Organize Women's World Banking, 26
    on DFC, 133
Rothermel, Tim, 24–26
Royal Tropical Institute, 68, 72
Ruckelshaus, Catherine, 22
Rwanda, WWB-Africa regional office, 108

S

Saavedra, Lucy, 61–64
SAICO. *See* Trade Union of Swedish Academics (SIACO)
Sajjabi, Margaret, 100–101
Salzburg Seminar (1989), 129–32
    letter to trustees, 131–32
San Remo Conference (1981), 55–57, 150
Saurwein, Virginia
    Committee to Organize Women's World Banking, 14, 19, 23
    Mexico City Conference, 8, 11, 13
Schulz-Dornburg, Ursula
    "Eternal Wheat" poster, 135, *136*
Schumacher, E.F., 164
Second International Workshop of Women Leaders in Banking and Finance. *See* San Remo Conference (1981)
Sederlund, Leslie, 14, 18–19, 37

Self-Employed Women's Association (SEWA), 8, 119–20, 124–27, 147

SEWA. *See* Self-Employed Women's Association (SEWA)

Shahani, Leticia Ramos
    Committee to Organize Women's World Banking, 14, 161–62
    essay by, 179n4
    Mexico City Conference, 11–12

Shapiro, Joan, 34–35

Sheffield, Anne, 21–22

Sheldon, Tony, 22

Shorebank Corporation, 17–18

SIDA. *See* Swedish International Development Agency (SIDA)

Siebert, Muriel, 161

Simba, Khadija, 101

Small is Beautiful (Schumacher), 164

Snyder, Margaret (Peg)
    Amsterdam 1980 meeting, 36, 37
    Committee to Organize Women's World Banking, 14, 21, 23
    Copenhagen Conference (1980), 54
    Mexico City Conference, 8, 10–11, 13

Socorro, Maria del, 64

SOFINCO, 112

Sohl, Joyce, 149

Souza-Castro, Lucia, 125

"stagflation," 146

Starkey, Jacqui, 7–8

Status of Governments' Reactions on the Women's World Banking Protect as of 1 December 1980, *24*

Stevenson, Adlai III, 18

Stichting Steun Door Rabobanken, 102

Stichting to Promote Women's World Banking
    change of name, 91–92

Stichting Women's World Banking (SWWB)
    affiliates and affiliates-in-formation (1975-1990), 188–89
    Atlanta Global Meeting (1990), Board meeting following, 142
    Board of Trustees, 57, 83, 86, 122–23, 170
    bylaws, 64
    Capital Fund. *See* Capital Fund
    consultants (1980-1990), 187
    debentures, 153
    and Finance Committee, 150–51, 153–54
    formation of, 147
    Global Meetings (1980-1990), 182
    interns (1980-1990), 187
    Kuala Lampur, hosting of Board of Trustees (1988), 115, 127
    lawyer for, 54
    legal name, 20
    Organizing Committees, list of, 181
    San Remo Conference, 55
    staff (1980-1990), 187

    Trustees (1980-1990), 184–86
    Trustees Meetings (1980-1990), 182
    volunteers (1980-1990), 187
    Working Groups, list of, 181
    WWB-Thailand, 77

"Strategies for Achieving Self-Sufficiency" (Nairobi, 1989). *See* Nairobi Seminar (1989)

Stuart, Barkley, 13

Stuart, Martha
    and affiliates, 117
    Amsterdam 1980 meeting, 33, 37
    Committee to Organize Women's World Banking, 14
    Martha Stuart Communications Video, 37
    Mexico City Conference, 13
    San Remo Conference (1981), 55
    WWB-Africa regional office, 107

Stuart, Sara, 38–39, 137

Subijano, Cynthia V., 74

Swedish International Development Agency (SIDA), 106, 147

SWWB. *See* Stichting Women's World Banking (SWWB)

SWWB Capital Fund. *See* Capital Fund

T

Tabatabai, Zohreh (Zuzu), 6, 8–10, 135

Taconic Foundation, 4

A Tale of Two Cities (Dickens), 145

Tanchoco-Subido, Chita, 35, 74

Tan-Wong, Nellie, 92–93, 127

Tanzania, 101

Taylor, Eugene, 86

Thailand. *See* WWB-Thailand

TheThe Penny Foundation (Guatemala), 25

Thompson, William Irwin, 5

Tibulya, Rose, 99–100

timeline, financial history of WWB, *149*

Time magazine article about WWB, *144*

Tocqueville, Alexis de, 159

Toward a New Psychology of Women (Miller), 15

Trade Union of Swedish Academics (SIACO), 12

Trickle-Up, WWB-Africa regional office, 108

Triodos Bank, 16, 84–87, 118–19

Truman, Harry S., 1

U

Uganda. *See* WWB-Uganda

Uganda Women's Finance Trust (UWFT), 99–101

UNCTAD. *See* National Council of Women and Development (UNCTAD)

UN Decade for Women, 7, 146

UN Decade for Women Conference (Nairobi). *See* Nairobi Conference (1985)

UNDP. *See* United Nations Development Program (UNDP)

UN Economic Commission for Africa, 10–11
UN General Assembly of 1975, 6
UNICEF, 30
UNIFEM. *See* United Nations Fund for Women (UNIFEM)
UNITAR. *See* United Nations Institute for Training and Research (UNITAR)
United Methodist Church Women's Division, 147
United Nations Development Program (UNDP)
    and African countries, 94
    and Copenhagen Conference, 53–54
    Country Specific Program Development, 147
    and financial history of WWB, 147, 153
    and Mexico City Conference, 7
    pledge from, 147
    support by, 23–25
United Nations Fund for Women (UNIFEM), 11
United Nations General Assembly
    Resolution 3520, 179n3
    Resolution 3522 (XXX), 179n3
United Nations Institute for Training and Research (UNITAR), 7
United Nations World Conference on Women, 5
US Agency for International Development (USAID), 26
    Alternative Technology International, 32
    Citizen's Advisory Council, 29
    and financial history of WWB, 153
    and Mexico City Conference, 20
    WWB-Kenya, 97
    WWB-Thailand, 75–77
USAID. *See* US Agency for International Development (USAID)
UWFT. *See* Uganda Women's Finance Trust (UWFT)

V

Vietnam war, 146
Vivo, Queenie de, 23, 109–10

W

Walker, Anne, 7
Walsh, Frank P., 1, 179n1
Walsh, Michaela
    and affiliates, 122
    Atlanta Global Meeting (1990), 137, 139–41
    Bilderberg Hotel (Netherlands, 1984) meeting, 84–85, 88–90
    Committee to Organize Women's World Banking, 15, 161–62
    Dominican Republic, establishment of WWB-ADOPEM, 65
    Finance Committee, 149
    Gambia, 107
    letter to trustees (1989), 131–32
    McNamara, Robert, invitation to speak at the

Amsterdam meeting, 27–28
    Mexico City Conference, 5, 9–10
    Private Placement Memorandum (PPM), 153
    resignation letter, *176–77*
    Rockefeller Brothers Fund (RBF), 162
    Salzburg Seminar (1989), 130
    start-up costs (1977 to 1982), 145, 147, 148
    and Thailand, Princess, *74*
    vision of, 166
    WWB-Europe, 112
    WWB-Italy, 114
    WWB-Latin America Regional Office, 109–10
    WWB-Netherlands, 69, 72
    WWB-North America Regional Office, 110–11
    WWB-Thailand, *74,* 75, 79, 81–83
    WWB-Uganda, 101
Wang Ying, 123–25
Waring, Marilyn, 135
Watergate affair, 146
Weisblatt, Abe, 55
Weiss, Chris, 110–11, 118
Wells, H.G., 160
wheel, concept of WWB as, *71*
Whitlam, Gough, 8–9
WID. *See* Women in Development (WID)
Wilcott-Henry, Leslie, 89
Williams, Jacqui, 89–91, 135, 137
Winer, Susan, 57, 111
Women as Entrepreneurs, Women's World Banking (film), 69
Women at Work-Unity in Diversity (Bhatt), 118
Women in Development (WID), 7
Women in Finance and Entrepreneurship (WIFE), 56, 72, 74
Women's Bond Club, 4
Women's International Loan Guarantee Association, 16
women's liberation movement, 146
Women's Tribune, 101
Women's World Banking Background Paper (Cloherty), 41–52
Women's World Enterprise (WWE), 116
World Bank, 21, 27–28
    creation of, 14–15
    Young Professionals program, 173
World Conference of the United Nations Decade for Women (Copenhagen, 1980), 53–54
World Conference on Women in Mexico City. *See* Mexico City Conference
world events, 1960s and 1970s, 146, 161
World Federation of Women Entrepreneurs (FCEM), 113
World Food Conference, 6
world support received, 1984 and 1986, *155*
WWB-ADOPEM, 60, 65–66, 121–22
WWB Advisory Associates Committee, 83

WWB Africa Newsletter, 102
WWB-Africa regional office, 101–8
    affiliate representatives, 104–5
    Fundraising Manual for Affiliates, 104
    guidelines, 104
    "promoter," profile of, 104
    regional seminars, report covers, *102*
WWB Capital Fund Drive, 39
WWB-Europe, 112
WWB-Ghana, 94–96
WWB-Italy, 113–15
WWB-Kenya, 96–99
WWB-Latin America Regional Office
    Policy Guidelines for the Latin America/Caribbean
    Regional Representative (RR), 108–9

WWB-Nairobi, 103
WWB-Netherlands, 67–72. *See* WWB-Netherlands
WWB-North America Regional Office, 110–11
WWB-Philippines, 73–74
WWB-Thailand, 74–85
WWB-Uganda, 99–101, 125
WWE. *See* Women's World Enterprise (WWE)

Y
Young, Andrew, 135
Yunus, Muhammad, 29

Z
Zonta Club, 75

ABOUT THE AUTHOR

Photo by Gala Narezo

Michaela Walsh is an activist, scholar, mentor, educator, and author. She was a pioneer woman manager with Merrill Lynch in Beirut, Lebanon, in the '60s, the first woman Partner of Boettcher in the '70s, and in 1980, Founding President of Women's World Banking.

Throughout her career, Michaela has maintained a vibrant commitment to education and service. She was an Adjunct Professor at Manhattanville College and Director of Global Student Leadership programs there. Board appointments have included Synergos Institute and Union Theological Seminary, with advisory roles in a wide range of governmental and social-justice organizations over the decades.

She was Chairperson of the 59th United Nations DPI/NGO Conference in 2006. She received the Woman of Vision Award of the National Organization for Women, the UN Development Program's Paul G. Hoffman Award for outstanding work in development, and in 2012 was honored by Women's Funding Network for changing the face of philanthropy.

COSIMO is a specialty publisher of books and publications that inspire, inform, and engage readers. Our mission is to offer unique books to niche audiences around the world.

COSIMO BOOKS publishes books and publications for innovative authors, nonprofit organizations, and businesses. **COSIMO BOOKS** specializes in bringing books back into print, publishing new books quickly and effectively, and making these publications available to readers around the world.

COSIMO CLASSICS offers a collection of distinctive titles by the great authors and thinkers throughout the ages. At **COSIMO CLASSICS** timeless works find new life as affordable books, covering a variety of subjects including: Business, Economics, History, Personal Development, Philosophy, Religion & Spirituality, and much more!

COSIMO REPORTS publishes public reports that affect your world, from global trends to the economy, and from health to geopolitics.

CPSIA information can be obtained
at www.ICGtesting.com
Printed in the USA
FSHW022050190320
68220FS